- Includes a website with **online quizzes, assessment of key co** **video documentaries and interviews,** and **news feeds** so you aren't always stuck in the book

- Has a design that is sleek, friendly, and easy to use. Think BMW, but in paper form. OK, bad analogy. Really though, it looks nice.

And that's only the beginning. To help get the material across and make it easier for you, each chapter includes **Test Prep Questions,** a Marginal Glossary that gives you definitions right when you need them, **Key Terms** at the beginning of chapters, Marginal Icons that link you to web content, and a Learning Objectives Review so you know what's going to be covered.

Oh yeah, and the website is very cool.
It's got the stuff mentioned above plus **video interviews and documentaries from CNN, photo essays,** and **additional articles.** See people like Maria Stephan from the International Center for Nonviolent Conflict. Get a better handle on concepts like mutually assured destruction by watching a CNN video. If you're like me and learn better from visual information, you'll love this website . . . . !!!

website:
www.between
nations.org/

Some LAst Things
--> -> Before the Fun Begins

So what you end up with is a text that is well organized, easy to read, and maybe, just maybe, even enjoyable to use. It's been tailor-made to include the type of things you want so that studying (and your grade) come easier. When students were asked to compare a chapter from this book to another, they responded overwhelmingly in favor of this one.

So that's it. You can quit reading this and start using a book that's easier and more enjoyable. Yes, you still have to read it, but hey, at least students like you helped design it.

Greg

World Politics
in the 21st Century

World Politics in the 21st Century

Student Choice Edition

▶ **W. Raymond Duncan**
▶ State University of New York, Brockport

▶

▶ **Barbara Jancar-Webster**
State University of New York, Brockport

▶

▶ **Bob Switky**
▶ Sonoma State University

Houghton Mifflin Harcourt Publishing Company

Boston   New York

Publisher: Suzanne Jeans

Senior Sponsoring Editor: Traci Mueller

Marketing Manager: Edwin Hill

Discipline Product Manager: Lynn Baldridge

Senior Development Editor: Jeffrey Greene

Senior Project Editor: Nancy Blodget

Senior Media Producer: Lisa Ciccolo

Content Manager: Janet Edmonds

Art and Design Manager: Jill Haber

Cover Design Director: Tony Saizon

Senior Photo Editor: Jennifer Meyer Dare

Senior Composition Buyer: Chuck Dutton

New Title Project Manager: James Lonergan

Editorial Assistant: Evangeline Bermas

Marketing Assistant: Samantha Abrams

Editorial Assistant: Jill Clark

Cover Image Credits
Protesters: © Peter Turnley / CORBIS
Sumo wrestler: © Creasource / CORBIS
Student Choice logo: Trevor Hunt / iStockphoto

Printed in the U.S.A.

Library of Congress control number: 2007940571

For orders, use student text ISBNs:
ISBN 13: 978-0-547-05634-0
ISBN 10: 0-547-05634-6

1 2 3 4 5 6 7 8 9 – WEB – 12 11 10 09 08

Brief Contents

Contents

CHAPTER 8

POLITICAL GEOGRAPHY   230

CHAPTER 9

NATIONALISM'S POWER IN WORLD POLITICS   262

CHAPTER 10

GLOBAL VIOLENCE: WARS, WEAPONS, TERRORISM   290

Preface

▶ THE *Student Choice Edition*: A TEAM APPROACH: BUILT BY PROFESSORS AND STUDENTS, FOR PROFESSORS AND STUDENTS

Over the past two years Houghton Mifflin has conducted research and focus groups with a diverse cross-section of professors and students from across the country. The purpose of this endeavor has been to create the first textbook that truly reflects what professors and students want and need in an educational product. The result of this effort is *World Politics in the 21st Century, Student Choice Edition.* Everything in this textbook—from its structure and organization to its learning system, design, packaging and marketing—has been orchestrated to meet the teaching and studying requirements of today's instructors and students. We believe you will find this breakthrough textbook model provides a unique path for your students to advance their understanding of the complexities of twenty-first century world politics.

▶ WHAT STUDENTS TOLD US

Students have told us that they want above all a textbook that reflects the way they actually learn and study—as well as a price they can afford. This means they are looking for a textbook that has true value to them. Toward this end we have used their practical and creative ideas about how they study and gain knowledge to develop an educational learning model like no other on the market today. *World Politics in the 21st Century, Student Choice Edition* meets a student's primary goals: a price-conscious textbook/media package loaded with concepts presented in a way that makes learning more pleasure than pain.

We know that different students learn in different ways. Some learn best by reading, while others are more visually oriented. Still others acquire insight through practice and assessment. While students learn in different ways, almost all students told us the same things regarding what they want their textbook to "look like." The ideal textbook for students gets to the point quickly, is easy to understand and read, has shorter chapters, has pedagogical materials designed to reinforce key concepts, has a strong supporting website for quizzing, testing, and assessment of materials, is cost conscious, and provides them with real value for their dollar. And for more visually oriented students, we have developed a special website, **BetweenNations.org**, that provides video documentaries and interviews as well as news feeds from BBC World News and the United Nations.

▶ TAKING WHAT STUDENTS TOLD US TO CREATE THE *Student Choice* MODEL *World Politics in the 21st Century, Student Choice Edition*

World Politics in the 21st Century, Student Choice Edition provides exactly what students want and need pedagogically in an educational product. While other textbooks on the market include some of these features, this Student Choice Edition is the first international relations textbook to incorporate fully all of these cornerstones, as well as to introduce innovative new learning methods and study processes that completely meet the wishes of today's students. It does this by:

- Being concise and to the point
- Presenting more content in bulleted or more succinct formats
- Highlighting and boldfacing key concepts and information
- Organizing content in smaller, easier-to-manage chunks
- Providing a system for immediate reinforcement and assessment throughout the chapter
- Creating a design that is open, user friendly, and interesting for today's students
- Developing an integrated Web component that focuses on quizzing and assessment of key concepts
- Creating a product that is easier for students to read and study
- Providing students with a product they feel is valuable

When we asked students to compare a chapter from this new learning model to chapters from traditional competing textbooks, students overwhelmingly rated this new product model as far superior.

▶ ORGANIZATION OF THE BOOK

The central aim of this textbook is to address the wide range of 21st century issues that lie in the domain of world politics. With this goal in mind the text includes both topics that have been the traditional subject matter of international relations and those that commonly are considered non-traditional topics. The first category includes the concepts of the state, the nation, power, foreign policy decision-making and international organization. The second category includes topics that in many texts form a minor part of a chapter or are not presented in a comprehensive form. In this textbook you will find a whole chapter devoted to geographic factors that shape world politics, another dedicated to women, poverty, and human rights, and a third that looks at the environment as a key international issue in itself, rather than an addendum to the problem of economic development.

The text is organized to introduce the study of these issues in a systematic and logical manner. Chapters are in three parts. *Part One* explores the foundations of world politics, with chapters on the importance of how to study and what to analyze in this field. *Part Two* examines the major driving forces in world politics, such as power, foreign policy, intergovernmental actors, nongovernmental actors, political geography, and nationalism. *Part Three* looks at significant issues in 21st century world politics—global violence, wars, weapons and terrorism, human rights, women and global justice, the international political economy and developed countries, the political economy of development, and the global environment.

Chapters move from the more basic concepts and principles—such as how to think about and analyze world politics in terms of the state, power, and foreign policy—toward a discussion of the multiple dimensions of today's world politics arena. Each chapter contains learning objectives to make clear the important points to keep in mind, mini quizzes to make certain key elements are grasped, a debate to sharpen understanding of major issues and a case study at the end of the chapter to give deeper meaning and relevance to the chapter's discussion.

World politics today poses a real challenge to our understanding, yet this textbook offers keys that will open the doors for us. The main theme of this book is that we can make sense of world politics by finding patterns in world events. The principal pattern is *centralization* versus *decentralization*.

Centralizing tendencies of international relations are found in the twin processes of globalization and global interdependence—and in international organizations. Decentralization tendencies show up in forces such as nationalism, religious fundamentalism, terrorism, and divisive ideologies. Spreading *globalization* and *interdependence* have made state boundaries less relevant to commerce and finance and have undermined old concepts of state sovereignty. Intergovernmental organizations (IGOs) that tie states together now span the globe, while a host of new non-governmental organizations (NGOs) unite people across state boundaries and work tirelessly to solve age-old problems, such as race, religion, economic degradation, and territory disputes that threaten to tear the world apart.

Decentralizing forces, on the other hand, are mirrored in numerous driving forces examined in this text. They include ethnic national groups that seek to fragment states into even smaller land areas—a legitimate endeavor from the perspective of the individual groups in search of control of their lives. The Palestinian drive for statehood inside Israel—with all its explosive violence in that part of the world—is a case in point. Iraq, meanwhile, illustrates the volatile and divisive influence of religion as Sunnis battle Shiites, while the Kurds would like independence from both these groups. Nuclear and conventional weapons proliferation, not least of which is the spread of ballistic missile technology as well as chemical and biological weapons, fall into the category of decentralizing forces. North Korea and Iran hence become natural points of concern by much of the world community when it comes to nuclear weapons.

▶ SKILLS-FOCUSED PEDAGOGICAL FEATURES

The text contains an array of pedagogical tools designed for student self-assessment and reinforcement, including *chapter-opening outlines* and *learning objectives* that correspond to each major section of the book; *Test Prepper* questions at the end of each section to check for understanding; *key terms* that appear at the beginning of each chapter, and then again in the margins of the text pages; *marginal icons* linking students to website material, which includes online quizzing and multimedia assets; a *marginal glossary* to define unfamiliar terms; and a *learning objectives review* at the end of chapters to help students review the chapter's main points.

► AN EFFECTIVE TEACHING AND LEARNING PACKAGE

FOR INSTRUCTORS

Online Instructor's Manual. Written by the authors and based on their extensive classroom experience, each chapter contains a wealth of active and collaborative learning techniques, Internet projects, home assignments, and case study teaching techniques.

HMTesting Instructor CD. This CD-ROM contains electronic Test Bank items. Through a partnership with the Brownstone Research Group, HMTesting—powered by *Diploma*®—provides instructors with all the tools they need to create, write/edit, customize, and deliver multiple types of tests. Instructors can import questions directly from the Test Bank, create their own questions, or edit existing questions, all within *Diploma*'s powerful electronic platform.

Instructor Website. This website offers valuable resources for course preparation and presentation, including downloadable Instructor's Manual files and classroom response system ("clicker") slides. A news feed provided by the Associated Press provides a steady stream of current events for classroom discussion. Visit the Instructor Website at **college.hmco.com/pic/duncanWP**.

BetweenNations.org. This website is an online learning tool designed specifically to engage students in the international political process through a variety of media, including original videos, short-form documentaries, writing excerpts, and additional resources. Students are asked to answer a series of questions in the online "Notebook," which records their answers and allows you to keep a record of the assignment. Correlated to the Table of Contents in the text, the site offers instructors two to five quality homework assignments per chapter and content that engages students and invigorates class discussions. In addition, to keep your students current with world affairs there are news feeds from BBC World News and top stories from the United Nations News Centre.

FOR STUDENTS

BetweenNations.org. Each copy of this book includes passkey access to the valuable resources of **BetweenNations.org**, a dynamic and user-friendly website providing an array of multimedia content and web-based assignments for students. With a narrative approach featuring real people in real-world political environments, the site's video clips and interactive resources bring concepts to life and directly complement the textbook chapters. Students complete assignments on the website and submit their work to instructors with the click of a button. Students will also have access to flashcards to check their comprehension of key terms, practice tests, audio concept study tools for download, and the news feeds from BBC World News and the United Nations.

► PROFESSORS AND STUDENTS: WE COULDN'T HAVE DONE IT WITHOUT YOU

We are very grateful to all the students across the country who participated in one form or another in helping us to create and build the first educational product pedagogically designed specifically for them and their learning and educational goals. Working with these students was an honor, as well as a lot of fun, for all of us at Houghton Mifflin. We sincerely appreciate their honesty, candor, creativeness, and interest in helping us to develop a better learning experience. We also appreciate their willingness to meet with us for lengthy periods of time and to allow us to videotape them and use some of their excellent quotes. We wish them much success as they complete their college education, begin their careers, and go about their daily lives.

STUDENT PARTICIPANTS

Acosta, Pricilla, *University of Texas at Brownsville*
Adamec, Christopher J., *Indiana University, Bloomington*
Aiken, Katie, *Miami University*
Albert, Chris, *California State University, Sacramento*
Allen, Laura, *Carroll College*
Araujo, Javier H., *University of Texas at Brownsville*
Arreola, Jose, *University of Texas at Brownsville*
Back, Hillary, *James Madison University*
Baker, Elaine, *Iowa Lakes Community College*
Barrett, O'Neil, *Borough of Manhattan Community College*
Barron, Joe, *Providence College*
Beal, Laura, *Miami University*
Belle, JaLisha Elaine, *Adrian College, MI*
Beverly, Carolyn, *Southwest Tennessee Community College*
Bis, Ryan, *Boston University*
Boyd, Shawn, *Southwest Tennessee Community College*
Brantley, Gerius, *Florida Atlantic University*
Brewster, Angie, *Boston College*
Brez, Cyleigh, *Miami University*
Bruss, Joy, *Carroll College*
Buchholz, Mike, *James Madison University*
Butters, Amy, *Carroll College*
Calvo, Veronica, *Keiser College*
Campbell, Jessy, *James Madison University*
Chester, Elaine, *Columbus Technical College*
Chimento, Kristin, *Miami University*
Coker, Nadine, *Columbus Technical College*
Collins, Shayla, *Southwest Tennessee Community College*
Connolly, Catie, *Anna Marie College*
Cooper, Angelique, *DePaul University*
Cooper, Jolinda, *Beaufort County Community College*
Counihan, Mallory, *James Madison University*
Day, Brian, *Georgia State University*
Delaney-Winn, Adam, *Tufts University*
Denton, Justin, *California State University, Sacramento*
DiSerio, Stephanie, *Miami University*
Diz, Rita, *Lehman College*

Dolcemascolo, Christine, *California State University, Sacramento*
Dolehide, Maggie, *Miami University*
Dripps, Matthew, *Miami University*
Duran, Gabriel, *Florida International University*
Ebron, Clara, *Beaufort County Community College*
Espinoza, Giovanni, *Hunter College*
Fahrenbach, Tanya, *Benedictine University*
Fargo, Sarah Louise, *Indiana University, Bloomington*
Faridi, Muneeza, *Georgia State University*
Fischer, Christina, *University of Illinois at Chicago*
Fisher, Emily Katherine, *Indiana University, Bloomington*
Fleming, Linda, *Columbus Technical College*
Frazier, Sharita, *Georgia State University*
Gabri, Holli, *Adrian College, MI*
Gagnon, Danielle, *Boston University*
Gamez, Iris, *University of Texas at Brownsville*
Garza, Brenda, *University of Texas at Brownsville*
Gillispie, Renata, *Southwest Tennessee Community College*
Glater, Paulina, *DePaul University*
Gonzalez, Donna, *Florida International University*
Goulet, Michelle, *Carroll College*
Greenbaum, Barry, *Cooper Union*
Griffis, Jill, *Carroll College*
Hall, Rachel, *Miami University*
Harris, Emma, *Miami University*
Hawkins, Roy, *Southwest Tennessee Community College*
Hightower, Kendra, *Southwest Tennessee Community College*
Hill, Erika, *University of Florida*
Hoff, Joe, *University of Wisconsin–LaCrosse*
Hooser, Ginny, *Western Illinois University*
Huang, Jin, *Georgia State University*
Janko, Matt, *University of Massachusetts–Amherst*
Johnson, Peggy, *Iowa Lakes Community College*
Johnson, Stella, *Columbus Technical College*
Keltner, Travis, *Boston College*
Khan, Javed, *University of Central Florida*
Knowles, Mary, *University of Central Florida*

Konigsberg, Matthew, *Baruch University*
Kozeibayeva, Leila, *Indiana University, Bloomington*
Krouse, Molly, *James Madison University*
Kuhnlenz, Fritz, *Boston University*
Lambalot, Lindsey, *Northeastern University*
Lanier, Mary, *Southwest Tennessee Community College*
Largent, Thomas, *Adrian College, MI*
Lawrence, Lucy, *Beaufort County Community College*
Lee, Cheng, *University of Wisconsin–LaCrosse*
Lippi, Steven, *Boston College*
Long, Crystal, *Iowa Lakes Community College*
Lopez, Henry, *Florida International University*
Ly, Bryant, *Georgia State University*
Lynch, Jessie, *Miami University*
Mancia, Mario, *Georgia State University*
Marcous, Michael, *University of Central Florida*
Marith, Sarah, *Boston University*
Marshall, Nichole, *Columbus Technical College*
Mavros, Nichelina, *Fordham University*
McLean, Chad, *California State University, Sacramento*
McNamara, Meghan, *California State University, Sacramento*
Medina, Jose A., *University of Texas at Brownsville*
Michalos, Marika, *City College of New York*
Miller, Evan, *Parsons School of Design*
Monzon, Fernando, *Miami Dade College*
Moore, Donald, *Beaufort County Community College*
Nitka, Matt, *University of Wisconsin–LaCrosse*
Noormohammad, Rehan, *Northeastern Illinois University*
Offinger, Caitlin, *Amherst College*
Ortiz, Laura, *University of Texas at Brownsville*
Paredes, Idalia, *University of Texas at Brownsville*
Paruin, John, *Adrian College, MI*
Queen, Durrell, *University of New York*
Randall, William, *Southwest Tennessee Community College*
Rayski, Adrienne, *Baruch University*
Rederstorf, Melonie, *Adrian College, MI*

Ringel, Kevin, *Northwestern University*
Rodriguez, Juan F., *University of Texas at Brownsville*
Rodriguez, Uadira, *University of Texas at Brownsville*
Rosenwinkel, Wendy, *Iowa Lakes Community College*
Royster, Megan, *Indiana University, Bloomington*
Savery, Alison, *Tufts University*
Schaffner, Laura, *Miami University*
Schiller, Raquel, *University of Central Florida*
Schlutal, Aubrey, *James Madison University*
Silgvero, Jesus Javier, *University of Texas at Brownsville*
Silva, Miriam, *University of Texas at Brownsville*
Simkovi, Jordan, *Northwestern University*
Smith, Christine, *James Madison University*
Smith, Everrett, *Southwest Tennessee Community College*
Smith, Karl, *Western Illinois University*
Smith, Letesha, *Southwest Tennessee Community College*
Staley, Ahmad, *Columbus Technical College*
Stenzler, Michael, *University of Central Florida*
Stondal, Adam, *Adrian College, MI*
Teekah, Karissa, *Lehman College*
Thermitus, Patrick, *Bentley College*
Thurmon, Lorie, *Beaufort County Community College*
Toft, Gregory, *Baruch University*
Tolles, Rebecca, *Miami University*
Tran, Vivi, *University of Central Florida*
Trzyzewski, Sam, *Boston University*
Uribe, Vanessa, *Florida International University*
Vayda, Kristin, *Miami University*
Werner, Michael, *Baruch University*
Wesley, Adrian, *Southwest Tennessee Community College*
White, Robert, *DePaul University*
Williams, Jen, *Carroll College*
Williams, LaTonya, *Southwest Tennessee Community College*
Wong, Helen, *Hunter College*
Yusuf, Aliyah, *Lehman College*
Zittcricsch, Steve, *Iowa Lakes Community College*
525 Students in MKTG 431: Principles of Marketing, San Francisco State University

We are equally grateful to all the professors across the country who participated in the development and creation of this new textbook through content reviews, advisory boards, and/or focus group work regarding the new pedagogical learning system. As always, professors provided us with invaluable information, ideas, and suggestions that consistently helped to strengthen our final product. We owe them great thanks and wish them much success in and out of their classrooms.

PROFESSOR PARTICIPANTS

Blakely, Malika, *Georgia State University*
Boeckelman, Keith, *Western Illinois University*
Brown, Paula E., *Northern Illinois University*
Eliason, Robert, *James Madison University*
Fine, Terri Susan, *University of Central Florida*
Fisher, Bruce, *Elmhurst College*
Fox, Mark, *Indiana University South Bend*
Hensley, Kermelle, *Columbus Technical College*
Hladik, Paula, *Waubonsie Community College*
McConnel, Lisa, *Oklahoma State University*
Nalder, Kimberly Love, *California State University, Sacramento*
Peterson, Suzanne, *Arizona State University*
Schultz, Debbie, *Carroll College*
Silver, Gerald, *Purdue University–Calumet*
Thannert, Nancy, *Robert Morris College*
Thomas, Ron, *Oakton Community College*
Thompson, Kenneth, *DePaul University*
Weeks, Benjamin, *St. Xavier University*

▶ **ACKNOWLEDGMENTS**

We are grateful to the following reviewers and consultants who provided feedback
for this and previous versions of this book:

Linda S. Adams, *Baylor University*
E. Perry Ballard, *Brescia University*
Amanda Bigelow, *Illinois Valley Community College*
Patricia Bixel, *Maine Maritime Academy*
Merike Blofield, *Grand Valley State University*
J. Barron Boyd, *LeMoyne College*
Sophie Clavier, *San Francisco State University*
Jane Cramer, *University of Oregon*
Michael Deaver, *Sierra College*
Mark Denham, *University of Toledo*
Jeff Dense, *Eastern Oregon University*
Rado Dimitrov, *University of Minnesota*
Manochehr Dorraj, *Texas Christian University*
David V. Edwards, *The University of Texas at Austin*
Larry Elowitz, *Georgia State College and University*
Rick Foster, *Idaho State University*
Erich Frankland, *Casper College*
Andrea Grove, *Westminster College*
Nancy Haanstad, *Weber State University*
Steven Jones, *University of Charleston*
Kelcchi Kalu, *University of Northern Colorado*
Roger E. Kanet, *University of Miami*
Patricia Keilbach, *University of Colorado, Colorado Springs*

George Kent, *University of Hawaii*
Deepa Khosla, *Willamette University*
Bertin K. Kouadio, *Florida International University*
Lawrence LeBlanc, *Marquette University*
Christopher Leskiw, *Cumberland College*
Guoli Liu, *College of Charleston*
Domenic Maffei, *Caldwell College*
Vince Mazzeo, *Everest College*
Zach Messitte, *St. Mary's College of Maryland*
Matthew Morehouse, *University of Nebraska at Kearne*
Joel C. Moses, *Embry-Riddle Aeronautical University*
Michael Nojeim, *Prairie View A&M University*
Richard A. Nolan, *University of Florida*
Christopher Prososki, *University of Nebraska at Kearney*
Jeffrey Ross, *Yale Gordon College*
Joseph R. Rudolph, *Towson University*
Christopher Scholl, *Wheeling Jesuit University*
Thomas Schrand, *Philadelphia University*
Charles Sewall, Jr., *Robert Morris College*
Shawn Shieh, *Marist College*
Adam Silverman, *University of Florida*
Robert E. Sterken, Jr., *University of Texas at Tyler*
Paul E. Sum, *University of North Dakota*
David Van Heemst, *Olivet Nazarene University*
Peter M. Volpe, *Meredith College*
Carol Woodfin, *Palm Beach Atlantic College*
Raymond F. Wylie, *Lehigh University*

A special note of appreciation goes to Dr. Nikolai V. Semin of Moscow State University for his invaluable help in PowerPoint design and presentation, and in his ability to reformat for Microsoft Word virtually any text we put in front of him. Our deep thanks as well to the many students who assisted in Web research, proofreading, collating, and doing the countless things that a book this size demands. Our thanks go to Ty Haussler, James Schledewits, Eric Okanović, Paul Ferland, Kara Gable, Alison Schweicher, Mary Buggie-Hunt, Marian Gentzel, and Carrie Labell. We would also like to thank Marcelle Stickles, Secretary, Department of Political Science and International Studies, SUNY–College at Brockport. Any errors that remain of course are our own.

Last but not least, we must thank our ever-patient spouses without whose constant support and encouragement we could not have brought this book to a successful completion.

W. Raymond Duncan
Barbara Jancar-Webster
Bob Switky

World Politics
in the 21st Century

Our Rapidly Changing World

LEARNING OBJECTIVES

1 *Define world politics and be able to understand current political events through the competing forces of centralization and decentralization.*

2 *Understand how world politics affects your life and how studying international affairs will help you develop analytical skills to better see patterns in the complexity of current events.*

> *"Politics is the authoritative allocation of values."*
>
> —David Easton

Chapter Outline

▶ **WHAT IS WORLD POLITICS?**
Politics as the Authoritative Allocation of Values
An Overview of World Politics
Current Political Trends

▶ **WHY STUDY WORLD POLITICS?**
Relating International Affairs to Your Life
Interconnections and Patterns in Politics

▶ **WHAT NEW FORCES ARE SHAPING THE PLANET?**
Information Technology
The New Global and Transnational Issues
The Increasing Inability of the State to Solve Problems
The Rise of Ethnic Nationalism and Religious Fundamentalism
New Citizen Activism

---

3 ▶ *Identify the five most significant forces shaping the world today and understand how these forces have centralizing or decentralizing effects on world politics.*

Globalization The process by which economic, social, and political institutions become worldwide in terms of activity, influence, and application.

World Politics Today

In the first decade of the twenty-first century, rapid change and **globalization** dominate our world. *Rapid change* is all around us. At the end of World War II, intercontinental plane service was a rarity, and a flight from New York City to Shannon, Ireland, took over nineteen hours with stopovers. Today, you can fly nonstop from Seattle to Tokyo, a far greater distance, in thirteen hours. The increase in airplane speed and the universality of air travel has made the planet smaller and brought previously inaccessible places within the reach of virtually every traveler. It also made possible the horrors of the World Trade Center catastrophe of September 11, 2001, and facilitated the lightning spread of the Severe Acute Respiratory Syndrome (SARS) epidemic around the world in 2003.

Between Nations
For more information see
The Treaty of Westphalia
www.BetweenNations.org

Authority   The right or power to enforce rules or give orders. In the modern world, who has this authority is usually decided by elections.

Treaty   A contract in writing between two or more political authorities, such as states, formally signed by representatives of those states, and most commonly ratified by the legislature of the signatory states.

Sovereign   No higher authority can control the state's decision. The state has a monopoly on the use of force.

The high-tech revolution of the 1970s and 1980s brought the personal computer, the Internet, the cell phone, and hand-held personal digital assistants, which are now commonplace throughout the world. The days of media companies or government-owned organizations that gathered, monitored, and controlled information flow have given way to news that is transmitted over TV and the Web as it happens. In the last thirty years, there has been a similar revolution in biotechnology. Modern advances promise cures for many of humanity's ailments and at the same time raise the threat of biological warfare.

Global interconnectedness shapes our experiences. Rapid technological change makes the world a global village, where what one group of people does in one part of the planet can be immediately acted upon in another part. The collapse of the World Trade Center towers was filmed as it happened and instantaneously transmitted around the globe in real time. On a more positive note, the high-tech revolution has brought great economic benefits. A college student's purchase of a T-shirt with a particular design at a Wal-Mart in Des Moines, Iowa, or a Grande Surface in Lyons, France, triggers a computer-programmed merchandise accounting-and-ordering system that crosses continents with the speed of light and generates new orders from China that are shipped out the next day. For the college student in the West, this high-tech ordering system enables him or her to buy goods at the lowest possible price. For the Chinese factory owner, the system ensures a constant demand for the product, and for the worker, steady wages.

The absence of an overarching world **authority** is a third characteristic of the modern international system. Rapid change is taking place in a world where there is no overarching authority that can use force to restrain the violent or bring the offenders to justice. We live in a world whose outlines were set by the Treaty of Westphalia, a seventeenth-century treaty signed by the states of Europe that were eager to work out ways to stop the violence that had been tearing their continent apart for thirty years (see chapter 3). The **treaty**'s program for peace was based on the twin notions of state sovereignty and noninterference in the affairs of other states. Three and a half centuries later, the principal world actors remain the sovereign states, or independent countries, like China, Japan, Russia, France, and the United States. When we call a state **sovereign**, we mean no higher authority can control its decisions: the state has a monopoly on the legitimate use of force. Almost all of the world's states are members of the world organization of states, the United Nations (UN), but UN decisions are not binding on its members because the UN's institutions have no coercive means to compel compliance.

Sovereignty thus presents states with opportunities for conflict or cooperation. In particular, sovereignty engenders political forces within states that promote cooperation with other states, as well as forces that emphasize the state's individuality, uniqueness, and national interest. World politics today is push-and-pull between the forces of **decentralization** and forces of **centralization**; you will find this theme recurring throughout this book. Since the 1970s, non-state actors have played an increasing role in influencing subgroups within states one way or the other. These actors include international intergovernmental organizations (IGOs) and non-state actors representing groups of individuals rather than governments. These actors have taken advantage of rapid change and global interconnectedness to undercut the longtime dominance of states in world **politics**. Through their activities non-state actors have challenged the viability of actions long accepted as lying solely within the jurisdiction of states, such as war, treaty making, and diplomacy.

This text is designed to give you the analytical and factual tools to develop your own appreciation of how the interaction of these forces shapes world politics. To help you understand your world better and to address its challenges, chapter 1 introduces you to the subject matter of world politics. It gives you three major reasons for studying world politics. The chapter closes with a discussion of the significant forces currently at work in the world. This discussion will help you find patterns in current events and to locate yourself and your place in the world today. At the end of the chapter, we provide a case study on *The Report of the 9/11 Commission of the U.S. Senate and New Forces Shaping the Planet*. The case study draws together and puts into practice the chapter's main points. ■

Decentralization The spreading or distribution of functions and power from a central authority to regional and local authorities. In world politics, decentralization infers the strengthening of the functions and powers of the various entities that make up the international system, including states and non-state actors.

Centralization The concentration of political or administrative power in a central authority with diminished power at lower or local levels of government. In world politics centralization infers the concentration of political power in some kind of central institution with the states giving up some of their powers of self-rule.

Politics The theory and practice of government at all levels of organization. The total complex of relations between humans in society.

WHAT IS WORLD POLITICS?

> **1** Define world politics and be able to understand current political events through the competing forces of centralization and decentralization.

The ancient Greek philosopher Aristotle (384–322 BC) wrote, "Man by nature is a political animal."[1] *Politics* comes from the Greek word for the principal form of state organization in ancient Greece, the city-state, or *polis*. Aristotle took for granted that a primary feature of a political community is authority to make decisions for the well-being of the community. This authority or power may be exercised in a legal or dictatorial manner, and it may be located in one person (a king or dictator), a few people (oligarchy), or many people (representative government or mob rule). The nineteenth-century thinkers Karl Marx and Max Weber emphasized the importance of power deployed within a given territory as central to the concept of a political association.

Politics as the Authoritative Allocation of Values

Twentieth-century political scientists have built on these theories. We discuss two definitions that are particularly useful to world politics today. Political scientist Harold Lasswell defines *politics* as a power struggle about "who gets what, when, and how."[2] His colleague David Easton says, "Politics is the authoritative allocation of values or scarce resources."[3] Let us examine these definitions to understand aspects of relations among the world's states and non-state actors.

The Major Actors

The major actors in world politics are the ones *who,* in Lasswell's definition, compete to gain sufficient power to have a say in determining *what* the issues of political power struggle are and *how* the struggle will be played out.

a. As we saw at the beginning of the chapter, the principal group of actors are the 191 sovereign and independent states located around the globe. The governments of these states make decisions in the name of the state based on what the government determines are the national interests of the country. While in principle these decisions are independent of the influence or actions of other actors in world politics, in practice a state's decisions are based on the ebb and flow of the international political activity in which that state is engaged (see chapter 5 on foreign policy).

Intergovernmental organizations (IGOs) Organizations composed of representatives appointed by state governments that have agreed to become members of the organizations.

b. The second group is composed of **intergovernmental organizations (IGOs)**. These intergovernmental organizations are made up of representatives of state governments that have agreed to participate in them. The largest of these entities is the UN, of which almost all the world's states are members. Then there are regional IGOs, such as the European Union (EU), as well as regional trade, economic, and cultural organizations such as the North Atlantic Free Trade Association (NAFTA), which includes Canada, the United States, and Mexico and the Association of South East Asian Nations (ASEAN), a loose association of Southeast Asian states interested in pursuing common economic and, to a lesser degree, social policies.

Non-state actors (NSAs) Members of groups of individuals with shared economic, social, religious, or environmental interests.

c. **Non-state actors (NSAs)** are the third group of major actors in world politics. The members of these organizations are not representatives of states but of groups of individuals with shared economic, social, religious, or environmental interests. NSAs are a diverse group ranging from paramilitary and terrorist groups to international business corporations to scientific and professional organizations, humanitarian groups and religious movements. NSAs are the most recent arrivals on the international scene and among the most significant, as you will see throughout the book.

d. Finally, we should not fail to mention the importance of individuals as actors in world politics. History is full of people who change the course of history by virtue of their military, economic, or scientific genius. We talk about some of them in chapter 2.

Interactions among the Actors

If politics is about who gets what, when, and how, interactions among the actors are the *when* and the *how.* Timing and the ability to carry out a decision economically and efficiently are key determinants of the struggle for political power.

a. *Timing: When* a state decides to undertake an action on the international stage is critical to the probability of its success in that action. Throughout the 1930s, Chancellor Adolf Hitler of Germany engaged in small invasions into the territory of other European countries, starting with the Rhineland and ending with his takeover of Czechoslovakia in 1938. With each invasion, he tested the response of the Western democracies. After almost ten years of little or no response, Hitler judged the time was ripe for a full-scale invasion. His timing was perfect. The United States and Great Britain were not prepared to go to war.

b. *Ability to Carry Out a Decision:* Hitler underestimated the capabilities of his opponents. He invaded Poland and started World War II in 1939 because he wrongly thought that the Western democracies were so weak that they lacked the capability to oppose his superbly trained armies.

c. *The Struggle for Power:* This World War II example illustrates the hard fact that politics everywhere is a struggle for power. In the game of who gets what and how, power is exercised by somebody over someone else. Politics, in Easton's definition, is the *authoritative* allocation of **resources**. Some actor or group of actors must gain sufficient power to be able to decide what the other actors in the game get. How political actors understand the exercise of power determines, to a large extent, their sense of timing and the way they develop and utilize their capabilities. These issues are raised in the discussion of the modern state in chapters 3 and 4.

> **Resource**   A source of supply, support, or status; a natural source of wealth or revenue.

Theoretical approaches to understanding how power is exercised divide into two main viewpoints. The so-called realist approach sees the struggle for power as a game between players in which there is a clear winner and loser. While other players may improve their situation, the game is always about who wins and who loses. The idealist approach to power says while the struggle for power is a fact in world politics, states do not need to resort to violence or force to get what they want. In this view, peaceful cooperation for long-term gain is a vital component of any state's vision of its future. We talk more about the theoretical approaches to world politics in chapter 2.

Allocating Resources

Resources constitute the final component of Lasswell's definition, the *what,* or the *values* of Easton's definition. These resources may be conveniently divided into three types: political resources, economic resources, and social and cultural resources.

a. *Political resources* refer to a country's power, prestige, and status, backed by military power. We call these *scarce resources* because of the internationally perceived hierarchical arrangement of world order. As we show in chapter 3, we tend to perceive the international system as a four-tiered structure with the developed industrial states at the top and the poorest and failed states at the bottom. Developed countries can leverage their status and prestige to gain their objectives even if they lack military power. Poor and failed states can only use their weakness as bargaining chips. One state, the United States, is a superpower. Other industrialized states, like Japan, the United Kingdom, France, and Germany, are world powers. All these states have in common stable political systems. Although elections may be hotly contested, the transition of power from one leader to the next is peaceful. States with stable political systems are less likely to collapse or fail than states with weak political institutions. States like Russia and China are harder to categorize because they are in the midst of enormous political as well as economic transformation. However, Russia's nuclear weapons and China's large military gives these countries more power and greater status than very poor countries, like Chad, or failed states, almost non-states, like Somalia.

b. *Economic resources* include a state's financial resources, such as wealth, annual national income, supply of capital, and investment opportunities; industrial and agricultural production; and natural resources (oil, coal, soil, water, and mineral resources). Like political resources, these are also scarce resources not equally distributed around the globe. For example, most of the world's capital is located in the hands of the top 1 percent of the world's population, living primarily in the United States, Japan, and Western Europe. The United States attracts foreign investment, especially from Asia, because of its huge financial resources and relatively free financial markets, which make it easy to invest. Asia, by contrast, has become the global industrial powerhouse, producing the majority of consumer goods for the rest of the world.

By far, the most significant scarce economic resources are energy resources. So important is oil to the developed world's economies that many of us tend to explain world politics simply in terms of the struggle for control of the world's oil supplies. We look at this issue in chapter 7. Water is another scarce resource whose availability is grossly under appreciated. The world may eventually learn to do without oil, but human beings can never do without water. From California to Mexico, to Australia, China, and the Middle East, the Earth's water supply is increasingly failing to meet the needs of the Earth's large population. The twenty-first century is likely to see water wars (see chapter 14).

c. *Social and cultural resources* may not seem directly related to the global **struggle for power**, but they most certainly play a huge role. Like all other resources, these are scarce and unequally distributed around the globe. They include health, education, a clean environment, and a population that agrees on the major values of its government so that ethnic or religious diversity adds to the power of the state rather than undermines it. Once again, the United States, Japan, and Western Europe lead the world in these resources. They have the most educated populations, the healthiest people, and relative harmony between diverse ethnic and racial groups within national borders. A sick population has little strength to engage in economics or politics. For example, the AIDS epidemic in Africa is so severe that it is wiping out the middle generation of Africans, the very individuals who should be actively engaged in the economic and political life of their countries. Despite its political instability, Russia remains a powerful state, able to project itself on the world stage because it has a highly educated population with high-tech skills that are valuable all over the globe. What keeps Russia in a secondary power position is the declining health of its citizens. AIDS is becoming widespread throughout the country, and, as in Africa, threatening to wipe out much of that educated population.

We see, then, that who gets what, when, and how in world politics depends, in large measure, on which states can demonstrate sufficient power to determine or dominate decisions on the distribution of the world's scarce resources. It should come as no surprise that the wealthiest states with a strong military, high educational and health levels, and relative ethnic harmony should be the states in the best position to make their decisions prevail.

An Overview of World Politics

In world politics, as we have said, there is no authoritative institution—no world government—that is recognized as such by its member states and that has the power to make decisions about the distribution of the world's scarce resources.

Struggle for power   The struggle to compete for and reach dominance in an organization, a state, a region of the world, or the whole world.

Between Nations
Audio Concept
Cultural Resource
www.BetweenNations.org

Hence, throughout history, world politics has been characterized by the struggle for power. The international system has provided the jungle-like setting where force, conflict, and violence have often played key roles. We discuss the nature and exercise of power in chapter 4. Traditionally, power has been the exercise of brute force by a dominant and dominating authority to maintain order.

The Struggle for Power in European History

The struggle for power is an historical fact. Europe in particular has been the scene of bloody conflicts about which dynasty or state was to control the continent. So much has conflict characterized European interactions that the ruling European governments frequently tried to mitigate the violence by creating institutions promoting peace.

■ *Birth of the Modern State System:* In 1648, the leading states of Europe ended the Thirty Years War that each of the combatants at last realized it could not win. In the Treaty of Westphalia, signed that year, the competing states agreed not to try to overthrow each other's governments, not to interfere in each other's internal affairs, and generally to work toward a more peaceful Europe. The treaty was a landmark in that it set up mechanisms through which new states could be recognized and all the signatories could interact peacefully. Diplomacy became a regular practice in Europe, and although wars continued, some progress had been made to curtail the use of brute force to decide what was going to happen, when, and to whom.

■ *Balance of Power:* At the beginning of the nineteenth century, Napoleon Bonaparte of France led his triumphant armies to the gates of Moscow, overthrowing long-established governments in his path. To stop him, the leading states of Europe banded together and, in 1815, dealt Napoleon his deathblow at the Battle of Waterloo. Napoleon was exiled to a remote island for good. That same year, the European powers came together again, this time in Vienna, to negotiate the composition of Europe after Napoleon. One of the concepts that played a determining role in the negotiations was that of the **balance of power**. No one or even two states should be allowed to grow as powerful as France had. To prevent this, states chose their allies with an eye to seeing that the military might of one alliance was roughly equal to that of another. (Balance of power is discussed more fully in chapter 4.)

World War I marked the demise of the balance-of-power concept as a way to lessen or resolve conflict. Not only did the two major alliances at the end of the nineteenth century fail to prevent war, they may have actually promoted it. Germany, Italy, and Austro-Hungary were allied on one side, and England, France, and Russia on the other. When the heir to the Austrian throne was murdered in Serbia, Germany sprang to the rescue and said it would go to war for the honor of its Austrian ally. Russia protested, saying it had a paternal interest in the Slavic populations of Eastern Europe and would protect its Slav cousins if anyone invaded Serbia. (The Russians and the Serbs are two of many Slavic ethnic groups.) The British said a treaty was a treaty, and they backed their Russian allies. And so one of the bloodiest wars of the twentieth century began. The war was fought to a stalemate in 1917, with huge losses on both sides. The entrance of the United States into the war on the British and French side swung the balance of forces, and Germany was forced to surrender.

Between Nations
For more information see
The View From:
Lost Empires
www.BetweenNations.org

Balance of power The distribution of power among two or more nations where the pattern of military and economic dominance among them is balanced such that no single nation has dominance over the others.

Collective security   The maintenance of peace and prevention of war through the united action of nations.

■ *Collective Security:* At the Peace Conference at Versailles, outside Paris, France, the nations of Europe once again came together to talk about the organization of a postwar world. Europe was in a shambles, its economy in ruins. France had spent all the wealth accumulated in the previous century and lost 20 percent of its population. Because the Americans had had the decisive power to stop the Germans, U.S. President Woodrow Wilson, a former political science professor and president of Princeton University, presented to the Conference his view of an international organization where **collective security** would replace the old alliance system and the nations of the world would resolve their conflicts peacefully in a global assembly. The Conference delegates agreed somewhat reluctantly to form a League of Nations. However, despite Wilson's efforts, the United States Senate refused to ratify the treaty. With the most powerful world player absent, the League had a short life. In 1933, Hitler became chancellor in Germany. Just two decades after signing the Versailles peace treaty, Europe was at war again.

The vision of an international institution that could deal with conflict remained alive through the horrors of World War II and the Holocaust. In 1945, a new world organization came into being, the United Nations. This organization is still in existence. On balance, it has achieved a great deal and done much to alleviate world poverty and conquer disease. However, it has proved unable to stop conflict. We discuss the UN and its current role in world politics in chapter 6.

Terrorism and the Changed Face of the Struggle for Power

In the twenty-first century, as we learned, the world faces a new kind of war, a war launched by a faceless NSA, a group or groups of individuals who may reside anywhere on the globe. They recognize allegiance to no state or national government but are able to influence governments to support them or cease to oppose them. Because these individuals are networked all over the globe, they have the capability to launch an attack at any time and any place. One of the central questions of our time is how to cope with this new kind of terrorist threat (discussed in chapter 10). Can or should the UN be given more authority to pursue the issue? Should one state, such as the United States, be allowed to take the lead, as the empires of old did? Is the mobilization of national police by each country the answer? We have returned once again to the focus of politics: Who gets what, when, and how?

Terrorism   Politically motivated violence, usually perpetrated against civilians. Terrorists and terrorist groups normally want to change by force or by threat of force a political context that they oppose.

North Atlantic Treaty Organization (NATO) A military alliance, initially formed in 1949 between Belgium, the Netherlands, Luxembourg, France, Canada, Portugal, Italy, Norway, Denmark, Iceland, and the United States. The alliance created a system of collective defense whereby the member states agreed to mutual defence in response to an attack by an external party. At its beginning the attack was expected to come from Soviet Russia. Greece and Turkey joined in 1952 and West Germany in 1955. France withdrew from the alliance in 1959 to pursue an independent defence. After 9/11 NATO expanded its area of activity to include taking charge of the mission in Afghanistan.

Current Political Trends

The current world situation returns us to the major theme of this book, the push and pull of the forces of centralization and decentralization. The 2006 elections in the United States revealed the frustration and weariness with the global war on **terrorism** and the war in Iraq felt by the majority of the electorate of the United States. In October 2004, the Afghan people voted for a president in the first free election in decades. Free parliamentary elections were held a year later. The elections constituted a major achievement for the Afghan government in cooperation with the United States and its allies in the UN and **North Atlantic Treaty Organization (NATO)**. By 2007, the Taliban had regrouped from their safe bases inside Pakistan and threatened to undo this progress. The increasing sectarian violence in Iraq presents an even more complex picture, demanding a high level of international cooperation that so far the international community has not come together to provide. Europe and the United States have two very different approaches to internationalization. Europe prefers to see the UN as the authoritative decision maker in the world, doubtless because of that continent's horrific experience with an aggressive Germany trying to carve out a greater living space in two world wars. As the planet's sole superpower, the United States prefers to consider the UN's deficiencies in its calculus of that organization's role as world decision maker. The United States is thus less ready for the world to become more centralized politically than it already is. On the other hand, the United States is one of the leading advocates of economic globalization, whereas large groups of Europeans and Asians are not so ready to embrace that reality. Let's look at the world's experience with central world organizations. We begin with historic attempts to form central world organizations and the possible consequences of centralization. We then consider the rise of non-state actors in the post–World War II era and the possible consequences of decentralization.

A Peaceful World Order under a Central World Organization

If the struggle for power and dominance has been a central feature of world politics, the efforts to create order in place of conflict cited above suggest another dynamic that has also been at work, the push and pull of two opposing forces: centralization and decentralization. Forced centralization was a primary condition of the traditional empires of China, India, and Rome. However, each emperor had to allow some expression of regional differences to keep the empire intact. The empires fell apart under pressure from outside invaders and regions seeking more say in imperial affairs.

In the history of Europe, as we have seen, the movement since 1648 was toward voluntary centralization, culminating in the League of Nations and the UN. But the road was littered with the dead of European wars. In 1957, the Europeans took perhaps their most innovative and challenging step in forming the European Common Market, whose supranational governing institutions had the authority to impose rules and regulations on the governments of the member-states and to make sure those rules and regulations were enforced. Today, the Common Market has become the European Union (EU), with a membership of twenty-five states. We talk about the EU in chapter 6.

The Consequences of Centralization

Ultimately, the tendency toward centralization could lead to world government and the globalization of the world economy. Global economic integration (discussed in chapter 12) is well on its way. However, while world government has many supporters, it is unlikely to occur any time soon. Those in favor of it argue that a world government would more easily solve the planet's most urgent problems of violence, hunger, disease, poverty, and environmental decay. Those against it hold that because these problems can't be solved even on a national level, it is pie-in-the-sky thinking to believe a world government could solve them. They further argue that a world government would not end the power struggle that characterizes all of politics. Moreover, such a government would be so huge and create such a huge bureaucracy that no one on Earth would be able to identify with it. World citizenship is a long way off. Nevertheless, both sides would probably agree that the UN could be given more authority to make binding decisions on some of the more critical global issue areas, such as economic development, poverty, and disease.

 Between Nations
Audio Concept
Centralization
www.BetweenNations.org

The Rise of Non-state Actors and Increasing Decentralizing Tendencies

The movement toward voluntary centralization initiated by the European states was supported by the victorious powers of World War II, the United States, and Soviet Russia. The UN was designed to include all the states in the world so decisions about global issues could be made centrally by delegates from every government on the planet meeting in an inter-nation or inter-state assembly. However, the founders of the UN made no provision for the rise of non-state actors, and it is precisely these actors who form the core of the decentralizing and fragmenting forces at work in the world today. Not only terrorist groups, but religious organizations and even humanitarian or environmental groups sometimes seek to change social structures and political outcomes in the countries where they are working. On March 11, 2004, just prior to national elections, a terrorist group bombed one of Spain's main railways, killing more than 200 people. The action had a decisive influence on the outcome of the elections and encouraged the new Spanish government to pull its troops out of Iraq.

The Consequences of Decentralization

At the extreme end of decentralization is the descent of the world into prolonged chaos, where non-state actors have succeeded in bringing down or destroying national governments and have weakened the resolve of the powerful nations to take action. Niall Ferguson, a professor of history at Harvard University, suggests the defining movement of our time is not a shift of power *upward* to a centralized international organization like the UN but rather a shift of power *downward*. States have lost their monopoly over the means of violence and, with the advent of the Internet, can no longer control how and what individuals communicate to each other. Ferguson posits that the non-state actors now wield the power to decide who gets what when and how. The resultant scenario, as he sees it, is the plundering of the wealthiest countries of Europe, North America, and Asia, limited nuclear wars, pirate attacks on the high seas, an AIDS plague in Africa, and other horrors.[4]

Others argue that decentralization is not such a bad thing, as it allows non-state actors and individuals access to influence and decision making that was impossible before the Internet and the World Wide Web. In the last twenty years alone, citizens have overthrown dictatorial governments in the Philippines, Nicaragua, the Soviet Union, and Eastern Europe, and staged a massive protest in Tiananmen Square in Beijing, the capital city of Communist China (1989). Instant photos and replay enabled these events to be transmitted immediately around the globe, so the whole world could see what was happening. Decentralization has its positive aspects, they argue.

TEST PREPPER 1.1

ANSWERS APPEAR ON PAGE A12

True or False?

_____ 1. IGOs (intergovernmental organizations) are the principal actors in international politics.

_____ 2. NSAs (non-state actors) have only recently become major players in the international system, yet are among the most significant.

_____ 3. The idealist approach to power attempts to obtain as much power as possible by focusing on elevating a state's status and prestige.

_____ 4. Social and cultural resources are significant factors in whether a state will have power in the international system.

_____ 5. A state using the balance of power approach to international politics will attempt to balance its political and economic resources as much as possible.

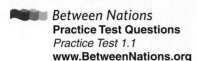

Between Nations
Practice Test Questions
Practice Test 1.1
www.BetweenNations.org

Multiple Choice

_____ 6. Which of the following makes the Treaty of Westphalia a landmark treaty for international affairs?

   a. Allowed for recognition of new states and for peaceful interactions between states

   b. Ended a war that had gone on longer than most other wars during that period of history

   c. Bypassed traditional diplomatic practices in favor of the use of force

   d. Allowed states to band together to form collective security alliances

_____ 7. Which of the following is *not* an example of centralizing tendencies in international politics?

   a. The League of Nations

   b. The United Nations

   c. The European Union

   d. Non-state-actor influence in the international system

WHY STUDY WORLD POLITICS?

2   *Understand how world politics affects your life and how studying international affairs will help you develop analytical skills to better see patterns in the complexity of current events.*

Among the many reasons that might be given for studying world politics, we offer three: The study of world politics will help relate the world's future to the rest of your life. World politics will help you see the connections between international issues and the politics of individual states. And studying world politics will help you find patterns in the complexity of current events.

Relating International Affairs to Your Life

Before 9/11, you might have thought about taking a course in world politics to satisfy some core college requirement, or because you wanted to understand your world better so you could choose a career or be directed toward a rewarding job. For example, you might have read about the high-tech jobs shifting to India, or the transfer of manufacturing jobs to China and Mexico, and wondered whether an understanding of the global forces behind such events could save someone (you) from a similar fate. Or you might have been planning to study or work abroad and wanted to know more about the place in world affairs of your country of destination. One of the most common reasons for studying world politics is in preparation for a career in the foreign service or the United States Department of State.

World Politics and International Events

Perhaps one of the most important reasons for studying international relations is the hard truth that ignorance is not bliss. World politics affects every aspect of your daily life—the clothes you wear, the food you eat, the technology you buy, and the gas you put into your car. Before 9/11, Americans had so little grasp of international affairs that they couldn't begin to understand the event. "Why do they hate us?" they asked.

Today, you need world politics more than ever to enable you to understand the forces that are shaping your life and your future. You must live and breathe world politics to grasp what may be in store for you. The 9/11 attacks were a tragic demonstration of the main theme of this book, namely, the increasing tension between the centralizing forces of globalization and the decentralizing forces of religion and ethnicity, which extend to every corner of our Earth. The U.S.–led war in Iraq and the subsequent transfer of sovereignty back to an Iraqi government turns the world spotlight on the role of the UN as a centralizing force for peace and stability and the proper exercise of power by member-states, like the United States, to compel regime change in states ruled by tyrants.

World Politics and Your Career

The economic downswing of 2001–2003 illustrates a second aspect of how world politics affects your life: the interdependent and transnational character of the issues. In 2002, Enron, a huge global corporation with deep ties to the powerful in Washington, suddenly went bankrupt. Its chief executives were accused of fraud, and its employees lost their life savings. Other major American corporations followed Enron into bankruptcy, their chief executive officers exhibiting the same fraudulent behavior as Enron's. The news of corruption in the U.S. economy quickly went out over the TV, radio, and Internet. Europe congratulated itself that its more regulated companies could not behave in the same way—until *its* business executives were charged with the same kinds of actions. The value of stocks on the U.S. stock market rose and fell in violent swings, and foreign stock exchanges experienced similar confusion. This confusion further reduced the value of stocks on Wall Street.

The stock decline made U.S. consumers fearful that their pensions and life savings, invested in the stock market, might disappear. So they decided to buy less. Fewer consumer orders to U.S. companies forced those companies to reduce their orders of supplies from foreign companies. Receiving fewer orders, the Asian and Latin American factories were forced to cut both expenses and production and to fire their employees. Unemployment rose and consumption fell around the world. International uncertainty about the U.S. economic future was increased by the war in Iraq and fear of oil shortages. In the United States, this international uncertainty translated into higher heating and energy costs, further raising the cost of production and discouraging consumer spending.

In this discussion of an economic downswing we circled the globe and introduced issues ranging from local production decisions to global war and peace. The modern world is so complex and interconnected that you cannot begin to know how to act without understanding the connections.

Studying World Politics and Developing Analytic Skills

In this book, we address

▮ The building blocks of world politics (the international system, power, foreign policy, international organizations, the global economy)

▮ The major issues (political geography, global justice, the environment)

▮ The theoretical and factual background that can enable you to answer those questions most important to you:

- What role should the United States play in world affairs?

- How can we ensure that we won't run out of energy?

- How can we ensure that the planet will continue to be hospitable to human life?

- How can we reduce the huge gap between the rich and the poor nations?

- What can be done about terrorism?

To help address these and related questions, each chapter contains a "Join the Debate" box that you can use to argue the theoretical points made in the chapter, or a box that invites active participation. If you work on these questions, when you have finished the book, you will be able to work out your own answers to questions of importance to you.

In summary, the study of world politics helps you make sense of your world. It gives you a set of tools with which to assess the world situation, whatever the crisis or driving forces at work may be. World politics provides methods of analysis to help you understand the diverse positions of the world's leaders and peoples, and it proposes frameworks for evaluating the media sound bites that flood the daily news. Last, studying world politics shows you how the world "out there" is closely tied to your world "at home" and how the interaction between the two affects your life.

Interconnections and Patterns in Politics

In the modern world, no country conducts its domestic affairs in a political vacuum but there are real differences between international relations and comparative government.

World Politics and Comparative Government

World politics is the study of interactions between international actors, such as those listed earlier in the chapter. Its focus is on who gets what, when, and why in the international arena. World politics thus differs substantially from comparative government whose subject area is the contrasts and similarities between who gets what, when, and why in different types of national governments. If we want to compare the role of the chief executive, like the president in the United States to the role of the president in Russia, we would turn to the tools of **comparative government**. The boundaries become confused, however, when we seek to compare national foreign policies, and the actions of state governments in the global arena. The fact is that in the real world, we cannot make a total separation between the conduct of actors within states and the conduct of these same actors between states. Domestic politics impacts on world politics and vice versa.

Comparative government The comparison of interactions of state actors within state borders.

World Politics and Domestic Politics: Intermestic Issues

Political scientists have coined the word *intermestic* to describe the interconnectedness of international and domestic political issues. You have seen this linkage in the discussion of the 2001–2003 international economic downswing. Here is a specific example.

In the 2006 U.S. elections, the Democratic Party won majorities in both the House of Representatives and the Senate. The new majority interpreted the election results as a mandate to get U.S. troops out of Iraq as soon as possible. Republican President George W. Bush responded by initiating a surge in troops to Iraq to reduce the violence and bring more law and order to the capital city of Baghdad. The Democrats in the House reacted to the initiative by passing a budget that included stipulations and dates as to when the troops in Iraq were to be withdrawn. As is his prerogative under the U.S. Constitution's system of checks and balances Bush vetoed the budget, which then had to go back to the legislature for reconsideration. Bush argued that the Constitution made him commander-in-chief, and in that capacity, he had the right to initiate any action he considered necessary in the war in Iraq. We have been talking about this situation so far in *comparative-government terminology*: the separation of powers according to the U.S. constitution, the powers of the separate branches of government, and the checks and balances on these powers. How does the tension between the legislature and executive in the United States differ from an analogous tension between Prime Minister Gordon Brown and the British House of Commons? Where does tension between the legislative and executive lie in France? Can such tension exist under the more autocratic Russian constitution?

As students of world politics, however, our question is not about relations between branches of government as a comparative-government issue, but how these relations impact on the conduct of U.S. foreign policy. How does the bickering and bargaining between the executive and legislature in the United States structure foreign policy inputs and outputs? What effect does all the infighting have on the Sunni-Shiite conflict in Iraq? When we ask these questions, we are treating the current legislative-executive standoff in the United States as an *intermestic issue*.

Between Nations
For more information see
*The Beginning of
the Cold War*
www.BetweenNations.org

Cold War The great ideological and power conflict between the Soviet Union and its allies and the United States and its allies, which lasted roughly from 1946 to 1991.

Religious extremism The use of religion to rationalize extreme actions such as terrorism or militancy against a recognized government.

Finding Patterns in the Complexity of Current Events

Perhaps the most important reason you need to study world politics, as we noted at the beginning of the chapter, is that the world of the twenty-first century is changing at a more rapid pace than at any other time in history. In the final decade of the twentieth century, we witnessed a revolution in communications and technology, and the end of the **Cold War**. The Cold War between the United States and the Soviet Union, the two major powers in the world at that time, lasted almost fifty years (from 1946 to 1991), and the global bipolarity of that era seemed a permanent fixture of the international landscape. Suddenly, the war was over, leaving the international community grasping for a definition of the new era. Too soon, however, terrorism supplied some of that definition, as did **religious extremism**, which has become a major ideological factor in world politics in the new century.

Giving students tools for understanding the complex, rapidly changing circumstances around us is an important goal of this book. Despite the seeming chaos of the events portrayed on the nightly news, patterns *can* be found. The principal patterns on which we focus in this book are the centralizing and decentralizing forces at work in world politics today. Forces for centralization can be seen in the twin processes of globalization and global interdependence. In contrast, forces for decentralization are those that insist on their own identity, self-worth, and autonomy of action. They can be found in ethnic nationalism; in individual, group, and state terrorism; religious militancy; and in immediate citizen access to information. The 9/11 terrorist attacks on the United States are a dramatic example of the centralizing/decentralizing tensions in the modern world. Islamic terrorists justified their murderous actions through references to Islam and the Koran. In so doing, they energized supporters of Islam in the Middle East, and Central and East Asia (decentralizing force). The rallying of the whole world around the United States in its moment of tragedy was a centralizing force that focused world attention on the need to deal with terrorism. In the course of this book, we return to this theme of centralizing/decentralizing tensions repeatedly in our study of the structure, actors and issues of world politics.

When you are asked why you have chosen to study world politics, you can now give at least three important answers:

▌ World politics provides you with a framework with which to evaluate and define your life and future.

▌ World politics also enables you to see the interconnectedness of international and domestic politics, and to understand that decisions made in one country may one day profoundly affect you.

▌ You need to study world politics to find the patterns that can make sense of those forces that are so rapidly changing our fast-moving world.

The last section of the chapter looks at the main forces at work in world politics today that are shaping your future and the future of the planet.

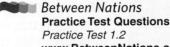 **Between Nations**
For more information see
Globalization and Sovereignty
www.BetweenNations.org

TEST PREPPER 1.2   ANSWERS APPEAR ON PAGE A12

True or False?

_____ 1. Religion and ethnicity act as centralizing forces leading to increased peace and stability in international politics.

_____ 2. The bankruptcy of corporations in America has the potential to lead to the increase in unemployment and reduced consumption throughout the rest of the world.

_____ 3. Comparative government—the study of political processes internal to governments around the world—can be clearly separated from the study of international affairs, which focuses on politics between states.

Multiple Choice

_____ 4. Which of the following is not a proposal from the UN Commission on Global Governance?

    a. A system of global taxation for individuals and companies that burn fuels emitting carbon dioxide

    b. A standing UN army to intervene in states that abuse human rights

    c. A system that allows individuals to sue states that engage in economic policies that counter free trade practices

    d. UN authority over global commons such as the oceans

_____ 5. Intermestic issues deal with:

    a. The intersection between politics of developed countries and developing countries

    b. Internal political processes influenced by domestic lobbying groups

    c. Issues that have both a domestic and international component

    d. International economic situations that affect the UN's ability to provide funding for its internal operations

 Between Nations
Practice Test Questions
Practice Test 1.2
www.BetweenNations.org

WHAT NEW FORCES ARE SHAPING THE PLANET?

 Identify the five most significant forces shaping the world today and understand how these forces have centralizing or decentralizing effects on world politics.

In this book, we discuss five forces that are important in shaping our world at present. These are not the only forces, but to our mind, they are the most significant. They are:

▌ information technology

▌ new global and transnational issues

▌ increasing inability of states to solve their problems individually

▌ rise of ethnic nationalism and religious fundamentalism

▌ new citizen activism

Whether these forces will push the world closer together or farther apart it is too soon to tell. But it is safe to say that at present, each of them can be either centripetal or centrifugal. They can work toward greater cooperation or toward more global fragmentation. Let us look at each of these forces in turn.

Information Technology

Since 1980, the industrialized nations have shifted to what are termed *postindustrial technologies*. These technologies make distances shorter and increase the speed of communication. They range from currency-exchange transactions via the computer to the transfer of ideas and pictures via satellite, fax, E-mail, and the Internet. Our lives have been transformed by the information revolution. How have these technologies affected international relations? Here are a few examples.

The Global Village: The Internet and Videotechnology

On September 11, 2001, thanks to an array of improved information technologies, TV viewers around the world watched in disbelief as two airplanes crashed into the twin towers of the World Trade Center in New York City, causing them to collapse. The film sequence was played over and over again in the days and months that followed.

Since then, Osama bin Laden's organization, al Qaeda and other terrorist groups have made consistent use of the mass media to publicize their goals, their view of the world, and their selected killings of those who would be against them. They have successfully planned and executed terrorist attacks—not only in the United States but also in Saudi Arabia; in the port city of Aden on the Red Sea; at a Jewish synagogue in Morocco; at a vacation resort in Indonesia; on the fast rail line between Madrid and Seville, Spain; in London, UK; in resort towns in Egypt; and all over Iraq. Behind their success lies a skillful, coordinated usage of old and established technologies such as bombs and airplanes with the new technologies of rapid communication, instant replay, and mass audiences.

Information Technology and Global Financial Markets

In 1987, the U.S. stock market fell more points in a single day than on Black Friday in 1929. In 1998, the stock market went on a roller-coaster ride, leaving investors breathless. In March 2007, volatility on the Shanghai stock exchange caused mar-

High-tech Meets Low-tech
High-tech cell phone mixes with low-tech begging bowl as this Hindu sadhu or holy man in Allahabad, India, connects with the faithful by phone. His begging bowl recalls his poverty and his dependency on others, just as all living things are connected in the divine web of being.

kets around the world to fall. There was talk of a possible crash. In both cases, computer technology and instant satellite communication of corporate and market news played a role in market volatility. Let's look at how.

Computer programming and instant recording of stock sales have played a major role in the roller-coaster market that characterized the beginning of the twenty-first century. Before the Internet, brokers handled all stock dealings. Today, individuals may manage their own stock transactions over the Internet, or they can send instructions to their brokers to program the computer to trigger the automatic sale of a stock when it rises or falls to a specified value. The computer has thus enabled thousands of people to enter the stock market who never had participated before. Information technology has created twenty-four-hour virtual stock markets. When the real stock market closes in Tokyo or Hong Kong and before it opens in New York, computer stock traders are already trading stock based on activity in the Asian markets.

In international financial dealings, information technology, in a very real sense, is a force integrating global financial markets, even risking the replacement of real stock exchanges with virtual ones. On the other side of the coin, information technology is a decentralizing force, as it provides access to information previously obtainable only by being physically present at the stock market and thus enables individuals to play the market independently of a stockbroker or exchange.

Information Technology as a Decentralizing Tool

A third example of the impact of rapid information technology on world events is the incredible speedup of information exchange. Anyone who perpetrates a terrorist act can immediately evaluate the results of a bombing, shooting, or killing by watching how the media report the event on that day's evening news program. Of key importance is the media's assessment of the action's impact on public opinion. The bombing of the World Trade Center provoked universal horror and sparked a major U.S. offensive against terrorist camps in Afghanistan. The bombing of a Spanish train in March 2004, however, produced an opposite reaction. In this case, horror moved the Spanish people to give in to terrorist demands that Spain withdraw its troops from Iraq. Because the effect of terroristic acts on public opinion within states and around the world is immediately visible through the intensity of public outcry and government response, terrorist groups quickly learn to exploit the weak links in the chain of opposition to them to influence world opinion in their favor.

Information Technology: A Tool for World Centralization or Decentralization?

Today, we find ourselves in the middle of the information revolution and can only begin to assess its impact. Change occurs so fast that we may not be able to understand the dimensions of this revolution until we have experienced its unintended consequences. A search on the World Wide Web will locate virtually any information one could want and bring together like-minded people around the world. The information revolution has liberated individuals from dependence on some authority for information and, thus is a powerful decentralizing force. So much information is available, in fact, that individuals have difficulty separating reliable and trustworthy information from erroneous hearsay. The revolution thus risks producing a worldwide population of information junkies who lack the tools for finding meaning in the message but who are ready to react to it.

On the centralizing side, the new technology has the ability to disseminate information around the globe, permitting governments and corporations to make

 Between Nations
For more information see
*Why It Matters to You:
Why Shouldn't I Download
Music from the Internet Free?*
www.BetweenNations.org

instant global connections. Equally important, it can unite individuals in one chat room for discussion on a subject of mutual interest. So we must wait and see before we make a final judgment on information technology.

The New Global and Transnational Issues

In the twenty-first century, events in one part of the world can reverberate on the global level. They differ from the old issues in that they are **transnational**, freely crossing state borders.

The Global Economy

One example, in the new global economy, is the transnational corporation. This is a corporation that can use communications technology to run a global business without having a national home. It can invest and locate anywhere on the planet, benefiting the people who live in that location with jobs, but it is ready and willing to pull capital out and move elsewhere if the business climate in that country shifts to its disadvantage. When global capital pulled out of Indonesia in 1997, the Indonesian people were quickly reduced to poverty. In some regions and countries, such as Russia, corporations are reluctant to invest global capital. Other countries seem to attract capital. We talk more about transnational capital transactions in chapters 10 and 11.

A main feature of our world today is the large gap between the world's rich and the world's poor, both within countries and transnationally. This problem highlights one of the paradoxes of the tension between centralization and decentralization. Global capital responds to the global market. In so doing, it acts at odds with attempts by the international community to put weak or failed states back on their feet. Hamid Karzai, the president of Afghanistan, has made frequent appeals to the international community to invest in his country, with few responses from global capital sources.

The global economy allows corporations of the major industrialized countries to take advantage of low costs and cheap labor in the developing countries in order to manufacture products to market around the world. On the plus side, people all over the globe benefit from the quantity and quality of goods produced by global corporations. On the downside, the economies of mass production can drive out local companies and local products causing large-scale unemployment whenever a local industry shuts down.

Environmental Degradation

Environmental degradation is another transnational and interdependent problem. Early environmentalists such as the English poets William Blake,[5] and William Wordsworth[6] deplored England's "satanic mills" and "stagnant waters." In the New World, John James Audubon painted and Henry Thoreau[7] decried the disappearing flora and fauna of the rapidly expanding American frontier.

Transnational Going beyond state borders or unstoppable at state borders. Air pollution, for example, may be confined within the boundaries of one state, or it may be transnational, crossing state boundaries. We call this instance *transboundary air pollution.*

McWorld Is Here

At the end of the twentieth century, large corporations produced and marketed literally around the world. McDonald's was the first to market fast food successfully by selling a standardized hamburger and French fries in California. The company expanded operations throughout the United States and prides itself in maintaining the same quality of food service around the world today. This photo was shot in Ortokoy, Istanbul, Turkey.

In 1969, we went to the moon and for the first time appreciated how fragile and small our planet really was. In the industrialized countries, environmental degradation has become increasingly obvious in the pollution of waterways, and smog in the larger cities. At first, these problems seemed to be solvable by the action of national governments—where a problem such as pollution of a river involved several states—or by a group of states. Now we know that these problems require a transnational approach to their solution.

The 1980s brought recognition of a new dimension to environmental pollution: the degradation of the **global commons**. The global commons are areas of the planet, such as oceans and the Earth's atmosphere, which are shared by all the world's population. Soil erosion, deforestation, and water pollution are more than local problems; they are transnational as well. Not only does the cutting down of forests lead to local soil erosion but also to reduced rainfall caused by deforestation that contributes to regional droughts, as in Saharan Africa, and to global warming. The jury is still out as to whether reduction in our consumption of fossil fuels would significantly slow down the process. Nevertheless none of us would wish by our actions to contaminate the atmosphere in such a way as to risk life on Earth. At the opening of the twenty-first century, climate change and sustainable development have become international priorities. (We talk more about these issues in chapter 14.)

> **Global commons** Areas of the Earth's biosphere that are shared by all the world's population, such as oceans and the atmosphere.

International Terrorism

Finally, terrorism recognizes no state borders and has no single source. In recent years, the face of terrorism has changed. Terrorists are now networked all over the globe, and their attacks have become more deadly. They come from a diverse set of countries—Iran, Iraq, Pakistan, Libya, Egypt, Saudi Arabia, Afghanistan, Peru, and Central America. Fifteen of the nineteen hijackers who commandeered the four planes on 9/11 were Saudi citizens. Identifying terrorists and preventing attacks are transnational tasks that necessitate timely coordination of both large amounts of information from all parts of the world and action among countries.

Can you identify other transborder problems? Do not overlook international drug trafficking, the global child and sex trade, and the large migrations of refugees who seek to escape the consequences of global problems. These, as well as the issues that we have identified, have acquired a life of their own, demanding international agencies to assure maximum benefits and minimum hardships to all the world's people. The new issues thus operate as a powerful force pushing the world toward cooperation and international community building.

The Increasing Inability of the State to Solve Problems

The twenty-first century has seen the ability of the state to resolve serious problems both within and without its borders decline. Not only are governments finding it harder to solve transnational problems on their own but they are also discovering they can no longer solve basic domestic problems. Why is this so? Let us first consider transnational problems, and then domestic.

Transnational Problems and Transnational Solutions

An important theme that runs throughout this book is that no state can solve the new transnational problems on its own. Solutions to terrorism, migration, drug trafficking, environmental degradation, and the global child and sex trade require the cooperation of the major governments around the world, including the

Garment Workers in a Factory, Seeduwa, Sri Lanka

A negative aspect of globalization has been the setting up by transnational corporations of manufacturing plants in countries, like Mexico, where wages are low. The practice takes jobs away from workers in the United States, while offering the low-wage earners between $1.00 and $3.00 a day. The pay for the workers in the developing countries is often the difference between want and subsistence, but it puts workers in the affluent, higher paid, industrialized countries out of work.

exchange of sensitive information, the standardization of laws relating to these issues, and the coordination of national police forces.

We have seen the difficulties faced by states trying to solve transnational problems on their own. Even a nation as powerful and wealthy as the United States cannot stop terrorism or drug trafficking by unilateral action. In the case of the environment, it is clear that no one country can undertake the cleanup of the world's oceans or air by itself. Some reduction of domestic levels of carbon or sulfur dioxide emissions into the air can be achieved through the passage and enforcement of national emission standards. But these reductions are generally limited to local areas. The achievement of worldwide reduction of emissions requires a global agreement on the nature of the problem and its solution, with stipulations on which country is to do what to contribute to the solution.

Inability of States to Solve Problems at Home

If states are limited in what they can do to solve the new transnational problems, they are also limited in their ability to solve problems that were once viewed as purely domestic single-handedly. This is an entirely new situation requiring rethinking of what noninterference in the affairs of other states mean. Problems such as a fair wage for workers, the right price for wheat, and standards for industry and consumer goods are now enmeshed in the politics of globalization. The U.S. Congress could raise the minimum wage to $10 an hour, but many U.S. industries would quickly move to Mexico, the Caribbean, or Southeast Asia, where the cost of labor averages a dollar a day. The result would be rising unemployment in the United States and a further increase in the gap between rich and poor, as more unskilled workers are thrown out of the U.S. work force. In addition, the $10 hourly labor cost would increase the cost of products made in the United States to a level where they could not compete with cheaper products on the world market. The United States could try to push China and India into adopting a higher wage scale, but clearly, both countries would see this as interference in their domestic affairs. Globalization has been one of the strongest forces in reorienting state problem solving in the direction of international organizations (centralization). On the other hand, the perceived erosion of the state's control of the domestic agenda has contributed to an increase in decentralizing tendencies within state borders.

The Rise of Ethnic Nationalism and Religious Fundamentalism

The weakening of centralized state power has encouraged decentralization in many parts of the globe. For examples, please take a good look at Table 1.1.

Where state power has dramatically decreased, ethnic nationalist and religious movements have sometimes succeeded in breaking that state into national ethnic entities, as happened in Czechoslovakia and Yugoslavia in the 1990s after the collapse of communism. More frequently, the inability of the central government to quell ethnic tensions has resulted in a persistent low-level state of civil war. For example, each of the Central Asian states that arose from the fall of the Soviet

TABLE 1.1

Some States Experiencing Internal Dissension

State	Source of Dissension
Mexico	Low-level conflict between Mexican government and the Native Americans of Chiapas for greater autonomy of the Chiapas region
Great Britain	Conflict in Northern Ireland between Roman Catholics and Protestants
Spain	Basque separatist movement wants either independence or more autonomy
Belgium	Continuous dissension between Flemish- or Dutch-speaking Protestant North and French-speaking Catholic South
Russia	Chechnya seeking independence
Georgia	Conflict between majority Christian Georgians and minority Muslim Abkhazi demanding independence
Azerbaijan	Conflict between majority Muslim Azeris and minority Christian Armenians who want the Armenian-controlled part of Azerbaijan ceded to Armenia
Israel	Delineation of a Palestinian state
Iraq	Conflict between minority Sunni Iraqis, ethnic Kurds, and majority Shiite Iraqis
India/Pakistan	Conflict between Muslims, supported by Pakistan, and Hindus, supported by India, for control of the territory of Kashmir
China	Fifty-year-old conflict between Chinese government and Tibetans over Tibetan desire for independence
Sri Lanka	Ongoing conflict between the majority Sinhalese and the minority Tamils
Sudan	Two conflicts: 1) A civil war between the black Christian south and Arab Muslim north that has been going on for decades 2) In Darfur, in western Sudan, raids and mass murders of black Muslims by Arab Muslims
Rwanda	Ethnic rivalry between Hutus and Tutsis
Ivory Coast	Civil war between largely Christian south and Muslim north

Union has a multiethnic population. In many of them, the larger ethnic minorities would prefer their own independent country, or at least a large share of self-rule. Since 1991, civil wars have raged in Azerbaijan, Georgia, and Tajikistan, as has a war for independence in Chechnya a region of Russia. (To understand the differences among state, the nation, and ethnic groups, review Figure 1.1.)

Ethnic and Religious Tension

Ethnic and religious tensions have increased in many parts of the world. In Africa, the most salient examples are the civil wars in Sudan, Somalia, Rwanda, the Ivory Coast, and the Democratic Republic of Congo. An example of seemingly irresolvable religious nationalism is the century-old conflict between Jews and Palestinian Arabs in what is now Israel and the Palestinian territories. The conflict is made more complex by the division between the Palestinians themselves over

FIGURE 1.1

Do You Know the Difference Between . . . ?

State

▮ A geographic territory with internationally recognized boundaries

▮ An internationally recognized and identifiable population that lives within those boundaries

▮ An internationally recognized authority structure or government

Nation

▮ A group of people linked together in some manner, such as by a common territory (Estonians, Czechs, Norwegians), although not necessarily by a common territory (Arabs, Tamils, Kazaks)

▮ Common culture that may or may not be based on religion

▮ Common language

▮ Common history or understanding of the past

▮ General desire for independence

Ethnic Group

▮ A group of people linked together similarly to those of a nation, EXCEPT:

  • No expressed desire for independence

  • Most important unifying or identifying factor is language

▮ Religion is often a unifying factor.

Multinational State: A state such as China, India, Nigeria, Russia, or the United States, which contains more than one nation within its territory. Most states are multinational.

Multistate Nation: A single nation occupying more than one state boundary. The German, Russian, and Kurd nations are classic examples.

Ethnic Nationalism: An ethnic group that seeks independence and bases its right to independence on the right to speak its own language (the Hungarians in Slovakia and Romania; the Kurds in Iraq, Iran, and Turkey; the Basques in Spain and France; the Albanians in the Yugoslav province of Kosovo). In contrast to the American fight for independence, which was based on self-rule over a specific territory regardless of language, most modern nationalist movements are language oriented. We call groups seeking independence under such conditions ethnic national groups.

Race: A division of humankind possessing biological traits that are transmissible by descent and are sufficient to characterize it as a distinctive human type. Based on the criteria of pigmentation, color and form of hair, shape of head and nose, and stature, anthropologists generally agree on three major races: the Caucasoid, Mongoloid, and Negroid. To classify humans on the basis of race is highly problematic, for there has been an intermingling of races since earliest human history.[8]

---

whether to follow a more traditionally nationalist path to self-government represented by President Abbas and his party, al Fatah, or to take the more extreme religious nationalist route of Hamas (the majority in the legislature) and become a Muslim state.

In Kashmir, Indian Hindu soldiers have faced Pakistani Muslim soldiers since 1948 in a bloody drama of hostility, over which country (and religion) is to prevail. In Sri Lanka, the Tamils, a minority ethnic group, want independence from the Sinhalese ethnic majority. The French-speaking Catholic Canadian province of Quebec has held several referendums on whether it should become independent of Canada.

The driving force behind the rise of religious fundamentalism has been the rise of militant Islam. While militant Islam is composed of many diverse terrorist groups, its primary leader is Osama bin Laden. Scholars differ as to the objectives of militant Islam, but it is generally conceded that its goal is to end the domination of the world by the Western, highly industrialized countries that militant Islamic groups consider decadent and corrupt, and to replace the existing world order with a Muslim universal caliphate rooted in the Muslim holy book, the Koran, and Islamic law known as the *Shari'a*. To achieve these goals, terrorists groups have attacked strategic sites in Europe, Asia, Africa, and North America. Nowhere is the struggle for power being more fiercely fought than in Afghanistan and Iraq.

New Citizen Activism

The fifth and last new force we discuss as influencing world politics is the rise of citizen activism. People around the world appear frustrated by what they see as the weakness and failure of the state to pay attention to their concerns. They may blame their governments for corruption, for abandoning traditional values or traditional religion, or for failing to take sufficiently radical measures to either create or halt change.

Citizen Activism and Citizen Empowerment

The efforts of citizens to take power into their own hands and change the politics of their country has markedly increased since the 1970s. In Iran, angry citizens in 1978 protested against what they perceived as their government's inhuman and absolutist methods of rapid industrialization. In 1979, within a little more than two weeks they ousted the ruling shah and welcomed home Ayatollah Khomeini, a cleric urging the return to fundamental Islamic values. In Indonesia in 1998, thousands of young people took to the streets to demand democracy as a solution to the collapse of the Indonesian economy. In 2003–2005 citizens in the Republic of Georgia and Ukraine in what became known as the Rose and Orange Revolutions, organized massive sit-ins in their main squares demanding a more democratic government. The mass demonstrations against the World Trade Organization (WTO) at every meeting it has held since November 1999 provide another illustration of this new level of citizen activism with the protesters demanding the end of globalization. In the first four examples, citizen activism brought changes in the government of the country where the demonstration took place. Iran became an Islamic Republic, Indonesia embarked on its democratic road. In Georgia, the new government has brought economic growth and greater political freedom, while Ukraine has been forced to learn the value of compromise and national reconciliation.

The Green Belt Movement
Nobel Peace Prize Winner Dr. Wangari Maathai of Kenya working with volunteers from the Green Belt Movement planting trees to reforest Kenya's degraded environment.[9]

Citizen empowerment is thus more than a passing phenomenon. Unlike any other technology, the personal computer or cell phone linked to the Internet gives the individual the ability to seek and send information and to communicate with individuals who have similar views but live in other countries and cultures. Messages flowing across the Internet provide the infrastructure necessary to support citizens' organizations.

Rise of Non-state Actors

Citizen activism is not only a matter of mass demonstrations. Increase in citizen activism has gone hand in hand with the accelerated growth of individual initiatives and **non-state actors (NSAs)**. Non-state actors are actors on the international stage that are not states. NSAs may be subdivided into four main groups: international paramilitary and terrorist groups such as the Shining Path (Sendero luminoso) in Peru or al Qaeda and its associated terrorist groups; firms and business with a global reach, such as multinational corporations (MNCs); the international media; and **nongovernmental organizations (NGOs)**. The 2006 Nobel Peace Prize

Non-state actor (NSA)   In international relations, these are actors on the international level that are not states.

Nongovernmental organization (NGO)
An international organization made up of groups or individuals, recruited across state boundaries, joined either by profession or interest.

winner exemplifies the individual and non-state-actor dimensions of citizen activism. The 2006 prize went to Bangladeshi native, Muhammad Yunus for his founding of the Grameen Bank, the first bank to give microcredit to poor people.

As noted earlier, NGOs are organizations of citizens with a common agenda or set of demands they would like a government to implement. NGOs are discussed in more depth in chapter 2 and chapter 7. Some NGOs go back to the nineteenth century, but most got started in the 1970s or later. NGOs may be organized at the grass-roots level, or at the state and international levels. Grass-roots groups commonly organize around a local issue. National NGOs organize to pressure national governments to adopt certain policies or legislation, while the newest of the NGOs, international NGOs, aim to influence international organizations, such as the UN. NGOs are as diverse as Mothers Against Drunk Driving (national), Friends of the Earth (international), the Adirondack Mountain Club (local), Sister Cities International (international), and al Qaeda, an international terrorist organization.

Pressure exerted by global NGOs became so strong that in the late 1980s the UN agreed to give legal standing to NGOs that registered with them. Legal standing means that the registered NGOs are represented in an official capacity at world conferences and in deliberations about UN activities. Such a practice would have been unthinkable one hundred years ago.

As you can see, the new citizen activism can reinforce the centralizing tendencies at work today through the formation of like-minded NGOs that can influence policy at the local, national, and international levels. It can also strengthen the fragmentation of world politics through the proliferation of groups with specific agendas. International terrorism is not the product of one large terrorist organization but rather a collection of smaller groups that are loosely associated and tend to act on their own volition for their own goals.

Test Prepper 1.3

Answers appear on page A12

True or False?

_____ 1. Forces such as information technology either act as centralizing or decentralizing forces in world politics, but not both.

_____ 2. Transnational corporations operate in multiple countries but do not possess a national home.

_____ 3. While the origins of transnational problems may lie across multiple countries, oftentimes it is possible for just one powerful country (such as the United States) to solve the problem.

_____ 4. Ethnic or national movements leading to internal dissent is a problem faced by many different countries, including countries in the developed world such as Great Britain and Spain.

_____ 5. With the changing world landscape after the attacks in the United States on 9/11, the world has seen a significant decrease in citizen-based efforts to take power into their own hands.

Multiple Choice

_____ 6. The global commons are:
   a. A variety of affiliated IGOs dealing with transnational economic issues
   b. A subdivision of the UN that focuses on bridging the gap between divergent viewpoints throughout the world
   c. Issues, such as human rights, that generally act as centralizing forces in world politics
   d. Areas of the planet shared by all the world's population

_____ 7. A geographic territory with internationally recognized boundaries is one element of a:
   a. state   c. race
   b. nation   d. ethnic group

Between Nations
Practice Test Questions
Practice Test 1.3
www.BetweenNations.org

CASE STUDY

The Report of the 9/11 Commission of the U.S. Senate and New Forces Shaping the Planet

See **www.BetweenNations.org**   **Between Nations**

JOIN THE DEBATE

Should There Be One World Government?

OVERVIEW

In 1995, the United Nations Commission on Global Governance published *Our Global Neighborhood*. This report was commissioned after a meeting in 1991 in Stockholm, Sweden, entitled "Common Responsibility in the 1990s: The Stockholm Initiative on Global Security and Governance." The report suggests changes in the way the world community goes about running its affairs in order to promote a more just and equitable world society. It presents a cogent argument for consolidating our current international organizations by giving more power to the organizations of the United Nations. The concept of global governance is opposed by those who see the road to one world government as the end of state sovereignty and an opening of the door to tyranny on a scale the world has never seen, all overseen by a gigantic, faceless, unelected bureaucracy. You are just starting your course on World Politics. It is more than likely you have never given any thought or marshaled any arguments in favor of one world government or national sovereignty. Below, we give you some arguments to start you off. Go ahead. Try it. What about one world government?

Most Important Proposals

- A system of global taxation based on the levy of special-user charges, such as a carbon tax, for individuals and companies that burn any kind of fuel that emits carbon dioxide
- A standing UN army that would have the sole authority to intervene in states that abuse human rights
- An Economic Security Council that would oversee more equitable payment for labor, the promotion of sustainable development around the world, and policies to alleviate poverty and disease

- UN authority over the global commons—the oceans and the atmosphere
- An end to the veto power of permanent members of the UN Security Council
- A new Petitions Council to which individuals and NGOs could bring suit against states for noncompliance with international law
- A new International Court of Criminal Justice, whose verdicts would be binding on all the member states of the UN. (This court, established in July 1998—but without binding jurisdiction on all UN member states—is now located in The Hague, the Netherlands.)
- Expanded authority for the secretary-general of the UN.

Arguments for a Stronger, More Powerful United Nations Organization

- *A small world needs a world government.* The world is already so small that we can fly around it in supersonic planes or satellites in three hours or less.
- *The world's economy is already globalized.* What better way to promote more equitable labor conditions and conservation of environmental resources than through a central organization empowered to oversee the planet's human and natural resources?
- *Intervention by one country in the affairs of another is unacceptable.* Decisions on the invasion of member-states must be made collectively within the UN Security Council.
- *There already exist UN military forces with specific orders for specific places and targets.* The upgrading of these forces into a permanent army would give more clout to UN decisions on the resolution of global conflicts.

∎ *The International Court of Justice should have mandatory jurisdiction over all member-states of the UN.* How else is the world to fight criminal abuses of authority by heads of state, national armies, and international terrorists?

Arguments against a Stronger United Nations

∎ *The larger the government, the more likely it is to rule tyrannically.* We don't need global government; we need honest national governments willing to act first and foremost in the national interest.

∎ *There are no internationally recognized global values and no consensus on how a world government should be organized.* One of the most severe value conflicts in the world today is over the rights of women and children. If the UN cannot resolve these conflicts today, a more centralized UN will have to impose its values throughout the world.

∎ *Regulation of the world economy by a UN economic institution would promote a global welfare state in which resources are taken from the most productive global citizens and distributed to the least productive.* What is needed is to step up the training of the poorest members of the global community in effective methods of food production and technology development. Education, not welfare, is the answer.

∎ *People are not prepared to surrender their national sovereignty and to entrust the security of their homes and families to a UN army.* If states give up their military and police forces, how secure will we be against terrorists, criminal gangs, drug rings and sheer cranks?

∎ *Sovereign states must have the right to intervene and invade other states whose expressed policies and interests are opposed to their own and threaten the world community.*

The arguments pro and con highlight the basic problem: that the formation of a global government with its own military force and court of justice to enforce decisions of a global legislature means each state must surrender its sovereignty. This surrender is made all the more problematic by the report's proposal to form a separate parliament composed of recognized

NGOs. That would put al Qaeda on the same parliamentary standing in the NGO assembly as the United States is in the current UN General Assembly. You will discover as you debate that the issue of global governance is more complex than it seems at first and that it demands some heavy thinking.

QUESTIONS

1. How could a world government more efficiently and more equitably handle such global issues as regional conflict, poverty, and environmental degradation?
2. How readily do you think any state would be persuaded to give up voluntarily the right to control its own political, economic, and social affairs?
3. How do you understand the term *global governance*? Do you see the centralization of the world's economic and political activities as a positive or negative step? Why?

SELECT READINGS

United Nations Commission on Global Governance, *Our Global Neighborhood* (Oxford University Press, 1995).

Peter Singer, *One World: The Ethnics of Globalization* (New Haven, Conn.: Yale University Press, 2002).

Victoria Wise and Dloyd Hedrick, *Global One: The New World Government* (New York: Morris, 1999). A novel written by a housewife about an astronaut who runs afoul of the Organization of Nations and faces persecution by the Prince.

SELECTED WEBSITES

www.sovereignty.net/p/gov This site provides the total text of *Our Global Neighborhood*, plus material supporting the con side of the global governance debate.

www.lse.ac.uk/Depts/global The Centre for the Study of Global Governance at the London School of Economics provides information, links, and evaluations of materials published on global governance.

http://globalization.about.com/od/globalgovernance/ This site provides a bibliography of articles and reports on the institutions and practice of global governance.

LEARNING OBJECTIVES REVIEW

1 ▶ *Define world politics and be able to understand current political events through the competing forces of centralization and decentralization.*

- We defined *world politics* as the global allocation of the planet's scarce political, economic, social, and cultural resources.

- Because there is no world government, this allocation takes place through the struggle for power and dominance by international actors, including states, international intergovernmental organizations, nongovernmental organizations, and individuals.

- Over the past centuries, various institutions have been created by European governments to promote peace, including: the birth of the modern state system, the balance of power, and collective security.

2 ▶ *Understand how world politics affects your life and how studying international affairs will help you develop analytical skills to better see patterns in the complexity of current events.*

- The study of world politics is important to you. It is not just a subject for diplomats and experts. As a voter, a future player in the global economy, a future professional or businessperson, and as a consumer concerned about your health, your present and future lifestyle are profoundly affected by international relations.

3 ▶ *Identify the five most significant forces shaping the world today and understand how these forces have centralizing or decentralizing effects on world politics.*

- The five most significant forces shaping the world today:
    - The new information technology
    - The transnational character of the new issues, such as AIDS and other pandemics, terrorism, and global environmental degradation
    - The inability of traditional states to solve these problems on their own
    - The rise of ethnic nationalism and religious extremism
    - The new citizen activism promoted and sponsored by the new information technology

RESOURCES ON THE WEB

To use these interactive learning and study tools, including video and audio multimedia resources, go to **www.BetweenNations.org**.

Practice Tests	Case Studies	Current Events
Audio Concepts	Primary Sources	Daily Newsfeeds from *The Washington Post*
Flashcards	Historical Background	Weblinks for Further Exploration

 Between Nations

Understanding Complexity through Theory

LEARNING OBJECTIVES

1 ▶ *Understand and be able to summarize the key assumptions of political realism, idealism, and the ecological paradigm.*

2 ▶ *Identify and understand the key theories that result from realism, idealism, and the ecological paradigm.*

Chapter Outline

3 ▶ *What are the subjective approaches
to world politics? Understand how
such approaches differ from realism,
idealism, and the ecological
paradigm.*

International Relations
Theories and Paradigms

In chapter 1, we said that world politics was the struggle for power among the world's sovereign states in the absence of a world government to enforce the rules of the game. We further said that this struggle over the world's scarce resources was the continuation of a historic phenomenon that has been going on since the human race began. This struggle takes place within the framework of movement toward centralization countered by movements toward decentralization. However, the struggle at the beginning of the twenty-first century differs from those in the past due to new forces that are shaping the planet. These include the high-technology revolution; the globalization of political, economic, and social issues; the inability of one state to solve even

Paradigm The framework of assumptions from within which we derive theories about the natural and the social world.

domestic problems without taking a global perspective; the rise of ethnic nationalism and religious extremism; and the new citizen activism.

How do you make sense of all that is happening in the world today? What does all the news in the media add up to? Do the rapid changes taking place provide any idea where the world is heading? What are your predictions based on Figure 2.1?

Here is where theory can help. Chapter 1 supplied numerous bits of information. The only way to make the information intelligible is by organizing it in a systematic way. All such systems are rooted in the assumptions you make about human behavior in relation to the world around you. A group of those assumptions is called a **paradigm**. Philosopher of science Thomas Kuhn has defined a paradigm as "an entire constellation of beliefs, values and techniques . . . shared by the members of a given community."[1] In the case of international relations, members of the given community would be scholars in the political science discipline.

A paradigm is thus the intellectual framework from within which we derive theories about the natural and social world. As shown in Table 2.1, theories, in turn, provide the lens through which we are able to describe events, explain them, and, less accurately, make predictions about them. Theories also help us make policy recommendations; this is a very important way in which theory and reality are linked.

FIGURE 2.1

The Difficulty of Prediction

Theories Help Us To

▌ Describe things

▌ Explain things

▌ Make predictions

▌ Make policy recommendations

The year was 1984 and a political prophet was asked to predict what would happen in the world in twenty years' time. He looked into his tea leaves and prophesied in twenty years that communism would have collapsed, that China would be a member of the World Trade Organization, that the biggest threat to the United States would be from militant Muslims then being supported by the United States, that apartheid would have ended in South Africa, and that Germany would be reunited into one state. People at that time would have thought the prophet was a lunatic.

In fact, in 1984 no one predicted the collapse of the Soviet Union.

You be the prophet.

What do you think the international system will look like in 2024? Which states will be the major powers?

What will be the major alliances and trading blocs?[2]

TABLE 2.1

International Relations Paradigms, Theories, and Assumptions

Parent Paradigm	Assumptions	Theories Derived from Assumptions
Realism	Human beings are imperfect. The international world is a jungle characterized by an anarchic struggle for survival and power. War is inevitable. The only thing that stops power is power.	Political Realism Balance of Power Hegemonic Stability Neorealism (structural) Offensive Realism
Idealism	Utopianism: The world is getting better. Human beings are basically good and perfectible. Caring and compassion are innate. Everyone has equal value and human dignity. We can cooperate to build a better world. We must restructure flawed institutions to create good ones.	**Markism** Imperialism Dependency theories **Liberalism** Democratic Peace Theory Collective security Regime Theory Neoliberalism **Subjective Approaches** Critical Theory Constructivism Some feminist theories
Ecological Paradigm	The human world is a subset of the global ecosystem. Resources on Earth are finite. Humans cannot exceed an ecosystem's carrying capacity or that system will collapse. Sustainable development is the answer to a planet at risk.	Sustainable Development Theory Deep ecology Ecofeminism Ecojustice

In this chapter, we present three of the major paradigms with their accompanying theories. In the first section, we present each of the paradigms, and in the second, the theories that derive from them. In the last section, we look at theories that are critical of the assumptions behind the major paradigms and are starting to play a larger role in analyses of world politics. ■

WHAT ARE THE TOOLS OF ANALYSIS IN WORLD POLITICS?

1 *Understand and be able to summarize the key assumptions of political realism, idealism, and the ecological paradigm.*

In this section, we discuss three paradigms that underlie theory building in world politics today and help us understand the international world: **political realism**, **idealism**, and the **ecological paradigm**. In many ways, the three paradigms differ dramatically from each other. You must read and decide which worldview best suits your outlook on life. Keep in mind as well that each can offer useful insights into how the world works.

Political realism A philosophical position that assumes that human beings are imperfect and possess an innate desire for power. The international system is composed of states and other entities whose primary interest is to survive and thrive in an anarchic jungle whose competing actors are constrained by no higher authority. The fundamental purpose of the state is to use its power to further its interests while containing the power of other states that might prevent this from happening.

Idealism A philosophical position that argues that human beings are basically good. War can be prevented when the proper international institutions are created. States can cooperate to solve problems and improve the existing world order, given the right institutions.

Ecological paradigm The approach to international relations that assumes that the world of humans cannot be studied apart from its natural environmental context and that sees the human world as a subset of the global ecosystem. Central to this paradigm is the view that planet Earth, with its surrounding atmosphere, represents a finite ecosystem.

Between Nations
For more information see
The View From:
The Indian Realist Thinker
Kautilya
www.BetweenNations.org

Between Nations
For more information see
The Melian Dialogue
www.BetweenNations.org

Between Nations
For more information see
"The Prince" by
Niccolò Machiavelli
www.BetweenNations.org

Political Realism

Political realism is the dominant paradigm in international relations. The paradigm is based on the twin assumptions that human beings are imperfect and that they have an innate desire for power. Realists thus like to theorize about the uses of power, the consequences of power, and the containment of power. Central to this view is the belief that we live in a world of anarchy, where only their offensive and defensive capabilities keep states from each others' throats. Security is thus the big issue in realist analysis.

An Overview of Political Realism

The realist approach to international affairs traces its origins to the ancient Greek historian Thucydides, who wrote what was probably the first systematic analysis of war, titled *The Peloponnesian Wars.* The work recounts the story of the thirty-year war between the Greek city-state of Athens and its great rival, Sparta (431–404 BC). In a celebrated passage, Thucydides has the Athenian Assembly debate the fate of a rebel colony, Mytilene on the island of Lesbos. The angry response of the Athenian army to the revolt was to order the whole colony put to death. The Athenian citizens protested that order, and they called for another meeting of the Assembly. Using arguments based on political realism, the ruler of Athens, Cleon, urged that the punishment be carried out and the colonists executed. He claimed that the rebels had known what they were doing and had planned the whole thing. Here are three of Cleon's arguments:

- "One only forgives actions that are not deliberate." (That is, we should not feel pity for the rebels.)
- "A sense of decency is only felt toward those who will be our friends in the future." (That is, give these people what they deserve.)
- "It is a general rule of human nature that people despise those who treat them well, and look up to those who make no concessions." (That is, punishment is the best medicine.)[3]

These arguments and others like them have been used to justify the use of force throughout history.

The realist path runs through the Indian philosopher Kautilya (3rd Century BC) to Niccolò Machiavelli (1469–1527) and his famous book, *The Prince*. Written to gain favor with the Medici rulers of Florence, Italy, the author describes an ideal ruler very similar to the cruel and cunning prince of the Papal States, Cesare Borgia. The Medicis rejected the book, and it outraged the Florentine public. Since that time, Machiavelli has had a bad reputation. Machiavelli wrote of the realities of state power through an analysis of the means by which individuals have tried to seize and keep power in the highly volatile and fragmented environment that was Renaissance Italy. Perhaps his best-known statement is "It is better for a prince to be feared than loved," but a wise ruler will take care not to be hated. His central idea was that power was so changeable, a single mistake could topple a ruler. To stay in power, the ideal prince must enforce his will through a combination of strong character, ruthlessness, a love of risk taking, and an ability to calculate the consequences of his actions. Machiavelli was the first major Western thinker to uncouple politics from ethics. To him, politics was solely about getting and keeping power.

A century later, Thomas Hobbes (1588–1679), an adviser to another prince—Charles II of England—set forth his realist approach in his treatise on government, entitled *Leviathan, or the Matter, Form, and Power of a Commonwealth.* Hobbes's use of the Hebrew word *leviathan,* or sea monster, as a metaphor for the state's power over its citizens, gave the word a negative connotation. When we speak of a leviathan state today, we are probably referring to an authoritarian state with a huge bureaucracy to enforce its rule. Hobbes based his arguments for the leviathan state on his realist view that human nature is imperfect, rooted in the senses, and prone to strong emotional reactions and imprudent decisions. He argued that to be happy, human beings needed "a common power to keep them all in awe"; otherwise, every person would be the enemy of every other person. Hobbes saw the causes of conflict as endemic in the nature of human beings: competition, distrust, and desire for glory.[4]

Modern Political Realism

Political realism has become synonymous with the practices of Otto von Bismarck, the Prussian prime minister who engineered the unification of modern Germany in 1871. Bismarck, in fact, coined the term **realpolitik** ("politics of the real") to characterize his foreign policy. Bismarck was a leading supporter of the balance-of-power principle, discussed later in the chapter and in detail in chapter 4. As a realist, he saw power primarily in terms of armaments and military preparedness. He did much to build up Germany's military so that Germany quickly became a leading European power that challenged Great Britain's supremacy.

In the United States, Hans Morgenthau probably made the largest contribution to the development of American political realism after World War II. Morgenthau argued that events that occurred between the two world wars, as well as World War II itself, demonstrated that human beings do not come into the world inherently good. They are capable of both good and bad, but the drive for power is innate and instinctive. War is thus a certainty. Governments and individuals must devise their actions and responses in the international world based on the worst-case scenario. The central event in Morgenthau's life was the onset of the Cold War between the United States and the Soviet Union (USSR). If the United States wanted to keep out of a hot war with the USSR, he argued, national security required it to have superb offensive and defensive capabilities, and to be dedicated to opposing communism.

Political Realism Today

Drawing on the work of Bismarck, Morgenthau, and others, realists today emphasize the primacy of foreign policy over domestic policy, the importance of a strong military force and cutting-edge military technology, and the centrality of national security. The major player in the international arena is the state. States operate on an international stage where anarchy rules. With no higher power to constrain their behavior, states struggle to increase their power and prestige at the expense of other states. World politics is a **zero-sum game**, where the winner takes all and is the most powerful state. Where idealists argued that we should do away with nuclear bombs because they present a hazard to humanity, realists argued that the only way to keep power-hungry states like the USSR from attacking was through

The Father of Modern Realism
Hans J. Morgenthau (1904–1977), the leading proponent of realism in America after the Second World War and author of Politics Among Nations.

Realpolitik A term coined by the nineteenth-century German chancellor Otto Von Bismarck to describe his foreign policy for Germany—namely, the building up of the military to make Germany one of the leading European powers, rivaling Great Britain.

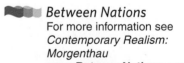 *Between Nations*
For more information see
Contemporary Realism: Morgenthau
www.BetweenNations.org

 *Between Nations*
Audio Concept
Zero-Sum Game
www.BetweenNations.org

Zero-sum game The concept that in politics, the winner takes all; if one side gains, the other must lose.

Mutually assured destruction (MAD)
In the context of the rivalry between the United States and the Soviet Union, both sides were deterred from attacking each other because they believed the destruction of both countries was be assured if one initiated a nuclear attack.

the building of a nuclear arsenal on each side that guaranteed the other would not attack. This situation was known as **mutually assured destruction (MAD)**.

In summary, political realism:

▌ Starts from the premise that human beings as well as the world in which they live are imperfect.

▌ The games of states take place in an arena dominated by the struggle for power.

▌ Realists tend to support a strong military and to put national security ahead of international cooperation.

▌ In aligning themselves with national sovereignty and independence, realists are skeptical of a centralized world order, preferring a more decentralized and flexible relationship among states.

Idealism

Idealism is the second major approach to international relations. Idealists differ from realists in that they ask what the world could or ought to be and how to get there. In contrast to realists, they believe that human beings are basically good. Therefore, institutions must be developed that will enable them to be the best they can be. The two great transforming ideologies of the nineteenth and twentieth centuries, Marxism and liberalism, stem from the idealist view of the world. Many scholars would not place Marxism in the idealist camp. Karl Marx was an idealist, however, in the sense that he was a utopian and believed the world would become more just and more equitable by means of fundamental changes in the way human society is organized. In addition, the subjective approaches discussed at the end of the chapter also derive from Marxism.

In January 1918 ten months before the end of World War I, U.S. president Woodrow Wilson in a speech to the U.S. Congress presented fourteen points that announced a new approach to international relations. These ideas came to be known as *liberalism.* The central tenet was that war could be prevented. It was not inevitable if the proper international institutions were created. Rather than the balance of power keeping nations from war, nations would join a League of Nations dedicated to collective security: "An attack against one is an attack against all." The League would operate on the principles of international law, provide a forum for discussion to prevent war, and threaten the potential aggressor by collective military action.

World War II demonstrated that neither international law nor the League of Nations was capable of preventing war. Still, idealists were not disheartened. Human beings may be imperfect, but they are perfectible. The League was a badly conceived institution, they argued. It was open only to democratic nations—and, unfortunately, the largest democratic nation, the United States, did not join. After the war, idealists, both Marxists and liberals rallied around the formation of a new international organization, the United Nations (UN; see chapter 6). This time, membership was open to any duly recognized state. The United States and the Soviet Union were among its founding members, and the United States took the lead in designing the organization. Although some may argue the point, other international institutions and agreements formed after World War II, including the International Monetary Fund (IMF) and the General Agreement on Tariffs and Trades (GATT), owe their existence most analysts believe to the analogous liberal

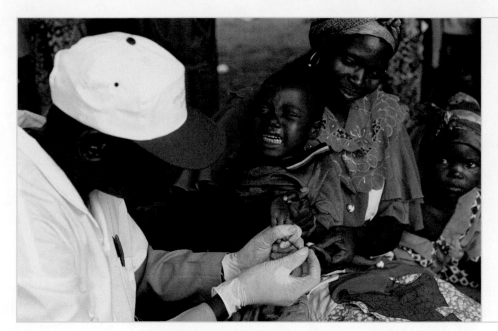

Screening Patients for Sleeping Sickness in Chad
The World Health Organization has done a superlative job in cooperation with national health organizations such as the U.S. Center for Disease Control, monitoring contagious diseases around the globe. Early warning from the IGO alerts governments to a possible epidemic. The national responses to the warning help contain some of the deadliest diseases, such as SARS, saving millions of lives. WHO's most significant success has probably been the eradication of smallpox.

conviction that cooperation can be achieved in the economic sphere and is a rational alternative to bankrupting nations and starting trade wars.

The Importance of Cooperation to Build Peace

Idealists share the conviction that altruism is as fundamental to the human condition as competition and rivalry. Human beings through the centuries have understood the benefit of cooperation to minimize risks and maximize benefits for all the participants.[5] Governments and states can and should work together to develop policies and strategies that call humankind to a world order of justice, compassion for the less fortunate, and concern for basic human values.

A common concern of most idealists is the horror of modern war. If the two world wars were terrible in general, the dropping of the atomic bombs on the Japanese cities of Hiroshima and Nagasaki, which killed more than 140,000 people, was especially horrific. Idealists were fierce critics of nuclear war and the nuclear buildup between the United States and the USSR. During the Cold War, Marxist thinking provided the ideological underpinnings for many Western peace movements.

Throughout the second half of the twentieth century, idealists (liberals and Marxists alike) fought for more international cooperation, more international regulation, and the value of multinational treaties such as the Nuclear Non-Proliferation Treaty and the Montreal Protocol, which limits the emission of chlorofluorocarbons into the atmosphere. Idealists are often active members of peace movements, women's movements, and environmental and human rights movements.

Today, many idealists center their hopes for a cooperative future on the extraordinary increase in the number of international treaties that have been signed and ratified by the world's governments. These treaties cover a wide range of subject matter. Generally, they outline a procedure or identify a process that the treaty signatories agree to follow. The process or procedure that is born of a treaty

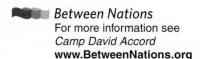

Between Nations
For more information see
Camp David Accord
www.BetweenNations.org

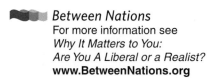

Between Nations
For more information see
Why It Matters to You:
Are You A Liberal or a Realist?
www.BetweenNations.org

Regime   The process or procedure that is born of a treaty that the signatories agree to follow. The treaty usually sets up a goal to be reached, a process by which to reach the goal, a timeline, and a permanent organizational framework to monitor progress.

is termed an international **regime**.* The existence of international regimes challenges the realist assumption that only the struggle for power can characterize international relations. Each state may be out for itself. But the existence of regimes is an indication that cooperation between states without coercion from a global authority is not only possible but also an effective way to resolve or promote international concerns.

The idealist paradigm builds on the notion that altruism is a fundamental characteristic of human behavior. It just needs the right kind of social and government structure, to be released. States can and should cooperate among themselves with the aim of constructing a more just and cooperative world order. Violence can be prevented by binding states together through international treaties and addressing the causes of violence through the combined efforts of the world community.

The Ecological Paradigm

The third approach to international relations that we present is the ecological paradigm. Of far less prominence than realism or idealism, it dates from the late 1970s and was developed by political scientists Herman Daly and Dennis Pirages, along with many others. The element that differentiates the ecological paradigm from any variant of idealism or realism is its insistence that the world of humans cannot be studied apart from their natural environment. The human world, in fact, is a subset of the physical universe; humanity survives or disappears according to its ability to adapt to the global ecosystem. Central to this approach is the realization that planet Earth and its surrounding atmosphere are finite. Most important, the planet possesses finite resources. No amount of money can substitute for the exhaustion of these resources. If humankind is to continue to exist, it must conduct its global transactions in such a way as to sustain or build up the **ecosystem** and not destroy it.

Ecosystem   A community of interacting organisms and their natural environment.

Sustainable Development

Sustainable development   In the interests of its own survival, the human race must not undertake any economic development that leaves a larger footprint on the environment than the ecosystem can successfully accommodate without breaking down.

A vital concept for the ecological paradigm approach is **sustainable development** (see Figure 2.2).

Sustainable development means that in the interests of its own survival, the human species must not leave a larger footprint on the environment than the ecosystem can successfully accommodate without breaking down. If we overgraze our fields, erode our farmlands, cut down our forests, and use up and pollute our water, our species will disappear, like the dinosaurs. In the context of the theme of this book, the ecological paradigm posits that many decentralized regional or national acts of environmental degradation ultimately add up to global pollution. In other words, the domestic policies of individual countries, such as rapid deforestation, the promotion of farming on marginal soils, the spread of the urban metropolis, and the concentration of the world's populations in cities *combine* to, produce intermestic environmental issues that can only be solved on a global scale.

---

*Political scientist Oran Young was the first to look at regime formation resulting from environmental treaties and to ask how we can determine whether or not a regime will successfully complete or follow the process demanded of it by its treaty.

FIGURE 2.2

Pirages's Five Capitals and Three Pillars of Sustainability

Sustainability: Community control and prudent use of five types of capital supported by what Pirages calls "the three pillars of sustainability."

The Five Types of Capital

1. *Nature's capital* = natural resources
2. *Human capital* = people and the body of knowledge they contribute to community and production
3. *Human-created capital* = products and technologies created by humans
4. *Social capital* = civic trust and civic involvement in a place; participation in the political life of a particular community, newspaper readership, membership in associations from sports clubs to the Lions Club, from unions to choral societies. Social capital defines where you are and the importance of that place to you.
5. *Cultural capital* = a community's culture, including factors that provide it with the means and adaptations to deal with the natural environment and modify it, such as creation myths and dreams of a better world.

The Three Pillars of Sustainability

1. *Economic security* = the control that individuals have over their own economic lives and the degree to which they are capable of shielding themselves from external economic shocks
2. *Ecological integrity* = living in harmony with natural systems: clean air, water, and land use that meets human needs and maintains the essential elements of the ecosystem
3. *Democracy* = citizen participation in community decision making. The three pillars are created and supported by the five forms of capital.

From Dennis Pirages, *Building Sustainable Societies* (Armonk, NY: M.E. Sharpe, 1996), pp. 43–48.

In 1988, the former president of the Soviet Union, Mikhail Gorbachev, was the first world leader to put sustainable development at the top of the global political agenda. His placing of planetary survival on the international agenda encouraged politicians and scientists in other countries to address the issue.

Think Globally, Act Locally

In 1998, Hurricane Mitch brought torrents of rain down on the Central American countries of Honduras and Nicaragua. In the resulting floods and horrendous mudslides, some 10,000 people died. One of the principal reasons for the scope of the tragedy was the rapid deforestation of tropical forests in both countries. Another was the pressure on the poor peasants to till marginal land, because the good land had all been dedicated to export agriculture. In December 2004, a submarine earthquake in the Indian Ocean and attending **tsunami**, the deadliest ever recorded, killed upwards of 187,000 with 43,000 missing in the Indian subcontinent, Sri Lanka, and Indonesia.[6]

In August 2005, Atlantic Hurricane Katrina devastated the city of New Orleans causing at least 1800 deaths, and $81.2 billion in damages. A major reason for the lethal destruction caused by the two storms was the human alteration of natural coastlines and watersheds, such as the Mississippi River, to the benefit of industry, pisciculture, and the resort business. Similar tragedies might be avoided in the future if the international community presses forward in its promotion of

Tsunami An ocean wave produced by a submarine earthquake, landslide, or volcanic eruption. These waves may reach enormous size and travel across entire oceans.

The Three Gorges Dam on the Yangtze River, China
Research is showing that dams may frequently do more harm than good. On the positive side, they generate electricity from falling water, one of the cleanest ways to generate power. On the negative side, they store water in huge reservoirs, completely changing a river's ecology. Environmentalists all over the world have been protesting the construction of huge hydroelectric projects like this one in China.

Anthropogenic   Caused by humans or originating from human actions.

Carrying capacity   Carrying capacity is usually defined as the maximum population of a given species that can be supported indefinitely in a defined habitat without permanently impairing the productivity of that habitat.

sustainable development programs and prevails on the nations of the world to agree to them.

Hurricanes, earthquakes, floods, typhoons, and ice storms are natural phenomena. They become human tragedy when the **anthropogenic**, or human-created, impact exceeds the **carrying capacity** of the at-risk ecosystem, causing the ecosystem to collapse.[7] Sometimes we can predict the collapse. Sometimes it comes as a surprise. We talk more about the surprise factor in the environmental paradigm in chapter 14.

In summary, the environmental paradigm believes:

▌ That world politics is essentially environmental politics.

▌ Individual states need to recognize that their domestic and foreign policies have significant environmental repercussions for the global community.

▌ On their part, centralizing world-order institutions, like the organizations affiliated with the UN, must be able and willing to assist states in ensuring not only their environmental security but also the security of the world as a whole.

The proliferation of natural disasters in the twentieth century resulting from human activities suggests that the ecological paradigm may well take center stage in the international politics of the twenty-first century.

True or False?

_____ 1. The dominant theories of world politics allowed scholars to predict the fall of the Soviet Union.

_____ 2. Proponents of realism believe that the international system is characterized by anarchy.

_____ 3. Idealism argues that international institutions should be developed in order to allow human beings to be the best they can be.

_____ 4. Marxists and idealists basically believe the same things when it comes to explaining international politics.

_____ 5. Because of increased environmental concerns in the past decade, the ecological paradigm has become the dominant approach to international politics in recent years.

Multiple Choice

_____ 6. Which of the following does theory help us do?
   a. Describe things
   b. Explain things
   e. Make predictions
   d. Make policy recommendations
   e. All of the above

◥◣ *Between Nations*
   Practice Test Questions
   Practice Test 2.1
   www.BetweenNations.org

_____ 7. A zero-sum game refers to which of the following situations?
   a. When both countries in a nuclear arms race are devastated completely through nuclear war
   b. When anything gained by one country must come at the expense of another country
   c. When the absolute gain made by two countries through economic trade "zeroes out"
   d. When the relative gain by one actor is reduced to zero through excessive military spending
   e. None of the above

_____ 8. A central idea in the ecological paradigm is that:
   a. The environment should take precedence over all other living things as life cannot survive without a hospitable environment.
   b. Global warming is the single most threatening environmental problem faced by humanity.
   c. The planet Earth and its surrounding atmosphere are finite and possess limited resources.
   d. The environment must be studied apart from the humans that occupy it to truly understand the environment's impact on world politics.

WHAT THEORIES OF WORLD POLITICS FLOW FROM THE PARADIGMS?

2▶ *Identify and understand the key theories that result from realism, idealism, and the ecological paradigm.*

How do these basic paradigms about the human condition influence the theories one adopts to explain the international world? Throughout this book, we explain a variety of global events and issues based on one or a combination of theories derived from these paradigms. Take another look at Figure 2.1 to get a better understanding of what political theories have been developed from the three paradigms. Now let us take each of the paradigms in turn to explore the theories each has spawned. Keep in mind that the chapter looks only at the *dominant* paradigms and theories in world politics, with realism and idealism rivals for first place.

Political Realism

Realism's central concerns are war, peace, and security. War may be inevitable, but we can limit the desire of enemies to wage war by appropriate military preparedness and by diplomatic maneuvers to redirect that country's interest. We use diplomacy as long as it promotes our state interest but are ready for war if diplomacy fails. In the words of the nineteenth-century Prussian general Karl von Clausewitz, "War is nothing but the continuation of politics by other means."[8] In every international interaction, the gains of one state come as a loss to another.

To give you a sense of realism as a tool to understand world politics, we present three modern theories that derive from the realist perspective. Many others also come from realism, some of which were mentioned earlier. The theories presented here are balance-of-power theory, hegemonic stability theory, and neorealism or structural realism.

Balance-of-Power Theory

Balance-of-power theory   Posits that peace and security are best preserved by a state of equilibrium between the major players in a potential war.

According to the realist **balance-of-power theory**, war is avoided by a condition of equilibrium between the main players in the potential war. Just as we can find out a baby's weight by placing him or her on one side of a scale and adding increments of pounds or kilos to the other side of the balance until the two sides of the scale are in equilibrium, so we can measure global or regional equilibrium by weighing the power attributes of one state or set of states against the power attributes of a second state or set of states. Power attributes of states include:

▌ Military and economic potential

▌ Nature of a state's leadership

▌ Extent of international involvement

If the power attributes of one side outweigh those of the other, the balance goes out of equilibrium and war ensues.

Balance-of-power theory dominated diplomatic and international military and economic relations throughout the nineteenth century. Using this theory, Admiral Alfred Mahan of the United States and English geopolitician, Sir Halford MacKinder argued late in the nineteenth century that power was determined by strategic and geopolitical factors. Geopolitics is now a subdiscipline of international relations that we discuss in chapter 8.

The theory was also used to justify the formation of the two alliances that dominated Europe prior to World War I: the Triple Alliance and the Triple Entente. According to the theory, World War I was caused by a breakdown in the rough equality or balance between the Triple Alliance of Germany, Austro-Hungary, and Italy, and the Triple Entente between France, Great Britain, and Russia, as shown in Figure 2.3.

A number of scholars, including Paul Kennedy, George Modelski, Immanuel Wallerstein, and Chase Dunn have questioned whether in the rise and fall of world systems, the United States today is historically in decline as a world power and how that decline might affect the international balance of power. Balance-of-power theory is also a good tool to use in investigating regional conflict, such as Iraq's invasion of Iran, or the difficulties in finding a solution to the century-old conflict between Jews and Arabs in the Middle East.

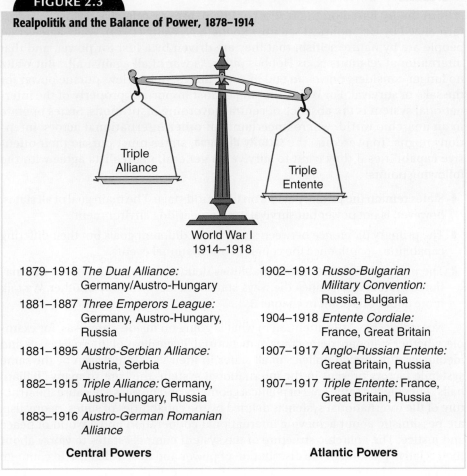

FIGURE 2.3

Realpolitik and the Balance of Power, 1878–1914

Triple Alliance

Triple Entente

World War I
1914–1918

1879–1918 *The Dual Alliance:*
Germany/Austro-Hungary

1881–1887 *Three Emperors League:*
Germany, Austro-Hungary,
Russia

1881–1895 *Austro-Serbian Alliance:*
Austria, Serbia

1882–1915 *Triple Alliance:* Germany,
Austro-Hungary, Russia

1883–1916 *Austro-German Romanian
Alliance*

Central Powers

1902–1913 *Russo-Bulgarian
Military Convention:*
Russia, Bulgaria

1904–1918 *Entente Cordiale:*
France, Great Britain

1907–1917 *Anglo-Russian Entente:*
Great Britain, Russia

1907–1917 *Triple Entente:* France,
Great Britain, Russia

Atlantic Powers

Hegemonic Stability Theory

A second theory in the realist paradigm argues that economic and/or political stability in the world or in a region requires a strong power, termed a **hegemon**, from the Greek word for "leader." Contrary to balance-of-power theory, hegemonic stability theory (HST) does not fear an imbalance of power but rather argues that the imbalance, is necessary. Why were the Asian countries of Japan, Korea, and Taiwan able to industrialize as rapidly as they did in the last quarter of the twentieth century? HST says they were able to do so because there was a hegemon (the United States) in the Pacific basin that provided the military and economic security necessary for these states to develop. Moreover, the United States was strong enough economically to keep its markets open to the products of Asian countries, which a weaker power could not do.

HST thus argues in favor of a dominant political, economic, and military state that can guarantee the order necessary for weaker states to develop, provide the force necessary to secure the peace in a given region, and commit its influence to treaty implementation.

Hegemon A country whose overwhelming military, political, and economic power gives it the ability to write and enforce the rules of the international system. A powerful regional state that tries to use its military or economic power to dominate countries in the region—as in Iraq's invasion of Kuwait in August 1990.

Neorealism An approach to international relations, developed by Kenneth N. Waltz, that argues that while humans may be selfish by nature and driven by a lust for power, power is not the true end. States really pursue power in order to survive. The goal is national survival.

Security dilemma Because the international system is characterized by anarchy, any attempt by a country to increase its security results in a corresponding decrease in other countries' security. The dilemma faced by states, then, is how to increase one's own security without threatening other states and thereby making yourself less secure as a result.

Neorealism

A third theory based on the realist paradigm, **neo-** or **defensive realism**, was first formalized by U.S. political scientist Kenneth N. Waltz (1979). Waltz agrees that people are by nature selfish, that they are driven by a lust for power, and that international relations is, as Hobbes put it, "a war of all against all." But Waltz no longer considers power an end in itself. States, in his view, pursue power for the sake of survival. For Waltz, the single most important property of the international system is the absence of central governing institutions. States operate in an anarchic world, where uncertainty of other international actors' intentions reigns. To overcome the **security dilemma**, states must pursue their offensive capabilities if they want to survive. In general, neorealists agree with the following points:

▌ States remain the primary actors on the world stage. The main goal of all states, however, is not power but survival in a dog-eat-dog environment.

▌ The primary difference between states is not different goals but their differing capabilities to influence the course of international events.

▌ The unequal distribution of capabilities defines the structure of the international system and shapes the ways states interact with one another. We talk more about this point in chapter 3.

Neorealists pay little attention to what is going on inside states—as, for example, whether states are democratic or dictatorial. Regardless of internal beliefs and ideologies, the foreign policies of all states in their view, are driven by the same systemic factors present in the international system; they are so many "billiard balls" obeying the same laws of political geometry and physics.[9] Because the structure of the international system is defined by the capabilities of states, neorealists are pessimistic about achieving international cooperation and a world of peace and justice. The anarchic structure of the system compels states to worry about their relative position in the distribution of power and in self-defense to compete to improve or just maintain their position. For neorealists, permanent insecurity is the major impediment to global cooperation, and it is built right into the anarchic international system, whether we admit it or not.

Offensive Realism

Offensive realism A theory that blames conflicts in the world on the anarchy of the international system, not on human nature. Great powers tend to seek hegemony to limit or destroy challenges from other great powers.

Of the fourth theory, **offensive realism**, turns neorealism on its head. Its leading proponent, John Mearsheimer, holds that states are not content with the power they have, but seek dominance or "hegemony," to satisfy their sense of vulnerability in an insecure world. Mearsheimer argues that there is no such thing as the status quo. Every great power faces the problem of determining how much power is enough for its survival and thus is constantly striving for world dominance to eliminate the possibility of challenge by another great power. Offensive realism contrasts with Waltz's theory of defensive realism, where insecurity forces states to compete to keep their relative position in the global distribution of power.[10]

Realism in Perspective

Political realism has its gloomy moments. Its predictions for the future are not hopeful. Realists do not want to be discouraging, but they do insist we look at reality as they see it. That reality is an anarchic world where, in the absence of a central authority or world government, states and other international actors compete in a fierce and brutal struggle for survival. The only way to contain power is with power. During the Cold War, nuclear war was prevented through the realpolitik of mutually assured destruction. In the post–Cold War world, the insecurity brought about by the changed landscape of states, the globalization of the economy, and other problems all call for the state to maintain its vigilance to look out for Number One.

Idealism

Idealists are nowhere near as skeptical of international cooperation as are realists. Their assumption, that the world can be made better if we can only get the institutions right, leads us to two important theoretical perspectives on international relations. Idealists believe that the world, or at least its human institutions, is perfectible. In this sense, idealism is utopian. Idealists ask, What is wrong with human society? How can it be improved? Idealists are convinced that change is for the better and that human beings can become more caring, more mindful of others' needs than they generally are. They believe that human beings can be perfected through education and by changing institutions and their relationships. The right structuring of institutions, they assert, enables human beings to bring about a better world, free of greed and envy.

The two great transforming ideologies of the twentieth century, **Marxism** and liberalism, stem from the idealist view of the world. Many scholars would not place Marxism in the idealist camp. Karl Marx was an idealist, however, in the sense that he was a utopian and believed that the historical process, as it unfolded, would bring about a more just and equitable world through transformative changes in the way human society was organized. In addition, many modern critiques of the tenets of realism and idealism derive from Marxism. We discuss a few of these approaches in the last section of the chapter, "What Are the Subjective Approaches to World Politics."

Marxism

History, according to Marxist theory, is a one-way street from the past into the utopian future. As we move from the past to the present, we see that certain thresholds in human experience mark turning points, or decisive changes, to a different form of socioeconomic and political organization. The historic instrument of these changes was what Marx called the *class struggle*. Every major socioeconomic change in the history of humankind, Marx said, occurred as a consequence of the struggle between the two most important socioeconomic groups in that period of time: the property-owning class, or haves, that controlled the key economic assets and made all the rules, and the property-less class, or have-nots, that owned none of the assets and worked for and obeyed the ruling class.

Marx argued that the changes were typically violent because they involved real struggle between the haves and the have-nots. But the changes were always a change forward and indicated a progressive betterment of the human condition. Communism, for Marx, was the end-state of human social organization. Under communism, he asserted, all exploitation would cease; there would be no rich or poor and no class divisions, and the state would no longer possess coercive and oppressive authority. All humankind would live in harmony according to the principle "From each according to his ability, to each according to his need."

Marxism The theory that history is a one-way street from the past to the future. As history progresses, thresholds in human experience mark a turning point in terms of socioeconomic and political organization. These changes are always a change forward and indicate the progressive betterment of the human condition. The engine driving the change is the class struggle—the tension between the class that possesses the means of production in a given society and the class that works for it. Marx identified the human race as having gone through prehistoric society, slave-holding society, feudal society, and capitalist society. The end condition of human society would be the classless society of communism.

The Fathers of Communism

Karl Marx (left) wrote his Communist Manifesto *in 1848 and started two movements to improve the conditions of the working class, socialism and communism. Vladimir Ilych Lenin (right), the leader of the Russian Revolution of 1917 and first communist ruler of the Soviet Union, introduced the theory of imperialism into Marxist thinking.*

The ideas of Marx inspired both the democratic socialist democracies, with their pluralist, multiparty systems, in Western Europe and the dogmatic communist regimes in Eastern Europe, Eurasia, and Asia. In Western Europe, the social democratic party was the party of the have-nots, the working class, whose aim was the improvement of the worker's life by peaceful means, such as elections and legislation. A central assumption of communist regimes is that improvement of the lot of the working majority of a population can come about only through violent means.

Once the communist regime comes to power, the state can create a "new man" (or woman) who will have all the best qualities. To achieve these goals, capitalism, with its emphasis on individual and private gain, must be abolished and a new system of state ownership of the economy established. Once the revolution has been achieved, the state can then focus its vast powers on the education of the new man or woman and provide work in the new working environment—which is no longer governed by the profit motive but by the worker's enthusiasm for work.

Imperialism

Imperialism   A theory developed by Vladimir I. Lenin, who described it as the highest stage of capitalism (see *Marxism*). Under imperialism, national states driven by economic success and the need for more and more raw materials acquired colonies. These they proceeded to exploit for cheap labor and natural resources and to use as an expanded market where they could sell their goods.

The application of Marxism to the international arena produced two corollary theories. The first was developed by the first leader of the Soviet Union, Vladimir Ilych Lenin. Lenin used the term **imperialism** to describe the division of the nineteenth-century world by the European powers into colonial empires for each power. Imperialism, he said, was the most advanced stage of capitalism. Imperialism involved the movement of domestic capital abroad to Asia, Africa, and the Americas, in search of cheap raw materials, cheap labor, and new markets that the mother country no longer or never had possessed. Lenin was quick to see the disruption of traditional lifestyles brought about by the transfer of the industrial system to the colonies. The class struggle that Marx had identified between worker and capitalist in one country, Lenin saw transferred to the international world. The capital-exporting countries were the imperialists, and the peoples of the colonial countries were the proletariat.

Until the late 1980s, the USSR and China based their foreign policies on antagonism to imperialism. They endorsed Lenin's view that the institution of private property inevitably led to wars and rivalry for power. Socialism, they believed, brought the end of private property and thus opened the door to peaceful international cooperation.

Unfortunately, history proved otherwise. For years, these two communist nations conducted a foreign policy hostile to the world's industrialized countries and to the United States in particular. For years as well, Soviet and Chinese leaders each claimed that their country represented the leading edge of the world march toward communism. Interstate rivalry produced a mini-cold war for leadership of the so-called socialist states that at times broke out into hot wars along the Soviet-Chinese border.

In the new century, the word *imperialism* still resonates in the expansion of the U.S. and European transnational corporations' production, distribution, and retail facilities around the globe. This concept of economic imperialism is matched by the concept of political imperialism. Many states, both Muslim and non-Muslim, believe the United States attacked Iraq for purely imperialist reasons. In 2003, for example, France considered the United States such an imperialist threat that it forged a coalition with Germany and Russia to threaten to use their veto power in the UN Security Council to try to stop the United States from invading Iraq.

One reason that Americans do not like to admit that the United States is an imperial power is because of Marxism's association of imperialism with the resource- and territory-grabbing European powers of the nineteenth century. By contrast, Harvard historian Niall Ferguson argues that empires are the great engines of world history, and that they can accomplish positive things, like maintain law and order among rival ethnic groups, and promote a civilizing mission around the world.[11]

Dependency Theories

A second derivative of the dogmatic Marxist branch of idealism is **dependency theories**. In the two decades following World War II, most of the colonies of the European powers became independent states and were admitted to membership in the United Nations. The end of colonialism was a major event of the time. One of the big problems of the new states was how to develop their economies, prompting the elaboration of scenarios of how states could become industrialized as efficiently and quickly as possible. As time went on, many of the new states seemed to be growing economically, but they were not developing in the sense of becoming industrialized states. A new theory, *dependencia*, or "dependency," was born. The term comes from Spanish because the concept evolved in Latin America.

Dependency theorists use state classifications similar to those of imperialism: industrial states (core countries) and the developing states (periphery countries). They address questions such as, Why don't the developing states becoming industrialized? Why do they remain sources of raw materials and cheap labor? These questions are examined in detail in chapter 13.

Dependency theories   A set of related theories that have in common the belief that less-developed countries can never develop because they are dependent on the industrial states for capital and technology. The argument is that foreign investment in developing countries is a means of dominating and extracting capital from weaker states.

Liberalism

Liberalism A philosophical approach that argues that human nature is basically altruistic and that human altruism enables people to cooperate. In the international arena, compassion and caring for the welfare of others should motivate state actions. War is not a certainty because violence and selfishness are not part of the human condition but rather the result of flawed institutions. In addition, all wars are a matter of collective concern.

Consistent with the idealist approach, the core assumption of **liberalism** is that the world is perfectible and, by choosing the right institutions, human beings can make it so. In contrast to Marx, who saw the perfectibility of human institutions and human beings rooted in immutable historical laws, liberals emphasize the individuality of each person and the fundamental human ability to choose. The liberal argument may be summarized as follows: Human nature is basically good and—more important—altruistic; we care about others. These qualities make us perfectible. Through education, we can learn to use our reason. We can learn to consider the whole of humankind and not just our national or local problems. Liberals believe government can create institutions that will train citizens to greater tolerance and produce a society dedicated to social justice. One of the main goals of a liberal democracy is to provide universal education to all its citizens so they can make rational choices about their leaders and the policies they would like to see adopted. Participation in government also develops our reason. According to liberal thinking, democracy is the best and ultimate form of government because citizens elect representatives to make decisions for them based on their understanding of the candidates and the issues. The election process makes elected officials accountable to their constituents and thus limits their power to act arbitrarily. The result is a stable political system and a prosperous economy. Democracy provides sufficient security to its citizens so they can develop their capacity to care for others.

Liberals also assert that our natural altruism lies at the heart of international cooperation and trust. Because their citizens feel secure, democratic states are less prone to make war on other states. And thanks to democracy's internal stability, trade prospers among democratic states, improving the standard of living for all. One part of the liberal reform program insists on the merits of free trade to replace the economic nationalism that liberals believe propelled Hitler's Germany into World War II.

Compassion and concern for the welfare of all should inform all actions taken on the global stage. An example of the world's compassion is the humanitarian aid given to states experiencing famine or natural catastrophe. Another example is the enormous outpouring of sympathy for the families of the victims of 9/11 and for the United States as a whole from people and governments all over the world.

In addition, according to liberalism, violence and selfishness result from flawed institutions rather than the human condition. Agreements made between states in secret—what is called *secret diplomacy*—is one example of a flawed institution that can lead to war, as was the case with World War I. Liberals believe dictatorships are flawed institutions that promote violence and oppression, and they therefore urge the promotion of democracy worldwide. The United States asserts its liberal philosophy when it calls states that have oppressive dictatorships, such as North Korea, "rogue states."

Democratic Peace Theory

Democratic peace theory Democratic peace theory argues that although liberal democracies may go to war with non-liberal states, they remain at peace with each others. To put it another way, democracies do not fight each other.

This theory holds that although liberal democracies may go to war with non-democratic states, they typically do not fight each other. A key issue is the extent to which democracy has been consolidated in a country. History shows that new or transitional democracies can be war-prone in their international politics. In addition, democratic peace theory does not explain the impact of democratization on internal conflict. Iraq today illustrates high internal conflict as the democratic process struggles forward.

Collective Security

Liberals are convinced that war is not a certainty. It can be avoided by perfecting institutions designed to control violence. Liberals are strong advocates of the United Nations and seek to extend and strengthen the Security Council's mandate of **collective security**, the second offshoot of liberalism we address.

Collective security holds that individual agreements between countries are no guarantee against war. As a consequence, all wars are a matter of collective concern. The two world wars of the twentieth century demonstrated that agreements between states are no guarantee against war. The best guarantee is when all countries subscribe to the notion that "an attack against one is an attack against all." When Iraq invaded Kuwait in 1990, U.S. President George H. W. Bush immediately called together the UN Security Council and secured a UN mandate to drive Saddam Hussein's army out of Kuwait. The UN action against Iraq in 1991 may be viewed as a success story of collective action from the liberal point of view.

> **Collective security** A concept of world order maintaining that aggression can be deterred by promising overwhelming collective retaliation by the combined power of the world's states against any community member that pursued aggression. In other words, an attack against one is an attack against all. Collective security first took form in the League of Nations—which the United States refused to join—immediately following World War I.

Regime Theory

A third derivative of liberalism is regime theory. This theory assumes that international policy making can be organized in such a way as to promote cooperation. It is possible to devise treaties and international agreements that will set up a process or regime to implement the aims of the signatory parties. Once the process is initiated, the states can move forward toward the treaty's goals by making little modifications, one by one, over an extended period. For example, the 1973 Polar Bear Treaty provides for specific action by the signatory states, a joint research program, and periodic consultation. The U.S.–Russian extension of that treaty in 2000 goes further in establishing a joint commission to supervise and coordinate activities. Regime theorists believe that if states can agree on a general direction of action, subsequent meetings and consultations can refine and direct that action into increasing cooperation between states.

Neoliberalism

A third offshoot of liberalism is **neoliberalism**. Neoliberalism developed as a response to what liberals saw as the failure of realism. Realism proved unable to predict or explain the peaceful disintegration of the USSR in the early 1990s, the enormous transformation of global society that took place in the late twentieth century, and the emergence of global problems, such as environmental pollution, the AIDS epidemic, mass migrations, population growth, and failed economic development. The neoliberals proposed a new look at liberalism based on the following assumptions:

▌ Progress in international relations can be achieved only through international cooperation.

▌ International institutions can help countries resolve their differences peacefully. This is one reason why neoliberals are sometimes called *neoliberal institutionalists.*

> **Neoliberalism** A philosophical position that argues that progress in international relations can be achieved only through international cooperation. Cooperation is a dynamic rather than a static process. By focusing on understanding the dynamics of the web of relationships driving the international system, states and other international actors can use the international institutions spawned by the system to promote peace and cooperation. More recently, the neoliberal economic argument in support of a global free market has come under criticism.

❚ The world may look chaotic, but it has patterns that can be found by studying the dynamics of international relationships.

❚ Peace and cooperation can be promoted if we focus on understanding the dynamics of the web of relationships and influences driving the international world, such as democratic government, free trade, international law, international organizations, collective security, arms control, and moral decision making.

Neoliberals, ask questions like these:

❚ What kinds of political and economic processes promote cooperation?

❚ How can negotiations lead to a cooperative solution for all parties?

❚ What types of governments or institutions tend toward cooperation rather than going it alone?

❚ What are the elements of conflict resolution?

❚ What kinds of economic institutions lead to stability and greater prosperity?

Neoliberalism claims not to be a theory per se. Its basic assumption is that process determines outcome.

Neoliberalism's economic aspect has come increasingly to the fore since the 1990s. Advocates argue that neoliberalism promotes universal prosperity through free trade, a balanced budget, and stable currencies. Critics respond that global market liberalism is just another term for global capitalism, whose chief international institutions are the World Bank, the International Monetary Fund and the World Trade Organization (WTO). In their insistence on a deregulated global market, these institutions have been the main contributors to the world's increasing social and economic inequalities. In addition, the assumption that the operation of the market can be the main guide for human activity in developing countries, replacing traditional religious or moral beliefs belies the pain and suffering globalization has inflicted on the world's weaker citizens. Opposition to the economics of neoliberalism inspired the creation of the anti-globalization movement and led to the mass demonstration at the WTO meetings in Seattle and Genoa. We discuss this approach more in chapter 12.[12]

If we look at the theories derived from idealist assumptions, we can see that, essentially, they all aim to transform the world in some way—to make it better. They provide a theoretical framework that explains how and why the world is badly organized and how and why reforming or modifying the appropriate institutions will bring the desired world harmony.

On the negative side, both Marxism and liberalism, especially neoliberalism, have a strong utopian component. The goal of each is a perfect social system within which everyone lives in harmony. History suggests that that goal will not be achieved any time soon.

The Ecological Paradigm

The main tenet of the ecological approach is that you cannot separate humankind from nature either in theory or in fact. Humankind sprang from nature and depends on nature for survival and sustenance. From a tiny group, *Homo sapiens* gradually spread over the globe until the human species dominated the Earth. From the ecological approach, then, any theory of global politics that does not put Earth first underestimates the interdependence between humankind and the planet. From this perspective, new theories have emerged.

Taos Blue Lake
Hidden in the mountains of northern New Mexico lies Blue Lake or Ba Whyea, an ancient sacred site for the Taos Pueblo community. Deep ecologists hold only veneration of the sacred in nature can deter the human race from annihilating its most treasured landscapes and keep it in touch with the wellspring of human existence.

Sustainable Development Theory

Sustainable development theory evolved from the development theory, a concept which did not exist until the 1940s and which found its most enduring expression in W. W. Rostow's book, *The Stages of Economic Growth: A Non-Communist Manifesto,* published in 1960. Rostow posited that economic growth went through a series of well-defined stages, starting with traditional society through development takeoff, economic maturity, and high consumption. At first the focus of development was on industry and agriculture with the goal of improving living standards. In the late 1970s Paul Streeten and others advocated a focus on basic needs, such as education, sanitation, health care, employment. Growing awareness of the unevenness of the development process, the gap between rich and poor within and between countries, and the realization that development was putting inordinate demands on local ecosystems and the global environment called for a new approach to development. By the mid-1980s scholars were questioning whether Earth's ecosystem would survive the increased strains on its resources, if all nations reached satisfactory levels of GDP by, say, 2050. When the UN World Commission on Environment and Development published its report, *Our Common Future*, it sought to address the problem of competing environmental and developmental goals by formulating a definition of sustainable development. In her forward to the report, Gro Harlem Brundtland, prime minister of Norway and chair of the commission, defined *sustainable development* as development that "meets the needs of the present without compromising the ability of future generation to meet theirs."[13]

While a definitive definition of sustainable development does not exist, a definition has emerged around three important features:

▌ *Economic:* An economically sustainable system provides goods and services on a continuing basis equitably to all Earth's citizens.

■ *Environmental:* An environmentally sustainable system maintains a stable resource base, avoiding both the depletion of nonrenewable resources and the over-exploitation of renewable resource systems. An environmentally sustainable system further ensures the continuation of biodiversity, atmospheric stability, and clean watersheds.

■ *Social:* A socially sustainable system ends the imbalance between rich and poor, provides adequate social services, and promotes gender equality, and political accountability and participation.[14]

As you can readily see, sustainable development theory is more a set of goals to be reached than basic assumptions about the functioning of the world economy or international relations. The goals raise questions of how to balance competing objectives and how to judge success. Despite these drawbacks, sustainable development as a theoretical model dominates our thinking today about how human kind can continue to live on this planet without causing its ecosystem to crash. We will discuss the concept more in Chapters 13 and 14.

Deep Ecology

Deep ecology developed out of the thinking of Norwegian environmentalist and philosopher Arne Naess[15] and others like him who saw the ecological concepts of complexity, diversity, and **symbiosis**, as the way to relate human life to all things on the planet. For the deep ecologist, the environment has its own value independent of human needs. Human beings need to rediscover their place in nature's web of interdependent elements and treat nature reverently.

The deep ecologist sees human beings in a living relationship with their environment. The environment has its own reasons for being. It speaks to each of us and assigns us our identity. Modern society has lost this sense of identity. Many of us are indifferent to where we live. But to the Mohawk, the Huron, or the Navaho, a particular mountain or stream, or a particular lay of land, is sacred. A tribal member finds renewal by going back to the natural home revered by his ancestors. Deep ecology proposes to reconnect modern humans to their natural home.

In international affairs, the deep ecologist tends to oppose large earth-moving projects, such as the construction of the Three Gorges Dam in China, extensive logging, the paving over of swampland for parking lots, and the destruction of habitat for agriculture or a new factory. For the deep ecologist recognition and acceptance of our rootedness in nature is the ultimate wisdom.

Ecofeminism

A third offshoot of the ecological perspective is **ecofeminism**. The ecofeminist argues that women are more closely associated with the natural world than men because they are the child bearers and thus actively participate in the renewal of the species. Men, the ecofeminist argues, have an instrumental attitude toward nature. What can nature do for *me*? Women, on the other hand, have a reverence and empathy for nature, containing within themselves the secrets of birth and regeneration.

Ecofeminism holds that capitalism is the last and worst outgrowth of a patriarchal, male-dominated society. The division of labor that capitalism calls efficient divided men and women into two separate worlds, one the world of paid work, and the other the world at home. Men, with the aid of male-dominated modern

Deep ecology A worldview that promotes a reverence for nature, a concern for ecological principles such as complexity, diversity, and symbiosis, and that sees human beings in a living relationship with their environment. The environment does not exist for human use alone; we gain our identity from it. Deep ecology proposes to reconnect humankind with nature.

Symbiosis The living together of two dissimilar organisms in a mutually beneficial relationship.

Ecofeminism A theory whose proponents argue that women are more closely associated with the natural world than men are. Men have an instrumental attitude toward nature and ask, How can I use it? Women have a reverence and empathy for nature, as they contain within themselves the secrets of birth and regeneration.

science, proceeded to rape the planet in search of raw materials to satisfy their always-hungry industrial machines. As a result, the world has lost most of its forests and biodiversity.

Ecofeminists relate male domination of nature to male domination of women, arguing that the structure of domination is the same in both cases. Women and nature are considered instrumental to the achievement of male goals, be they pleasure or power, and are treated accordingly.

Some scholars dismiss ecofeminism as irrelevant. But ecofeminists are quick to point out that at the local level, where women are most active politically, women are in the forefront of local environmental groups. Women organized the movement in India to save the subcontinent's tropical forests. The most vocal opponent of the Three Gorges Dam in China is a woman.[16] Women were the principal protesters against the dumping of chemical wastes into Love Canal in Niagara Falls, New York, and maintained their vigilance until the U.S. government agreed to buy the homes contaminated by toxic waste.

Ecofeminists argue that the global environment remains at risk as long as the international community continues its primarily male view of it. At the Fourth World Conference on Women in Beijing in 1995, women's NGOs argued without success with national delegates to include phraseology guaranteeing indigenous peoples the right to benefit as much as the international drug companies from the scientific extraction of useful medicine from a local herb. (See chapter 11 for more details on the women's movement.)

To the male ecologists' argument that males can also feel a special closeness to the natural world, the ecofeminists answer that males who do develop an intimacy with nature are in essence discovering the women's world. Ecofeminists would like to see the major international organizations give up their patriarchal emphasis on economic development as primarily industrial development and begin to assess the impact of development in terms of our place in nature and our spiritual need to connect with it.

Ecojustice

The fourth theory derived from the ecological paradigm is **ecojustice**. Ecojustice theory starts from the observation that environmental quality is not equally distributed around the globe. Some environments are more desirable than others. Some environments, like the world's forests, belong to a few states but are essential to all humankind to protect our common atmosphere. The ecojustice movement originated among working black women in Warren Country, North Carolina, on land that had been predominantly owned by black people since the end of slavery in 1865. The movement began when Warren County was selected to be the final burial site for over 32,000 cubic yards of soil contaminated with PCBs (polychlorinated biphenyls). A woman named Dollie Burwell objected to the location of the site, which was just behind her and her neighbors' backyards.

The merging of race, poverty, and pollution in a single issue rapidly picked up followers all over the United States and around the world, most notably in Kenya, Nigeria, and Russia. In Russia, in 1991 women lawyers took the initiative in organizing an ecojustice group, Ecojuris, to publicize the inequity of pollution in Russia's major cities. The lawyers filed suit in a number of landmark cases, arguing that the principal victims of industrial pollution were women and young children.

Ecojustice   The concept that, as environmental quality is not equally distributed around the world, methodologies and procedures must be developed to address the environmental inequalities that are the result of lack of natural resources, poor location, and poverty.

Today, international relations scholars in the environmental field have added ecojustice to their theoretical tools of analysis. Ecojustice theory drives the argument of the developing nations that because today's industrial pollution was generated by the industrialized countries, those countries must therefore pay for the cleanup. At the Third Conference of the Parties to the United Nations Framework Convention on Climate Change, commonly known as the conference on global climate change, in Kyoto, Japan, in 1998, China and other developing countries opposed a treaty to limit emissions from the use of fossil fuels because it was not fair. In China's view, the industrialized nations were eager to prevent global warming and reach an international agreement because they already had achieved full development by polluting the planet at no cost to themselves. An adoption of the treaty would prevent developing countries from reaching their development goals.

Ecojustice theory attempts to develop methodologies and procedures to answer those questions by analyzing the connections between poverty and environmental degradation. A leading ecojustice theorist, Andrew Szasz, found, for example, that "toxic victims are, typically, poor or working people of modest means. Their environmental problems are inseparable from their economic condition."[17] In Russia, ecojurists have documented connections between environmental degradation, the living conditions of low-paid workers, and high mortality rates. In accordance with the environmental paradigm, ecojurists believe that justice in human society cannot be divorced from a search for a just distribution of environmental goods.

The environmental paradigm is the newest arrival in international relations. Many texts on world politics do not mention it at all. After reading about ecotheories, you may very well say, So what? Sure, the environment is important, but let's be real. It has nothing to do with power relations between states. Is this a fact? What about mass famines created by the expansion of the desert in Africa? What about torrential rains and mudslides in Central America? What about earthquakes in San Francisco? No one emigrates to Mexico after a California earthquake. But you may be sure that thousands moved northward from Nicaragua and Honduras after the disastrous rains of 1998.

The environmentalists argue that citizens in the industrialized world are living the good life in a clean environment because they have transferred their most polluting industries to the developing world. The industrialized states have not tried sustainable development and so far have shown little desire to do so. To achieve sustainable development, the industrial states must recognize the primary importance of the environment to all humans, and not just a privileged few. The inequitable transborder effects of environmental pollution are already causing increased tension and conflict in the world. This recognition demands both a retreat from the instrumental view of the environment as a human resource and a deeper understanding of the functioning and value of the environment in and of itself.

TEST PREPPER 2.2

True or False?

_____ 1. Balance-of-power theory argues that war is most likely to occur when states in the system have reached balance.

_____ 2. According to realists, the only way to contain power is through power.

_____ 3. Marxists argue that class struggle is the key dynamic that fosters socioeconomic change over time.

_____ 4. Democratic peace theory refers to the belief that liberal democracies typically do not fight one another, although they may go to war with non-democratic states.

_____ 5. Ecofeminists believe that women are more closely associated with the natural world because they bear children while men view the environment as an instrument for achieving material objectives.

Multiple Choice

_____ 6. Which of the following statements would a neorealist agree accurately represents international politics?

   a. States are the primary actors in the international system.

   b. All states have the same goals, but they differ in their ability to influence world politics.

   c. The structure of the international system is defined by the unequal distribution of power among the countries of the world.

   d. None of the above

   e. All of the above

_____ 7. Neoliberals believe which of the following statements about international politics?

   a. Progress in international relations occurs through the good will of individuals.

   b. The chaos of world politics can only be addressed using economic theories of behavior.

   c. International institutions are effective at assisting countries resolve their differences without resorting to conflict.

   d. A combination of a focus on power in the military realm and cooperation in the economic sphere is the most effective way to analyze the international system.

   e. None of the above

 Between Nations
Practice Test Questions
Practice Test 2.2
www.BetweenNations.org

WHAT ARE THE SUBJECTIVE APPROACHES TO WORLD POLITICS?

3 *What is a "subjective approach to world politics"? Understand how such approaches differ from realism, idealism, and the ecological paradigm.*

In the last quarter of the twentieth century, philosophers and political scientists launched increasingly sharp attacks on the basic assumption of political realists, idealists, and ecologists that the world and its political, economic, and social structure could be objectively known. The assumption that there is a real world out there, independent of ourselves, that all of us, using our reasoning power, can discover and use to our benefit, underlies all Western philosophy from the Greeks to the Enlightenment. Realists and idealists may disagree as to whether humankind is basically imperfect or basically cooperative and develop contrasting theories as to whether world politics is continuous anarchy or can become a cooperative venture. Ecologists and realists may disagree about whether the Earth is warming or not, but both groups base their arguments on empirical evidence drawn from objective observations of the real world.

Critical theory, constructivism, and most feminist theories in international relations question the ability of human beings to look objectively at the world. All people, they argue, are shaped by the society and culture in which they live. Our perceptions are formed by our society's dominant attitudes about wealth, race, gender, and religion. This assumption that our background and upbringing totally inform our perceptions of the world derives from the Marxist teaching that all science, art, and culture reflect the interests of a given society's ruling class. Throughout history, each social class that rose to power imposed its prejudices, its ethics, its way of doing things on the society it governed. In their struggle against the ruling class, the other classes developed their own class culture and identity in response to the reigning status quo. Critical theory and constructivism carry this logic to its conclusion and hold that every individual's perception of reality is determined by personal experience of a given society's dominant culture relative to that person's position in its social structure.

Critical Theory

▰▰▰ *Between Nations*
Audio Concept
Critical Theory
www.BetweenNations.org

The term *critical theory* was first used by members of a scholarly group that formed at the Institute of Social Research at the University of Frankfurt in the 1920s and lasted into the 1950s. These scholars were appalled by the rise of what they saw as the lack of freedom and irrationality in European capitalist societies in the 1920s and 1930s, culminating in fascism in Germany and Italy.[18]

Herbert Marcuse (1898–1979) and Jürgen Habermas (1929–) are two major contributors to the ongoing evolution of critical theory in the latter half of the twentieth century. The common thread between them is that in modern society, human beings are increasingly losing their autonomy, their capacity to make independent individual decisions exclusive of outside control. Marcuse argued that "advanced industrial society" creates false needs to integrate individuals into the existing system of production and consumption. Mass media and contemporary culture, advertising, and industrial management all reinforce the political and suppress opposition.[19]

Habermas posited that the technological revolution had contributed to the suppression of individual freedom by forcing humans to learn and adapt to new technologies that function on the machine's inner logic. The market, the state, and social and economic organizations: all operate on some form of "strategic/instrumental rationality" based on how technology *works* rather than on how humans really *live*. Habermas argued for social change through communication. A freer, more democratic world was possible not through revolution, as the Marxists taught, but through people finding community through communication.[20]

Constructivism

Constructivism Constructivism is a philosophy of learning founded on the premise that, by reflecting on our experiences, we construct our own understanding of the world we live in.

The critical theory started by the Frankfurt School leads directly into constructivism. Constructivism, like critical theory, posits that because human beings exist within society, knowledge can never be objective, only subjective. We all can use reason to try to figure things out, but *how* we reason is culturally determined—that is, it is shaped, or "constructed," by the society and culture in which we live. Thus, all perceptions and all cultures reflect the worldview and social structure of a given social group, be it tribe or nation. We can never know what reality is, only what our perceptions of it are. Because reality cannot be known, every culture, every society presents a worldview that is equally valid. Contrary to the neorealist and neoliberal viewpoint, constructivism holds that the structure and institutions of the international system function only insofar as the international actors *think* they function and so do not influence states' behaviors per se. Rather, the political culture, the diffusion of ideas circulating in the international system, informs, or "constructs," the interests and national identities of states that, in turn, shape the dynamics of world politics.[21]

Constructivism in international relations leads to a focus on an individual or group's experiences both as regards their understanding of the world and the actions they choose to take. Political scientist David Campbell uses the constructivist approach in his analysis of the emergence of Bosnia as an intractable ethnic problem. How did a once successful multicultural society turn into an international nightmare? Campbell finds that both the peacemakers of the North Atlantic Treaty Organization (NATO) and the belligerents in Bosnia failed or refused to take into account the possibility of overlapping identities. For example, a man could simultaneously be Bosnian, and a Serb, and a Muslim, or he could be a Bosnian, a Croat, and a Catholic. But instead of recognizing this fact, both sides shared the same misperception of identity: namely, that a national grouping had to have a self-contained shared history and culture, speak the same language, and live together in definable borders. Campbell faults the poverty of Western thought in developing concepts that promote identity politics within heterogeneous communities (national, ethnic, or linguistic groups that do not live in separate, culturally distinct, social enclaves). He concludes that Europe and the United States intervened in Bosnia not in the interests of saving a once vibrant multicultural community but to support the nationalist idea in order to prevent the spread of multiculturalism beyond national state borders at home.[22]

Feminist Theories in International Relations

There is no single feminist theory of international relationships but rather several different and often conflicting theories. We look at some of these theories more closely in chapter 11.

While the roots of feminist theory go back to Mary Wollstonecraft (1759–1797) and the struggle for women's suffrage, the European Marxist women's movement of the nineteenth century bequeathed a powerful legacy to modern feminist theory building. Most feminists today agree that basic attitudes and behaviors are culturally determined. Western civilization is a patriarchy, a male-dominated enterprise. Males have dominated politics, science, economics, and the arts. Realism and idealism are constructions of the male imagination. Traditional Western male thinking perceives reality as a set of mutually exclusive dichotomies: black, white; rational, irrational; weak, strong; chaos, order; war, peace. Every term has a definition that limits its meaning to a specific thing. States have identifiable borders that separate them from other states. International governmental and nongovernmental organizations have constitutions, identifiable memberships, and identifiable goals. State organizations operate at different and distinct levels in the world system.

Feminism refuses to see the world in these terms. Instead of seeing it as a rather static dichotomous (either/or) hierarchical international system, feminists approach world politics as a to-be-determined, unstructured, interdependent, dynamic set of interrelationships, similar to those in their personal and family lives.

Constructivists and feminists alike understand political theory not as an approach to understanding objective reality but as a prescription, a recipe for

The Rebuilt Bridge at Mostar

Stari most, *the old bridge, crosses the Neretva River at Mostar, where Bosnian Muslims and Croat Catholics lived side by side for centuries. Built in 1566 by the Ottoman Turks, it was destroyed by Croat fighters during the bitter fighting between Mostar's Muslims and Croats in 1993. It was reconstructed using the same methods and materials employed by the original builders 500 years ago. Its reopening in 2004 is living witness to the concept that ethnic rivalry is not a given but is a subjective assumption that can be deconstructed.*

action. They see information and communication about world events as data to feed into an activist agenda directing what should be done rather than a framework within which to analyze facts describing what actually happens.

Critiques of Constructivism

Critical theory, constructivism, and feminist theories have played a decisive role in shifting our focus from external, state-to-state relations to a closer look at the subjective dynamics of international affairs. But in so doing, they have produced what one educator has called 'the evidential dilemma."[23] If there is no empirical evidence, on what does an individual, tribe, or state base a decision for action?

Critical Theory in Perspective

This section has looked at three critiques of subjective approaches to international relations theory. Constructivism and feminist theories have been important in drawing attention to the gap between what a culture says the world is like and actual individual experience. If, however, realist and idealist international relations approaches lead to excessive concerns about the struggle for power and the nature of war or peace in an anarchic world, the critical theorists can lead us into a quagmire of uncertainty about whether or not we can know anything about the nature of global issues and why states behave as they do in the international system.

TEST PREPPER 2.3

True or False?

_____ 1. Subjective approaches to world politics are so named because they rely strictly on opinions and are opposed to collecting data of any kind.

_____ 2. Constructivist approaches to world politics tend to focus on the state level of analysis because they combine the impact of various entities when analyzing political behavior.

_____ 3. Rather than having a single approach to world politics, there are multiple and conflicting feminist theories of international relations.

_____ 4. Generally speaking, critical theory questions the objective nature of reality, arguing that each individual constructs their own reality based on their own perception.

Multiple Choice

_____ 5. Most feminists argue which of the following?
   a. Basic attitudes and behaviors are biologically determined.
   b. Western civilization is a patriarchy (or male-dominated enterprise).
   c. Males have dominated the military while women have had an opportunity to control the arts.
   d. All of the above

 Between Nations
Practice Test Questions
Practice Test 2.3
www.BetweenNations.org

CASE STUDY

The Future of Afghanistan

See **www.BetweenNations.org**

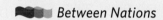 *Between Nations*

JOIN THE DEBATE

Looking Out for Number One

OVERVIEW

Traditionally, realists argue that it is necessary for states to focus on their own self-interest. Kautilya, an Indian scholar writing in the third century BC consistently advocated the need to, in essence, "Look out for Number One."

Advocates of the U.S. invasion in Afghanistan and the preventive military action in Iraq might make a similar case. Osama bin Laden has been organizing and masterminding terrorist actions since the early 1990s. For an entire decade the United States took little aggressive action, even when U.S. ships and seamen were bombed and embassies blown up. The attacks of 9/11 changed all that. By doing nothing, the United States encouraged bin Laden to think it were scared to use its power. If the United States had waited until the UN agreed it should go to war in Iraq, Saddam Hussein would have thought the same thing and launched possibly a terrible preemptive strike of his own. Each nation has the right to use its power to defend itself. The UN cannot look out for all its members. A state either looks out for itself and forcefully uses its power, or it goes into decline.

Advocates of collective security and international cooperation look at the U.S. action in an entirely opposite light. Iraq was a country where international sanctions had been in place for a decade. During that period the people became impoverished and Saddam Hussein's military preparedness decreased. Iraq was not a threat to any country, least of all to the United

States. Negotiations were in progress. The United States broke international convention by rushing headlong into a venture—one that has proved costly in lives and materiel—contrary to the counsel of the world's major powers. There is no indication that negotiation would not have worked. The proper way to conduct national affairs in a global community is through the global institutions established by that community. The United States has acted like a global bully, trying to push weaker states around.

A realist looks after Number One. An idealist looks to international cooperation as the only way to secure peace and prosperity for all states. In essence, the debate focuses on two key questions: (1) What does looking after Number One entail? Does it mean only using a state's own power resources, or can it include cooperating in international organizations? (2) In what ways can cooperation contribute to a state's prosperity? In what ways could it be a hindrance?

Pro: Arguments for Number One Looking after Number One

▌ There is no world government, only other states testing you and ready to move against you in the struggle for power.

▌ States that openly declare their hostility to you are your enemy.

▌ Each state has the right and obligation to act in its own interests.

▌ Self-defense is vital to a state's preservation and should not require either international approval or catastrophes like Pearl Harbor or 9/11 to attack an enemy. Preemption is sound survival strategy.

Con: Arguments for Collective Security and International Cooperation

▌ Looking out for Number One to the exclusion of the interests and needs of the global community leads to needless violence and suffering by innocent people.

▌ War is to be avoided at all costs. Any war can lead to nuclear war, as nuclear weapons are readily available.

▌ War directed at one state puts at risk the independence and political stability of neighboring states and escalates violence to surrounding countries.

▌ In the modern world, one state can no longer impose its will on another and risk such consequences.

▌ Negotiation and diplomacy remain the best instruments of peaceful solutions.

▌ If war seems necessary to avoid the consequence of a widening war, military intervention should only be allowed with UN approval.

QUESTIONS

1. Depending on which side you took, did you find that all the arguments you used came exclusively from either the liberal or realist approach?

2. In what areas did your arguments cause you to change approach?

3. Did you find yourself arguing in favor of more centralized global oversight of state behavior or for the right of states to be the main actors in global politics? What reasons did you give?

LEARNING OBJECTIVES REVIEW

▶ 1 *Understand and be able to summarize the key assumptions of political realism, idealism, and the ecological paradigm.*

- *Realism* holds that human nature is, by definition, imperfect. We all have an innate drive for power. National governments, therefore, should concentrate on promoting the national interest through a strong military to defend against aggression and a "what's-in-it-for-me" posture in the conduct of foreign policy.

- *Idealism* posits that human beings are perfectible. With the right institutions to guide them, individuals and states can learn to cooperate and to prefer peace to war.

- The *ecological* paradigm posits human society as a subset of the natural environment. This environment has limits, and we must learn what those limits are and accommodate our institutions to them if humankind is to survive.

▶ 2 *Identify and understand the key theories that result from realism, idealism, and the ecological paradigm.*

- From the realist perspective, we derive the theories of the balance of power, hegemonic stability, and neorealism. These are theories that explain the management of the international system as a decentralized, many-sided process that takes place among states.

- From the idealist perspective come the theories of Marxism and liberalism (the two major theories of the past 150 years) and the more recent dependency theory, collective security, and neoliberalism. Liberal theories tend to argue in favor of centralized cooperation by states in global organizations and to downplay the importance of national identity.

- Within the ecological perspective, we find deep ecology, ecofeminism, and ecojustice. These theories seek to bridge the gap between the human footprint on the local environment and its impact on the global community.

▶ 3 *What is a "subjective approach to world politics"? Understand how such approaches differ from realism, idealism, and the ecological paradigm.*

- Critics of these approaches have developed critical theory, constructivism, and feminist theories of international relations that focus on the psychological and social components of state identity and behavior.

- These theories seek to explain how the identities of cultures and societies are formed and how these relate to their behavior on the international stage

RESOURCES ON THE WEB

To use these interactive learning and study tools, including video and audio multimedia resources, go to **www.BetweenNations.org**.

Practice Tests	Case Studies	Current Events
Audio Concepts	Primary Sources	Daily Newsfeeds from *The Washington Post*
Flashcards	Historical Background	Weblinks for Further Exploration

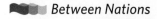 Between Nations

Different Lenses for Different Pictures

LEARNING OBJECTIVES

1 ▶ *Identify the primary characteristics of a state. Understand how the state has developed over the past centuries and its current role in world politics.*

2 ▶ *Understand what is meant by levels of analysis and who are the primary actors that operate at each level.*

> *"All the world's a stage."*
>
> —William Shakespeare

Chapter Outline

3 ▶ *Understand how the levels of analysis
are used to understand international
relations; apply the levels to the case
of Afghanistan.*

Analysis as a Tool to Understand Our World

In chapter 1 you learned that one of the five forces shaping the planet is the increasing inability of the state to solve problems because of decentralizing ethnic, religious, and economic tensions. You further learned that most issues today are transnational and transboundary in character, promoting a centralizing tendency in the international system—as, for example, the tendency for states to turn to the United Nations (UN) and other international agencies for regulations and guidelines. What is this entity called a state, and why does international politics seem to revolve around it? How can we understand the tensions that push states *toward dissolution* and the tensions that push them *toward international cooperation*?

This chapter enables you to address those questions. We first look at the state—what it is, how it arose, and why it plays such a central role in international relations today. We then look at the structure of the international system by applying levels of analysis. For example, we may study the international system in its entirety, as we might study the solar system as a whole. That's one level. But we can also study the international system at the regional level by looking at regional organizations of states such as the European Union (EU) and the North American Free Trade Agreement (NAFTA). For a third perspective, we can study the international system at the state level—that is, by looking at the world from the standpoint of the behavior of individual states. This is a very important level because the basic unit of analysis in the international system is the state. We can also study the international system at the substate level, looking at ethnic conflict or civil wars and how these tensions affect the state and its ability to function at the regional and international levels. Finally, we can look at the international system through the role individuals play in moving and shaking world politics. We conclude the chapter by showing that by understanding what the state is and how it functions at these five levels, we can begin to understand the centralizing and decentralizing tendencies at work in the world today. ■

THE STATE: THE BASIC UNIT OF ANALYSIS IN THE INTERNATIONAL SYSTEM

 Identify the primary characteristics of a state. Understand how the state has developed over the past centuries and its current role in world politics.

For all the paradigms, states are the basic building blocks of the international system. Chapter 1 presented three characteristics that differentiate a state from a tribe, an ethnic group, or a nationality. To review, a state is:

1. a geographic territory with internationally recognized boundaries
2. an internationally recognized and identifiable population that lives within those boundaries
3. an internationally recognized authority structure or government

Let us look more closely at these characteristics.

The State and Its Primary Characteristics

The modern state, as we understand it, grew out of rivalry for power and wealth among the ruling dynasties of Europe from the fifteenth to the seventeenth centuries. The concept of an international system dates from the 1648 **Treaty of Westphalia**, which ended the Thirty Years' War. The war had decimated large sections of Europe, and, important for our purposes, left no clear victor. Our modern understanding of state, then, is derived, essentially, from the European experience.

The treaty recognized that none of the rival European powers at war could achieve a decisive win to dominate the other powers. The treaty thus called for the

Treaty of Westphalia   The treaty, signed in 1648 at the close of the Thirty Years' War, called for the recognition as sovereign states of territorial entities that could no longer be dominated and that had fixed borders, a recognized population, and an acknowledged government.

recognition of these territorial entities as states, with fixed borders, an acknowledged government, and a population identified as living within that state's borders. The treaty recognized these states as *sovereign,* or self-ruling, and promised that the government of one state would not interfere in the affairs of another. Relations between states would be characterized by diplomacy and regulated by international law in the form of treaties and agreements.

Definition of a State

The modern definition of *state* is based on the principles set forth in the 1648 treaty. Central to the definition are the concepts of legitimacy, sovereignty, and formal obligations.

▌ *Legitimacy* means that all states have a right to exist and that the authority of the government in that state is supreme and accepted as lawful.

▌ *Sovereignty* means that no higher authority than the state exists, or in Max Weber's words, the state has "a monopoly of the legitimate use of physical force."[1] The United Nations is made up of states, yet it has no authority to compel member-states to take any action or refrain from any action. It has no army of its own and must rely on the member-states to contribute their armed forces when any UN armed intervention takes place. In the last analysis, each state decides its own course of action.

▌ States have *formal obligations,* or *expectations* vis-à-vis one another. States agree to rules drawn up according to international law for declaring and fighting a war, for implementing treaties, for continuing to recognize the legitimacy of the governments of other states, and for exchanging and treating diplomatic representatives. In recent years, however, the new global and transnational issues have prompted new thinking on this front. Although at an operational level the state still retains full control over the actions of its police and military, the conditions for their use are increasingly shaped by rules and regulations receiving their legitimation from the UN and other international institutions.[2] For example, the U.S. invasion of Iraq in 2003 was considered illegitimate by many (but not all) because the United States failed to secure the approval of the UN Security Council for the action.

 Between Nations
Audio Concept
Sovereignty
www.BetweenNations.org

The Nation-state and the Multinational State

A discussion of the state and its characteristics would not be complete without distinguishing between two kinds of states that appear frequently in this text. The first is the *nation-state.* The nation-state is composed primarily of one ethnic or nationality group or nation. The common definition of **nation or ethnic group** is a group of people who have a common language, common ethnicity, common culture, common territory, and a desire for independence. Ethnic groups like the Kurds and the Palestinians in the Middle East or the Chechens in the Caucasus form ethnic nations. All demand independence in a specific territory, based on a common language and common culture. A nation-state is that nation once it has gained political independence, as East Timor eventually did. Examples of older nation-states are Germany, the Netherlands, France, and Japan.

The second kind of state is the **multinational or multiethnic state**, as it is often called. As the name suggests, the population in this kind of state is composed of two or more ethnic groups or races. Most of the world's states fall into this category. The world's largest states—Russia, China, India, and the United States—are

Nation or ethnic group   A group of people linked together in some manner, such as a common territory, with a shared culture that may or may not be based on religion. This culture can be monocultural or multicultural—a shared language, a shared history or understanding of the past, and a general desire for independence.

Multinational or multiethnic state A state—such as Nigeria, the United States, Russia, and India—that contains more than one nation and/or ethnic group within its territory. Most states are multinational in nature.

all multinational. So are some of the world's smallest states, such as Switzerland, Belgium, and many states in Africa and Asia. Multinational states frequently suffer from the desire of the component ethnic groups to live their own lifestyle or obtain more power in the central government.

The Vulnerability of the Modern State

While the principles of legitimacy, sovereignty, and duty are still in force today, the forces of change discussed in chapter 1, particularly the new global and transnational issues, the inability of the state to solve problems on its own, and the technology revolution, have undermined sovereignty. Increasing state vulnerability is one of the most visible decentralizing forces in the world today. First, state sovereignty has been weakened through the growth of networks of communication and linkages among non-state actors that are beyond the state's immediate control. These interdependent networks have grown most rapidly among non-state actors in the global economy and non-state actors such as Greenpeace and al Qaeda.

The 9/11 attacks highlighted two additional important dimensions of a state's vulnerability: the dangers posed by *failed states* and the insecurity of even the most powerful state in the world. Not all states are successful. Some fail to maintain law and order within their borders or to provide the level of economic well-being, education, housing, food, and security their populations demand. Failed states today include Angola, Burundi, the Democratic Republic of Congo, Liberia, Sierra Leone, Somalia, and Sudan. In each of these states, economic and political chaos reigns. Failed states, such as Afghanistan before 9/11, offer havens for criminals, terrorists, drug trafficking, and cross-border mayhem. In so doing, they promote global insecurity. The United States bombed Afghanistan in 2001 not because it had declared war on the state of Afghanistan but because this failed state harbored Osama bin Laden's terrorist organization. In the interests of guaranteeing security at home, the United States, for the first time since the Treaty of Westphalia, declared war, calling it a war on terrorism, against a *non-state actor,* who had been given sanctuary in Afghanistan, arguably violating the internationally recognized sovereignty of that state.

The war in Iraq that started in 2003, departed from the Westphalian norms governing state sovereignty in two ways.

1. The war was billed as a preventive action, intended, according to the U.S. government, *to prevent* the Iraqi dictator, Saddam Hussein, from completing the development of weapons of mass destruction and distributing them to terrorist groups.
2. The declared U.S. goal of regime change in Iraq undermined Iraq's state sovereignty, and the legitimacy of its internationally recognized government. The invasion of Iraq marked the fifth time in recent history that the United States took preventive action to force regime change in another state.

   ▌ 1961: The United States sponsored a failed attempt to bring down Fidel Castro's communist government in Cuba.

   ▌ 1983: The United States invaded the state of Grenada to prevent the consolidation of a Marxist regime on the island.

   ▌ 1989: The United States invaded the state of Panama to replace the dictatorship of Manuel Noriega with a pro-American government. While the world community was not happy with these actions, they occurred during the Cold

War and, to a certain extent, could be justified by the necessity of preventing the further projection of Soviet power into the Western hemisphere.

▮ 1999: Similarly, Western Europe accepted the U.S. bombing and invasion of Yugoslavia in 1999 because of the perceived need to prevent a worst-case scenario, namely, genocide of the Kosovar population in that country.

▮ 2003: In contrast, the United States was unable to present a rationale for its invasion of Iraq that was acceptable to the other power centers of the international community. France, Germany, and Russia felt their power threatened by the prospect of the dominant world power taking military action whenever it perceived its national security to be at risk. The Iraqi invasion thus brought home the hard fact that, in the absence of a world government, the concept of sovereignty is a political football in the decentralized struggle for power among the world's states.

The Interdependence of States

Like a two-edged sword, the three forces mentioned above as contributing to decentralizing tendencies promote centralizing tendencies as well. Some analysts of the liberal persuasion hail the increased vulnerability of states as testimony to the growing **interdependence** of states. These analysts consider the coming of globalization and interdependence a good thing. In their view, states that depend on other states for raw materials and export markets are less likely to go to war to resolve differences and are more likely to cooperate.

> **Interdependence** The linking of states together in a web of wide-ranging interactions. These include: international finance, trade and commerce, environmental pollution, the information revolution, transnationalism, intergovernmental organizations (IGOs), and nongovernmental organizations (NGOs.)

Neorealist Kenneth N. Waltz and others criticize this position as simplistic. We need to look at *how* states depend on one another, they say, and honestly admit that the United States can probably get along without the rest of the world better than most states can get along without the United States. Waltz argues that the low level of U.S. dependence on other countries is a primary source of its great power status and the relative facility with which a great power can unilaterally control the behavior of less powerful states.[3] We return to this idea in chapter 4.

A third position on globalization, derived again from the liberal paradigm, is reflected in the work of James Rosenau, who sees the growing loss of sovereignty as signaling the end of the dominant role of states in the international system. The salient characteristics of the emerging post-Westphalian system, he argues, are the inclusion of non-state actors and the development of global civil society. After the 9/11 attacks, Rosenau's perspective seems most convincing and also most terrifying.[4] How can any state control the behavior of non-state actors whose membership is largely invisible? We talk more about the behavior of non-state actors in chapter 7.

The Origins and Development of the State—
The European Experience

How did the world come to be dominated by states where ethnicity and nationalism play such a strong role? The state is both a relatively new arrival on the international scene and an old form of social organization that appeared for relatively short periods of time in antiquity. Today, the **international system** has outgrown its European origins and expanded to include the entire globe, with 191 states[5] and a growing number of non-state actors.

> **International system** A concept that includes a number of key actors (states, nations, IGOs, and NGOs) and the patterns of actions among them that can be explained by the distribution of power and other factors. The state plays a pivotal role within this system, because the system has no central authority to maintain order and dispense justice.

The state derives from a diverse heritage of independent self-governing city-states in ancient Sumer in Mesopotamia, Greece, China, and classical Rome. The

Sumerian city-states flourished at the dawn of human civilization in Mesopotamia in what is now Iraq. The city-states of Greece, Rome, and China were at their height between the fifth century bc and the second century ad.

The modern state had its rise in the Middle Ages, long after Rome fell. The history of Europe is the history of rivalry—war and conquest—among feudal chieftains, with the periodic ascendancy of a strongman. These rulers were eager to expand their domains. To do so, however, they needed to create sufficient wealth to raise an army. The medieval city was just coming into its own as a commercial power. Some cities, like Venice and Florence in Italy and Dubrovnik in modern Croatia, flourished as independent city-states. Others, like Prague, London, or Paris, accepted the rule of the prevailing strongman. Through patronage, royal subsidies, and the granting of imperial or royal charters, these cities became centers of trade, finance, and learning. In return for their liberties, the cities paid taxes to the king to support his armies. With tax money rolling in and helped along by marriages of convenience to princesses with large land holdings, the kings gradually became stronger than the feudal chieftains, whose power largely resided in their agricultural land base. The consolidation of royal power in the fifteenth century put Europe well on its way to playing midwife at the birth of the modern state. Additional factors that led to the evolution of the modern state include the following:

▌ *Ideology and a Common Culture:* We cannot be sure that modern states would have evolved out of this process if it had not been for the long political conflict between the rising nation-states of France, Spain, and England, on the one hand, and, on the other, the pope in Rome, who called himself Vicar (deputy of Christ) of Christendom, by which he meant Europe. Over the centuries, the royal powers challenged the temporal or non-religious authority of the medieval Church and carved out a space where they could rule independent of its control, eventually leading to the development of Protestant and Catholic sects. Each sect's acknowledgment of its king as the guardian of the one true faith led to the identification of a national leader and, by extension, the nation-state with a particular belief or ideology. Eventually, the ideology of nationalism replaced Christianity as the glue that bound European peoples together.

▌ *Technology and the Growth of Nationalist Sentiment:* Perhaps no other development had as great an impact on the rise of the national state and the promotion of a common language as the printing press.

In one month, Johannes Gutenberg could turn out more German bibles than the monks could write by hand in Latin in several years. Thus, the printing press made literature in the *vernacular* (the language people spoke in a particular locale) easily available and readily disseminated in the form of the printed book. People rushed to learn how to read and to buy the new books. Printing thus gave nationalism a big boost. With the appearance of books in vernacular languages such as English, French, and Spanish, people began to buy only those books whose language they could understand. In the process, some languages were winners. Some were losers.

Because the printing press made it easy to distribute the printed word and booksellers made more sales with books printed in the local language, the press prompted kings to standardize the language throughout their domains. By the sixteenth century, in part due to having acquired a set of common languages, Western Europeans had developed a strong sense of nationality, territory, and common history. The French Revolution of 1789 spread the ideology of nationalism as far as Russia with

The Inventor of the Printing Press

Printing was actually invented in China, where the emperors disseminated their edicts and orders through a printed text composed of ideographs or picture symbols. European written languages use an alphabet representing the sounds or phonemes present in the spoken language. The advantage of the alphabet is that many combinations of sounds can be written down using a few letters. Johannes Gutenberg's achievement was the invention of movable type. Instead of carving a font of a word or ideograph, as the Chinese had to do, Gutenberg used a line of type that could be filled with different letters, depending on the word appearing in the text. Just before the year 2000, Time-Life conducted a poll asking worldwide leaders in science, education, government, technology, medicine, and other fields to name the most important events of the last 1,000 years. The printing press was voted the most important event.

the march of Napoleon's armies eastward, thereby awakening the East European peoples to the possibilities of independence and the right to speak *their* own language, rather than the language of their German and Russian imperial masters.

▎ *Europe Becomes a Continent of Nation-states:* In 1815, the European powers united to defeat Napoleon. But Napoleon's legacy lived on. In Western Europe, England and France emerged as the two leading states promoting democracy as an integral part of their nationalist ideology. Throughout the rest of Europe, still under the rule of autocratic empires, nationalism assumed a more cultural aspect, leading to the consolidation of German states into a unified German Empire and the creation of the Austro-Hungarian Empire, based on two ruling ethnic groups. Other nations living under imperial rule also demanded national recognition. In their push for their own separate national state, they turned to the European great powers for support. The instability and threat to the status quo posed by these developments resulted in the Triple Alliance (made up of

Germany, Austro-Hungary, and Italy, 1882) and the Triple Entente (England, France, and Russia, 1907). Great-power rivalry and the fear that one European state might gain the ascendancy over all the others led to a balance-of-power game that played out in a domino-like series of events culminating tragically in World War I.

World War I marked the fall of the Ottoman and German empires and the ascendancy of nationalism as the basis of the state. These two empires were replaced with nation-states. The one remaining traditional empire was the Russian Empire. Although instability caused by the Bolshevik Revolution in 1917 forced the new leader, Vladimir Ilych Lenin, to give up the Baltic territories as well as Russia's share of Poland, the remainder of the empire was reformed as the Soviet Union. In the twentieth century, the great overseas empires of Britain, France, Germany, Spain, and Portugal were replaced by independent states. From 1989–1991, the last European land empire, the Soviet Union inherited from the Russian tsars and enlarged after World War II, broke up to be replaced by independent states.

▌ *The Modern International System:* The founding of the United Nations in 1945, at the end of World War II, formalized the concept of a global international system composed of national states. The UN began its existence with fifty signatory states. Amazing as it may seem, most of today's states have come into being since then. Of the 191 UN member-states today, some are very small, like the African states of Sao Tomé and Principe. Others are large land masses, like the United States, Canada, Russia, and Australia. As we show in chapter 8, geography—including size, location, and shape—plays a big role in the ability of states to participate in international politics effectively.

Because most of the new states came into being as a result of the breakup of the colonial empires, virtually all their borders were drawn by the colonial powers. The citizens of the new states had virtually no say. With the exception of some island states, many of the new states contain more than one ethnic group. Some do not have a common language or a common ethnic group. As a result, a major problem is developing citizen loyalty to the new country and a sense of belonging among people who, just a generation earlier, were living under their tribal leaders in an imperial system of government imposed by rulers from far away. Nigeria is an excellent example of this kind of problem where over 300 ethnolinguistic groups were consolidated into one country by an imperial ruler.

Under the principles of international law, the new states are as sovereign and independent as the older and more established powers. The principle of equality is recognized through the mechanism of "one country, one vote" in the UN General Assembly. In practice, however, the newer states can do little to oppose the power of the major states. The best they can do is to play one power off against the other to assure they do not fall under the control of one state permanently. In addition, today's states are living in a period of U.S.–superpower dominance. It is hard for small, weak states to oppose the United States or larger regional entities, such as NATO, in their part of the world. The dynamics of the modern international system remain the same as in the days of the Treaty of Westphalia, at least in terms of the interaction between strong and weak states. Weak states must decide the merits of forming regional alliances, giving in to the superpower, or going it alone. The difference between 1648 and today is that the international action now covers the entire globe. In 1648, it covered only the continent of Europe.

True or False?

_____ 1. The state is the primary actor in the international system because no other actor in the system has the ability to harm the state.

_____ 2. State sovereignty allows the United Nations to force its member-states to take actions when it is in the interests of the UN to do so.

_____ 3. Both China and the United States are examples of multinational states.

_____ 4. The majority of the 191 states that have membership in the United Nations today did not exist when the UN was first formed in 1945.

_____ 5. The 2003 United States invasion of Iraq followed the traditional Westphalian norms governing state sovereignty.

Multiple Choice

_____ 6. Which of the following is NOT a characteristic of a state in the international system:

    a. A geographic territory with internationally recognized boundaries

    b. An internationally recognized and identifiable population that lives within those boundaries

    c. An internationally recognized authority structure or government

    d. An entity with membership in the United Nations' Security Council

    e. None of the above

_____ 7. Which of the following was a factor leading to the evolution of the modern state:

    a. The temporary slowdown of technological advancement leading to a focus on national unity rather than economic self-interest

    b. The feudal nature of European society in the early 1800s

    c. The development of a common culture and/or ideology among a group of people constituting the nation

    d. The devastating effects for the average person during the War of 1812

 Between Nations
Practice Test Questions
Practice Test 3.1
www.BetweenNations.org

WHAT ARE THE LEVELS OF ANALYSIS?

2▸ *Understand what is meant by levels of analysis and who are the primary actors that operate at each level.*

How are we going to analyze the interactions of 191 states and various regional governmental and nongovernmental organizations? Because doing so is extremely complex, political scientists have developed a tool for getting a handle on the international system, its players, and how they relate to one another. It is called **levels of analysis**, a system for organizing the players into five levels of international activity (see Table 3.1). Let's begin with the highest level.

Levels of analysis   A method of classifying the players in the international system and how they relate to one another on five levels.

The International System as a Whole

System level analysis enables us to make generalizations and predictions about patterns of interaction among the actors in the system. The basic assumptions underlying system level analysis are:

1. The international system is considered as a single whole.
2. Within this whole, actors interact with and respond to one another in ways that are predictable.

An analogy might be a forest. A forest is composed of trees, but if you're interested in the system, you do not look at each individual tree but rather at the

TABLE 3.1

Levels of Analysis

Levels	Actors
1. International system level	States, non-state actors, and individuals
2. Regional level	States, regional NSAs, individuals
3. State level	States, state-level NSAs, individuals
4. Substate level	Interest groups, ethnic groups, individuals
5. Individual level	Individual people

component parts of the forest, such as the deciduous trees and the coniferous trees. By identifying the behavior pattern of each component, you can classify the deciduous trees into oak, maple, larch, or birch. The coniferous trees might be pine, hemlock, and spruce. Through study of the forest, we can make generalizations about the conditions necessary for the survival of all forests—and of species of trees within the forest.

In similar ways, though with considerably less accuracy, we can consider the international system as a whole and identify its components. Among the most important components are the types of actors within the system.

Grouping the State Actors

As you already know, the principal actors are the states. We commonly group these states into categories, based on the level of economic and political development a state has attained. As Table 3.2 presents, we categorize states into four sets:

1. The *first set* contains the *industrialized states,* such as the United States, the West European states, Japan, and Australia.
2. The *second set* consists of the *former communist countries in transition to a democratic society and market economy:* Russia, the countries of East Central Europe, and the independent states formed from the former Soviet Union and located in Central Asia and the Caucasus.
3. The *third set* comprises the *developing states,* including countries in Latin America, the Caribbean, Asia, and most of Africa.
4. The *fourth set* are the *at-risk states,* or those that may not develop the economic and political institutions necessary for survival. The at-risk states include Somalia, Chad, Ethiopia, the Central African Republic, and other African states that are desperately poor and possess virtually no natural resources.

It is important to understand that Table 3.2 represents a classification of states, not a rank order. The second set of states are all those states that experienced communist rule in the second half of the nineteenth century. Most developing states never experienced communist rule, Vietnam and China being the most visible exceptions. And most developing states do not fail. There is an expectation that developing countries will want to develop further into developed states, but probably not all those states will do so.

This classification is far from perfect, as many states don't readily fit into the categories, and there is no agreement among scholars on an appropriate terminology. The International Monetary Fund (IMF) assigns three categories: the advanced economies, countries in transition from communist one-party regimes, and developing countries. This set of categories uses level of economic and political development as the principal criterion. Some political scientists prefer just two classifications, developed states and developing states. But this classification lumps all the world's states—with their wide array of incomes per capita, political systems, and economic development—into just two groups. Finally, scholars have increasingly come to refer to very poor states and those states that have either

---

TABLE 3.2

The Four Sets of State Actors in the International System

Set One (Developed or Industrialized States)	The states that have experienced substantial industrial development: North America, Western Europe, Australia, New Zealand, Japan
Set Two (Countries in Transition)	Countries in transition from communism to a free market economy: Russia, states of East Central Europe and Central Asia, and the independent states formed from the former Soviet Union in Central Asia and the Caucasus
Set Three (Developing States)	States undergoing the process of development: Latin America, the Caribbean, Asia, most of Africa
Set Four (Failing or At-Risk States)	States that are so poor that they may never be able to take the road to development

collapsed or are in danger of falling apart because of political, social, or economic circumstances as *failed* or *failing states*. For the purposes of this book, the terms *developed states, countries in transition* from communism, *developing states,* and *failing states* are used.

As you can see, the groups of states are not equal in power and wealth, and some states don't readily fit into the categories. Because of its low gross domestic product (GDP) per capita, China is in many respects a developing country, but its military and the unparalleled growth of some parts of its economy put it among the industrialized states. In terms of its political system, it belongs in the second set, but not economically so, because of its extensive capitalist reforms. Although in theory all states are defined by the same characteristics, and each has one vote in the General Assembly of the United Nations, in practice we automatically assume differences based on economic and political factors. Indeed, the classification suggests a rank order, with the industrialized states at the top and the at-risk countries of the fourth set at the bottom. We thus may expect the leading states of the international system to be found in the industrialized world.

Lead State Actors of the International System

Lead actors or great powers at any time in history have always come from the most economically advanced regions. In the first century AD, India, China, and Rome were the most economically advanced regions and world leaders. In the fifteenth century, China, the Ottoman Empire, the Netherlands, Portugal, and Spain were the world leaders. In the eighteenth and nineteenth centuries, the major European powers were the movers and shakers. In the international system of that time, England, France, Germany, Austria, and Russia maintained a fragile balance of power at the top, and they divided the rest of the world between them as parts of their colonial empires.

As a result of World Wars I and II, the power position of the European countries substantially weakened. The United States and the Soviet Union emerged as the two superpowers, each possessing the capability to destroy each other and the world. What is fascinating to students of the international system is that neither country sought the superpower role.

TABLE 3.3

Types of Non-state Actors

International government organizations (IGOS)
International organized crime and drug groups
International paramilitary and terrorist groups
Public interest and professional nongovernmental organizations (NGOs)
Firms and businesses, especially multinational corporations (MNCs)
The international media
Transnational diaspora communities

Non-state Actors

Realists hold that the international system level of analysis includes states only. Liberals see the arrival of non-state actors as the evolution of a new global civil society where non-state organizations and groups both complement and challenge the state system. The category of non-state actors divides into several groups as shown in Table 3.3.

▮ *Intergovernmental Organizations (IGOs):* IGOs are those whose members are national or multinational states (see chapter 6). Examples of IGOs are the United Nations, the World Health Organization, the World Bank, the International Monetary Fund, and the International Court of Justice, as well as regional IGOs such as the European Union, the North American Free Trade Agreement, and the Organization of African States.

▮ *Organized Crime:* The second group of non-state actors are organized crime and drug groups, such as the Mafia.

▮ *Paramilitary and Terrorist Groups:* Including al Qaeda, Basque terrorist groups, and U.S.–based groups like the anti-abortion Army of God, and the Earth Liberation Front. These organizations operate in a shadow world, recruiting and training volunteers to carry out acts of terrorism or protest. While it would be great to excommunicate them and put them beyond the pale of global civil society, we still have to deal with them. In both the Muslim and the non-Muslim worlds, al Qaeda exerts an almost magical influence. Some see al Qaeda as unabashedly bad, but many see it as their rescuer from the wretchedness of personal lives or the visible and extensive corruption in high places.

▮ *Nongovernmental Organizations:* These are generally described as not-for-profit organizations and their members are individuals rather than representatives of states. Four categories of NGOs may be identified.

1. *Professional and scientific NGOs* whose members are professionals in their fields and address issues generally related to their professional expertise. Examples are the International Political Science Association and the International Union of Concerned Scientists.

2. *Religious or faith-based NGOs*, whose members advocate responses to an array of topics supported by shared religious convictions. Examples include the World Council of Churches, and the American Jewish Committee.

3. *Environmental NGOs* represent the third category. Members of Greenpeace, the Sierra Club, or Friends of the Earth promote the goals and purposes of the NGO's charter.

4. *Single-issue NGOs* are exemplified by women taking leading roles in not-for-profit activities and forming NGOs focused specifically on women's issues, such as Virtual Sisterhood and the Women's Jurist Association/Women's Advocacy Center.

▮ *Transnational Corporations (TNCs):* TNCs do business in the global economy. Many of these have budgets larger than those of some states (see chapter 7). A TNC branches out internationally and may set up headquarters in one state, build plants in others, and conduct business around the globe, depending on the business climate in a given state. Its sales are worldwide.

Examples are McDonald's, Wal-Mart, Exxon Mobil, IBM, Microsoft, Intel, General Motors, and Toyota. Because of their wealth and economic clout, TNCs have long been the target of heavy criticism by neoliberal scholars for exploiting poor countries where labor is cheap, robbing them of their resources, and maximizing corporate profits. Realists prefer to argue that TNCs are the glue of the global economy, providing jobs in one state and inexpensive, high-quality products in another.

▌ *International Media:* Media such as CNN and al Jazeera, the Arabic language TV network, now present broadcasts in most European languages.

▌ *Diaspora Communities:* Diasporas are international migrations, both forced and voluntary, of diverse ethnic groups and individuals. Members of these groups may organize to represent their group interests in the domestic or international community. An example of such an organization is the American-Jewish Public Affairs Committee, with member units in Europe, Canada, and the United States.

Opinions vary on the assessment of the activities of NGOs in the international arena. Many international relations experts, such as James Rosenau, see the emergence of NGOs as a positive development. In Rosenau's view, they operate as active lobbying groups in a global civil society that reaches out to everyone. Others argue that these groups are not representative of any interest, as their members are non-elected individuals and, as such, merely represent themselves. In addition, some of them, like the terrorist NGOs, are dedicated to destroying the international system as we know it.

Relations between Actors in the International System

A first important generalization that emerges from this discussion is that relations between states and, indeed, between states and non-state actors are characterized by power relationships. At any given time in history, one or several states are on top. Pick any date in the past, and the international system may be characterized by how the powerful states relate to one another and to the rest of the world.

The emergence of non-state actors does not significantly change the power relationships between the weak and strong states. Weak states, however, can and do use both the IGOs and NGOs as advocates for, negotiators of, or simply extensions of their foreign policy.

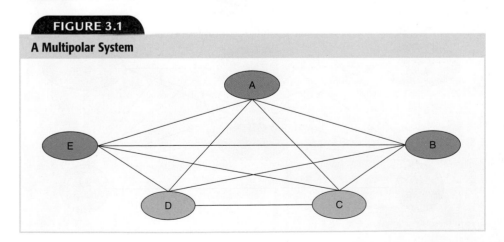

FIGURE 3.1

A Multipolar System

A second generalization derives directly from the notion of power relationships among lead actors, supporting actors, and very weak actors. At the system level of analysis, the strong states may be defined as those that attract weaker states into their orbit as the system's *poles of power*.

During most of the nineteenth century, several powerful European states were rivals for power. The international system of the period may thus be described as a European **multipolar system**. As each state sought to prevent others from acting too aggressively and disrupting the system, it entered into an alliance with what it perceived to be like-minded states (see Figure 3.1).

A so-called **balance of power** was produced through the alliances of two opposing groups of states. Because England was an island apart from the continent of Europe and had by far the largest empire, it saw its role as a balancer of power to prevent France, Germany, or Russia from dominating the European continent.

The European multipolar system gave way after World War II to the **bipolar** (two-pole) **system** of the Cold War, where the two poles were the United States and the Union of Soviet Socialist Republics (USSR). But the latter collapsed in 1991, and entering this century, no other country—with the possible exception of China—comes close to challenging the United States either militarily or economically.

The current system could be classified as **unipolar** (see Figure 3.2). However, although there may be only one superpower, many *regional* powers are economically strong. Thus, the current system may be redefined as overall unipolar with one superpower but with a multipolar regional structure. An in-depth discussion about the balance of power and power relationships follows in the next chapter.

As mentioned, interacting with the groups of states are the increasing number of non-state actors. Since 9/11, there is some question as to whether groups like al Qaeda—and others, such as Friends of the Earth—are eroding the sovereignty of the state, as James Rosenau and other neoliberals contend. For example, the events

Multipolar system   An international system based on three or more centers of power (poles) that may include states or IGOs, such as the European Union. The nineteenth-century international system may be described as multipolar.

Balance of power   A foreign policy principle that world peace and stability is best preserved by way of a basic equilibrium among the world's major actors—typically states.

Bipolar system   A balance-of-power system in which states are grouped around two major power centers.

Unipolar system   When a single superpower dominates the international system.

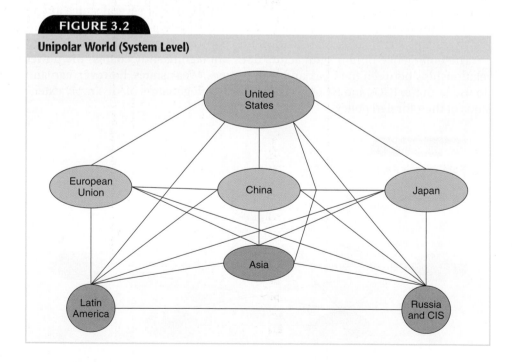

FIGURE 3.2

Unipolar World (System Level)

of 9/11 entailed an attack against the United States—a member of the UN—by al Qaeda, a group whose members, numbers, and location are unknown but that can strike anywhere at any time. No member-state of the UN has these privileges. If you recall, states have formal obligations to one another. The UN was founded to keep aggressor states in line and to promote collective peace, but the UN document says nothing about protecting states from NGOs—and NGOs have no obligations to states. The fact is that a non-state actor has attacked a sovereign state and forced that state to respond as a state, not as a police power. This is a totally new event in the modern world.

Moreover, NGOs may now apply and receive formal NGO status at the UN. Every major international conference, such as the Seventh Global Forum on Reinventing Government held in Vienna, Austria, in June 2007, has a set of officially recognized NGOs in attendance, which lobby the UN delegates and promote their point of view. Do these developments minimize the importance of states in the international system? Many scholars argue that the international system is fast becoming a civil community of state and non-state actors recruited from all over the globe who appeal to the UN with multiple proposals for the collective resolution of world problems. In practice, however, *states alone have the combined economic, political, and military authority* to implement solutions to these problems.

The Regional Level of Analysis

The regional level of analysis compares one region to another, or *across* regions, and compares *one state with another within a region.* As with the systems level of analysis, the focus is on the actors that make up the system and the generalizations that can be made about them. The major regions of the world are shown in Table 3.4.

The regional level looks at the same actors as at the international level. The difference is that at the regional level—comparing, for example, economic growth in Southeast Asia with economic growth in sub-Saharan Africa—involves looking at specific states and non-state actors in those specific regions. At the international systems level, the emphasis is on how the actors behave in the overall power structure.

Comparing the combined economic and industrial capacity of states grouped as regions confirms, on further study, the hypothesis made earlier in the chapter that although the current system may be a unipolar system with one superpower, there is also a strong multipolar distribution of economic power within regions. To prove the point, compare the wealth of the **European Union (EU)** with that of the continent of Africa, or the per capita income of Kenya or South Africa to that of Ethiopia or Chad, in northern Africa. At the regional level, the dynamics of regional organizations—of IGOs and NGOs—in various parts of the world may also be studied—for example, the structure, organization, and activities of IGOs with similar goals but with differing ranges of function and jurisdiction, such as the EU, the North American Free Trade Association (NAFTA), the African Union (AU), the Organization of American States (OAS), and the Association of Southeast Asian Nations (ASEAN).

Finally, a study of the international reach of regional organizations, such as the North Atlantic Treaty Organization (NATO) and the EU, may attempt to predict from the behavior of the most active regional IGOs a general future pattern of regional IGO behavior.

TABLE 3.4
Major Regions of the World

Africa
Australia and Oceania
Latin America and the Caribbean
North America
East and South Asia
West and Central Asia
Europe

European Union (EU)　A multipurpose international organization comprising twenty-seven Western European countries. It has both supranational and intergovernmental characteristics.

Analyzing Regional NGOs

Regional NGOs are not quite as visible as their international cousins. They seem most active in the EU, where a supranational government has the authority to make laws and regulations binding on the member-states. For example, the European Social Action Network focuses on developing coherent European policies on human rights, and the European Union Migrants Forums unite and provide representation at the EU level for some 190 migrant organizations throughout Europe. Regional NGOs can and often do influence regional agreements. Environmental NGOs such as the Union de Grupos Ambientalistas, a federation of thirty-eight Mexican environmental NGOs, and the U.S.–based Sierra Club, which unites groups in Canada, Mexico, and the United States, played a decisive role in ensuring the attachment of an environmental agreement to NAFTA, that went into effect in 1994. Regional women's groups, particularly in Africa and South Asia, have been instrumental in making governments in those regions aware of the problems women face in agriculture and commerce both within the region and in interregional trade.

Some paramilitary and terrorist groups operate exclusively at the regional level. These include the Latin American terrorists groups operating in Columbia, Peru and Equador, and the Basque terrorists groups in Spain and France.

The State Level of Analysis

As its name suggests, the *state level of analysis* looks at and contrasts the behavior of individual states. But how do you compare and contrast states to understand better their position in the international system? What specific features do states have in common? The four factors most often considered are power, wealth, status and prestige, and population.

Northern Border Crossing
Trucks entering the United States from Canada at the Ambassador Bridge connecting Windsor, Ontario, and Detroit, Michigan. Since NAFTA went into effect in 1994, trilateral trade between the United States, Canada, and Mexico has increased. Canada and Mexico send more than 80 percent of their exports to NAFTA partners. U.S.–Canadian trade represents the largest bilateral flow of income, goods, and services in the world. Mexico is the second-largest trading partner of the United States. Ninety percent of the goods that are traded are moved by service transportation and three-quarters of that movement is by truck.

▌*Power:* The way that *power* is organized and distributed within a state relates to its system of government, its constitution and legal system, and its requirements for citizenship and participation in politics, such as the right to vote or the minimum age for holding public office.

▌*Wealth: Wealth* and its distribution involve all aspects of a state's economic system. Wealth factors include the quality and quantity of natural resources, agricultural and industrial output, labor indicators, external and internal trade, gross domestic product (GDP), taxation policy, public finance, and technological development.

▌*Status and Prestige:* The concept of *status and prestige* relates to a state's social system, health and education policies, and the distribution of justice. Comparing status and prestige among states provides an investigation of who's on top—that is, which group most influences the conduct of government.

In modern democratic states, education is a determining factor in assessing the kind of profession or job you have and your ability to exert influence in your local community or at the national or international level. Health is another determinant of status and prestige in today's world. Epidemics and serious health problems weaken a state, sometimes threatening its very existence. In determining whether to invest in a state, the international investor needs to know how healthy its population is. Statistics tell us, for example, that most of the world's AIDS cases are found in sub-Saharan Africa. If you compare the health of the population in Uganda with the health of the population in Thailand, another of the states most threatened by AIDS, you will find that Thailand has started a public health project to educate its citizens about AIDS and also has a more comprehensive public health care system than does Uganda.

▌*Population:* The last factor used at the state level of analysis, *population,* includes much more than the size of a state's population and its demographic characteristics. Besides such factors as the age profile, the rate of population growth, the birth rate, and age of marriage, an analysis of a state's population is also concerned with the level of unity. What is a state's ethnic and/or religious makeup? How much harmony or disharmony exists among groups? How productive are its people? What level of education do they possess?

For example, a state whose population has a very low level of literacy is at a distinct economic disadvantage in comparison with states that invest in education and require high levels of educational achievement in its people. The new technologies all require highly educated people. As the whole world participates in the technological and communications revolution, the opportunities for workers with a low education level is steadily diminishing.

Just these four factors, compared across states, can yield generalizations regarding the capability of each to be a strong and effective player in the international system. For example, one hypothesis to test is whether or not states with strong government institutions and a more equal distribution of wealth tend to be more active and aggressive players than those with weak government institutions and an unequal distribution of wealth. Or a question may be asked about the correlation between a state's level of economic development and the health and education of its population. What is the impact of AIDS or any other serious health threat on the stability of government institutions in such diverse states as South Africa and the United States? In conducting foreign policy, governments make such analyses every day. These questions are taken up later in the chapter.

The Substate Level of Analysis

Beneath the state level of analysis is the *substate level*. At this level are all the units that make up a state or that act as players in a regional organization. The discussion looks first at the actors at the substate level and then turns to the generalizations that can be made about them.

The Actors and Their Issues

The subunits of the United States are the fifty states. In Germany, the subunits are the Länder (Lands) similar to the U.S. states. Belgium is divided into Flemish-speaking provinces and French-speaking provinces. The United Kingdom is composed of England, Scotland, Wales, and Northern Ireland. Russia is composed of a multiplicity of overlapping administrative units that are based on the uneven distribution of more than 160 ethnic groups. Until recently, scholars paid little attention to the substate level. As discussed in chapter 1, however, as the new forces shaping the planet have tended to make states more vulnerable, their central governments have come under pressure from both without and within to loosen central control. These decentralizing tendencies have given new life and power to the state's subunits.

Increased Prominence of the Substate Level

Increased activity at the regional level has also contributed to new vitality at the substate level. For example, over the past forty years, the states of Europe have been gradually harmonizing their markets, legal systems, and monetary systems to form a European Union. The EU is a supranational authority to which the member-states have yielded some of their sovereignty in specified legal areas. If a law of one state within the EU does not meet the requirements or specifications of EU regulations, it must be revised to meet those standards. The subordination of the state governments to the institutions of the EU has, to a large degree, weakened the extent to which they can dictate to their subunits. These, on the other hand, have recognized the transfer of member-state sovereignty to the EU as an opportunity to assert their powers and privileges at the substate level.

A similar phenomenon may be taking place in the United States. The United States and Canada have an international agreement, binding on both countries, regarding the conservation and use of the Great Lakes. Initially, this agreement primarily regulated water use. In the 1970s, the agreement was amended to include the harmonization of pollution control. However, neither the United States nor Canada has taken much action in this regard. Most of the work has been done at the substate level, with U.S. states bordering the Great Lakes forming an organization and inviting their Canadian counterparts, the provinces of Ontario and Quebec to join them. Moreover, substate NGOs, such as the Great Lakes Consortium, are pursuing agendas to link the two countries in a single environmental management effort.

As you can see, the environmental paradigm is particularly relevant at the substate level. The Great Lakes basin forms a natural ecosystem. The political entities within that basin, both states (used here, in the sense of subunits of the United States) and provinces (subunits of Canada), recognize the vital importance of that ecosystem to their survival and future livelihood. They thus have a greater interest in working out cooperative arrangements than do the more distant federal governments, which have a great many international interests to address.

A Good One
Fisherman checking his line under the five-mile long Mackinaw Bridge over the Straits of Mackinac connecting the state of Michigan's Upper Peninsula with its Lower Peninsula. The Straits link the upper Great Lakes to the lower Great Lakes and thence via the St. Lawrence River to the Atlantic Ocean. Canadians and Americans cooperate in preserving the beauty and history of the Great Lakes, and local NGOs take especial pride in promoting the conservation of this largest body of fresh water in the Americas.

Decentralizing Elements at the Substate Level

China provides another interesting case of the power and importance of emerging substate actors. China is divided into rich and poor provinces. China's rich provinces are on the country's east coast. These provinces have been granted special rights, as free enterprise regions, to enter into agreements with foreign corporations and sell directly abroad. As foreign capital has poured into these provinces, the economies have grown by leaps and bounds, the populations have been lifted out of the grinding poverty of the rest of the country, and the provincial governments have grown wealthy through the taxation of their upwardly mobile people. One of the great fears of the central Chinese government is that these provinces will grow so wealthy that they will refuse to pay taxes to the central Chinese authorities and choose to secede from the rest of the country.

The arrival of substate actors on the international scene adds yet another dimension to the growth of international civil society. To be players in the international arena, substate entities need to attract and keep the attention of the major players in the international system. To give legitimacy to their push for greater self-rule within the state or for complete independence from the state, these substate units often turn to a superpower like the United States, a regional actor like the EU, or an IGO such as the United Nations, to request recognition and assistance. The Autonomous Republic of Chechnya in Russia is one example; Kosovo in Serbia and Montenegro is another.

In their struggle for international attention, the substate actors play on the same themes that brought the state of which they are a part into being: legitimacy, sovereignty, and the obligation and expectation to live up to international rules and laws.

Conflict at the Substate Level

Often the issue that divides a substate from its mother state (Kosovo from Serbia) or one substate from another (Dagestan from Chechnya) flows from disputes over territory, ethnicity, language, and/or religion (see chapter 1). *Boundaries,* closely related to the issue of territory, can cause serious problems. In the nineteenth century, the colonial powers—Great Britain, France, and Germany—carved up Africa. They drew boundaries that were useful to themselves, but these had little relation to the living patterns of the inhabitants.

This situation is not limited to Africa. In Asia, India and Pakistan have clashed a number of times since the two states were created from British India in 1947. The issue is where to draw the boundary between them in the Himalayan territory of Kashmir. Neither state appears to care that a large majority of the actual inhabitants of Kashmir would probably prefer independence.

History shows that boundary lines can be very important to the people who live within them. It also shows that not everybody who lives within a set of boundary lines wants to be part of the state those lines describe. Quite often, ethnic groups are spread out beyond the confines of one state. Sometimes one state has lost territory or lays claim to territory it believes it owns. Such situations can create **irredentist** pressures upon the home state to extend its political power to include lands lying within a neighboring state, more often than not inhabited by ethnic cousins. The Italian term, *terra irredenta* means unredeemed land. For example, when the Austro-Hungarian Empire broke up at the end of World War I, Hungarians were living in all parts of the Empire but considered Hungary their homeland. The victorious Entente powers carved up Austria and Hungary, and distributed the land to other states. Suddenly some Hungarians found themselves a minority ethnic group in another country. As a consequence, irredentist feelings ran high in Hungary in the period between the First and Second World Wars. The nationalist policy to regain lost territories, or irredentism, drove Hungary to ally itself with Nazi Germany during World War II.

When a people or ethnic group within the borders of a recognized state, like the Kurds in northern Iraq, wishes to carve out a part of the recognized state and set up its own sovereign government, we call this a movement for *self-determination*. In 1991, for example, the Kurds rose up to demand self-determination from Saddam Hussein. The Iraqi regime bloodily repressed the nascent civil war, using poison gas, bombing, torture, mass killings, and deportation. The regime's tactics forced NATO to establish a no-fly zone in northern Iraq, declaring the area off limits to Saddam Hussein's bombers and protected by NATO troops. See Table 3.5 for an overview of substate movements.

Ethnicity   Probably the single most significant factor in substate conflict is the presence of a heterogeneous population, meaning that a variety of ethnic groups are represented. An *ethnic group,* as discussed in chapter 1 is a group of people linked by a common bond. Most frequently this bond is language, but it may also be one of belonging to the same tribe or religion. Less frequently, **race** is a common bond. Language is the most common bond of ethnicity. If you have ever traveled to Europe, you will remember that in Paris the Americans tend to group together in one corner of a café, the Germans in another, and the French somewhere else. Language is obviously an important reason for these divisions. When you visit Switzerland, you will find that it is separated into three distinct areas, each of which is primarily populated by a different ethnic group. In each part—the French cantons, the German cantons, and the Italian cantons—the signs are in the language of the majority population.

Irredentism   A foreign policy directed toward the incorporation within one state's boundaries territories that historically or ethnically were related to it but are now subject to another political authority. Irredentism can lead to war when one state claims the people, and a part or a whole of another state.

Race   A division of humankind possessing biological traits that are transmissible by descent and that are sufficient to characterize it as a distinctive human type. Skin color is the major trait identified with race today.

TABLE 3.5

Substate Movements

Independence	breaking away from the host country
	(Slovakia broke away from Czechoslovakia, Slovenia and Croatia from Yugoslavia, East Timor from Indonesia)
Civil War	occurs when
	a. Ethnic groups in the substate unit disagree over seeking independence or staying with the host country.
	b. Ethnic groups in the substate unit fight the army of the host country for independence (Kosovo, East Timor).
Irredentism	a foreign policy directed toward the incorporation within one state's boundaries of territories that historically or ethnically were related to it but are now subject to another political authority
	(Hungary in between the First and Second World Wars, Hitler's *Anschluss* in 1938, Armenia's current desire to annex the Armenian enclave in Azerbaijan, Nagorno-Karabakh, China's goal to get back Taiwan)

In Afghanistan, one of the main problems in creating a national state is that each of the country's ethnic groups speaks a different language. The largest group, the Pashtuns, would like to control the government and have their language, Pashtun, become official. The ethnic Tajiks and others disagree. And so tension between the tribes and their chieftains threatens the existence of the fragile state.

Religion   A third major reason people want to live apart is *religion*. Religious conflict tends to occur wherever two religions neighbor each other and where the boundaries between the two are *porous* (or not well defined, meaning that people can easily cross the boundary and move from one region to another). The island of Ireland is a prime example. The Irish people in the independent Republic of Ireland and Northern Ireland, which is part of the United Kingdom, all speak the same language or languages. The 100-year-old civil war in Northern Ireland is over religion.

 Between Nations
For more information see
*The View From:
The Holy Land: The Israeli-
Palestinian Conflict*
www.BetweenNations.org

▌ The Republic of Ireland is Catholic and wants to remain so. About half the people in Northern Ireland are Catholic, and most of these would like to join their Catholic relatives and neighbors in the Republic of Ireland. They also would like to share in the good economic times that country is enjoying.

▌ The other half of the people in Northern Ireland are Protestant, the descendants of English and Scottish immigrants. They are afraid that the Catholic Irish will take over the province and vote to join the Republic of Ireland. Protestants then would have, in the Protestant Irish view, no rights at all. A peace accord signed on Good Friday, April 10, 1998, promised resolution of this conflict. In 2006, the British and Irish governments and all the major political parties in Northern Ireland agreed to a permanent end of the fighting and the formation of a new Northern Ireland executive.

Religion can be a source of conflict between Muslims as it is between some Christians. Among the critical challenges to the future of Iraq are constitutional decisions relating to the sharing of power between the Shiite majority and the

Religion with a Vengeance
The market in the Shiite neighborhood of Sadriya, Baghdad, Iraq, April 18, 2007, after a Sunni-driven truck exploded, killing 140 people, smashing cars, and shattering buildings.

Sunni minority, in particular the sharing of oil revenues. The same is true in Kosovo, where ethnic cleansing first by Orthodox Serbia and then by Muslim Kosovars make the presence of NATO's armed force indispensable to the area's security.

In conclusion, when you combine territorial, religious, and ethnic issues into one package, you often discover a substate/state conflict of seemingly irresolvable proportions. This is the case with the Israeli–Palestinian conflict. This conflict between Jew and Arab is now entering its second century.

History offers a rather brutal lesson. Any government that has tried to create one nation from a multiethnic population has, in the main, had to rely on force to achieve its goals. You encounter this lesson again and again when reading the history of France, Britain, and Germany or when exploring the story of white expansion across the American continent. The Native American tribes were beaten back until the few that remained were sidelined onto reservations. The United States prides itself today as a multiethnic state that celebrates cultural diversity. But its history has several chapters on ethnic cleansing, including this significant one about the people who reached the Americas first.

The Individual Level of Analysis

At the *individual level of analysis,* we examine the role individual human beings play in the international system. In reading this section, note that this role can be more important and critical than you may have expected.

The Actors

The first actors usually considered at this level are powerful government officials or leaders with a world reputation, such as the president of the United States, the pope, or the head of the World Bank. But inventors, artists, actors, and athletes also fall into this category: people like Bill Gates, the chairman of the board of a large U.S. corporation, or a famous rock or opera singer. At the individual level of analysis, any person who exerts influence on world politics may be considered an actor.

The tendency is to think of an individual's power and influence based on the role he or she plays. Anyone who becomes president of the United States exercises a tremendous amount of individual influence by virtue of the office. Individual influence is also generally associated with roles played in large established institutions.

But how would you rate the influence of the Saudi financier Osama bin Laden, alive or dead, the mastermind behind al Qaeda who organized a worldwide network of terrorists and established training camps for terrorist activities in Afghanistan? And how do you assess the influence of Mother Teresa as compared with that of bin Laden, Bill Gates, or Saddam Hussein? Would the power of the United States be more or less if the president today were Teddy Roosevelt, who led a group of volunteer soldiers known as the Rough Riders to defeat the Spaniards in Cuba in 1898? Does President Bush have the influence to persuade the American people to fight the war on terrorism indefinitely? Clearly, the personality and beliefs of a national leader have a decisive impact on both the input and the outcome of an international event. The individual level of analysis attempts to measure or assess the relative influence on world politics of one individual against another on the basis of his or her personal characteristics.

The Impact of Individuals on World Politics

It is possible to make several generalizations about the impact of individuals on world events. First is the basic proposition that individuals do have the ability to influence world affairs in a unique direction, although much depends on the time and place. At the beginning of World War II, Winston Churchill galvanized the British to fight rather than capitulate to the Nazis with his rousing speech on "blood, sweat, and tears." As soon as the war was won, however, the British people threw him out of office at the next election. Clearly, they did not think he was the right person to be in charge of rebuilding the war-torn British economy.

Former U.S. President Bill Clinton wanted to stamp his image on world history when he used force for humanitarian purposes and sent the U.S. military into the Balkans. President George W. Bush would doubtless like to go down in history as the winner of the war against terrorism. Clearly, the personality and beliefs of a national leader make a difference in the outcome of international events.

Political Psychology

The second generalization to be made about the role of individuals in world events is that their perceptions and motivations play a key role in their decisions. Political psychology, a branch of international relations, is devoted to understanding these aspects of decision making, and the field has produced testable hypotheses about the attitudes and thought processes of leading international political actors.

▌ *Misperception and Groupthink:* One of the leading proponents of political psychology is Robert Jervis. Based on his study of the Cuban missile crisis, Jervis developed a series of hypotheses on the role of misperception in the management of crisis situations. For example, he claims that "actors tend to see the behavior of others as more centralized, disciplined, and coordinated than they are," and that "actors tend to overestimate the degree to which others

Groupthink   A mode of thinking that people engage in when the cohesiveness of their group is high and the members' striving for unanimity overrides their motivation to evaluate alternative courses of action.

 Between Nations
Audio Concept
Groupthink
www.BetweenNations.org

are acting in response to what they themselves do."[6] In his analysis of the decision-making process of the principal U.S. actors during in the crisis, Jervis expanded on another important concept in political psychology: **groupthink**, earlier identified by Yale social psychologist Irving Janis in his seminal work, *Victims of Groupthink* (1972). The term describes a situation where each member of the group attempts to conform his or her opinions to what they believe to be the consensus of the group. This results in the group ultimately agreeing on an action, such as the Kennedy administration's attempted invasion of Cuba, which individual members by themselves might normally consider unwise.

▌ *Cognitive Dissonance:* Cognitive dissonance theory, developed by Leon Festinger in 1957, explains the psychological phenomenon of discomfort an individual experiences when he or she discovers a discrepancy between what he or she already knows or believes and new contradictory information. Cognitive dissonance occurs when there is a need to accommodate new ideas. When individuals are confronted with new facts that contradict what they knew before, they tend to resist the new learning or the new reality. Political leaders are no different. An example of cognitive dissonance might be the Pentagon's initial picture of a swift and decisive American military victory in Iraq despite information that U.S. forces would meet a very different kind of reception.

▌ *Leadership Typologies:* The final aspect of political psychology mentioned here is the typologies of leadership offered to explain a leader's choice of certain kinds of decisions and actions rather than others. Some scholars like to talk about leadership styles based on a state's political development: the traditional leadership of a prince or a monarch, the charismatic leadership of a modernizing leader like Fidel Castro or Franklin Roosevelt, or the organizational leadership of a leader in an already operating pluralistic polity, like former U.S. President Jimmy Carter or Helmut Kohl of Germany. Others scholars follow Sigmund Freud's typology of three dominant personality types: the erotic personality that needs to love and to be loved, the obsessive or inner-directed personality, and the narcissistic or charismatic personality that aims to change things for the better or the worse. A third typology used by scholars is the Myers-Briggs personality model based on four personality continua: introversion-extroversion, sensing-intuition, thinking-feeling, and judging-perception.

The analysis of why certain individuals exert influence or act as they do is fascinating, and if you are drawn to the topic, you may want to take a course in political psychology. Decision making is discussed in more detail in chapter 5.

The Power of Individual Actors

Between Nations
For more information see
*Why It Matters to You:
Powerful Sayings*
www.BetweenNations.org

The third set of generalizations that may be formulated about individuals has to do with the amount of power they have. Indeed, almost all questions about individual actors on the international stage center on power: What is it, who has it, and how is it used?

The word *power* comes from the Latin word *posse,* meaning "to be able, to have the ability to act or to do." In politics, power involves the ability to get someone to do something that he or she otherwise would not do voluntarily.

The common way for individuals to acquire power is "out of the barrel of a gun," to quote the father of Communist China and former dictator, Mao Zedong. The majority of powerful people since the dawn of time have gotten that way largely through conquest. Although rare, a few individuals are recognized as powerful for their influence on our thinking or for their example of human goodness (such as Socrates, Saint Francis of Assisi and Mahatma Gandhi). Finally, certain people become powerful through their recognized role as head of a people, a nation, or a state. For example, no matter who fills the role, the president of the United States is one of the most powerful persons in the world today. Regardless of personality, the president exercises organizational leadership over the U.S. government.

How do individuals *exercise* power? Throughout history, there are only two ways: through force or through persuasion. Frequently, the two may be combined. Force is customarily violent: military might, terrorism, or compelling economic means (hostile takeovers, embargoes). Persuasion may be achieved through negotiation and bargaining, propaganda or advertising, by direct one-on-one influence over someone less powerful, or by persuasive example, as in the case of Saint Francis. Political scientist Theodore White first focused our attention on the notion of power as influence in his studies of the making of the U.S. president in the 1960s. When someone easily persuades others to do something they otherwise would not do, we say that person has *charisma*.

Ordinary People as Global Actors

Finally, in our explanation of the role of the individual in the international system, generalizations can be made about average people. Believe it or not, many people

Two People Who Have Made a Difference in International Affairs
At the turn of the twenty-first century, two of the major players on the world scene were George W. Bush, president of the United States, and Osama bin Laden, Saudi terrorist.

Volunteers for Habitat for Humanity Building Homes in the Philippines

Dr. Robert T. Potter, along with 200 other volunteers, went to the Philippines to help Filipinos build a home for themselves. Volunteers are found in every NGO and provide home, food, and clothing to the millions of poor, sick, and homeless in our world today. The global community cannot do without them.

Source: Courtesy of Dr. Robert T. Potter.

whose names are unknown exert considerable influence. For example, many states agreed to give money to alleviate the suffering of the 2004 tsunami in Indonesia. Large financial institutions pledged billions of dollars in loans that have taken a long time to process. In the meantime, individuals from humanitarian NGOs, such as the Catholic Relief Organization and the International Red Cross, have long been at work, caring for the needy. Tsunami victims in South Asia, hurricane victims in Nicaragua and Honduras, refugees returning to Kosovo, famine victims in Rwanda and Ethiopia, the victims of earthquakes in Iran, and refugees in Darfur are all causes that individuals support. Some people help by sending a check, others by giving personal time to an organization that is raising money. Still others actually go to the area that needs help and volunteer their labor. In 1995, after the Fourth UN Conference on Women, held in Beijing, American and Canadian women who had heard about the murder of girl babies in China spent their own money to go to that country, adopt baby girls, and save their lives by bringing them back to Canada and the United States. Volunteers organize and manage the countless sister city programs, like the Albany/Tula Alliance and the New York City/Tokyo program, that connect local administrations, organizations, and individuals in a web of citizen diplomacy.

Without the involvement of individuals at the grass-roots level, many international projects that alleviate suffering or promote cultural dialog could not be realized. When individuals care about someone or some problem in the world and act upon their feelings, they have an impact. You too can be a player at the individual level in the world today.

True or False?

_____ 1. The levels of analysis allow us to organize inter-national actors and events into five distinct levels of international activity.

_____ 2. Non-state actors include groups as diverse as the United Nations, al Qaeda, Greenpeace, international drug cartels and transnational corporations.

_____ 3. Because they rob the state of power, realists view transnational corporations (TNCs) as a disruptive force for the international economic system that should be regulated.

_____ 4. The most important factors used when focus-ing on the state level of analysis are power, wealth, and geographic location.

_____ 5. Generally speaking, there is a lack of conflict at the substate level of analysis—most conflict occurs at the international system.

Multiple Choice

_____ 6. Which of the following categories would you use to place China so that all of its attributes are accurately represented (political, economic, military)?
   a. Developing states
   b. Industrialized states

   c. Former communist states
   d. Failing or at-risk states
   e. None of the above

_____ 7. Which of the following best describes the level of analysis that focuses on organizations like the EU, OAS, NAFTA, and the AU?
   a. International system
   b. Regional
   c. State
   d. Substate
   e. Individual

_____ 8. Which of the following is NOT an example of an approach used to study the individual level of analysis?
   a. Misperception
   b. Groupthink
   c. Cognitive dissonance
   d. Power balancing
   e. All of the above

 Between Nations
Practice Test Questions
Practice Test 3.2
www.BetweenNations.org

APPLYING THE LEVELS OF ANALYSIS TO UNDERSTAND INTERNATIONAL RELATIONS

3 ▸ *Understand how the levels of analysis are used to understand international relations; apply the levels to the case of Afghanistan.*

The discussion of the five levels of analysis—the international system as a whole level, the regional level, the state level, the substate level, and the individual level—leads to a number of questions. What is the best use to make of them? Do analysts look at only one level at a time? Can levels be combined?

By this time in your studies of international relations, you can probably answer those questions on your own. The levels can be used in any way. Analysts focus on a particular level of analysis on the basis of three things:

1. The type of situation
2. What they want to find out
3. What paradigm or political theory they intend to use to determine what they want to find out.

Between Nations
For more information see
Democracy and Peace
www.BetweenNations.org

Applying the Levels of Analysis: The Example of Afghanistan

How can using the levels of analysis shed light on the problems of Afghanistan? Let us start at the *state* level. Only rarely in its history has Afghanistan been under the sole rule of a single leader. Its rugged geography and harsh climate facilitated the rise of tribal chieftains and helped perpetuate their hold on the local peoples. In addition, Afghanistan is landlocked, with powerful neighbors to the north, east, and west.

At the *substate* level, the social structure of Afghanistan is still tribal with power residing in the tribal chieftains. Seven tribes, each with its own language and belonging to its own ethnic group, form the bulk of the population. Their size and location are determining factors in the Afghan distributions of power. Each of the seven has ties with relatives of the same tribe beyond the Afghan border. Members of the Pashtun tribe, the largest tribe in Afghanistan, live across the Afghan border in Pakistan, a relatively weak country. The Taliban, defeated in the U.S.–led invasion of 2001, were from the Pashtun tribe. The relatives of the Uzbeks and Tajiks live in the new states of Central Asia, which are supported by Russia and, to a lesser extent, the United States. This support explains why the two tribes forming Afghanistan's Northern Alliance were given three prestigious ministries in the interim Afghan government and why they will continue to exert power under the new government. While the Afghan elections of 2004 spoke volumes about progress made toward a viable Afghan state, elected officials need a power base from which to operate. With the Taliban prevented from returning to power, the Northern Alliance, with its powerful tribal chieftains, is well placed and organized to fill the power vacuum. Finally, the entire country embraces Islam, a religion that has shown a strong preference for traditional values. The United States has insisted on promoting a regime change to a democratic government based on Western experience and has a relatively free and fair election to show for its efforts. But the path to democracy is experiencing severe roadblocks. As a budding international relations expert, you immediately suspect that something is going on at the system level that is impeding progress.

Afghanistan from the Systems Level of Analysis

From 1948 to 1991, the international system was bipolar, with a cold war between the United States and the Soviet Union. In 1979, the Soviet Union invaded Afghanistan to shore up a communist coup in the country. The United States responded by working with Saudi Arabia and other Muslim countries to promote an Afghan resistance to Soviet occupation organized around local chieftains. In 1989, the Soviets were forced to withdraw from Afghanistan.

In 1991, the Soviet Union collapsed, and the bipolar system ended. You might think that the climate would then have been ripe for the development of a pro-Western government in Afghanistan. But in supporting the local chieftains in their fight against the USSR, the United States had been promoting an emerging new force on the international stage: militant Muslim guerrillas drawn from Arab and Middle Eastern volunteers. During the 1980s, the United States armed and trained Muslim groups in Pakistan to operate across the border in Afghanistan. Many of these groups were associated with al Qaeda. With the collapse of the Soviet Union, al Qaeda and the militant Islamist movement emerged as a global power in its own right. The financing for the movement came from Muslim states, particularly Saudi Arabia, and Iran, a neighbor of Afghanistan.

From 1992 to 1996, Afghanistan was torn by a violent civil war between the very chieftains who had fought *together* to evict the Soviet army. The Taliban victory, while unexpected, was not surprising, as the Taliban came from the majority Afghan tribe with ties to Pashtuns in Pakistan. The Taliban imposed a rigid Islamic government on Afghanistan and permitted al Qaeda and other militant groups to re-form and train there. With the Russians out of the country, the Taliban and their terrorist associates thought to expand their efforts to rid the entire Muslim world of foreign influence. Once again, the Muslim oil countries, along with the lucrative domestic poppy industry, provided the financing.

The result is that even though the bipolar international system gave way to a unipolar system led by the United States, the United States cannot dictate the terms of the current or future Afghan government for a multitude of reasons:

1. Real power continues to reside in the same tribal leaders who led the fight against the Soviet Union (individual level of analysis).
2. Rivalry for power among the tribes inhibits any from making a compromise (substate level).
3. The United States alone has not the military, material, or financial resources to impose a solution while guaranteeing an ever-improving lifestyle back home. It has to seek allies (state level of analysis).
4. The existing relationship between the terrorist NGOs in Afghanistan and Pakistan and the Muslim states that finance them means that no solution will be permanent unless it is Islamic (regional level of analysis, distribution of power).
5. The United States needs Pakistan to wage its war on terrorism in Afghanistan to find the perpetrators of 9/11, yet it cannot alienate the Muslim oil-producing countries upon which it relies for energy. Russia cannot meet all the energy needs of the United States and send oil to Europe at the same time (international system as a whole).

In the preceding case, we have used the levels of analysis like a lens on a camera, zooming in on the individual level, out to the system level, and moving freely between the centralizing tendencies of the system level and the decentralizing elements at the state and substate levels? With the levels of analysis as a structure and the state as the main unit, you now are ready to try to figure out what it would take for a democratic regime to emerge in Afghanistan.

This chapter has been about the building blocks or fundamental units of the international system. It thus has done more describing than theorizing. We use theory much more in the coming chapters, but these basic concepts—the levels of analysis and the way power is used within each of them—recur as essential themes. In fact, so important is the concept of power that the entire next chapter is devoted to that one idea.

TEST PREPPER 3.3

ANSWERS APPEAR ON PAGE A12

True or False?

_____ 1. The state level of analysis is the most effective at explaining the situation faced by Afghanistan.

_____ 2. When looking at Afghanistan's tribal structure we are using the substate level of analysis.

_____ 3. The international systems level of analysis cannot be used to explain the lack of democracy in Afghanistan.

_____ 4. The United States does not possess the military or financial resources to impose a solution in Afghanistan without the assistance of allies.

_____ 5. The Taliban's role in Afghanistan can be viewed strictly from the regional level of analysis.

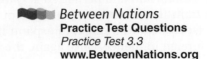

Between Nations
Practice Test Questions
Practice Test 3.3
www.BetweenNations.org

CASE STUDY

North Korea's Pursuit of Nuclear Weapons
See **www.BetweenNations.org**

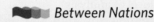 *Between Nations*

JOIN THE DEBATE

The New Global Civil Society Is Great!

BACKGROUND

States remain the principal actors on the international stage, but since World War II, they have increasingly been challenged by a growing set of non-state actors claiming to speak for specific interests and concerns in global society. Seven sets of actors are identified in this chapter: Among these are the international governmental actors (IGOs), terrorist and paramilitary groups, nongovernmental organizations (NGOs), and transnational corporations (TNCs). Representatives to IGOs are officially appointed by their member-states and must promote the position of their government. As such, the IGOs do not represent the global civil society but continue the tradition of state domination of the international system.

The other non-state actors are different. Drug and terrorist groups have their own violent agendas and operate in a shadowy world that is difficult for states to penetrate but whose actions serve to expose the state's vulnerable underside. NGOs operate in the full light of international scrutiny. Some are organized around professional interests, some have religious agendas, while others are primarily service organizations that provide

humanitarian aid as needs arise around the globe. Published charters or constitutions setting forth the NGOs' goals and procedures guide most of them. Professional groups like the International Meteorological Association have members from many countries who are experts in their field and are not duty bound to speak for their country. Decisions are reached on the basis of a vote in a governing body that comprises the most influential individuals in that particular area of expertise. Humanitarian groups like the International Red Cross and Doctors Without Borders recruit large numbers of volunteers from any country or region.

TNCs have been heavily criticized for exploiting the cheap labor, widespread political corruption, and lax environmental laws of developing countries. However, it is generally recognized that globalization is here to stay. Among its benefits are cheap goods for the industrialized world and jobs for the developing countries.

Many political scientists welcome the arrival of non-state actors on the international scene. In their view, these organizations provide input into international problems that go beyond the pure national interests of any one state, speaking for the global community as a whole. The World Wildlife Foundation (WWF), for example, works toward the improvement of habitat for endangered species all over the world. Its scientists speak for the conservation movement as a whole, not for any one country. Others say the NGOs do not represent people but rather push their own agendas with no accountability. The WWF may demand the preservation of the Siberian tiger, for example, but only states can guarantee that action will be taken to preserve them.

What do you think? Join the debate!

Arguments for the Benefits of a Global Civil Society

▮ NGOs are composed of like-minded people around the globe who share an interest, a goal, and a need.

▮ A large number of NGOs perform vital humanitarian functions that no other type of organization is capable of performing. Without the International Red Cross, who would organize relief for victims of disasters around the world?

▮ States have their own agendas. Many issues would fall off their radar screens, particularly in the environmental and human rights areas, if NGOs did not speak up and make the issue public. Look at Darfur. Would the UN Security Council have made any resolution if humanitarian organizations had not publicized the terrible conditions there?

▮ People contacting others around the globe are able to influence actions of individual governments and bring about needed change in a peaceful, positive manner. One of the best examples is the cooperation between East European, West European, and American NGOs that challenged the existing dictatorships and contributed to their destabilization prior to the fall of the Berlin Wall in 1989.

▮ National governments think and act only in the interests of the state they rule; nationalism and national interest destroy peace and cooperation.

Arguments against the Benefits of a Global Civil Society

▮ NGOs and TNCs are not elected bodies. The leadership speaks for no one and is not accountable to anybody. Being self-appointed, it acts in the interests of a small clique of individuals interested in pursuing a particular goal.

▮ If you know where an NGO gets its money, you know what it stands for. To a large extent, NGOs are sim-

ply the hidden arm of the major states' foreign policy and are paid accordingly, or they are carrying out the wishes of well-endowed foundations and corporations.

▮ NGOs, particularly the international environmental groups, have come under criticism recently for making matters worse in the interest of making them better. The international environmental NGOs have been the most vocal opponents of the construction of large dams anywhere in the world, arguing that the electricity produced by them goes to the TNCs and not the poor people dislocated by the projects.

▮ TNCs may provide jobs, but they destroy local economies and local lifestyles and ruin the livelihood of local merchants who cannot compete in price with the global giants. They also exploit workers, hiring them at the lowest possible wage in developing countries, where TNCs do not have to provide benefits, such as health care, as they would in the developed states.

QUESTIONS

1. What role do you see NGOs playing in world politics? How can they promote contrasting views to problems? How do they hinder the formulation of solutions?

2. If you were the head of a Western government and wanted to spread education about diseases to a developing country, what kind of organization would you use to develop the program? Why?

3. What vital roles do states play in world politics that NGOs and TNCs cannot?

SUGGESTED READINGS

David C. Korten, Nicanor Perlas, and Vandana Shiva, "Global Civil Society: The Path Ahead," The People-Centered Development Forum, http://www.pcdf.org/civil-society/default.htm.

Sebastian Mallaby, "How NGOs Hurt the Poor," *Foreign Policy* (September/October 2004): 50–58.

Jessica T. Mathews, "Power Shift," *Foreign Affairs* (January/February 1997).

See also the websites of NGOs fighting World Bank efforts to fight poverty: Friends of the Earth, www.foe.org; Environmental Defense, www.environmentaldefense.org; Swedish Society for Nature Conservation, www.snf.se/english.cfm.

LEARNING OBJECTIVES REVIEW

1▶ *Identify the primary characteristics of a state. Understand how the state has developed over the past centuries and its current role in world politics.*

- A state is defined as a territory inhabited by a people with a common language and a common culture. The characteristics of the state are *sovereignty, legitimacy,* and *formal international obligations.* States are either national, multinational, or multiethnic.

- The origins of the modern state, which emerged in Europe in the fourteenth and fifteenth centuries, lie in the city-states of antiquity in Mesopotamia, Greece, and Rome. Its current evolution can be tied to the following factors:
  - ideology and common culture
  - technological advancement
  - Europe becoming a continent of nation-states

- The structure of the international system is based on states. Under the principles of international law, all states are equal in sovereignty.

- Today, state domination of the international system is challenged by the large number of states (191) and their vulnerability to events and NGOs they cannot control.

2▶ *Understand what is meant by levels of analysis and who are the primary actors that operate at each level.*

- *The system level of analysis.* The basic assumptions at this level are that the international system is considered as a single whole and within this whole, actors interact with and respond to one another in ways that are predictable.
  - The principal actors are the states with non-state actors playing a secondary role. Key non-state actors include intergovernmental organizations (IGOs), whose members each represent a participating state, and nongovernmental actors (NGOs), whose membership is global and voluntary.
  - Non-state actors have become increasingly visible in the post–Cold War world.

- The *regional level of analysis* enables us to compare *across* regions and to compare states *within* regions.
  - At the regional level of analysis, we can generalize about economic and political capacity across regions, the structure of power within a region and across regions, and the dynamics of regional IGOs and NGOs.

- The *state level of analysis* looks at and contrasts the behavior of individual states, which are the actors at this level. Common factors to compare and contrast about individual states are *power, wealth, status and prestige,* and *population.*

- *The substate level* includes the units that make up a state (provinces, states such as those of the United States, or Länder) or that act as players in a regional organization, as well as IGOs and NGOs active at this level.
  - The issues around which substate conflicts revolve are most often of an ethnic, religious, or linguistic nature and frequently involve boundary disputes.
- The *individual level of analysis*:
  - Investigates the role individual human beings, including average people, play in world politics, based on time period, location, and power position.
  - Political psychology has produced testable hypotheses that generalize about the attitudes and thought processes of leading international political actors.

3 ▶ *Understand how the levels of analysis are used to understand international relations; apply the levels to the case of Afghanistan.*

- We use the levels of analysis like the lens of a camera to zoom in and out of a situation, looking at:
  - The international system level of analysis for the broadest view of power relationships.
  - Zooming in on the state or substate level for an analysis of the variables that explain why a state or substate unit acts the way it does.
  - Zooming further in to the individual level to understand the characteristics and abilities of the individuals who seem most involved with the situation under analysis.
  - And returning to the regional level for an analysis of the power relationships at the level that may support the state or substate unit under investigation.

RESOURCES ON THE WEB

To use these interactive learning and study tools, including video and audio multimedia resources, go to **www.BetweenNations.org**.

Practice Tests	Case Studies	Current Events
Audio Concepts	Primary Sources	Daily Newsfeeds from *The Washington Post*
Flashcards	Historical Background	Weblinks for Further Exploration

 Between Nations

4 Power in World Politics

The Primacy of Power

LEARNING OBJECTIVES

1 *Define power, focusing on both hard and soft forms; understand the dynamics of power that make defining power a difficult task.*

2 *Understand the difference between objective and subjective elements of power. Be able to describe each of the key objective and subjective power capabilities possessed by states.*

Chapter Outline

3 *Understand what is meant by balance of power and identify key types of balance that may exist in the international system. Understand the concept of collective security and its prospects for securing peace in the international system.*

Preventive war A preventive war is undertaken in order to prevent a possible future attack. A preventive war is initiated for purposes of national defense, but not in response to an imminent attack—as when the United States attacked Iraq in 2003. Although the Bush administration described its attack as preemptive, it more accurately can be classified as preventive, given the circumstances.

Understanding Power Is Critical to Understanding World Politics

Most questions addressed in world politics, as you learned in the first three chapters, tend to focus on power. This is so because *power* (the ability of actors to get other actors to do what they want them to do) is all about *politics*—the process of deciding "who gets what, when, and how." A second, similar, definition of *politics* as "the authoritative allocation of scarce resources" again brings us face-to-face with power. The point is that allocating resources and getting people to do what we want them to do requires power.

When President George W. Bush, for example, determined to launch a **preventive war** on Iraq on the grounds (later proved false) that Saddam Hussein had weapons of mass destruction that represented a possible threat to the United States, he employed a

Preemptive war   A preemptive attack occurs when State A believes that an attack by State B is imminent. State A attacks in order to pre-empt B's attack. An example of preemptive war is the 1967 Six-Day War, launched by Israel's preemptive attack on Egypt's air force at a time when Israel faced increased military activity near its border. The war was fought between Israel and its Arab neighbors of Egypt, Jordan, and Syria. Iraq, Saudi Arabia, Kuwait, and Algeria contributed troops and arms used against Israel.

traditional realist version of power: military force in the quest of security. So did Israel when it initiated a **preemptive war** against Egypt in 1967, because it faced immediate military activity on its borders.

Realists, you remember, believe the games of states take place in an anarchic global arena, dominated by a struggle for power. The only factor that will check power is power—not international law or appeals to moral behavior. By contrast, antiwar protests against President Bush's attack on Iraq immediately erupted around the world in another form of power, inspired by idealism: peace marches and street demonstrations. So politics and power play big roles in the paradigms used to study world politics—in these cases, realism and idealism. Because politics and power are so directly involved in world politics, they are underlying causes of centralization and decentralization in the international arena.

As we flesh out the concept of power, we will:

▌ Examine the nature of power and how to define it, with special attention to the concepts of hard and soft power.

▌ Explore the major elements of power, looking at its objective and subjective characteristics as well as the difficulties in measuring them.

▌ Explore power patterns that have existed among states, such as balance of power and multipolarity, both of which illustrate different combinations of power alignment among states.

▌ By the time you finish studying this chapter, you should be well grounded in one of the most important elements at work in world politics in the twenty-first century—and a major element in the understanding of unity and separation in the world political arena. ▨

WHAT IS POWER, AND HOW IS IT MEASURED?

 Define power, focusing on both hard and soft forms; understand the dynamics of power that make defining power a difficult task.

When power in world politics comes up for discussion, the first inclination is to think of military power, or brute force. This is not surprising, because in an anarchic system of states with no higher government to settle conflicts, the final option for self-help is military power. You see this impressive brand of power dramatically at work in most parts of the world. Yet, many observers make a compelling case that soft power should be used more effectively to spur cooperation.

Power literally jumps out of each day's news. On September 11, 2001, members of Osama bin Laden's al Qaeda terrorist organization hijacked U.S. commercial airliners and used them to crash into New York City's World Trade Center and the Pentagon in Washington, D.C., killing thousands of people. A fourth plane crashed in a field in western Pennsylvania after passengers and crew intervened to prevent the hijackers from diverting the flight to another target in Washington. Here was a case of raw power exercised by a group with far less military muscle than its target, the United States. The United States responded with classic military strength by bombing Afghanistan to dislodge the Taliban government, an Islamic religious group that had gained control of the government and provided sanctuary for bin Laden and his al Qaeda terrorist forces. The Taliban government collapsed in December 2001, but remnants of the Taliban and al Qaeda fled into neighboring Pakistan and subsequently began to regroup.

The United States next turned its attention to Iraq, which it alleged was hiding weapons of mass destruction (WMD) and allegedly had close ties with al Qaeda (both assumptions later proved false). In March 2003, the Bush administration launched its attack on Iraq (without support from the big powers in the international community or the United Nations) overthrew and subsequently captured its dictator, Saddam Hussein, and installed a military occupation (with the goals of rebuilding and bringing democracy to Iraq). Examining the context of this use of military power, however, the 9/11 Commission report, released in July 2004, found no credible evidence of strong al Qaeda ties to Hussein's Iraq and no link between Hussein and the 9/11 attack on the United States. Nor were WMDs discovered in Iraq after the U.S. invasion. Review the case study in chapter 1 for more on the 9/11 Commission report.

These events, however, are only part of the story of power and how it operates in world politics. Let's take a closer look at the nature of power, its definitions, and the differences between hard and soft power. Then we can examine the role of power in world politics.

The Nature of Power

Power lies at the heart of world politics. If politics is all about who gets what, when, and how, then power explains the political process as it plays out in the human drama of international relations. The politics of almost anything you can imagine—from education, energy, health care, and military spending to conflict management and cooperation on regional disputes—entails power and the human

Venezuela Is among the Top Four Exporters of Oil to the United States
With huge oil profits, Venezuela's President Hugo Chavez has become the self-appointed champion of anti-Americanism, given significant financial support to like-minded Latin American leaders, and delivered millions of gallons of heating oil at a significant discount to low-income residents in Philadelphia, Boston, the Bronx, and cities in Maine, Vermont, and Rhode Island.

struggle to seize and use it in order to accomplish objectives. It lies behind the foreign policy of states as they pursue their goals in world affairs, it affects international intergovernmental organizations (IGOs) and international nongovernmental organizations (NGOs), and it shapes the nature of decision making inside states. In a nutshell, power is at work around the globe twenty-four hours a day.

Power can be described in two distinct ways, objective and subjective. Objective sources of power include a country's assets that can be seen, touched, or measured, while subjective sources of power lie in the domain of human strengths or weaknesses. These objective and subjective capabilities represent the base of a country's index of power or strength and will be covered in more detail later in the chapter. When translated into action that affects the behavior of a country's population as well as that of other countries, those power assets become what might be called *kinetic power*, or power in motion. If potential power becomes kinetic power, it reaches the stage of **influence**. We speak of influence because at this point power capabilities are in motion to affect the behavior of others inside a country as well as leaders and followers abroad.

Power capabilities and influence also take hard and soft forms.

▌ *Hard power* generally refers to the tangible, measurable assets, such as military and economic strength, that give some countries more power than others. Hard power is the coercive kinds of power, such as economic sanctions applied by the United States to Cuba, or the military force used by the Israelis to occupy the West Bank.

▌ *Soft power*—comprised of the *subjective* types of power discussed below—are those elements that give a country the ability to get what it wants through its capacity to attract and persuade rather than by its capacity to coerce through military or economic might.

Power's Hard Profile

Power's hard military profile is visible around the world on a day-to-day basis. Taiwan, for example, looks across the Taiwan Strait at China's growing military capacity. Beijing's coastal weapons deployment is designed to remind Taiwan that it considers Taiwan part of China and that it should never declare its independence. Still, Taiwan's president, Chen Shui-bian, has continued to defy China by asserting Taiwan's sovereignty. Mainland China meanwhile continues to improve its navy, air force, and ground forces facing its rival across the Taiwan Strait. China raised its military budget by nearly 18 percent in 2007—the largest increase since 1995.

The use of hard military power, however, can have unintended negative consequences on a country's overall power. The United States, in the years since it invaded Iraq, has experienced a dramatic deterioration in its image around the world. It may come as no surprise that China is matching its expanded military budget with an orchestrated soft-power offensive to bolster its "peace-loving" image.

The Soft Side of Power

Whereas hard power is a state's economic and military capability to coerce, *soft power* is its ability to influence through cultural, ideological, and moral appeal. Soft-power factors constitute major elements of a country's overall power inventory. In part, soft power rests on the appeal of a country's ideals and culture and on its ability to establish an agenda that will persuade others to agree on values, institutions, and behavior.[1] Numerous critics of U.S. foreign policy believe the United States has not used its potential soft power adequately in recent years. Indeed, as

Influence   The capacity of one actor to change or sustain the behavior of another actor in the global system.

Between Nations
Audio Concept
Soft Power
www.BetweenNations.org

Information Technology Workers in Bengalooru [formerly Bangalore]
In India, Bengalooru's big draw for outsourcing is its deep pool of skilled technology workers who speak English. They cost one-tenth of what they would cost in the United States and Western Europe. Bangalore changed its name to Bengalooru in November 2006.

the U.S. occupation of Iraq continued many foreigners came to perceive the United States as arrogant, self-absorbed, self-indulgent, and contemptuous.[2] The image of the United States has not been helped by photos and reports of U.S. torture of prisoners at Iraq's Abu Ghraib Prison. By 2008, dislike of everything American was on the rise.

Other forms of soft power include:

Between Nations
For more information see
The View From:
Bengalooru
[Formerly Bangalore]
www.BetweenNations.org

❚ Information revolution: exemplified by the Internet and the World Wide Web, the information revolution clearly affects soft power. Consider that nearly a billion people now use the Internet on a regular basis. These relatively cheap flows of information have vastly expanded the number and variety of transnational channels of contact and have made state borders and other controls more porous. Indeed, terrorist organizations use the Web and the Internet to communicate and to incite violence.

❚ Economic growth and development: Outsourcing of U.S. corporate operations to places like India and China illustrate this changing nature of power in the twenty-first century.

❚ Investments in education: As for U.S. investments in science, in June 2004, forty-eight U.S. Nobel Prize laureates criticized the Bush administration for ignoring scientific evidence of global warming, for its negative stance of stem-cell research, and for cutting funding for scientific research.

Dynamics of Power

According to Hans Morgenthau, often referred to as the father of modern political realism, power refers to control over the minds and actions of others—a "psychological relation between those who exercise it and those over whom it is exercised."[3] A stunning example of this definition of power is the catastrophic March 11, 2004, terrorist railway bombings in Madrid that killed 200 people and injured some 1,800. The ten bombs that exploded on four trains in three Madrid stations during the busy morning rush hour were the work of an Islamic terrorist group associated with al Qaeda in Europe. In a letter faxed to the Spanish daily newspaper *ABC,* the group claimed responsibility for the attacks and warned that unless the country halted its support for the United States and withdrew its troops from Iraq, they would turn Spain into an "inferno." In reaction to the bombings, during which the government of Spain engaged in a colossal cover-up that failed—attempting to blame the attack on Basque terrorists—citizens launched a massive antigovernment protest. With public opinion already against the war in Iraq, three days after the terror attacks, Spain voted out the pro–U.S. ruling party of Spain and brought into power a new socialist prime minister. A month later, the last of Spain's 1,300 combat soldiers were pulled out of Iraq ahead of schedule. The terrorists had the capability to blow up trains, an act of power that influenced Spanish voters to throw out the pro–U.S. Prime Minister and elect a new prime minister more in tune with their overwhelming opposition (and that of the Islamic terrorists) to the U.S. war in Iraq.

Defining power is not as easy as it may seem. As we will see later in the chapter, measuring power is difficult because of its conditional nature. Multiple factors make the concept of power in world politics a subject difficult to pin down.

Differing Forms of Influence

While power is the major ingredient of political relationships, understanding how and in what ways it operates can be annoyingly elusive.[4] For example, we know that influence involves Party A getting Party B to do something it otherwise would not do; however, this endeavor can be less straightforward than it might seem. If Party A seeks to influence Party B to do something, it may try, for example, to persuade, reward, threaten, coerce, or punish.

An excellent example of power at work is the case of Libya's giving up its nuclear, biological, and chemical weapons programs in 2003. After months of secret diplomacy and intense negotiations with the United States and Great Britain, Libya announced in December 2003 that it had agreed to reveal and renounce its programs to build weapons of mass destruction. It did so in part as a result of U.S. economic sanctions on Libya after the bombing in 1988 of Pan Am Flight 103 over Lockerbie, Scotland. Libya acknowledged responsibility and promised to pay $10 million in compensation for each of the 270 victims—at first maintaining that it would not pay (applying its own brand of power) until all international sanctions were lifted. It caved in, however, in part because of the U.S. war in Iraq and what that war might mean for Libya in view of its perceived ties to terrorist organizations, and because it had become economically crippled and wanted foreign oil companies to return. In June 2004, as part of a carrot-and-stick power approach to Libya taken by the UN and the United States, full diplomatic relations with the United States were restored after a twenty-four-year break.

Power Is Shaped by Perceptions

Perceptions, as suggested earlier, play a major role in defining power. This is so for Party A, which intends to use some type of power capability, just as it is for Party B, the intended recipient of the influence. By *perceptions* we mean how policymakers interpret reality. Unlike computers, humans tend to simplify the outside world in order to organize it mentally and so deal with it. Compound this basic human limitation with all the components of perceptions that shape one's reality—values, beliefs, cognition (how individuals interpret incoming information), and stereotyping. For example, the brutal beheading of the American contractor Nicholas Berg in May 2004 in Iraq (one of several beheadings),while widely condemned and perceived as barbaric, was seen by many Arabs simply as an inevitable act of revenge for U.S. prisoner abuse at the Abu Ghraib Prison.

Perceptions, as the example above indicates, play a powerful role in world politics. Interestingly, although a power capability may not be in use, it still is in play if it affects the perceptions of leaders in other countries. Possession of nuclear weapons by one country, for example, typically deters others from launching a military campaign against it out of fear of retaliation. Such deterrent power is a key ingredient in world politics, especially in terms of how state leaders view each other. Remember, too, that the breakthrough with Libya in 2003–2004 no doubt was accelerated by Libya's perception of U.S. military power in Iraq, although military power had not been brought to bear directly on Libya.

Power Is Dynamic and Changing

As we saw in chapter 1, and as we are seeing as this century advances, rapid changes in power have occurred due to a number of driving forces. The Internet and World Wide Web have created a significant power shift. This technological power has made all state borders more porous, as demonstrated in the international communications that lay behind 9/11, thus weakening traditional power capabilities (the military) for maintaining territorial security. On the flip side, the information revolution has contributed to centralization by fostering globalization and state interdependence. Because of the connectedness of international finance, banking, and commerce, what happens in one country's economy can produce a chain reaction in countries around the globe, affecting the economic power of all.

Power shifts are created by other factors. The military's technological innovations, such as computers and global positioning systems, long-range aircraft, nuclear weapons, ballistic missiles, biological weapons, and chemical warfare, are cases in point. States that move forward in acquiring sophisticated equipment and WMDs assume strong power positions on the globe.

The power capabilities of states rise and decline over time. This chapter's case study about the United States illustrates that point. Meanwhile, China's economic and military power is on the rise, while Japan's economic strength waxes and wanes. Cuba's economy, military strength, and global reach went into a tailspin in the early 1990s with the collapse of its chief supporter, the Soviet Union. Russia's economy faltered after the breakup of the Soviet Union, as Russia struggled to replace a state-controlled economy with a market economic system. This is important because changing power relations create incentives for preventative attack and windows of opportunity to do so. Dale Copeland, in his book, *The Origins of Major War*, contends that war among major powers may likely occur when a dominant state's power has peaked—or is declining—and faces a growing threat from another state.[5]

Power Is Relative

Any one state's power can be evaluated in context only. For example, China has great economic power when compared to its next-door neighbors Vietnam or Taiwan, but not when compared to the United States. Mexico has much greater overall power in relation to Guatemala, which lies to its south, than in relation to its northern neighbor, the United States. Vietnam worries more about China's power than about Cambodia's, given the power difference in its two neighbors.

Power, then, is relative, not absolute. While Russia has suffered severe economic decline, it still has a powerful military capability, and its presence is felt in those countries that lie close to it geographically, which Moscow refers to as the "near abroad." The United States has vast objective power, but its perceived negative image abroad makes it vulnerable nonetheless. The relativity of power can also be seen in the capabilities of al Qaeda. Although this is an organization rather than a state, the will of its members and their readiness to commit suicide while killing as many people as possible have proven enormously effective in posing a threat to Western powers. Al Qaeda by no means possesses the colossal power of the United States, nor can it effect change through the use of commerce, finance, trade, or conventional military weapons. Nevertheless, it has demonstrated significant relative power in its ability to cause the United States to shift huge resources to homeland security and increased military spending and to pay attention to a war on terrorism.

Power Is Situational

Power is meaningful only within a specific policy context. Here is one example. One state's military capacity to win a war against another's state's military forces may be successful, but the so-called victor does not necessarily win the war against the defeated state's population. U.S. military power cleaned house on Iraq's military in March 2003, yet it would be difficult to claim the United States had won the hearts and minds of the Iraqi people. U.S. military and civilians were being killed weekly after the military victory. This example shows that while America's military power is very meaningful on the battlefield, it is much less capable of influencing the civil society of a defeated country.

TEST PREPPER 4.1

ANSWERS APPEAR ON PAGE A12

True or False?

_____ 1. Hard power refers to basic military weapons such as guns and conventional bombs while soft power refers to technologically advanced weaponry (nuclear bombs, aircraft carriers, etc.).

_____ 2. World leaders, like humans in general, are incapable of dealing with all the complexity of the world and thus are required to simplify the world in order to deal with it.

_____ 3. Power levels are relatively stable for most countries over the long run.

_____ 4. An absolute increase or decrease in a country's power is meaningless unless it is placed in context (which country gained or lost, what is the relative effect vis-à-vis its adversaries, etc.).

Between Nations
Practice Test Questions
Practice Test 4.1
www.BetweenNations.org

Multiple Choice

_____ 5. Which one of the following does *not* contribute to a country's soft-power capabilities?
   a. Cultural influence
   b. Moral influence
   c. Technological developments
   d. Investments in education
   e. None of the above

_____ 6. Which of the following accurately describes what is meant by situational power?
   a. A country that is located between two small powers is situationally powerful.
   b. A country that is located between two large powers is situationally weak.
   c. Power capabilities that are meaningful in one context are not necessarily useful in another.
   d. The most effective way for a superpower to maximize its power is to spread military bases across the globe.
   e. All of the above

WHAT ARE THE MAJOR ELEMENTS OF POWER?

 Understand the difference between objective and subjective elements of power. Be able to describe each of the key objective and subjective power capabilities possessed by states.

Objective elements of power have traditionally included those capabilities or assets that can be seen, touched, and measured—or, in other words, empirically verified. How and where these elements of power are distributed on the global stage establishes who will be the big players and who will be the small actors in the drama. Neither Haiti nor Bangladesh has much chance of making its voice heard in the daily political struggle over who gets what, when, and how, whereas the United States, the European Union, China, and Russia do. Saudi Arabia has oil that the United States, Western Europe, and Japan need. This gives Saudi Arabia power; for despite its past role in supporting schools that teach anti-Western Islamic fundamentalism, states that need petroleum count Saudi Arabia as an ally. Terrorism and suicide bombings are other forms of objective power, with the awkward caveat that they are difficult to count or measure until the bombs go off. That they possess armed force (objective power), however, and the will to use it (subjective power) is not in doubt.

Objective (Tangible) Sources of Power

Objective or tangible sources of power come in various forms. In trying to determine how much potential power a state may possess, scholars and policymakers look at the capabilities of a country—or a non-state actor. Capabilities—another word for "sources" or "assets"—means those resources available to an actor that can be used to influence others. The point is that because power is so complex to measure, one way to estimate how much potential power or influence an actor possesses is to look at the resources under the actor's control. A variety of resources can be used to measure an actor's influence in the international arena.

Military Capacity

Military preparedness has traditionally been the most compelling aspect of a country's objective power. This is so because military capacity has been the way in which a country protects its territory and people from threats of aggression and furthers its objectives abroad. The world has changed rapidly, with new threats from sources other than nation-states. Threats now include terrorists, black-market-weapons proliferators, organized crime affiliates, drug traffickers, and cyberspace outlaws. Longstanding ethnic and tribal conflicts generate civil wars not easily quelled by conventional weapons, and porous borders do not lend themselves to predictable responses by military doctrines. At the same time, the world's states continue to assemble weapons to defend against hostile or potentially hostile states. Military capability in our world of change still retains a high place in national leaders' perceptions of power.

That military capability occupies a priority position in terms of how state leaders calculate power is underscored by the level of global military spending. World military expenditures remain high; in fact, more money is spent on the military and the arms trade that on anything else in the world: over $1 trillion annually.[6] By comparison, the entire budget for the United Nations is only about 1.5 percent of this amount. The military budget of the United States for fiscal year 2008—nearly $650 billion—is larger than military spending by all of the other states in the world combined.[7] Figure 4.1 depicts U.S. military spending compared to some of the world's other military spenders.

States seek to acquire weapons despite porous borders and the numerous associated threats that seem to defy a military deterrent. South Korea worries about North Korea. Israel lives in a distinctly hostile neighborhood. India and Pakistan have their problems. Israel must deal with a two-war situation, one against Palestinian suicide bombings and another potentially waged by the surrounding countries. The Israeli situation is complicated by various terrorist organizations—Hamas, Fatah, Al Aksa Martyrs' Brigades, Islamic Jihad, al Qaeda, and Hezbollah—funded by nearby Middle Eastern states.

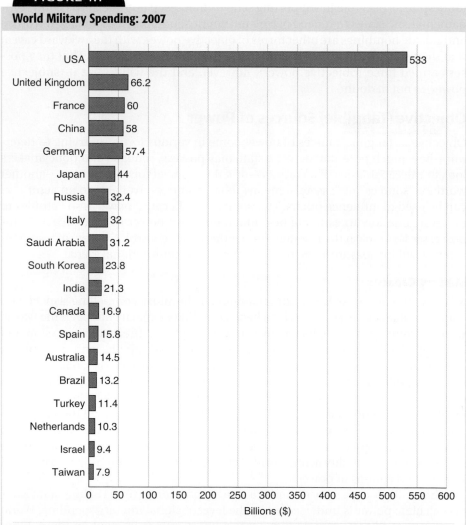

FIGURE 4.1

World Military Spending: 2007

Country	Billions ($)
USA	533
United Kingdom	66.2
France	60
China	58
Germany	57.4
Japan	44
Russia	32.4
Italy	32
Saudi Arabia	31.2
South Korea	23.8
India	21.3
Canada	16.9
Spain	15.8
Australia	14.5
Brazil	13.2
Turkey	11.4
Netherlands	10.3
Israel	9.4
Taiwan	7.9

The World CIA Factbook; SIPRI, Center for Defense Information and Center for Arms Control and Non-Proliferation, 2007, British Ministry of Defense and European Union government ministries. Experts at the International Institute for Strategic Studies, a military think tank, say that Beijing's official figures underestimated real spending. NB: The following countries are shown with 2006 figures: Italy, Saudi Arabia, Canada, Spain, Brazil, Turkey and Netherlands. Figures for Israel and Taiwan are 2005.

National Infrastructure and Level of Economic Development

National infrastructure is a major asset that must be factored into the power equation. This category includes a country's industrial base, scientific and technological development, transportation networks (railroads, roads, ports, air transportation), and information and communication systems (satellites, computers, cell phones). National infrastructure lies at the base of economic power.

▌ When we speak of a country's industrial base, we refer to the quantity and quality of its industries. These range from steel production to manufacturing and services. Industries lead to exports and thus income-generating activities and the ability either to exert economic pressure on others or to resist their economic pressures. Industrialized states are well situated in this respect compared to developing countries.

▌ A country's level of economic development is a key aspect of power because it reflects its ability to sustain itself, engage in finance and trade, and maintain a strong military establishment. A thriving economy, typically measured by a country's gross national product (GNP)—the total value of goods and services produced anywhere in the world by the residents of the country—indicates the strength of its international power. Figure 4.2 illustrates global per capita (GNP) to capture the world's economic power disparities.

FIGURE 4.2

Gross National Income Per Capita Map

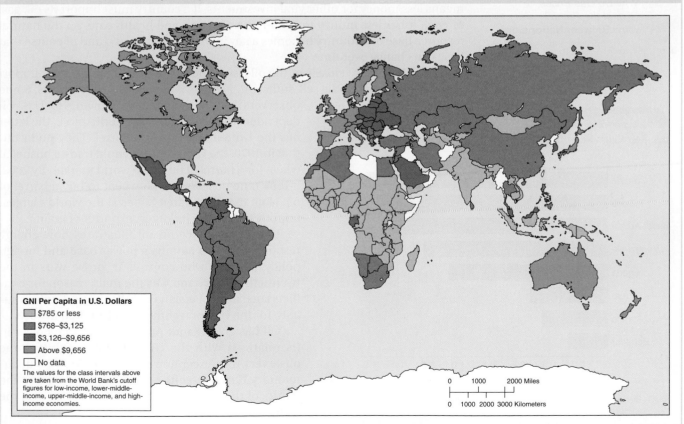

GNI Per Capita in U.S. Dollars
- $785 or less
- $768–$3,125
- $3,126–$9,656
- Above $9,656
- No data

The values for the class intervals above are taken from the World Bank's cutoff figures for low-income, lower-middle-income, upper-middle-income, and high-income economies.

0   1000   2000 Miles

0   1000 2000 3000 Kilometers

Geography

The geographic size and location of a state, as you might imagine, are extremely important as elements of objective power. Indeed, these factors are so important that a whole field of study centered on geography and politics, called political geography or **geopolitics**, has emerged over the years. As we show in chapter 8, a number of geographic factors affect a country's power capacity.

▌ A country with natural harbors and outlets to the sea, for example, is much more favorably located than a **landlocked state**.

▌ A country located in the **temperate zone** which lies between 23.5 degrees and 60.5 degrees north latitude and 23.5 degrees and 60.5 degrees south latitude has a climate more favorable for human and agricultural productivity than a country located near the equator or in the far north or south of the globe.

▌ Mountains can deter potential invaders, as in Switzerland, or they can impede a country's internal economic development, as in Bolivia and Peru.

Natural Resources

Natural resources constitute a key power capability closely associated with geography. These vital factors make it possible for a country to feed and shelter its population, industrialize its economy, and engage in trade. Access to natural resources like arable land for food production; coal, oil, and uranium; rivers for energy sources to run industries; or iron ore for steel production are the basis for comparative levels of GNP, levels and balances of trade, and military preparedness. If a country does not have sufficient land to raise food, then it must import it, which means less money for other vital investments. If a country must import its oil, gas, or coal, it has less money to spend on education and health care. So the natural resource base of a country becomes a key ingredient of power—and of course that base can change over time.

Let us look more closely at the oil issue. Today the United States must import oil, whereas it used to be self-sufficient. Figure 4.3 depicts U.S. oil imports. Some observers have concluded that owing to U.S. oil dependence on countries like Saudi Arabia, the latter has the United States over a barrel. They point out that in 1970, the United States could trade a bushel of wheat for a barrel of oil in the world market. By 2002, it took nine bushels of U.S. wheat to buy a barrel of oil. Note that the United States is the world's largest importer of oil and its largest exporter of grain.[8]

U.S. dependence on oil illustrates how energy resources affect a country's power base and foreign policy. Oil, and who controls it, drove wars in the twentieth century and was the main reason for conflicts such as the Persian Gulf War in 1991 and, arguably, for the U.S. preventive attack on Iraq in 2003.

Oil has given Saudi Arabia remarkable power in its relations with the United States. While some observers take exception to Michael Moore's documentary film *Fahrenheit 911,* the film depicted the nature of the Saudi kingdom's close oil ties with the United States.

Geopolitics   The study of the geographical distribution of power among states throughout the world, with specific attention to the rivalry of the major powers.

Landlocked state   As the term suggests, a state surrounded by other sovereign states and shut off from easy access to the sea; examples include Paraguay and Bolivia in South America.

Temperate zone   Two (north and south) areas of the globe that lie between 23.5 degrees and 60.5 degrees north latitude and 23.5 degrees and 60.5 degrees south latitude. They are temperate in climate and said to be prime territorial areas conducive to economic development owing to temperature and other climatic factors.

 Between Nations
For more information see
*Why It Matters to You:
Why Do Gas Prices
Rise at the Pump?*
www.BetweenNations.org

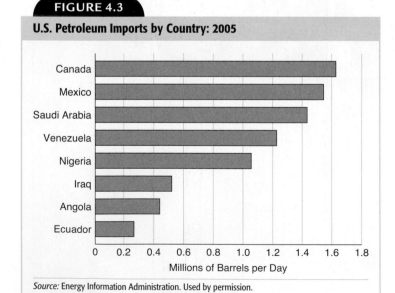

FIGURE 4.3

U.S. Petroleum Imports by Country: 2005

Millions of Barrels per Day

Source: Energy Information Administration. Used by permission.

Oil isn't the only energy source states have at their disposal:

▮ Nuclear power—given Middle East oil supply insecurity and global warming—is back on the agenda as a major source of energy. Nuclear power represents over 16 percent of the world's electricity, around 24 percent of electricity in OECD (Organization for Economic Co-Operation and Development) countries, and approximately 34 percent in the European Union states. Iran's effort to produce nuclear energy has been a major point of conflict with the United States out of fear Iran will use nuclear power to produce nuclear weapons.

▮ Rivers are another valuable natural resource that can add to a state's objective power. They provide drinking water and transportation, facilitate commerce, and serve as energy production (hydroelectric power) through the use of dams. A related consideration is a country's freshwater as a key source of power. Within twenty-five years, fifty-nine countries with a combined population of 3 billion people will experience freshwater difficulties.[9] We look at the question of the diminishing global supply of freshwater from the perspective of the ecological paradigm in chapter 14.

Geography and natural resources, then, are major sources of a country's power. The size of a country, its location, and its natural resources go a long way in enabling it to become powerful. Until recently, the three most powerful countries were also the three largest geographically: the United States, the former USSR, and China. Each of the three has significant natural resources.

Population

Population as a critical ingredient of power depends on factors including its size (relative to the land size of the state it occupies), age distribution, health, and education.

▮ Population size and density vary greatly from state to state, but, in general, a large population in a large territorial state can be an asset. It provides a base for selecting soldiers for military service and a work force for the economy. Small developing countries that face regional threats, however, may create large military forces despite their relatively small populations, as in the case of North Korea. With the high-tech smart weapons in today's military arsenals, however, big armies are no longer really as significant as they once were. Figure 4.4 illustrates the top ten countries in terms of population size.

The bottom line is that the large territorial states with huge populations—China, the United States, Russia, and India—tend to have substantial military forces with potential influence in their region or the world. While China is often viewed as a potentially powerful country because of its 1.3 billion people, India is second in the world with just over 1 billion. The United States, by contrast, has a population of roughly 300 million, less than a third of India's. Present-day Russia has roughly 143 million people. In keeping with our discussion in the preceding paragraph, keep in mind the geographic size of these

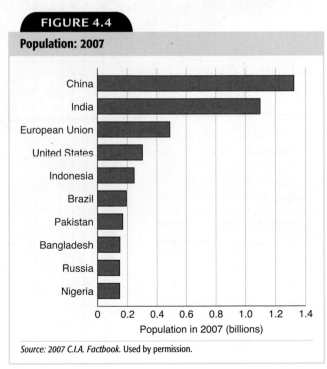

FIGURE 4.4

Population: 2007

Source: 2007 C.I.A. Factbook. Used by permission.

countries. Russia is vast (6,592,812 square miles); the United States and China are each just over half the size of Russia; and India is only one-third the size of these. That means that India is less than one-fifth the size of Russia but has *seven times* its population!

▌ Population demographics affect a country's power base. For example, if a large sector of the population is under fifteen years of age, a substantial percentage has not yet entered the work force and therefore is unlikely to participate in the country's economic productivity. Such is the case in many developing countries. A state's population in the sixty-five-and-older bracket also typically does not participate in economic productivity, yet it draws on social security programs and health benefits. The United States faces this problem—as does China with a rapidly aging population growing faster than its younger population. Figure 4.5 maps the average annual population growth rate for the years 2001 to 2015.

▌ A key aspect of population—in addition to its level of education—is its health. By 2008 the HIV/AIDS pandemic has affected the security of states throughout the world. Over 40 million people are living with AIDS, with nearly 8,000 dying every day during 2006. Figure 4.6 illustrates how the AIDS epidemic is impacting different regions of the world. A point to remember is that countries with a

FIGURE 4.5

Population Growth Rate

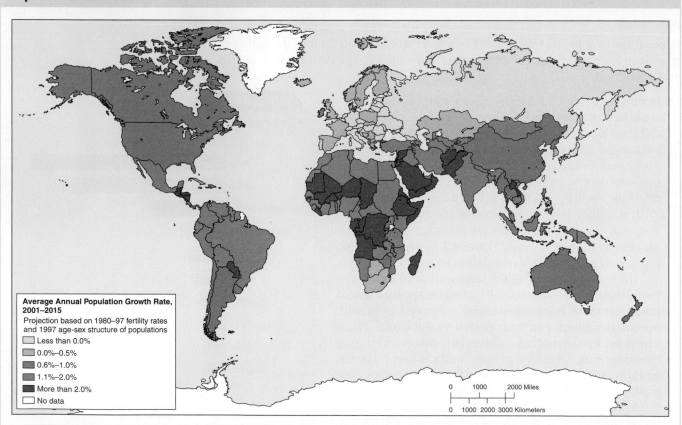

Average Annual Population Growth Rate, 2001–2015

Projection based on 1980–97 fertility rates and 1997 age-sex structure of populations

- Less than 0.0%
- 0.0%–0.5%
- 0.6%–1.0%
- 1.1%–2.0%
- More than 2.0%
- No data

0   1000   2000 Miles

0   1000 2000 3000 Kilometers

FIGURE 4.6

Global AIDS Epidemic Impacts Different Regions of the World: 2006

The HIV/AIDS pandemic is undermining the power and security of states throughout the world.

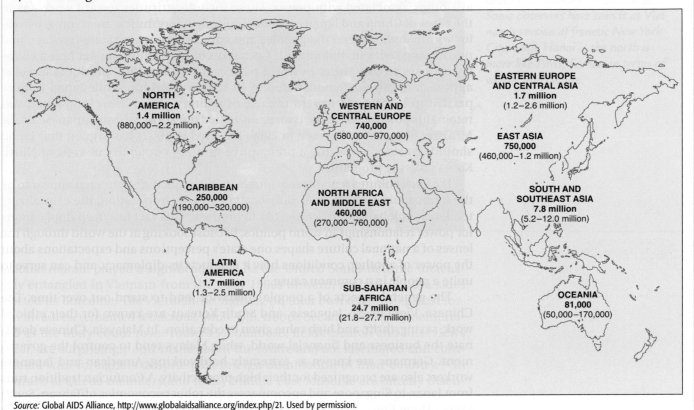

Source: Global AIDS Alliance, http://www.globalaidsalliance.org/index.php/21. Used by permission.

healthy, literate, and socially mobile population enjoy a solid base for economic and political development. Countries with an unhealthy, uneducated, and socially immobile population have a less promising base for economic and political power.

Subjective Power Factors

Subjective power factors—those that entail human values, beliefs, perceptions, and motivation—are less empirically measurable but remain enormously important in assessing a country's power base as we discussed above. Subjective factors also help us understand why conflict or cooperation arises among states, IGOs, NGOs, and other actors on the world political stage. Subjective factors are expressed in the ways people participate in government, express nationalism (see chapter 9), engage in diplomacy, display their work ethic, react to world events, and otherwise engage in political life. Let's turn now to a closer look at some of the major subjective power factors at work in world politics today.

■ Unemployment is high—a product, in part, of factory privatization—and more than 8 million people have lost their jobs in shut-down state-owned industries.

■ China's population is aging. This will place rising demands on the economy, as China must find ways to care for its elderly. This problem will be especially severe in the rural areas, where the elderly are not covered by pension plans. Given its massive aging population, it may not be able to sustain its level of economic growth and spend sufficiently on the military to overtake the United States.

■ China is plagued by low health and safety standards, underscored by frequent industrial accidents and epidemics like AIDS and Severe Acute Respiratory Syndrome (SARS). Dirty, unhealthy, overcrowded, highly polluted, and environmentally damaged urban centers contribute to China's health problems.

■ Corruption is widespread, despite government crackdowns.

■ Growth is straining China's infrastructure. The power grid is inadequate, reforming the state enterprises is taking much longer than anticipated, and the country is increasingly dependent on oil imports.

■ China's agricultural sector faces many problems. Although the country can feed itself today, its emphasis on food self-sufficiency has produced huge surpluses of types of grain not in demand abroad.

China's Military Power Is Less Impressive than It Seems

■ China's defense industry is state-owned and extremely inefficient, and it has a poor record of developing sophisticated weapons.

■ Much of China's weaponry is obsolete and outdated. Its oversize army is focused primarily on internal security.

China's Soft Power May Be Overrated

■ China's soft power is undermined by continued suspicions of China despite its peaceful and benign posture. Its political system is still opaque and can be perceived as threatening the economies and livelihoods of its neighbors.

■ China is not moving toward democracy. It remains controlled by the communist party (the CCP—the only political party permitted) and its high officials continue to exercise enormous power in defining and executing the rules of organized behavior, including the economy. This kind of power frequently leads to corruption.

■ With the current rapid pace of industrial development, China's oil consumption is likely to rise—and pollution levels with it.

Which factors do you think are most important? Where do you see China in, say, ten years from now?

LEARNING OBJECTIVES REVIEW

▶ *Define power, focusing on both hard and soft forms; understand the dynamics of power that make defining power a difficult task.*

• Power is a capability that, when translated into influence, enables one country (or IGO or NGO) to get another state (or IGO or NGO) to do something that it would not otherwise normally do.

• Power capabilities fall into two general categories: *hard and soft.*
  - Hard power refers to objective capabilities, such as military or economic power.
  - Soft power is the state's ability to influence subjectively through cultural, ideological, or moral appeal, or through its economic strength and information technology skills.

• Key dynamics of power make pinning down the concept difficult. These dynamics include the following:
  - Power translates into differing forms of influence.
  - Power is multidimensional in nature.
  - Power is shaped by perceptions.
  - Power is dynamic and changing.
  - Power is relative and not absolute.
  - Power is situational.

• It is important to note that changes in a state's power base can have dramatic effects in the international system, such as changing the overall distribution of power, shifting the system from bipolar to multipolar, producing hegemonic states, or contributing to regional wars or cooperation.

2 *Understand the difference between objective and subjective elements of power. Be able to describe each of the key objective and subjective power capabilities possessed by states.*

- Objective elements of power include those capabilities or assets that can be seen, touched, and measured, or, in other words, empirically verified. Objective power capabilities include the following:
    - Military capability
    - Economic development (national infrastructure, industrial base, technology, transportation systems, information, and communication systems)
    - Geography
    - Natural resources
    - Population
- Subjective power factors include the following: human values, beliefs, perceptions, and energy. They too help account for conflict or cooperation among states, IGOs, and NGOs in world politics. They include:
    - National culture
    - National morale
    - Quality of government
    - Political stability
    - Quality of diplomacy
    - Quality of intelligence

3 *Understand what is meant by balance of power and identify key types of balance that may exist in the international system. Understand the concept of collective security and its prospects for securing peace in the international system.*

- Power shapes different relationships among states, with power shifts and realignments common over time. The term *balance of power,* for example, has a variety of meanings with regard to patterns of power.
- Balance of power may be seen in terms of different distributions of power within the international system, such as bipolarity, multipolarity, and unipolarity.
- Among the most dramatic forces changing the nature of power are
    - Globalization
    - Interdependence
    - The information revolution—the Internet and the World Wide Web.
- The emergence of non-state ideological beliefs, specifically those of radical forms of Islamic fundamentalism, has produced a new form of terrorism power that threatens international stability. This threat was identified in the *Final Report of the National Commission on Terrorist Attacks Upon the United States* of July 2004.
- Collective security calls for the pooling of state power in one organization, like the UN. This power is used to deter or defeat any country that has attacked another. Collective security has not worked well because states have been reluctant to place their military forces under UN authority and because of competing versions of national-security interests.

RESOURCES ON THE WEB

To use these interactive learning and study tools, including video and audio multimedia resources, go to **www.BetweenNations.org**.

Practice Tests	Case Studies	Current Events
Audio Concepts	Primary Sources	Daily Newsfeeds from *The Washington Post*
Flashcards	Historical Background	Weblinks for Further Exploration

 *Between Nations*

Power into Policy

LEARNING OBJECTIVES

1 ▶ *Understand how foreign policy translates power into outcomes, and identify the associated core, middle-range, and long-term goals that accompany it.*

2 ▶ *Understand what factors at each level of analysis affect the formulation of foreign policy and identify the various perspectives used to explain foreign-policy decision making.*

> *"By this I mean that a political society does not live to conduct foreign policy; it would be more correct to say that it conducts foreign policy in order to live."*
>
> —George F. Kennan

Chapter Outline

3 *Identify the different phases in the U.S. war on terror; understand the key components of the Bush Doctrine, and be aware of the criticisms of that approach.*

Foreign Policy Is a Key to Survival in a Turbulent World

When you read daily newspaper headlines or watch television news, you quickly realize that at any given moment, foreign policy is a major aspect of world politics. Foreign policy is put into play by the world's states, but other players, such as intergovernmental organizations (IGOs) and nongovernmental organizations (NGOs)—including militant Islamic organizations like al Qaeda—may also make decisions that affect the foreign policy of states. Each of these actors tries to employ some form of power and influence—both hard and soft power—to achieve desired objectives.

When actors use foreign policy to interact and cooperate with other actors, it serves as a centralizing force. A good example of foreign policy as a centralizing force is Russian President Vladimir

Putin's decision in October 2004 to ratify the Kyoto Protocol, a step in the direction of cooperating with other states to combat climate change and global warming. Another example is the dramatic announcement of Libya's Colonel Muammar al-Qaddafi in December 2003 that Libya would disclose and dismantle all its weapons of mass destruction. This surprise foreign-policy move led the European Union in October 2004 to end eighteen years of economic sanctions against Libya—a remarkable example of centralization.

When foreign-policy decisions lead to conflict—as when the United States, backed by Great Britain, invaded and occupied Iraq in March 2003—decentralizing forces are at work in the international system. The Iraq invasion split the world into countries that supported the actions versus the large part of the international community that did not. Many foreign countries do not see terrorism as a war, even though they are opposed to terrorism and may cooperate in fighting terrorism as a police action by arresting suspects or freezing suspected financial assets.

Foreign policy can involve the actions of a country or maybe an organization (like Greenpeace) or an individual (think of Osama bin Laden) abroad and the manner in which those actions are carried out. Individuals and groups that hold decision-making authority inside the state (or IGO or NGO) play a major role in shaping its external behavior. An obvious example is the personality, perceptions, and background of big-power leaders. For example, on one hand, President George W. Bush of the United States and former Prime Minister Tony Blair of Great Britain both forcefully pressed for the war in Iraq. On the other hand, were the strong leadership personalities of former German Chancellor Gerhard Schröder and former French President Jacques Chirac, both of whom strongly opposed going to war with Iraq in 2003.

Given foreign policy's pivotal role in world politics, this chapter looks closely at its major characteristics and how it affects the international system.

▌ We begin with an examination of foreign policy's close links to various kinds of power capabilities, discussed in chapter 4 and to its principal goals and the kinds of issues it entails. Among the key factors that drive foreign policy are:

1. National interests (vital interests or core objectives)
2. Political and government leaders
3. Domestic economic and political structures
4. International influences

We show how these elements come into play, and how and why foreign policies change while basic core goals stay in place.

▌ Of great importance in this study is how foreign-policy decisions are made, and this chapter delves into that big question by examining four distinct dimensions of foreign-policy decision making:

1. Rational
2. Organizational
3. Political
4. Individual

▌ Finally, given the enormous impact of 9/11, we conclude this study of foreign policy with a look at the foreign-policy repercussions of 9/11. This discussion examines the Bush Doctrine, advocated by the Bush administration as it sought to maintain national security following 9/11. ▮

WHAT IS FOREIGN POLICY?

1 *Understand how foreign policy translates power into outcomes, and identify the associated core, middle-range, and long-term goals that accompany it.*

 Between Nations
For more information see
*Why It Matters to You:
Declining Concern Over
Foreign Student Enrollments
at U.S. Schools*
www.BetweenNations.org

To get a grip on why leaders of countries and other organizations pursue all kinds of goals on the world political chessboard, we need to understand the basic elements of foreign policy. Beyond simply trying to do this for its own intellectual attraction or because you are taking a course on the subject, it is important to understand the foreign policy of your own country, as well as that of others, because it matters greatly in our lives. *The Report of the 9/11 Commission of the U.S. Senate,* as examined in the online case study for chapter 1 (**www.Between Nations.org**), for example, shows how numerous flaws in U.S. national security intelligence gathering and processing—a major aspect of U.S. foreign policy—played a huge role in making possible the 9/11 terrorist attacks on the United States, with their horrendous loss of lives.

The following discussion illustrates another consequence of foreign policy in your life. Seeing how relevant it is to each of us, let us probe this subject by concentrating first on foreign policy as an approach to translating power capabilities into favorable outcomes, and then look at its core, middle-range, and long-range goals.

An Approach to Translating Power into Action

In chapter 4 we discussed the numerous power capabilities at the disposal of states and other actors in the world political arena. We looked at hard power (military and economic) and soft power (a country's core values and how other countries perceive them) as well as objective and subjective types of power available to leaders of states, IGOs, NGOs, and some individuals. Power as influence comes in multiple forms based on multiple capabilities, as discussed in chapter 4.

Foreign policy, as you can see, is a vital aspect of world politics, and power is one of its key components. To focus on the links between some kind of power/influence and foreign policy is a valid approach because without some type of power, it is difficult to have an effective foreign policy. Foreign-policy techniques and strategies—from diplomacy that promotes the legitimacy of a country's values or suicide bombings that express the radical ideals of a proselytizing Islamic crusade—are how key actors on the international scene pursue goals and objectives. They do so by translating available power into specific actions designed to influence other actors.

Power and Policy Tools

Once a state knows what their foreign-policy goals are, they have at their disposal a wide range of tools for translating available power capabilities into specific policies. The United States, for example, in response to the 9/11 attacks, used its military power first to bomb, then chase on the ground, the Taliban in Afghanistan, and later to attack and occupy Iraq. India and Pakistan have threatened to use nuclear weapons against each other in their dispute over Kashmir, although they have pursued peaceful negotiations, too. Islamic insurgents in Iraq have used the power of the sword—literally—to behead hostages in seeking to influence their home countries. How leaders translate available power into policies and the tools they use varies from state to state, actor to actor, and situation to situation.

The tools for translating power into policy range widely. Some are benign and peaceful, such as soft power, information programs, humanitarian aid, and diplomacy. Others are coercive: embargoes, economic blockades, espionage and sabotage, and military force. Each policy option requires underlying power to be put into play—money or goods for humanitarian aid, printing presses and film production for information programs, ships and naval weapons to establish an effective blockade. Figure 5.1 depicts this range and the types of foreign-policy tools available to state leaders and other actors.

Changes in the Diplomatic Climate

Diplomacy The negotiating process by which states and other international actors pursue international relations and reconciliation of competing interests by compromise and bargaining.

Note that **diplomacy** is the overarching tool at the disposal of state leaders. Diplomacy is the way a country negotiates with other countries—how a state conducts its political, cultural, economic, and security relationships. The issues on which states negotiate include everything from trade agreements to military conflict. Diplomacy establishes representation abroad. It defends a country's policies and observes other countries' behavior. As Figure 5.1 indicates, there are two kinds of diplomacy, benign and coercive; within each category is a range of actions from most benign to most coercive.[1]

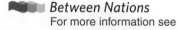 *Between Nations*
For more information see
The Marshall Plan
www.BetweenNations.org

The nature of diplomatic negotiations has changed, however, over the years. Before World War I, for example, Europe was the focus of much diplomacy. Few nationalist sentiments complicated the diplomatic process, and ideologies like communism or Nazism had not yet established a footing in world politics. Secret diplomacy was the name of the game, and the diplomats—that is, chief

---

FIGURE 5.1

Tools for Foreign-policy Implementation

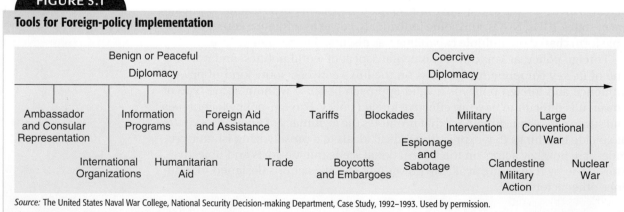

Source: The United States Naval War College, National Security Decision-making Department, Case Study, 1992–1993. Used by permission.

negotiators—tended to have a common aristocratic identity, with French as the key language. They represented governments, many of which were monarchies connected by intermarriage. This period before World War I is referred to as the era of **old diplomacy**.

After 1919, the world entered what is called the period of **new diplomacy**. New diplomacy is more open and public, with less secrecy and more public opinion and public press influence than during the earlier era. Furthermore, ideologies like Marxism-Leninism became more prominent, and although Marxism-Leninism largely died out in Russia, it continued in mainland China and in Cuba into the twenty-first century. Europe ceased to be the dominant geographic pivot of diplomacy as more and more sovereign states entered the international political playing field and as diplomacy became globalized.

Other changes are associated with new diplomacy. The United Nations became increasingly important as a forum for diplomatic representation and exchanges, and it gathered momentum in its global peacekeeping operations. Summit diplomacy—negotiations between heads of government and heads of state as opposed to negotiations between embassies, consulates, and diplomats—became more common. The world also saw the rise of **coercive diplomacy**: the threat and use of force in tandem with diplomatic pressure by an alliance like NATO. For example, the NATO alliance used coercive diplomacy to try to get Serbia to cease its military activities in Bosnia and Kosovo. The United States tried coercive diplomacy on Iraq in 2002–2003 to try to find hidden weapons of mass destruction, but it later resorted to a preventive military attack.

America's public diplomacy has suffered recently. The agency that has long dealt with public diplomacy, the U.S. Information Agency, has seen its resources reduced over the past decade, and in 1999 it was merged into the Department of State, where its functions have been fragmented and its resources even further depleted. This situation has weakened dramatically U.S. soft power, as discussed in chapter 4. At a time when the United States needs a healthy image for security in the post–9/11 period, its image remains broadly negative in Europe, Canada, Latin America, and in much of the Islamic world. The Bush administration's return to international diplomacy in May 2007 regarding what to do in Iraq—demonstrated by Secretary of State Condoleezza Rice's attendance at the May 2007 world conference in Egypt to launch the International Compact with Iraq (ICI)—may help to alter that negative image.

A Set of Core, Middle-range, and Long-range Goals

A sound approach to understanding the goals and objectives pursued by states in the international arena is to begin with the assumption that a country's foreign-policy objectives tend to be hierarchical and shaped by many forces. By *hierarchical* we mean that foreign-policy goals cover a range of (1) core or vital interest objectives; (2) middle-range objectives; and (3) long-range objectives. These three types of foreign-policy goals are defined easily enough.

Core Objectives

A country's most vital national interests guide its **core objectives**. They include maintaining its

1. territorial security,
2. economic strength, and
3. political independence.

Old diplomacy   The form of diplomacy that characterized the era prior to World War I. European-centered, it emphasized secrecy and was generally devoid of nationalism.

New diplomacy   The style of diplomacy that has evolved since World War I, with emphasis on open—as opposed to secret—negotiations and summit meetings, and in which nationalism has a greater impact on the negotiating process.

Coercive diplomacy   The threat and use of force in tandem with diplomatic pressure by one actor on another. The UN's coercive diplomacy on Saddam Hussein to reveal more information on Iraq's WMDs in 2003 is a good example. (Coercive diplomacy failed in this case.)

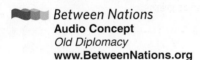

Between Nations
Audio Concept
Old Diplomacy
www.BetweenNations.org

Core objectives   A term used in foreign policy to identify a state's primary objectives (or interests), such as pursuit of its physical (territorial) security, economic vitality, and sovereign political independence.

Hardships of War

The Chechen capital Grozny, February 2000. Wars leave desolation and despair in their wake.

If a state is to remain a cohesive actor with some influence and some sovereignty and flexibility within the international arena, it must at all costs use foreign policy to serve its core or vital interests. No matter what a state's central belief system or ideological persuasion—from Iran's and Pakistan's Islamic beliefs to India's adherence to Hinduism and Israel's Judaism—each must attend to these three core interests if it is going to survive in the competitive international political system.

To determine what exact policy will best serve a country's core or "national" or vital interest can be difficult. Territorial security is a good case in point. The Bush administration decided to go to war against Iraq, first, to protect American territory against the threat of an attack by Iraq using weapons of mass destruction—which Iraq allegedly possessed. When it turned out Iraq did not possess such weapons, the justification for war and occupation switched to "build democracy" and make democratic Iraq a model for the Middle East. The more democracies the better, the theory went, because according to democratic peace theory (see chapter 2) democracies do not make war against each other. The war and occupation policies, however, rather than protecting American territory may have made it more insecure. Money and attention were diverted from Homeland Security, and the U.S. Army became weaker due to extended and repeated tours of service. America's soft power image abroad suffered.

We see this pursuit of core national interests in the U.S.–led attack on Afghanistan's Taliban forces, which protected bin Laden and al Qaeda insurgents, after the events of 9/11. The Taliban and al Qaeda represented an obvious security threat that had to be met. Core security interests equally were at stake in Israel's military assaults on Palestinians as a consequence of Palestinian suicide bombings inside Israel since 2002. Saudi Arabia's crackdown on radical Islamic insurgents in that country during 2004 underscores the royal family's focus on a rising national security threat.

When you think about the international political system, keep in mind the key points you learned in earlier chapters. States operate in a global arena that has no world government to regulate interstate relations, no legal authority higher than the sovereign state actors, no world executive to implement decisions, no world legislature or international legal system with teeth, and no world military to enforce peace within the system. We do have UN peacekeeping forces and the NATO military forces to try to deal with regional conflicts. But we do not have a global military organization capable of enforcing broad collective security, defending against international terrorists, or enforcing international law.

When the International Court of Justice (IJC) in July 2004 declared Israel's over 400-mile security barrier in the West Bank illegal and urged its removal from inside the occupied territories, Israel stated that it simply would not abide by the ruling. You can see that states, NGOs, and individual actors operate within what might be termed a *primitive political system*—not completely anarchic, but still primitive compared to life *within* most states, which have common internal belief systems, legal order, and power to enforce the law.

Middle-range Objectives

States also pursue a number of mid-range goals as a way of making certain their vital interests remain primary. For example, states may enhance their prestige and viability in the international system by engaging in foreign aid programs and cultural exchanges, by sponsoring trade shows and conferences of heads of states, by exploring outer space, or by exchanging diplomatic delegations. They engage in such activities while seeking to support primary core interests. Here are specific illustrations:

▌ China hosted its expensive fifty-fifth Anniversary of the Communist Revolution in October 2004, an event designed to portray China's image as a unified political state with a dynamic economic model of development—one way to project the perception of power.

▌ Russia continued to sponsor its outer space program after the Soviet Union collapsed and despite limited resources.

Opening Ceremony of the 2004 Olympic Games in Greece
In hosting the Olympic Games, Greece attained a middle-range foreign-policy objective.

■ President Vladimir V. Putin hosted a huge celebration in Moscow's Red Square on May 9, 2005, to commemorate the sixtieth anniversary of the defeat of Nazi Germany. Invited guests included U.S. President Bush and dozens of other leaders who watched a decked-out military parade replete with Soviet symbols and Russian pride.

■ Greece hosted the 2004 Summer Olympic Games to promote its middle-range objectives.

Long-range Goals

As part of their long-range interests, many countries promote their belief systems and overarching basic values abroad. You can see this agenda at work throughout history and certainly during the Cold War years following World War II. The Cold War, roughly 1947–1991 (when the Soviet Union collapsed) was a period of open rivalry without direct fighting (hence *Cold* War) between two groups of states practicing different ideologies and political systems. The Soviet Union led one group of states, frequently referred to as the Eastern bloc. Mainland China belonged to this group for a period of time before it began to develop its own tensions with the Soviet Union. The United States and its allies were on the other side, often referred to as the Western bloc.

During the Cold War the former Soviet Union, for example, sought to promote Marxist-Leninism, with its unique blend of economic determinism, permanent class conflict, and basic antagonism between communism and capitalism. Toward that end, it sought to promote socialism and socialist-oriented allies in the developing countries, like Cuba under Fidel Castro, and to undermine the United States wherever and whenever possible.

Containment   A U.S. foreign policy pursued during the Cold War that aimed at preventing the Soviet Union from expanding into Western Europe, Asia, and other regions of the Third World. President Harry S Truman announced it in 1947.

■ *Cold War Politics:* The United States, for its part, operates on a different belief system or worldview, one that is centered in a liberal, democratic orientation. This set of perceptions was played out time and again during the Cold War and has emerged strongly in the post–Cold War period. During the Cold War, the main focus of U.S. policy and its long-range objective was based on **containment**, or curtailing the expansion and spread of communism. Prolonged competition and confrontation, with brief periods of cooperation and conciliation, characterized Soviet-American relations during the Cold War. In a mirror image of each side, American domestic and foreign policy reflected virulent anticommunism, while deep suspicion of the "West" typified the Soviet leadership. The Soviets feared "capitalist encirclement," and the Americans feared an "international communist conspiracy." Each side, in mirror image, has seen the other as intransigent and aggressive.

Much of U.S. policy since the collapse of the Soviet Union has focused on the long-term promotion of democratic governments and market economies. We see this objective in U.S. policy toward Russia, Eastern Europe, China, and Bosnia, underscored by the 1995 Dayton Peace Accords, which aimed to bring democratic government to war-torn Bosnia.

■ *Promoting Islamic Principles:* Long-term objectives are at work in Iran's promotion of Islamic principles abroad, especially under Ayatollah Khomeini in the 1980s and during Afghanistan's Taliban regime in the 1990s. Al Qaeda seems bent on dramatically altering U.S. and Western policies toward the Islamic world, although not necessarily upon destroying the United States or its freedoms and liberties, and upon expanding Muslim beliefs and support for a traditional Islamic form of government.[2]

Osama Bin Laden and his supporters appear determined to generate worldwide Muslim identity and loyalty in support of militant action orchestrated to remove U.S. and Western forces from Saudi Arabia; Iraq, Afghanistan, and other Muslim territories; to end U.S. aid to Israel and ultimately eliminate that state; and to end U.S. protection of Muslim regimes that repress other Muslims in Egypt, Jordan, Kuwait, Saudi Arabia, and elsewhere.[3] Because the United States supports governments like those of Saudi Arabia and Egypt, al Qaeda sees the United States as the main obstacle to its goals.

The Wahhabi form of fundamentalist Islam sponsored by Saudi Arabia and mirrored in the teaching in Pakistan's *madrassas* (traditional Islamic schools) and in bin Laden's statements ironically is supportive of this long-term objective (see this chapter's case study), even though the United States has long-standing interdependent ties with Saudi Arabia.

A Focus on Key Issues Associated with Goals

Each core, middle-range, and long-range goal is tied to a range of issues associated with what scholars and policymakers term a country's **national interests**. This term typically refers to a country's (1) territorial security, (2) economic vitality, and (3) political sovereignty. Leaders must keep these goals foremost in mind in orchestrating their foreign policies. The challenge is to decide exactly what policies to pursue in order to protect the homeland's territory, build its economy, and guarantee its political cohesiveness and strength.

To illustrate this point, assume that policymakers are sitting around a conference table discussing how to defend their country. Defense, of course, is a vital aspect of territorial security. How will they be certain they have accurate intelligence—a big problem in the U.S. decision to go to war in Iraq? What will they do to protect the country's infrastructure (ports, airports, hydroelectric system, financial buildings)? Which weapons systems will they fund? How will they use their troops?

Economic vitality is another goal that must be promoted by specific policies. How much control should a government exert over the country's economy? The range is wide, from China's market socialism to the market capitalism of the United States. Should a country join in a common market or free trade organization, like NAFTA or the European Union, or should it remain aloof from such arrangements? Norway and Switzerland have remained independent of the EU, and North Korea has pursued a unique brand of independent economic foreign policy. How much should the country spend on social overhead capital (investments in elements of the economy that enhance the production of goods and services, such as roads, railways, sewerage, electricity, and education)? How much national spending should go to education, communications, and transportation, and highways and bridges?

What makes the concept of vital national interests so complex is the fact that policymakers around the world frequently find it difficult to determine the specific policies that will support their agreed-upon interests. The U.S. and British decision to go to war against Iraq was not widely supported. France, Germany, Russia, China, and most other countries across the globe did not support that decision. Inside America the U.S. Senate and House of Representatives voted for the war, but twenty-three members of the Senate and 133 members of the House voted against the Iraq War Resolution in October 2002. Indeed, in the buildup to this war—to rid Iraq of its alleged WMDs—the State and Defense departments differed strongly over what constituted the best course to follow.

National interests The principal priorities pursued by states in the international arena. Territorial security, political independence, and economic vitality are a state's key national interests. To determine national interests in precise policy measures, however, can be difficult.

Meanwhile, on economic policy, U.S. labor organizations have opposed strongly the accepted policy of allowing offshore tax shelters for American businesses as well as the whole range of outsourcing that has become widely publicized in recent years. Similar patterns are found inside many states, where internal foreign-policy differences can be profound—as, for example, inside China, France, Germany, Israel, and Russia. In today's globalized and interdependent world, defining the best way to protect a country's national interests and determining what issues to pursue have become exceedingly complex and difficult. The Soviet Union, for example, assumed that it was pursuing its national interests (and communism) in the most effective way possible by engaging in a weapons race with the United States. That quest, in the end, undermined its economy and environment drastically, as the world discovered in the 1990s after the Soviet Union collapsed.

Keep in mind that the task of ensuring core interests affects a state's internal or domestic activities as well as its external ones. Thus, as we have seen, foreign and domestic interests are in many ways interconnected. Examples of this **intermestic** phenomenon (international-domestic connection) include foreign policies in the arenas of international trade, defense spending, and the environment—all of which affect the job market, personal incomes of individuals who live in the home state, and quality of life in terms of air and water purity. Remember that the line between foreign and domestic concerns is often blurred.

Intermestic   Issues that affect both foreign and domestic policy, such as international trade.

TEST PREPPER 5.1

ANSWERS APPEAR ON PAGE A12

True or False?

_____ 1. States are not limited to coercive or hard power methods for translating power into policy.

_____ 2. The two kinds of diplomacy include defensive and offensive.

_____ 3. As a result of improved technology, new diplomacy is much more effective at maintaining secrecy so the objectives of foreign policy are met.

_____ 4. Territorial security, economic strength, and political independence are examples of long-range objectives in foreign policy.

_____ 5. Defining a country's core national interests is a fairly straightforward task.

Between Nations
Practice Test Questions
Practice Test 5.1
www.BetweenNations.org

Multiple Choice

_____ 6. Which of the following is a viable tool for translating power into policy:
   a. Use of information programs/propaganda
   b. Espionage
   c. Economic blockades
   d. Humanitarian aid
   e. All of the above

_____ 7. Which of the following activities would be directly related to the pursuit of core national interests?
   a. The U.S.–led attack on Afghanistan's Taliban forces
   b. The French sinking of the *Rainbow Warrior* vessel
   c. Participation in a United Nations Commission on refugees
   d. Greece hosting the Olympic Games
   e. All of the above

HOW IS FOREIGN POLICY FORMULATED?

> **2** *Understand what factors at each level of analysis affect the formulation of foreign policy and identify the various perspectives used to explain foreign-policy decision making.*

Many factors influence a state's foreign policy; its self-image (history, beliefs, and values), the availability of natural resources, and geographic location (see chapters 4 and 8) are three examples. Historically, the self-image of the United States has been composed of a sense of moralism and pragmatism. Russia's historic self-image has focused on conflict between its *Westernizers* (who thought Russia should adopt European practices) and its *Slavophiles* (who rejected Western thought in favor of Slavic culture), the drive for territorial expansion, and emphasis on great-power status.

While national self-images certainly change with time, we still can see elements of these historical self-images operating in foreign policy. The strong moral tradition of the United States is evident in its approach to Saddam Hussein's Iraq leading up to the 2003 war. Russia's leaders demonstrate the old conflict between Westernizers and Slavophiles in their attitudes toward NATO expansion. Asian countries like China, Taiwan, South Korea, and Japan have cultures that value hard work—a major asset when it comes to economic production.

The type of power resource possessed by a country, IGO, NGO, or individual actor is another crucial issue in foreign policy. Saudi Arabia has oil, and this fact deeply affects how Saudi Arabia can translate available power into policy. Argentina and Canada have food to export. France has nuclear-powered electricity to export. These different exports earn hard currency to help support core economic interests.

In exploring the many factors that influence foreign policy, with their multiple centralizing and decentralizing influence, we will:

- Examine the three levels where policy is made: the global, state, and individual levels.
- Look more closely at the dynamics of foreign policies—how they spring from human beliefs and are tied to concepts like nationalism and religion.
- Touch on the need to coordinate foreign-policy objectives and look at bureaucratic struggles in the formulation of foreign policy.

International System–level, State-level, and Individual-level Factors

As you learned in chapter 3, a useful frame of reference for analyzing the complex world of international relations involves five levels: the international system, regional, state, substate and individual. We will focus here on the international system, state, and individual levels. Let's begin at the international system level.

International System–level Factors

Many key forces operate at the international system level. One important factor is the international distribution of power. Which countries are the big powers? How is power shifting within the system? Here we need to remember our discussion of power in chapter 4. In the first decade of the twenty-first century, for example, we see the United States as a dominant player in military and economic terms. Russia under the leadership of Vladimir Putin has been rebuilding and reasserting its power in world politics. The question of power distribution, use, and potential, then, are central aspects of the international system arena.

Globalization The process of becoming worldwide in scope. When we speak of the globalization of industry, we refer to the process of industries going worldwide in scope, the internationalization of industry. The effects or consequences of globalization include the reduction of regional differences in lifestyle and the loss of distinctive regional identities.

Another major factor at work in the international system is the extensive worldwide impact of **globalization**—that is, the growing links between people, communities, and economies around the world. Globalization has increased the interdependence of a country and the international or regional trade system—for example, Mexico's membership in NAFTA or the participation of France and Italy in the European Union (EU). Now that it has joined the World Trade Organization (WTO), China's foreign economic policies will be affected by its rules. In short, countries that participate in regional trading groups must adapt their foreign policies to the dynamics of these organizations, just as membership in NATO shapes the foreign policies of member-countries.

Another aspect of globalization is the Internet. A compelling example of this transformation in the global context of foreign policymaking is the websites associated with al Qaeda, where its essays, articles, and editorials may be found.[4] Another example is the Middle East news media, *Al Jazeera*, which uses the Internet to broadcast major opinions, information, and attitudes coming out of the Middle East.

Other factors at the international level that affect foreign policy include:

▮ IGOs and NGOs: In 1995 the UN reported that around 29,000 NGOs were operating at the international level. By the year 2000, it was estimated that there were over 2 million NGOs in the United States alone. The most obvious high-level IGO is the United Nations, a giant actor in world politics that makes foreign policy and certainly affects the foreign policies of other countries.

▮ Worldwide climate change: The big question is how global warming—with its mega-droughts, coastal flooding, devastating hurricanes, food scarcity, and many other types of ecological disasters—will threaten national security in countries around the world.

State-level Factors

State-level factors refer to those elements inherent to a given country. They include such items as its geographic location and natural resources, with attention to its neighbors as well as its size, shape, topography, amount of arable land for growing food, climate, and a host of other factors that affect its power base. Other state-level factors include type of government (dictatorial or democratic), level of economic development (highly developed and rich, or underdeveloped and poor), military power, belief systems, and cultural underpinnings.

Democratic governments, for example, make policy by means of a process that differs sharply from that of authoritarian-style governments. The former, like the United States, have a system that includes checks and balances, separation of powers, numerous actors, lobbyists, a free press, public opinion, and many other factors. Authoritarian systems—like those in China, Iraq under Saddam Hussein, Syria, and Zimbabwe—are more likely to make decisions based on input from a limited number of people and in the context of a controlled press. Saddam Hussein, a dictator, had more individual control over foreign policy than the U.S. president does.

A state's culture operates at the state level. Japan's culture since World War II has reflected a posture of pacificism in terms of military power. Japan's rising nationalism, however, may foreshadow increased militarism in its future foreign policies. The United States has a distinct moral element in its approach to defining its national interests. Iran has a proud Persian historic legacy. So to understand how a state defines its national interests, we need to examine its national culture—or in some cases, its ideology as in the Soviet Union's communism during the Cold War or China's version of market socialism today.

Individual-level Factors

Individual-level factors include the role of political and government leaders, which is driven in part by their personalities, beliefs, and values. You can see this factor vividly when you consider the monumental role played by Adolf Hitler in leading Germany into World War II, Joseph Stalin's policies of occupying Eastern Europe after World War II—policies resisted by U.S. President Harry Truman, resulting in the Cold War. A more recent example is Osama bin Laden's role in orchestrating al Qaeda's infamous 9/11 attacks and the subsequent neoconservative ideological and religious beliefs of President George W. Bush in orchestrating the war on Iraq.

Beliefs Shape Foreign-policy Decisions: Ideology, Religion, and Nationalism

The predominant beliefs of states and individuals come in different forms that influence foreign-policy decisions. *Ideologies* are a collection of beliefs shared by a group of people. They can be divided into different categories, such as political ideologies—ideas about how to govern a country—and religious or philosophical ideologies regarding how people should make decisions. A case in point is Islamic socialism. A variety of socialisms are found in Africa. Christian Democratic ideology is a Latin American version. Marxism-Leninism in the Soviet Union and liberal democracy in the United States and the West converted the Soviet Union and the United States into natural enemies during the Cold War. The Bush administration's neoconservative ideology aptly illustrates how a set of beliefs shapes foreign policy.

Religion is another belief system that impacts foreign policy. Religious beliefs like the radical Islamic ideas of Osama bin Laden and al Qaeda have led to mortal combat with the United States and the Western world. Of interest to Middle East watchers, however, are the two versions of Shiite Islam vying for attention in Iran and Iraq. Whereas many of Iran's Shiite Islamic leaders advocate an all-embracing system of clerical rule personified by Iran's famous Ayatollah, the late Ruhollah Khomeini, other powerful Shiite clerics in Iraq propose a quieter brand of Islam, more **secular** in nature, and are less enthusiastic for an Islamic state.[5] In Iraq not all Shiite clerics are of the same mind, and disagreements exist among them. Muqtada al-Sadr, is a young leader who disagreed with the older Shiite Ali al-Sistani, who had avoided direct involvement in politics.

Nationalism and national identity affect how, and in what ways, a state defines foreign policy in pursuit of its vital interests. Nationalism (see chapter 9) refers to a people's sense of connection through their shared culture, language, history, and political aspirations. Nationalism is the emotive force these shared values generate as state leaders pursue foreign policies crafted to protect their people's aspirations, values, beliefs, and territory. (See chapter 9 for more detail.) National identity and **nationalism** have long been powerful in foreign policies and have become dramatically pronounced since the end of the Cold War. Chinese nationalism has been on the rise since the late twentieth century as its communism has been in decline—and the same could be said for Vietnam. Powerful Serb, Bosnian, Slovene, Croat nationalism led to the breakup of Yugoslavia in the early 1990s.

 Between Nations
Audio Concept
Ideology
www.BetweenNations.org

Secular The state of being separate from organized religion.

Nationalism A strong emotional attachment to one's nation that can be expressed in a range of behaviors from peaceful to violent.

Some Perspectives on Foreign-policy Decision Making

In trying to understand how states formulate their foreign policy, it helps to look at the decision-making processes that explain foreign policy from different perspectives. Different perspectives (rational, organizational, and individual) help explain why foreign policies are not easily coordinated, which is most notable in, but not exclusive to, democracies. Even in totalitarian governments such as Nazi Germany and the Stalinist former Soviet Union, several groups vied for power. Democracies, however, speak with more than one voice when it comes to making foreign policy. In the case of the United States, for example, the president is the chief diplomat and major player, but the Senate, House of Representatives, and other public and private groups have a say as well.

The November 2006 United States midterm elections produced a turnover of the House of Representatives, the Senate, and a majority of governorships and state legislatures from the Republican Party to the Democratic Party. The election has led Democratic Congressional foes of the Republican president to clash bitterly over a U.S. timed troop withdrawal from Iraq—and over House Speaker Pelosi's visit to Syria in April 2007.

Democracies have other difficulties, too, in coordinating their foreign-policy agendas. One is the clash between the need for secrecy in some foreign-policy issues versus the public's right to accurate information. Other factors include:

▌ the power of the press
▌ public opinion
▌ lobbying by interest groups in democratic systems
▌ separation of powers that creates checks and balances in democracies.

By contrast, totalitarian leaders and dictatorships do pretty much what they want, without concern for the population's likes or dislikes. The point here is that a number of organizations and groups influence foreign-policy decision making in most countries.

▌ In democracies you have a state's executive leaders, legislative leaders, defense industries and defense leaders, and a wide range of interest groups, plus the media and public opinion.

▌ In Islamic countries, different religious groups vie for power, as in Iraq, with its Sunni and Shiite divisions. In Iran, the authoritarian Shiite clerics have been at odds with more secular-minded educated Iranian citizens.

▌ Russia's President Vladimir Putin's harsh stifling of dissent and political power points to his increasingly strong authoritarian role in foreign-policy decision making. Anti-Kremlin rallies have led to dozens of protesters beaten and detained in 2007.

An International System Level Approach to Decision Making

Scholars have devised numerous models to analyze the decision-making process in foreign policy as discussed below. From among these, we look at four models, each of which gives us a different view of what happens in the foreign-policy–making process.[5]

Foreign-policy Input-Output Model   Figure 5.2 depicts the many actors, pressures, and forces shaping a foreign policy decision. Note their variety, like informal processes, situational factors, and information uncertainty.

FIGURE 5.2

Foreign-policy Input-Output Model

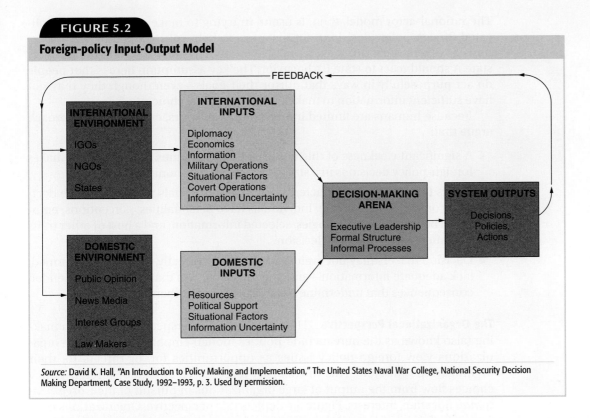

Source: David K. Hall, "An Introduction to Policy Making and Implementation," The United States Naval War College, National Security Decision Making Department, Case Study, 1992–1993, p. 3. Used by permission.

The Rational-actor Perspective   The rational-actor model focuses on the state as the key unit of analysis—and inter-state relations as the setting for analysis. Figure 5.3 depicts this model. In this model, the state is viewed from the perspective of its leader, whom the model assumes is a *rational* (purposeful) decision maker. The leader makes foreign-policy choices calculated to achieve *outcomes* consistent with his or her state's *goals* (for example, defending its territory). To achieve the state's goals, the rational decision maker examines which alternative choice takes priority. The top choice will be the one that will maximize the benefits and minimize the costs in achieving the country's goal. In other words, the decision maker selects the option that has the highest *payoff* in terms of achieving the state's goal. To summarize: people make the decisions for the state—decisions that have options, constraints, and information—so the rational-actor model takes a look at how a leader chooses among alternative courses of action.

An example of where the rational-actor model has been used to understand foreign-policy decisions is the Cuban Missile Crisis, of October 1962. At that time President John F. Kennedy learned that the Soviet leader, Nikita Khrushchev, had positioned nuclear missiles in Cuba. The rational-actor model was used to generate rational answers to the following questions:

1. Why did the Soviet Union decide to place offensive missiles in Cuba?
2. Why did the United States respond to the missile deployment with a blockade?
3. Why did the Soviet Union withdraw the missiles?

FIGURE 5.3

Rational-actor Model

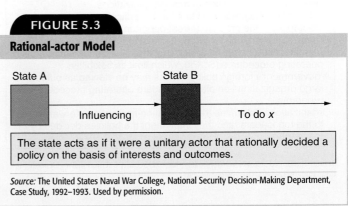

The state acts as if it were a unitary actor that rationally decided a policy on the basis of interests and outcomes.

Source: The United States Naval War College, National Security Decision-Making Department, Case Study, 1992–1993. Used by permission.

The rational-actor model, then, is useful in trying to make sense out of complicated foreign-policy decisions, for instance, to help construct rational explanations as to why a country's leader made certain decisions and to figure out how state A should react to state B's behavior. The key assumption here is that people do act purposefully in ways that mirror their goals—even though they may not have sufficient information to make the most rational choices.

Because humans are limited information processors, critics of this approach argue that:

▌ A significant weakness of this model is that it assumes a state's leader makes foreign-policy decisions in a strictly logical, unemotional manner.

▌ It fails to account for characteristics of the individuals who make these decisions on behalf of the state. Individuals have personalities, perceptions, emotions, beliefs, values, ideologies, selected information, and a host of other traits that affect their "rational" decision.

▌ Decision makers may not evaluate a situation correctly, may be misinformed, lack adequate information—and may make choices that produce unintended consequences that undermine a state's goals rather than advance them.

The Organizational Perspective   The organizational perspective of decision making (also known as the bureaucratic-politics model) emphasizes that large organizations view foreign-policy issues as opportunities for, or threats to, their organization's mission. This means that a large percentage of foreign-policy choices flow from the output of large organizations in pursuit of their *organizational*, not state, interests. Figure 5.4 depicts this perspective. Organizations have set ways of doing things, and they tend to focus on selected aspects of problems in terms of their own goals. Thus, foreign policy is the product of a power struggle between organizations. In addition, organizations determine the information and options available to the top leaders, and these too flow from organizational interests.

America's foreign-policy decision making relative to the Iraq War initiated in 2003 is rife with organizational in-fighting, turf battles, and conflicts of organizational interests. The Defense Department—under the leadership of Donald Rumsfeld before his resignation in November 2006—essentially ran the show with extraordinarily tight control. Former Secretary of State Colin Powell disagreed strongly with Donald Rumsfeld and Vice President Dick Cheney, both of whom were eager for war with Saddam Hussein—and disagreements between these parties continued after the war began and as it became increasingly unpopular.[7] Rumsfeld, for his part, had a low regard for the Department of State—and for Condoleezza Rice as National Security Adviser and as Secretary of State (after November 2004 when she replaced Colin Powell). A growing animus developed between the Central Intelligence Agency (CIA) and the National Security Council (NSC) during the war. In essence,

FIGURE 5.4

Organizational Model of Foreign-policy Decision Making

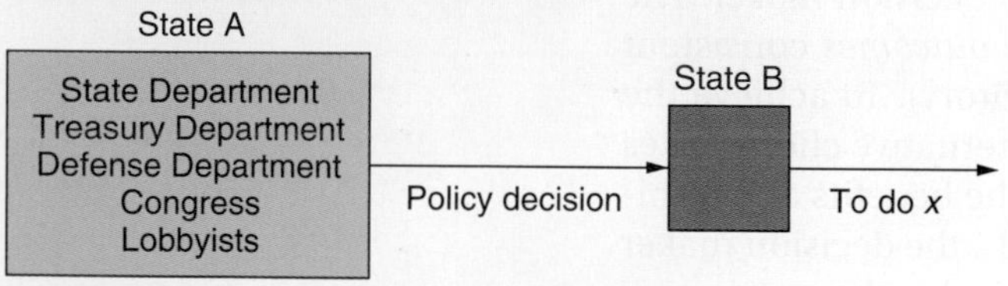

Organizations competing inside State A lead to a policy decision that seeks to influence State B to do x

Government is a collection of many organizations.
Each organization responds to a foreign policy problem in terms of the impact of the problem (threat/opportunity) on the organization.
Organizations are concerned with avoiding uncertainty.
An organization's policy decision is shaped by routine standard operating procedures (SOPs), which limit its flexibility.
A government's foreign policy actions may be viewed as outputs of large organizations employing standard operating procedures and programs.
Organizations determine the information and options forwarded up to the top leaders, and they implement the policies decided by the top leaders.

Source: The United States Naval War College, National Security Decision-Making Department, Case Study 1992–1993. Used by permission.

effective coordination of wartime policies among the relevant U.S. organizations essentially broke down.

The organizational model, as you can see, provides a far more complex and messier picture than does the rational-actor model. As for national decision making in the organizational management of the Iraq war, the coordinating of civilian and military efforts had become so complicated by 2007 that the White House sought to appoint a high-profile *czar* to oversee the wars in Iraq and Afghanistan.

The Individual Perspective   Remember that states do not make decisions, people do—as we saw in the rational-actor model. The individual perspective reminds us that people—wherever they are in the decision-making process—are subject to huge pressures. They must, for one thing, process gigantic quantities of often conflicting information. In dealing with such pressures, individuals such as presidents and foreign-affairs leaders differ in style, perception, and psychological reactions. The human mind has structures for selecting, sorting, storing, recalling, and comparing information to ease decision making. In essence, the goal is simplicity, consistency, and stability when solving problems. When reality is muddled and uncertain, people push even harder for simplicity. For this reason cognitive psychology is used by some political scientists to understand better the human factor in foreign-policy decision making. Cognitive psychology looks at a person's internal mental processes such as problem solving and memory.

U.S. presidents and foreign-policy leaders provide many examples of this process. James David Barber, a scholar of presidential personalities, has examined presidents in terms of "style" (habitual ways of performing political roles), "worldview" (politically relevant beliefs), and "character," or "the way the president orients himself toward life—not for the moment, but enduringly."[8] Barber's discussion of presidential personality types includes Active Positive and Active Negative. The essence of these two types is captured in the following display, which outlines two dimensions of presidential character:

Active Positive   Can-do people—energetic, accept responsibilities. Relatively high self-esteem. Emphasize rational mastery of their job. Self-respecting, happy, open to new ideas, and able to learn from mistakes. Best able to guide the country. Examples: Franklin Roosevelt, Harry Truman, John Kennedy, Gerald Ford, Jimmy Carter, George H.W. Bush and Bill Clinton.

Active Negative   Life seen as a hard struggle to achieve and hold power. Want to know if they are winning or losing, gaining or falling behind. They view their actions (if not the world) as being good or bad. They are gamblers, and their rigidity can plunge the nation into a tragedy. Examples: Woodrow Wilson, Herbert Hoover, Lyndon Johnson, Richard Nixon and George W. Bush.

While active-positive presidents, according to Barber, learn from their mistakes, this may not be so in every case. Some presidents, President George W. Bush, for example, may believe they have not made any mistakes to guide future learning. Note that recent research places George W. Bush in the Active Negative category.

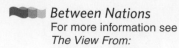
Between Nations
For more information see
The View From:
Mexico City, Mexico
www.BetweenNations.org

Foreign Policymaking in the International Arena

Let us now take a look at foreign-policy decision making in the global arena. Latin America is a good place to begin. Here we see the unintended consequences of America's focus on the war in Iraq with Latin America distinctly out of focus in American foreign-policy decision making. Some of the consequences include:

▌ Loss of U.S. influence in that region

▌ Mistrust of the United States

▌ Rejection of the U.S. posture in the world

It came as no surprise that President Bush's trip to Latin America in March 2007 led thousands to express their disapproval of the visiting president by protesting in city streets. Mayan priests in Guatemala vowed to purify an archeological site of Bush's "bad spirits" after he left, and around two thousand protesters tried to storm the U.S. Embassy in Mexico. Latin America's disenchantment with its northern neighbor stems from two driving forces.

▌ First, President Bush has virtually ignored the region since the 9/11 attacks, instead electing to go to war in Iraq based on false premises. As Latin Americans see it, President Bush simply has not offered effective leadership in helping to improve the quality of life in Latin America since he came to office—apart from trade and anti-narcotics policies.

▌ Second, the two-decades-old U.S.–sponsored drive to privatize state industries and lift trade barriers (neoliberalism's "free market" economics) has excluded vast numbers of the region's poor. Outside of sub-Saharan Africa, Latin America in the early twenty-first century has the world's most unequal distribution of wealth.

As a result of discontent with U.S. decision making and neoliberal economic choices, one Latin American decision maker after another has been elected on platforms dedicated to improving the lives of the lower classes. One in four Latin Americans live on less than two dollars a day, and crime and unemployment is running high.[9] New "Leftist" presidents have come to power—in Argentina, Chile, and Brazil where social democrats occupy the presidency, and in Peru, Mexico, and Colombia where the Left did not win presidential races but proved to be nonetheless powerful forces.

The fiery anti-American Venezuelan leader, Hugo Chavez, was reelected president in December 2006. Chavez called his election victory "another defeat for the North American empire" and has vowed to deepen his socialist revolution.[10] He has close ties with Fidel Castro's Cuba. He met Iranian President Mahmoud Ahmadinejad, when Iran's leader came to Latin America to court some of the leftist leaders of Latin American in his hope to gain allies in his fight against Washington. The objects of Ahmadinejad's courtship include the leaders of Venezuela, Nicaragua, and Bolivia. Chavez's decision making lends itself to the individual perspective model.

A major state-level and regional-level issue facing the United States is illegal immigration from Mexico. Spawned

Hugo Chavez of Venezuela and Lula da Silva of Brazil
They meet at the Latin American summit in Rio de Janeiro, Brazil, November 2004.

Ahmadinejad Embraces Latin America
Iranian president Mahmoud Ahmadinejad and Nicaraguan president Daniel Ortega wave to supporters in Managua. Ahmadinejad, on a January 2007 Latin American tour to round up anti-U.S. allies, promised closer ties to Nicaragua. "Rest assured that we will improve our relations to the point of fulfilling every wish and thing that we desire. It is our will to walk hand in hand," Ahmadinejad said after meeting Ortega. Earlier, the Iranian president had been in Venezuela, where he signed business agreements with President Hugo Chavez, an outspoken critic of George W. Bush. Each proclaimed the other an ideological "brother."

by deepening poverty, loss of land to giant agribusinesses profiting from market economics and the North American Free Trade Agreement (NAFTA), tens of thousands of Mexico's small farmers have been forced to sell their corn-growing land to the food giants. The food corporations have benefited from billions of dollars in subsidies that allow them to pump cheap corn into the Mexican market, where tortillas are a basic food substance. Poor Mexicans consequently have flooded illegally across the border in search of employment, while the United States government struggles with what to do with the estimated 12 million illegal Mexicans living in the United States.

How the United States reacts to this state- and regional-level problem will be shaped not only by America's top individual leaders, but also by U.S. organizations that have a stake in the decision, and by the political process. Then, there is Mexico. Decisions made by Mexico's leaders play a role in the evolving outcome, for example, whether or not Mexico can create more jobs to meet the challenge posed by thousands of unemployed or underemployed Mexicans. If not, the human tide across the border continues. Once inside the United States, having crossed the border illegally, Mexicans want amnesty (citizenship) and have taken to the streets in places like Los Angeles to demonstrate this desire—similar to the street protests against President Bush in Latin America during his March 2007 trip. Demonstrations about immigration policy have occurred across the United States, and have made the issue a factor in the 2008 U.S. presidential campaign.

Immigration Protests
Thousands of demonstrators gather in the streets of downtown Los Angeles to protest legislation that cracks down against illegal immigrants.

In addition to Latin America we can see how foreign-policy decision making plays out in other parts of the world.

▌ Japan: In the Far East, in Japan's new Prime Minister, Yasuo Fukada (elected in September 2007 after the former Prime Minister, Abe Shinzo, resigned) must contend with a complicated multiparty system ridden with many factions and prone to corruption. To stay in power and lead Japan, he must address this problematic internal system, which has contributed to over ten years of economic stagnation. That kind of economy affects the rest of world by holding back global growth. Not so long ago, Japan was the engine of Far East economic growth that helped propel the global economy.

▌ Middle East: Arab countries are non-democratic, with strong authoritarian rulers—albeit not without their own internal factions. Such forces have complicated democracy building in Iraq, to put it mildly, as in the civil war between Shiites and Sunnis, coupled with tribal and clan divisions. Two examples illustrate authoritarian rule as it will impact foreign policy. Egypt is dominated by President Hosni Mubarak, although he faces strong opposition from the Muslim Brotherhood. Saudi Arabia's king rules by decree in accordance with Islamic law (*Shari'a*), with the backing of senior princes and religious officials. The king acts as the ultimate source of judicial power. He is commander-in-chief of the armed forces. He approves and amends international treaties and agreements and regulations by decree. There are no institutional checks on royal authority. As a result, the king has enormous power in foreign policy.

▌ South and Southeast Asia: The links between domestic politics and foreign policy—and the usefulness of the four-perspectives model—are clear too. Although Indonesia, with the world's largest Muslim population, is experiencing a historic shift into democratic government, the country's political system comprises many political parties, ethnic and religious factions, and strong, charismatic individual leaders at the local and regional levels. With much constant political infighting, Indonesia's foreign policy will be subject to these internal domestic pressures as well as to those of the external environment.

▌ Pakistan's president General Pervez Musharraf leads a country notorious for its long record of military involvement in politics, religious political parties, and hard-to-control ethnic groups in its northern regions—a competitive domestic political setting, to say the least.

Pakistan is also well known for harboring al Qaeda and Taliban members, who are even embedded in the security and military forces Musharraf oversees—another complicating political factor in his domestic and foreign decision making. Because Musharraf has been the target of al Qaeda attacks himself, and because Pakistan closely supports the U.S. war on terrorism in return for substantial economic and military aid, Musharraf must crack down on al Qaeda militants now and then, capturing and arresting them when he can. Pakistan is also a good illustration of how individuals influence foreign policy.

▌ Afghanistan is notorious for its multiple ethnic groups, tribes, clans, factions, and warlords. Today these groups have made drugs the dominant feature of Afghanistan's economy, and the warlords have tightened their grip on power. They oversee 90 percent of the world's opium production and supply 90 percent of the world's heroin, connected to international cartels, crime, and large amounts of money.[11] Some people have termed Afghanistan's President Karzai

Afghan Warlord in Poppy Field
There has been a resurgence of chaotic conditions and opium production in Afghanistan.

the mayor of Kabul (Afghanistan's capital) rather than the president of Afghanistan, over which he has far less control.

All in all, then, using the concepts of foreign-policymaking discussed in this section is helpful in knowing what to look for in the settings that shape foreign policies across the globe.

TEST PREPPER 5.2

ANSWERS APPEAR ON PAGE A12

True or False?

_____ 1. While different in many respects, authoritarian and democratic governments use a mostly similar process when developing foreign policy.

_____ 2. For some countries, religion plays an active role in the formulation of foreign policy.

_____ 3. The president of the United States provides the sole voice for American foreign policy.

_____ 4. In most countries, a number of organizations and groups influence foreign-policy decision making.

_____ 5. One of the criticisms of the rational-actor model is that it views a state leader as capable of making foreign-policy decisions in a strictly logical way.

Between Nations
Practice Test Questions
Practice Test 5.2
www.BetweenNations.org

Multiple Choice

_____ 6. At what level of analysis do we focus when examining the role IGOs and NGOs play in influencing the foreign policy of states?
   a. Individual
   b. Substate
   c. State
   d. Regional
   e. International

_____ 7. Which of the following is NOT a difficulty faced by democracies when coordinating foreign-policy agendas?
   a. Clash between the need for secrecy and the public's right to accurate information
   b. Lobbying by interest groups
   c. The role played by an independent press
   d. Public opinion
   e. None of the above

WHAT ARE THE FOREIGN-POLICY REPERCUSSIONS OF 9/11?

 Identify the different phases in the U.S. war on terror; understand the key components of the Bush Doctrine, and be aware of the criticisms of that approach.

The foreign-policy repercussions of 9/11 are dramatic. President George W. Bush declared war on "terrorism" and developed a new national security strategy that became a major decentralizing force in world politics and a source of friction between the United States and much of the international community. The war on terrorism ultimately led the United States and Great Britain to spearhead an attack on Iraq on the mistaken assumption that Saddam Hussein had both WMDs and close links to al Qaeda. Following the invasion and occupation of Iraq, much of the Arab and Muslim world—and much of the rest of the world—distanced itself from these two countries. Several countries that initially joined the U.S., British, and other "coalition forces" in Iraq later pulled out when their citizens working in Iraq were kidnapped or killed by insurgents or when their homeland became the target of terrorist action. Spain is a case in point, as is the Philippines. We now turn to a closer look at the repercussions of 9/11.

America's War on Terrorism

America's war on terrorism, announced by President Bush following the 9/11 attacks on the United States, evolved through several phases. Much of the world *initially* sided with the United States as it directed military force at Afghanistan's Taliban government, which had allowed Osama bin Laden and al Qaeda forces to train and plan the 9/11 attacks in Afghanistan.

In the *second phase* of the America-led war on terrorism, the global alliance began to unravel as differences in strategy and tactics widened the distance between the United States and its allies. For example, the Europeans, as well as the Russians and the Chinese, differed sharply with the Americans, as did much of the Muslim Middle East, when the United States began to talk about attacking Iraq. The Muslim world was especially distressed over U.S. reluctance to intervene more directly in the Israeli-Palestinian conflict and for its perceived pro-Israel bias.

In the *third phase* of America's war on terrorism—as President Bush developed his perceptions of the "axis of evil" (North Korea, Iraq, and Iran), which he had introduced in his January 2002 State of the Union address—cracks between the United States and its previous allies opened still wider. By the end of the summer of 2002, as Congress returned from its recess, President Bush's more pronounced talk of attacking Iraq led to sharp splits between the United States and previous worldwide allies, although the UN did send weapons inspectors back to Iraq for a time.

The fallout from 9/11 was now producing decentralization in world politics, largely because the Bush team seemed prepared to go to war against Iraq even without support from France, Germany, Russia, and China, key members of the UN Security Council (UNSC). While none of these countries doubted that Saddam Hussein was "evil," they preferred to contain Iraq with more UN inspectors backed by UN peacekeeping forces rather than to initiate war. The United States and Great Britain argued that Iraq posed an immediate threat. Other countries of the UNSC did not appreciate the go-it-alone approach of the United States—basically a unilateral approach to a world security issue—even though Great Britain and less-powerful countries joined the U.S.–led action.

In the *fourth* phase, the Bush administration appeared to be moving toward more collective action in cooperation with UN Security Council members against Iraq. In September 2002, President Bush addressed the UN and challenged it to swiftly enforce its own resolutions against Iraq. The next month, the UNSC unanimously approved Resolution 1441, which imposed tough new arms inspections on Iraq and made clear it faced "serious consequences" if it did not cooperate. This phase ended in March 2003, however, when the United States and Great Britain realized they would not have UNSC backing to attack Iraq; in particular, France, Germany, and Russia wanted intensified UN inspections in Iraq instead. The United States and Great Britain then led the attack on and occupation of Iraq in March/April 2003—against the opposition of China, France, Germany, and Russia, members of the UNSC.

That rift between the United States and most of the international community continued to decentralize the world—up to, and after, the transfer of Iraq "sovereignty" to its new governing council in July 2004—and as the country spun out of control into deepening civil war. Several members of the U.S.–led coalition, including Spain and the Philippines, pulled out due to rising terrorist military actions in Iraq. As proposed elections approached in January 2005, Iraq remained in a high state of violent civil conflict. Meanwhile, with the U.S. Defense Department shift of attention (and troops) to Iraq, the situation in Afghanistan deteriorated.

A *new phase* began in May 2007 when the United States sent Secretary of State Rice to attend the international conference on Iraq, held in Iraq. With over fifty countries gathered, Secretary Rice and Iraqi Prime Minister Nuri al-Maliki urged the world to rescue Iraq from chaos and bankruptcy. In addition, the U.S. Secretary of State met with Syria's foreign minister, which was the first such high level meeting between the two countries in several years.

The Bush Doctrine

Let's now turn to what has been called by scholars and policymakers the **Bush Doctrine**—the foreign-policy strategy pursued by the Bush administration in its pursuit of U.S. national security. The term originally referred to the policy expressed by President Bush after the 9/11 attacks: that the United States would make no distinction between the terrorists who committed these acts and those who harbor them. The Bush administration applied this doctrine in its invasion of Afghanistan in early October 2001, once the Taliban government refused to hand over Osama bin Laden. Today the term generally refers to the broader set of policies announced by President Bush in his speech of June 1, 2002, to the graduating class of West Point and expressed in the official National Security Strategy of the United States, published in September 2002. The key components of this doctrine express how the United States will:

Bush Doctrine President George W. Bush's foreign-policy agenda, as published in a document titled "The National Security of the United States" (September 2002). The doctrine emphasizes that the United States will take unilateral preventive action against any country that poses a threat to U.S. security interests, and it may take unilateral action when its interests are threatened.

▌ Engage in a war against what it calls *global terrorism* conducted by terrorists or rogue states.

▌ Exercise its right of self-defense and extend that right in order to authorize a preventive attack if and when the United States or its allies are threatened by terrorists or by rogue states engaged in producing weapons of mass destruction.

▌ Exercise its right to pursue unilateral military action when acceptable multilateral solutions to security threats cannot be found.

▌ Keep U.S. military strength beyond challenge—that is, continue its status as the world's sole military superpower.

▌ Spread liberal democracy and freedom in all regions of the world and strive to build a balance of power that favors freedom. (While not explicitly stated, you can see the shadow of democratic peace theory at work here, namely that the assumption that the more democracies around the world the better.) Democracies, according to the theory, may go to war with non-democratic states, but they remain at peace with each other. (See chapter 2.)

In a global system without world government or enforced international law, the United States simply has to exercise a unilateral preventive war posture, based on military strength beyond challenge, according to the Doctrine. It must look out for its own vital security interests with the use of hard power, whether or not the rest of the international community agrees. Yet in the nation's sharp focus first on Afghanistan and then on Iraq, a number of foreign-policy specialists were deeply concerned that throughout this Bush-Doctrine period, Iran and North Korea were moving ahead in their development of nuclear-weapons programs. These countries could prove a greater threat to the United States and other countries than Saddam Hussein had been, given the on-site, ongoing weapons inspections in Iraq just before the U.S. attack.

Much of the rest of the world did not agree with the U.S. position. The doctrine of preventive war differed from the previous U.S. practice of the doctrine of containment, of deterrence, and of mutual assured destruction during the Cold War. As the U.S. war in Iraq continued after 2003, eventually morphing into a civil war, the Bush Doctrine produced increased criticism for its declaration of American hegemony, unilateralism, and the right to attack anywhere in the world when the United States decided alone that it was in its interests to do so.

Behind the scenes two schools of thought had developed within the U.S. administration. Then–Secretary of State Powell and then–National Security Adviser Condoleezza Rice, plus U.S. Department of State specialists, argued that existing U.S. defense policies should continue. This meant keeping in place the diplomacy of seeking multilateral consensus with the international community for actions against common enemies and the containment of such enemies, as during the Cold War. Opposed to this view were Vice President Dick Cheney, Secretary of Defense Donald Rumsfeld, and other influential neoconservative defense policymakers, including Paul Wolfowitz and Richard Perle. They argued for direct and unilateral action. Their views won the debate, as underscored in the key tenets of the Bush Doctrine.

Criticism of the Bush Doctrine

Critics of the Bush Doctrine, both at home and abroad, have been many and vocal. Among the sharper objections from a variety of sources are the following:

▌ It disrupts the balance of power by advocating that the United States use its military force unilaterally and preventively without international support for military action.

▌ The doctrine's "war on terrorism" is too vague and imprecise in defining the nature of the enemy. The adversary is a worldwide radical Islamic insurgency comprising ideological Islamic militants, not an enemy called "terrorism." Terrorism is a method of military strategy.

▌ The Bush Doctrine violates accepted (centralizing) international obligations and treaties, with actions such as pulling out of the Anti-Ballistic Missile Treaty, and advocating unilateral action and preventive military attacks without gaining acceptance in the international community.

▌ Undermines the UN—a policy that seems strange, given that the United States was one of the key countries pushing for its establishment after World War II.

▌ The doctrine justifies the U.S. attack and occupation of Iraq, which has dramatically alienated Muslims across the globe and decentralized the world. It has produced a foreign policy, bitterly resented by radical Islamic groups, that is generating rising hostility toward the United States and willing followers of radical Islam and recruits for al Qaeda ideology. It is not America's core values and belief system that al Qaeda followers resent but rather U.S. foreign policies in the Middle East.

▌ It has failed to unite the international community to fight radical Islamic militants and failed as well to recognize the role of soft power in world politics.

▌ By sanctioning a war against terrorism and not playing a more balanced role in the Palestinian-Israeli conflict, it has contributed to escalating conflict in that part of the world, notably by legitimizing Israel's war against Palestinian terrorists. As a consequence, the doctrine has created even deeper anti–U.S. sentiment in the Muslim world.

By 2007 the United States found itself virtually alone in a civil war in Iraq, fighting groups with widely different goals, whereas the original coalition in Iraq numbered forty-five—albeit deeply unpopular amongst the citizens of the coalition members. Since the announcement of the Bush Doctrine in 2002 and invasion of Iraq in 2003, the U.S. government has become increasingly alienated from many foreign-policy specialists in the United States and from much of the world. In October 2004, over 725 foreign-affairs specialists in the United States and allied countries signed an open letter opposing the Bush administration's foreign policy and calling for an urgent change in course.[12] The Pew Global Attitudes Project (AGAP) has tracked declining world support for Washington's "global war on terror" and its occupation of Iraq.

Consider the following observation. In 1958 authors William Lederer and Eugene Burdick published a book entitled *The Ugly American*. It became a best-selling fictional account of American arrogance and blundering, corrupt, and incompetent behaviors of Americans in Southeast Asia. It was a devastating portrait of how America was losing the struggle with communism in that part of the world. The book led President Dwight Dwight Eisenhower to study and reform U.S. aid programs in the region. Some would argue that "the Ugly American" is now the view held by many of America's former supporters around the world.[13] Figure 5.5 illustrates the percentage of those polled in countries around

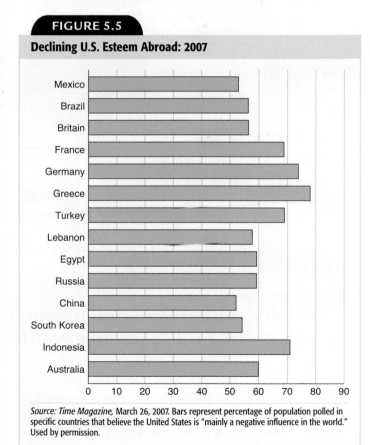

FIGURE 5.5

Declining U.S. Esteem Abroad: 2007

Source: Time Magazine, March 26, 2007. Bars represent percentage of population polled in specific countries that believe the United States is "mainly a negative influence in the world." Used by permission.

the globe that believe the United States is mainly a negative influence globally. Overall, the least admired countries were Russia (40 percent), North Korea (48 percent), the United States (51 percent), Iran (54 percent), and Israel (56 percent). The most admired countries were: Canada, Japan, France, Britain, and China. Still, an interesting point about this table is that none of the countries listed like the United States *less* than fifty percent.

TEST PREPPER 5.3 ANSWERS APPEAR ON PAGE A12

True or False?

_____ 1. Initially the broader international community supported the United States in its war against terror (when the United States was focused on Afghanistan).

_____ 2. While not supported by many countries, the March 2003 invasion of Iraq was supported by a majority of UN Security Council members.

_____ 3. The Bush Doctrine does not call for the United States to remain the world's sole military superpower.

_____ 4. The Bush Doctrine differed from previous U.S. policies of containment and deterrence through its advocacy of preventive war.

Multiple Choice

_____ 5. Which of the following is a criticism of the Bush Doctrine?
   a. The doctrine's war on terrorism is too vague when defining the nature of the enemy.
   b. It violates accepted international treaties such as the Anti-Ballistic Missile Treaty.
   c. It undermines the authority of the United Nations.
   d. It failed to unite the international community against the threat posed by radical Islamic militants.
   e. All of the above

Between Nations
Practice Test Questions
Practice Test 5.3
www.BetweenNations.org

CASE STUDY

The U.S.–Saudi Arabian Relationship

See **www.BetweenNations.org**

 *Between Nations*

JOIN THE DEBATE

Globalization Demands a New Foreign-policy Approach for the Sovereign State

OVERVIEW

The exponential expansion of globalization has raised a major debate in world politics. The big question is whether or not—and if so, to what extent—globaliza-

tion has rendered obsolete traditional foreign policies that sovereign states have pursued over the past three centuries. As we know, states have long been the source of physical security, economic vitality, and political independence for their citizens. Consequently, a state's foreign policy traditionally has focused on how to pursue its vital national interests: physical security, economic strength, and political security on the stage of world politics.

Over time, however, globalization has brought porous borders and interdependence, thus facilitating the exchange of goods, ideas, and information, financial transactions, and institutions to connect people in a global human community. Does this mean that globalization is displacing the older realism (power politics) and idealism (international legal norms to govern state behavior)—as well as traditional balance-of-power and collective security mechanisms—that have guided international relations over the past centuries?

THE PRO SIDE

Yes, globalization clearly has spawned a new international system. Porous borders and interdependence have undermined the capability of states to pursue security, economic growth, and political sovereignty through traditional uses of power, state-to-state relations, and balance-of-power or collective mechanisms.

Specific instances of the limitations of traditional power include:

1. Failures of military force, as demonstrated in the pitfalls of the U.S. rush to war in Iraq.
2. Economic interdependence, as illustrated when a downturn in a single state's economy affects the whole system. The Southeast Asian and Latin American debt crises in the 1990s led to a global economic downturn.

In addition, consider the following facts:

▮ Globalization has placed states in a strategic straitjacket, and national interests must be redefined. Globalized partners have a stake in maintaining their interdependent operations. The use of force to gain strategic advantage or to resolve disputes among globalizing states is irrational—and unlikely. War between the great powers (United States, West European states, China, India, and Japan) is almost unthinkable. Each operates with a strategic straitjacket imposed by globalization.[1]

▮ As Joseph Nye argues, the pawns on the world politics chessboard present the real challenges, such as

non-state actors. New power realities created by globalization include the information-technology revolution, interdependence, and porous borders, through which multiple forms of soft power flow. The new issues on national and international agendas cannot be solved by one country alone.[2]

▮ *New York Times* columnist Thomas Friedman writes that the "inexorable integration of markets, nation-states, and technologies to a degree never witnessed before—in a way that is enabling individuals, corporations and states to reach around the world faster, deeper and cheaper than ever before" simply means that we must think of foreign policies with new techniques and agendas.[3]

In his more recent book, *The World Is Flat*, Friedman argues that the economic playing field has been leveled by the global fiber-optic network into which some 3 billion people are rushing—from China, India, the former Soviet Union, and other countries whose economies have thrown off socialism.[4] These countries are recipients of U.S. outsourcing, while U.S. leaders, according to Friedman, are letting the country's scientific and engineering base erode.

▮ Globalization has produced "wars" that states are losing because they have not adopted new strategies.[5] The stateless, decentralized networks that cannot be fought by traditional foreign-policy techniques are terrorism, drugs, arms trafficking, intellectual property misuse, alien smuggling, and money laundering. Many would argue that the United States is losing its war on terrorism and that, in fact, attacking and occupying Iraq has increased the number of terrorists now opposed to the United States.

▮ The attacks of 9/11 highlight the point that the globalized world in which we live is one where traditional foreign policy and powerful defense systems (including long-range missiles and nuclear weapons) may not protect American citizens.

THE CON SIDE

While globalization may have created new realities within the international system, nation-states and their governments have not disappeared. They remain key players on the international landscape—and most certainly big-country realism and power politics in their foreign policies still make a difference. Consider the following:

▮ Rivalries and security concerns between great and small states still operate in world politics. The United States invaded Iraq in 2003. China is at odds with Taiwan, North Korea with South Korea, and India with Pakistan. States still seek conventional weapons as well as those of mass destruction; the traditional state of war still persists.[6]

▮ If wars between states have become less common, wars within states (civil wars) have been distinctly on the rise. Outside states have found it necessary to intervene through NATO or under UN auspices to prevent such civil wars from spreading regionally. Think of former Yugoslavia during the early 1990s.

▮ Globalization has not created an international society of global citizens, and IGOs frequently have little independence. Globalization has not seriously challenged the profoundly national nature of citizenship. When push comes to shove, national identity and national culture will trump global or international identity.

▮ Some states remain far more powerful than others, and their foreign policies are more dominant than others. Traditional U.S. foreign policy—and the power that backs it—is the prime player in this scheme.

▮ The major national security threat to the Western states today is terrorism. The primary responsibility of a state's government is to protect its people.

QUESTIONS

1. Which side of the issue strikes you as more compelling?
2. Do you see elements of truth on both sides, leaving you somewhere between the two opposing sides of the debate?

NOTES

1. This view is derived from Banning Garrett, Yale-Global, February 2004, http://yaleglobal.yale.edu/display.article?id=3311.
2. See Joseph S. Nye, "American Power and the 2004 Campaign." Project Syndicate, March 2004 Project Syndicate is an international association of 209 newspapers.
3. Thomas L. Friedman, *The Lexus and the Olive Tree* (New York: Farrar, Straus, and Giroux, 1999), 7–8.
4. Thomas L. Friedman, *The World Is Flat: A Brief History of the 21st Century* (New York: Farrar, Straus, and Giroux, 2005).
5. Moisés Naím, "Five Wars of Globalization," *Foreign Policy* (January/February 2003): 29–37.
6. Stanley Hoffmann, "Clash of Globalization," *Foreign Affairs* (July/August 2002): 104–115.

LEARNING OBJECTIVES REVIEW

▶ 1 *Understand how foreign policy translates power into outcomes, and identify the associated core, middle-range, and long-term goals that accompany it.*

- *Foreign policy* is the course of action pursued abroad mainly by a government but also by a nongovernmental organization or individual in quest of some goal. Foreign policy is put into play by the world's states and their governments, IGOs, and NGOs, including militant organizations like al Qaeda. Each tries to employ some form of power and influence—from hard to soft power—to achieve its desired objectives.

- The foreign policy of states involves three elements:
  - an approach to translating hard or soft power (see chapter 4) into policies to pursue core, middle-, and long-range goals
  - a focus on key issues associated with the goals pursued
  - the individuals and groups inside the state (or IGO or NGO) that play a major role in determining foreign policies

- *Power* refers to the objective and subjective capabilities discussed in chapter 4, and *policy* refers to how power gets translated into policies, such as using hard- or soft-power capabilities.

- The highest foreign-policy priority goes to core interests (also known as national interests): territorial security, economic vitality, and protection of the political system.

- Each goal can be achieved by a number of policies. Territorial security, for example, can be achieved via weapon use or acquisition, disarmament, arms control, or alliances. Problems arise in the course of choosing among policy options.

2 ▸ *Understand what factors at each level of analysis affect the formulation of foreign policy and identify the various perspectives used to explain foreign-policy decision making.*

- *Global-level factors* are those broad international influences on foreign policies (like the UN, the World Bank, globalization, and the Internet)

- *State-level factors* are those inherent to the country itself, such as its geographic location and belief system and core values

- *Individual-level* factors are the personality and perceptions of the leader of a country—or nongovernmental leaders who make a big difference in world politics.

- Key perspectives on how foreign-policy decisions are made:
  - The systems approach depicts the many actors, pressures, and forces simultaneously operating to shape a state's foreign-policy decision.
  - The rational dimension or aspect of foreign policy, which focuses on the state as a unitary actor, with no internal forces shaping its decisions.
  - The organizational dimension, which focuses on the important role of organizations in shaping policy outcomes.

  - The individual dimension, in which the focus is people—the unique beliefs, emotions, values, and cognitive processes (how they sift through information and reach conclusions) that each brings to the decision-making table.

3 ▸ *Identify the different phases in the U.S. war on terror; understand the key components of the Bush Doctrine, and be aware of the criticisms of that approach.*

- The foreign-policy repercussions of 9/11 are dramatic. The United States declared war on terrorism and developed a new national security strategy (the Bush Doctrine) that became a major decentralizing force in world politics and source of friction between the United States and much of the international community.

- The war on terrorism ultimately led the United States and Great Britain to spearhead an attack against Iraq under the mistaken assumption that Saddam Hussein had both WMDs and close links to al Qaeda.

- The attack on and occupation of Iraq has led to rising numbers of al Qaeda followers and the isolation of the United States and Great Britain from much of the rest of the world, including some of their traditional great-power allies within the UN Security Council and the international community (France, Germany, and Russia).

- The 9/11 attacks and other expressions of hatred directed at the United States stem not so much from objection to U.S. core values and beliefs but rather its policies in the Middle East, which have alienated many Muslims.

- The Bush Doctrine, with its emphasis on preemptive strikes, potential use of nuclear weapons, and unilateral foreign-policy implications, has decentralized world politics dramatically.

RESOURCES ON THE WEB

To use these interactive learning and study tools, including video and audio multimedia resources, go to **www.BetweenNations.org**.

Practice Tests	Case Studies	Current Events
Audio Concepts	Primary Sources	Daily Newsfeeds from *The Washington Post*
Flashcards	Historical Background	Weblinks for Further Exploration

 *Between Nations*

Intergovernmental Actors

Independent Actor or Tool of the State?

LEARNING OBJECTIVES

1 Define intergovernmental organization, understanding how scope and purpose differentiate organizations from one another.

2 Identify the factors that lead states to join intergovernmental organizations as well as the reasons why a state might not join an IGO.

3 Understand how the UN attempts to manage security, economic, and social issues in world politics as well as issues with the management of the UN itself.

The UN under Attack
The UN attempts to bring peace and security to many parts of the world, but it can also become a target in war-torn areas. In this photo, demonstrators in Kinshasa, the Democratic Republic of Congo, surround a burning UN van during a protest over the capture of the town of Bukavu by rebels.

five permanent members of the Security Council) still retain almost all decision-making power over what the UN does. In fact, among the basic principles of the UN is recognition of the primacy of the nation-state.

It is thus worthwhile reviewing the options that UN member-states have, especially the large ones, for preventing the UN from doing something they don't like.

1. Resolutions from the General Assembly (discussed below) are nonbinding, meaning a country is not obligated to follow them.
2. In the case of the permanent members of the UN Security Council, a veto is sufficient to prevent the UN from using military force.
3. Only the Security Council may make decisions that are binding on all UN members. However, the permanent members may, of course, veto any decision they do not like.
4. Member states may also withhold payment to the UN with a *de facto* financial veto that can prevent the UN from carrying out certain programs. This option is not available to UN members who make very small financial contributions.

To get a better understanding of the nonmilitary aspects of the UN, we now turn to its efforts at managing global economic and social problems.

Managing Global Economic and Social Issues

The UN has developed a number of special agencies to manage the diverse non-military activities of the organization. Table 6.1 lists some of the UN's nonmilitary activities. Some UN organizations help save children from starvation and disease, while others provide help for refugees and victims of disasters. The UN's World Health Organization (WHO) has been a leader in the eradication of diseases like smallpox and tuberculosis, and it is now helping to coordinate the fight against the worldwide AIDS epidemic. The UN has also advanced international rights to

---

TABLE 6.1

Nonmilitary Activities of the United Nations

The United Nations is an intergovernmental organization with an almost endless number of tasks to perform. While it certainly deals with military matters, especially in the Security Council, it also handles many nonmilitary activities, as the list below suggests. You are probably already familiar with some of them.

Branch of the UN	Function
The United Nations International Children's Emergency Fund (UNICEF)	Establishes child health and welfare services around the world.
United Nations Conference on Trade and Development (UNCTAD)	Promotes international trade.
The United Nations Development Program (UNDP)	Provides technical assistance to stimulate economic and social development.
The United Nations Educational, Scientific, and Cultural Organization (UNESCO)	Promotes cooperation in education, science, and culture.
The United Nations Environment Program (UNEP)	Promotes international cooperation on all environmental matters.
The United Nations Industrial Development Organization (UNIDO)	Promotes industrial development, especially among the members.
The United Nations Institute for Training and Research (UNITAR)	Assists the UN to become more effective through training and research.
The United Nations High Commissioner for Refugees (UNHCR)	Promotes humanitarian treatment of refugees and seeks permanent solutions to refugee problems.
The United Nations Population Fund (UNPF)	Assists both developed and developing countries in dealing with their population problems.
The United Nations Research Institute for Social Development (UNRISD)	Conducts research into the problems of economic development during different phases of economic growth.
The Universal Postal Union (UPU)	Promotes international postal cooperation.
The World Health Organization (WHO)	Improves health conditions in developing countries.
The World Intellectual Property Organization (WIPO)	Provides protection for literary, artistic, and scientific works.

protect children and migrant workers, and it has been a major global force for the advancement of the equal rights of women (see chapter 11). We talk more about these organizations in chapters 11–14.

Furthermore, the UN is involved in countering global crime and drugs. In some places, the UN's job is primarily to build democratic institutions. As noted earlier, the UN has sent impartial observers to ensure free and fair elections in many countries. It has also helped armed opposition movements transform themselves into political parties in El Salvador, Mozambique, and Guatemala. Typical examples of UN agencies or missions include the United Nations Angola Verification Mission (UNAVEM III), the United Nations Assistance Mission for Rwanda (UNAMIR), and the United Nations Disengagement Observer Force (UNDOF), which continues to observe a 1974 ceasefire agreement between Israeli and Syrian forces in the Golan Heights.

The General Assembly

The most important body in the UN for dealing with this diverse array of issues is the **General Assembly**. The General Assembly is the only UN body that directly represents all member-states. It is heavily involved in social welfare and economic matters, and it acts as the focal point of activity for the many agencies, committees, and institutions that deal with them. The General Assembly also serves the following functions, typical of national parliaments:

❚ It is a forum for airing ideas and complaints from constituents.

❚ It provides an arena for debate among member-states.

❚ It constitutes an environment for evaluating and approving the UN budget.

From a political perspective, the General Assembly has important internal challenges. As the European colonial era ended in the 1960s, more and more newly independent countries joined the UN. As a result, in many General Assembly debates, vocal opposition to the United States and other advanced industrial countries grew to such an extent that many Americans felt the General Assembly had become a place to bash U.S. foreign policies. Some UN opponents from the United States even complained that the UN was still largely "in the grip of a substantial majority of dictatorial, authoritarian and statist regimes."[17]

The clash within the General Assembly between many of the world's developing countries and the United States reflected a more profound division among UN members: the split between the industrialized countries of the **North** (the developed countries), and the mostly poor, often politically unstable countries of the **South** (the developing countries). This division is also related to how different countries view the mission of the UN.

❚ Southern countries complain that the rules of the international systems, established by the wealthy countries of the world, are structured against them. From their perspective, most of the world's problems, from political instability and ethnic conflict to the AIDS epidemic and population pressures, occur in the Southern states. Some of these problems, they argue, result from policies of Northern countries, especially the United States (see chapter 13 for more details). In their view, then, the UN's mission should emphasize solutions to the problems in the South.

❚ The Northern countries have resisted giving the UN a greater role in addressing Southern concerns. Some Northern states are reluctant, for political or financial reasons, to grant the UN significantly more powers. Many Americans, in particular, resent the anti–U.S. rhetoric of many General Assembly members, and others simply feel the UN is not the right vehicle for effecting change in the South. The North-South and other splits within the UN are likely to persist well into the twenty-first century.

The voice of Southern countries is enhanced by the voting system in the General Assembly. As we noted earlier, every country in the General Assembly is given one vote regardless of size. This puts small countries like Peru and Cambodia on the same level as the United States, India, and China. (The U.S. Senate works in a similar way; regardless of the size of the state, each gets two votes. California or Texas, for example, has no more influence than Rhode Island.) Because the poor countries of the UN vastly outnumber the wealthy states of the North, sheer numbers give the advantage to the South.

General Assembly   A branch of the UN in which each member-state is allotted one vote, regardless of size. It is heavily involved in social welfare and economic matters, and it acts as the focal point of activity for the many agencies, committees, and institutes that deal with UN matters.

The North   Loosely, the advanced industrial democracies of the northern hemisphere. Developed countries.

The South   Loosely, the less developed countries of the southern hemisphere. Developing countries.

Two important points about the General Assembly's influence must be made.

▌ First, unlike the Security Council, the General Assembly is weakened because, for the most part, *it can only make recommendations*. Even though it is involved in a wide variety of activities, it cannot issue binding legislation, and it does not have the legal clout to bring violators to justice. This, of course, also hurts the efforts by Southern countries to achieve their goals.

▌ Second, the General Assembly is weakened by the widely *diverse interests of its members*. Besides the North-South split, the General Assembly is fractured by countries with different religions, cultures, languages, and traditions as well as different territorial, political, and economic interests. General Assembly members even disagree on something the UN claims to uphold: human rights. Religious and cultural splits are particularly evident over issues involving the treatment of women (see chapter 11).

Other Important UN Bodies

There are many other important UN bodies designed for specific tasks. The Secretariat, for example, is the primary administrative organ that runs the UN on a day-to-day basis. It is headed by the *secretary-general* (currently Ban Ki Moon of South Korea), who acts as the UN's chief spokesperson and diplomat. The secretary-general is appointed by the General Assembly upon the recommendation of the Security Council for a five-year term. The Secretariat is also supported by a large staff from over 170 countries.

The Economic and Social Council (ECOSOC) is another of the UN's main organizational bodies. As mandated by the UN Charter, the ECOSOC is responsible for:

▌ promoting higher standards of living, full employment, and economic and social progress

▌ identifying solutions to international economic, social, and health problems

▌ facilitating international cultural and educational cooperation

▌ encouraging universal respect for human rights and fundamental freedoms

In carrying out its mandate, the Council consults with academics and representatives from the business sector. ECOSOC also plays a pivotal role in the UN's dialogue with over 2,600 nongovernmental organizations, many of which help carry out UN programs. As a consequence of its broad scope of responsibilities, ECOSOC receives over 70 percent of the human and financial resources of the entire UN system.

Another important branch of the UN is the International Court of Justice (ICJ). Located in The Hague, the Netherlands, the ICJ handles cases brought by states, not by groups or individuals. The Court is composed of 15 judges elected to nine-year terms of office by the General Assembly and Security Council. Note that the ICJ is different from the International Criminal Court (ICC), which is only loosely affiliated with the UN. The two courts are discussed in greater detail in chapter 10.

The World Bank and the International Monetary Fund

Two of the world's most important international financial IGOs, the World Bank and the International Monetary Fund (IMF), are part of the UN framework. Together with the World Trade Organization (WTO), these IGOs are designed to help manage the international political economy. Shortly after World War II, most of the world's major states felt that a selfish national strategy of "going it alone" in an anarchic world was ultimately destructive. Instead, states sought cooperative ways to rebuild after the destruction of the war and to build institutions and long-term rules that could guide international political and economic life into the distant future. Britain and especially the United States took the lead in setting up the IMF, the World Bank, and the precursor organization of the WTO.

The roles of the IMF and the World Bank (formally known as the International Bank for Reconstruction and Development) increasingly overlap, but their missions have traditionally been quite distinct. The IMF is responsible for overseeing the international monetary system by promoting exchange rate stability and orderly currency exchange relations among its member-states. The goal of the World Bank, by contrast, is to promote the economic development of the world's poorer countries. It assists these countries, for example, through long-term financing of a variety of development projects.[18] We reserve a more detailed explanation of the functions of the IMF and the World Bank for chapter 12.

Managing the UN's Affairs

Like many large organizations, the UN employs thousands of people. Think of the UN as a huge bureaucracy designed to tackle many issues. As with many bureaucracies, managing those thousands of people—scattered across the globe—and other resources can be quite a job. In the following pages, we discuss several management challenges facing the UN. In the 1990s and continuing today, the UN came under intense pressure to improve the management of its budget and streamline its administrative organs. Under separate sorts of pressures, the Security Council has been called upon to reform its membership to reflect better the global political balance of power. Let's now turn to these issues.

Between Nations
Audio Concept
Bureaucracy
www.BetweenNations.org

The UN's Funding and Its Controversies

In order for the UN to undertake any operations, military or otherwise, it needs money. Unlike a sovereign state, however, the UN does not levy taxes. The UN relies on dues and voluntary contributions from UN member-states. The UN budget has three main elements: the regular budget, the peacekeeping budget, and voluntary contributions for specific UN programs and activities. The General Assembly's Committee on Contributions assigns each member-state a percentage share of the budget, ranging from a minimum of .01 percent to a maximum of 25 percent. The top seven contributors to the UN in 2006 were:

- United States (22 percent, or almost $425 million, or $1.42 per person in the United States)[19]
- Japan (19.47 percent)
- Germany (8.66 percent)
- Britain (6.13 percent)
- France (6.03 percent)
- Italy (4.89 percent)
- Canada (2.81 percent)
- Spain (2.52 percent)[20]

Note that as a result of changes in relative economic influence, Japan's contribution drops to 16.6 percent while China's increases from 2.05 percent to 2.66 percent for the 2007–2009 period.

This kind of payment arrangement may seem unfair to the largest contributors, but how much a country pays depends on the size of the country's population, the size of its economy, and its per capita income. For example, because the United States is the wealthiest country in the world, it is expected to pay a higher share. In return, however, the United States is given more UN Secretariat jobs than any other member-state. Recently, for example, the United States has held the top posts at many UN agencies including UNICEF, the UN Development Programme, the World Bank, the World Food Programme, the International Court of Justice, and the Universal Postal Union. The UN has no legal obligation to provide specific jobs to the major contributors; it is more of a political bargain.

The regular UN budget has risen over the last four of five years from $1.48 billion to about $2 billion.[21] This covers the Secretariat operations in New York City and Geneva as well as offices in Nairobi and Vienna, plus five regional commissions. While this figure may sound large, one must put it in the context of the vast number of tasks the UN must perform. In addition, to understand the size of the UN's budget, it helps to compare it to the budgets of other organizations. For example, when compared to the scale of U.S. defense spending (over $600 billion) or even the budget of a major city, the UN's budget seems quite small.

Many countries (for example, the United States) fail to pay their dues to the UN for political reasons or for reasons of real or supposed economic hardship. The UN's budget situation was particularly bleak in 1999, when member states owed the UN almost $3 billion in dues: $1.7 billion for peacekeeping, almost $1.1 billion for the regular budget, and $148 million for international tribunals. In order to pay regular budget expenses, the UN often borrows from peacekeeping funds, which means the UN has been unable to reimburse those countries that have provided peacekeeping troops and equipment.[22] The largest debtor has been the United States, which at one point owed the UN $1.67 billion, or two-thirds of the total due. The United States actually risked losing its vote in the General Assembly by not paying its bill at the end of 1999. This predicament was resolved by a last-minute compromise. U.S. pressure on the UN to reduce its contributions from 25 percent of the UN budget to 22 percent finally succeeded in early 2001, and in September 2001, the United States finally agreed to pay its UN dues of $862 million. Many less developed countries did not understand why the world's most prosperous country, in the midst of unprecedented economic growth, should demand making fewer UN contributions. Nevertheless, by the end of 2006, the United States again owed the UN back dues, this time $291 million.[23]

The UN's Administrative Reforms

As controversial as the UN budget is, the bureaucracy of the United Nations may be even more so. We now turn to the politically charged, but unrelated, issues of mismanagement and membership in the Security Council.

Examples of UN waste and mismanagement are not hard to find. For instance, in the late 1990s, the Committee on Missing Persons in Cyprus hadn't found a single missing person in over twenty years. The committee was kept alive in part because Cyprus has considerable influence in the U.S. Congress.[24] Other cases have involved black-market operations, bribery, and egregious waste of resources.[25] It was primarily at the insistence of the United States that the UN cut down on waste, fraud, and mismanagement. From the U.S. perspective, reform essentially meant cutting back on UN staff resources and budgets. Kofi Annan, Secretary-General at the time, said in an interview in 1997 that after "50 years of existence, like all organizations, we've picked up some excess baggage that we are trying to shed."[26] By the end of the 1990s, the UN had, in fact, made major cuts in its labor force, and budget levels were frozen. Despite improvements, however, the UN still experienced important organizational problems. Investigations continue into the so-called oil-for-food program in Iraq. According to Annan, the oil-for-food program accomplished "one of the largest, most complex and unusual tasks ever entrusted to the [UN] Secretariat." Despite these positive aspects of the program and the praise from the former head of the UN, independent inquiries, led by the well-respected American Paul Volcker, found widespread corruption and mismanagement of the program. According to the U.S. Central Intelligence Agency, Saddam Hussein exploited the program, earning some $1.7 billion through kickbacks and surcharges, and $10.9 billion through illegal oil smuggling.[27]

Reforming the Security Council

Another administration issue, also highly politicized, is reforming the membership of the UN Security Council. The basic problem is that Security Council membership has barely changed since its founding sixty years ago. The permanent five members once spoke for about 40 percent of the world's population but now account for only 29 percent.[28] Some states that do not have permanent seats on the Security Council play significant roles in world politics and make important contributions to the UN. Moreover, membership is poorly represented geographically. For example, no Latin American or African country has a permanent seat, nor does an Islamic state. Hence the call to reform the membership of the Security Council.

Many Security Council reform proposals have circulated over the years. One potential solution to the Council's antiquated membership is to provide a permanent seat to a representative country from each region of the world. Three countries, one each from Africa, Asia, and Latin America, could then have a permanent seat. The seat could rotate among countries in each region. In late 2003, Kofi Annan set up a "high-level panel of eminent personalities" to examine other potential Security Council configurations. One proposal involved expanding membership from fifteen to twenty-four states in three tiers.

▌ The first tier would include the existing permanent members, each of which would retain the veto.

▌ The second tier would consist of seven or eight states elected on a regional basis for a renewable term of four or five years. Japan, Germany, Brazil, India, and South Africa could be in this tier.

▌ The third tier would involve rotating regional members elected for a nonrenewable two-year term (as it is now).

Negotiations have continued, and other plans have been debated, but no solution has been achieved.

The fall-back position, of course, is no solution. Often when countries cannot agree among themselves on how to reform their organization, they make no changes at all. Granting other states the special status of "permanent member" with veto power doesn't sit well with the existing permanent members, who would have to give up some of their influence to accommodate the new arrivals. Some states oppose granting permanent membership to one state because they feel just as worthy. Germany could make a strong case for permanent membership, but Italy could oppose the move until it, too, got a permanent seat. Or, for example, why should Brazil get a seat if Argentina does not?

In spite of the sometimes obvious flaws in the UN administration, public support for this IGO remains strong around the world. Support in the United States has been substantial over the last thirty years until recently. By the late 1990s, the vast majority of those polled in the United States—72 percent—thought the United States should not act alone to reduce international crises without the support of its allies.[29] According to a 2002 study by the Chicago Council on Foreign Affairs, 57 percent of Americans said it should be a very important foreign-policy goal to strengthen the UN.[30] Over the past several years, however, favorable attitudes toward the UN in the United States have declined. For example, in 2006, only 31 percent of those surveyed said that they had a positive opinion of the UN.[31] A Gallup Poll in 2007 found that 66 percent of Americans surveyed thought that the UN was actually doing a poor job.[32] Nevertheless, according to Daniel Drezner of Tufts University, the majority of Americans support giving up America's veto in the UN Security Council if it means a more effective global body.[33]

Assessing the UN's Effectiveness

Has the UN been an effective IGO? An assessment of its effectiveness depends on one's expectations. Despite a recent drop in the number of war casualties worldwide,[34] the number of wars since the founding of the UN has increased, and violence is still a core component of world politics. A partial explanation is that the UN does not have the military power to prevent or end complex disputes. For example, the UN's peacekeeping budget is around $5 billion a year which may sound like a lot of money, but it accounts for only 0.5 percent of global military spending.[35] In fact, the UN spends less each year on peacekeeping than the City of New York spends on its police department.[36] As we noted earlier, the UN does not have its own army. This reflects the fact that UN members are sovereign states that are unwilling to grant such important authority to the UN (see chapter 3).

Social and economic problems around the world also seem worse today than ever before. In addition, the UN was sidelined in one of the world's most important event in years: the U.S.–led war against Iraq. Not only was the UN bypassed in the decision to go to war, it played only a restricted role (helping put together the Interim Iraqi Authority, for example) in the stabilization of Iraq since the end of the main military operation. Thus, one might get the impression that the UN is relatively ineffective regarding both its security and non-security missions. However, as the UN's second Secretary-General, Dag Hammarskjöld, liked to say, the UN was not created to take humanity to heaven but to save it from hell. And as Pulitzer Prize–winning author Samantha Power asserts, "Even escaping hell requires an international organization that is up to the job."[37] In some ways, but not all, the UN has been effective. For an overview of the strengths and weaknesses of the UN, see "The United States Should Leave the United Nations."

When the UN has been ineffective, the root of the problem has often been linked to a problem inherent in all IGOs: when member-states essentially have full control over the actions of the IGO, *they should share both the credit and the blame for its successes and failures*. Moreover, the UN should not be blamed for every war that breaks out; that implies unrealistic expectations about its capabilities.

If we can't expect the UN to prevent all wars, what *can* we expect? The UN does have influence to foster peaceful relations between countries that previously were at war, thanks in part to its legitimacy among the nations of the world. Since 1945, the UN has been credited with negotiating over 170 peaceful settlements that ended regional conflicts. Some observers believe UN legitimacy would help achieve greater stability in Iraq.

What will be the role of the UN in the near future? As you learned in chapter 1, it is often hard to make predictions in world politics. The war in Iraq that began in 2003 may have permanently altered the role of the UN. Some observers argue that when large states act against Security Council wishes—such as the United States waging war against Iraq—the UN becomes politically irrelevant. And there are some in the United States who demand withdrawal from the UN. The UN's demise, however, is unlikely. For example, as the depth of postwar problems in Iraq became apparent to the Bush administration, the United States began turning more— although not much more—to the UN for help. It is likely that the UN will struggle along with scarce resources and a divisive set of member-states to address security, social, and economic problems. At least for now, the UN will remain an ambitious but restricted intergovernmental organization.

TEST PREPPER 6.3

ANSWERS APPEAR ON PAGE A12

True or False?

_____ 1. The primary goal of the United Nations is the establishment of a single world government.

_____ 2. The most powerful body within the United Nations is the General Assembly.

_____ 3. The Security Council uses a unanimity voting system while the General Assembly uses a majority voting system.

_____ 4. Plans for implementing Security Council reform are fairly uncontentious and have the approval of a majority of the permanent members of the Council.

_____ 5. The top seven contributors to the UN in 2006 were: the United States, Japan, Germany, Britain, France, Italy, Canada, and Spain.

Multiple Choice

_____ 6. Permanent members of the UN Security Council have what limitation placed on their membership?

   a. They may only use their veto power once per year.

   b. They are not allowed to vote on issues where they have a conflict of interest.

   c. They are required to provide foreign assistance to less powerful Security Council members in their geographic region.

   d. They must provide peacekeeping troops for any mission they authorize.

   e. None of the above

_____ 7. Which of the following is an option available to *all* UN member-states who wish to prevent the UN from doing something?

   a. Ignoring resolutions passed by the General Assembly

   b. Preventing the UN from using force by a veto vote in the Security Council

   c. Appealing to the International Court of Justice to prevent the UN Secretary General from taking his post

   d. Using the ECOSOC as a buffer to carve an exception to human rights regulations

   e. None of the above

_____ 8. The largest debtor to the United Nations has been:

   a. China   d. Russia

   b. France   e. United States

   c. Iraq

Between Nations
Practice Test Questions
Practice Test 6.3
www.BetweenNations.org

WHAT IS THE EUROPEAN UNION, AND HOW DOES IT WORK?

 Be able to identify and explain the functions of the key institutions that make up the European Union and discuss its prospects for the future.

While the UN is a *global* IGO, many *regional* organizations exist as well. The main example of a regional IGO that we present in this chapter is the European Union. Many other regional organizations, including the African Union (AU), NAFTA, the Organization of American States (OAS), and the Association of Southeast Asian Nations (ASEAN), are international organizations with more limited scope and jurisdiction. The AU, as we discussed earlier in the chapter, has existed for only a few years and has not developed the extensive degree of policy coordination found in the EU. NAFTA, for the most part, only addresses economic issues, notably freeing trade among its members. The EU, as you will see, goes much further than both of these IGOs.

The European Union is a unique phenomenon in the history of the world, especially because it brings together states that, throughout history, have waged war against one another. Remember, for example, that Germany and France went to war in 1870, and almost all of Europe fought in World Wars I and II. What began in the 1950s primarily as an economic-oriented organization of six West European countries has evolved into the most complex and integrated set of institutions anywhere in the world.[38] The EU now comprises twenty-seven democratic member countries from west, central, and eastern Europe representing 490 million people. The U.S. population, by contrast, is roughly 300 million.

The broad scope of the EU's responsibilities is reflected in its three "pillars."

- Economic aspects
- Common foreign and security policies
- Justice and home affairs

The *economic aspects* of the EU make up the first pillar in the EU's framework. Most EU laws deal with economic matters among the member-states. In addition, several EU countries have pushed economic cooperation to such an extent that they have even created their own currency, the euro. To manage the euro, the EU established the European Central Bank. So far, thirteen EU member-states have given up their national currency in favor of the euro. Thus, for example, there are no more French francs, German deutschemarks, and Italian lira. Notably missing from the euro-zone are Britain, Denmark, and Sweden.

The second pillar covers *common foreign and security policies*. Through the EU's third pillar, *justice and home affairs,* the EU states coordinate their policies to address immigration and drug trafficking and to cooperate more on border controls. This area has grown in importance with the threat of terrorism. The EU also has highly developed institutions including a trans-European parliament and Court of Justice.

Thus, no other IGO can match the EU in depth of institutional structure or the scope of policies under its jurisdiction. The next section of the chapter explores the historical roots of the modern EU. After that, we provide an overview of the main EU institutions, the impact of EU voting rules, and the EU's constitution.

This section of the chapter concludes by looking at the future opportunities and challenges facing the EU.

The Origins of the European Union

After centuries of warfare between empires and states, why did European countries create the most comprehensive set of international institutions of all time? We can offer five main reasons for why countries with a historical background of rivalry and warfare chose to work together. The first three are primarily economic; the others are more political and military in nature.

The Rationale for European Cooperation

1. European cooperation began in the late 1940s with the need to rebuild war-torn economies. Many European countries realized that going it alone would not be sufficient to transform their struggling economies. Assistance from the U.S. Marshall Plan was helpful in this regard.
2. A lesson from the Depression era and from World War II was that when states create significant barriers to trade, economic conditions worsen and international relations become more tense. Thus, the Europeans sought to lower trade barriers and enhance economic competition.
3. The six founding EU member states, as well as the states that joined later, recognized the benefits of *economies of scale*—that is, they saw the advantages of combining their resources in order to become more competitive internationally. Over time, this issue would become more prominent in the context of competition with the United States, Japan, the newly industrializing countries (NICs) of Asia, China, and others.
4. A more cohesive Western Europe was viewed as being better able to prevent the spread of communism, which was threatening on two fronts. In the 1950s, Western Europe was concerned about an invasion by the Soviet Union and its allies. In addition, communist parties had made strong inroads in the *domestic* politics of some European countries, notably France and Italy. During World War II, the French and Italian communists underground had fought heroically against the Nazis, and the postwar electorate rewarded them with many votes.
5. In the immediate post–World War II period, many feared a resurgent Germany—the country that had been fully or partially responsible for three major wars in Europe in two generations (1870–1945). By integrating Germany economically and militarily into the EU, it was hoped that German militarism would be tamed and World War III would be less likely to occur.

The Creation and Expansion of the European Community

The first step in the creation of the EU was the establishment of the European Coal and Steel Community (ECSC) in 1952. Created to manage the commercially and militarily important coal and steel industries, the ECSC also showed that the French and Germans could actually get along and that Germany and Italy could be trusted partners. The ECSC was also important because it created a set of institutions that would later evolve into the institutions of the EU that we know today. The ECSC thus taught its member states, some with historically deep animosities, that they could cooperate in a vital sector and that the new international institutions with independent political power could function to the benefit of all.

Between Nations
For more information see
European Union
www.BetweenNations.org

With the signing of the Treaty of Rome in 1957, France, Germany, Italy, and the Benelux countries (Belgium, the Netherlands, and Luxembourg)—the six members of the ECSC—formed three new European "communities": the European Atomic Energy Community (Euratom), the European Defense Community (EDC), and the European Economic Community (EEC). Unlike the EEC, both Euratom and the EDC proved ineffective, which is one reason why some old-timers continue to call the European Union the EEC.

EU Membership

EU membership has expanded—known as *widening*—on several occasions since 1957. Figure 6.3 shows the old and new members of the EU. In 1973, for example, the EU grew from the original six members to nine with the admission of Britain, Ireland, and Denmark. In the 1980s, Greece (1981), Spain (1986), and Portugal (1986) joined. Although not technically considered an expansion of the EU, East Germany became part of the EU in 1990 after it was reunified with West Germany. In 1995, Austria, Finland, and Sweden were admitted. The most ambitious widening occurred in 2004 with the addition of eight central and eastern European states

FIGURE 6.3

An Expanded European Union

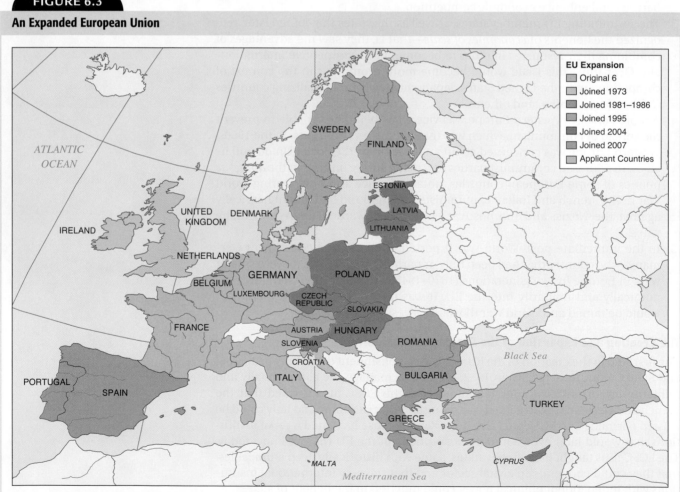

Unity in Diversity
The European Union holds one of its first major meetings after its enlargement from fifteen to twenty-five member-states in Rome, October 2004.

as well as Malta and Cyprus. The most recent additions to the EU were Bulgaria and Romania which joined in 2007.

The Main European Union Institutions

The functioning of the European Union is based on a shifting balance among the twenty-seven member-states and both intergovernmental and supranational actors. Five institutions together handle most of the EU's affairs. In some respects, some of these appear to act like the main institutions in a typical country that has judicial, executive, and legislative branches. Appearances, however, can be deceiving. We address each of these institutions in turn:

▌ The European Council
▌ The Council of the European Union (also known as the Council of Ministers)
▌ The European Parliament
▌ The European Commission
▌ The European Court of Justice

Of these, the two that are primarily intergovernmental are the European Council and the Council of Ministers.

The European Council

The European Council is a group that consists primarily of the heads of government and state (HOGS) and foreign ministers of the member-states. Every six months (or more frequently, if there is a crisis), the leaders of the twenty-seven member-states gather to discuss major political issues and practices. This is really the only time that national politicians (prime ministers and presidents) *directly* affect the governance of the European Union. Even though this is the only main EU organization that does not meet daily, its influence can be profound in setting the overall agenda for the EU.

The Council of the European Union

The Council of the European Union (often called the Council of Ministers) is a central legislative body that meets daily, unlike the European Council. This body has considerable influence because it has final say on most important pieces of EU legislation. The Council of Ministers is made up of at least one minister from each of the twenty-seven member-states; thus, each meeting should have at least twenty-seven people. In actuality, many councils exist, depending on the policy area. What helps give the Council of Ministers its intergovernmental flavor is that the ministers' main responsibility is to the home government first. The Swedish fisheries minister, for example, tries to push forcefully for what is best for Sweden at the fisheries council meeting.

Leadership in the Council of Ministers rotates among the member-states every six months. The country that holds the council presidency at any time is responsible not only for providing overall direction of the EU agenda but also for chairing (leading) all the council meetings. The six-month period was chosen in part because it allows many countries the opportunity to lead council activities. The time frame, however, is too short for any one country to dominate the others. A drawback, of course, is that the progress made by one council presidency may not be maintained in the subsequent presidency. This often happens because the country taking over the council presidency has a different agenda. The EU tries to get around this problem by having a *troika*—that is, cooperation among the current, past, and incoming council presidencies.

The European Commission

Whereas the Council of Ministers does a great deal of the EU's legislative work, most of the executive power in the EU resides with the Commission, whose members are nominated by the Commission president and then approved by the European Parliament.[39] It is made up of twenty-seven officials from all the member-states, and each commissioner is responsible for a different policy area, such as foreign policy, agriculture, fisheries, relations with less developed countries, and so on. The commissioners are supposed to act in the interests of the EU as a whole, independently of national governments. This contrasts with the Council of Ministers, whose members push what's best for their own country first. What are the functions of the Commission?

▌ The most important role of the Commission is to propose legislation. With a few exceptions, the Council of Ministers cannot pass legislation unless it is proposed by the Commission.[40]

▌ Another important function of the Commission is ensuring that EU treaties are being followed.

▌ The Commission plays a key role in ensuring that EU legislation is implemented. Most of the policy implementation is handled by the member-states (because they have the personnel and resources, and the Commission does not), but the Commission oversees the entire process.

▌ The Commission is a key player in the EU's budget process.

▌ The Commission helps varying sides (governments, companies, interest groups, or individuals) reach compromises when they have a dispute.

▮ The Commission mediates differences between the other institutions of the EU.

▮ The Commission represents the EU as a negotiating unit in trade negotiations such as those with the WTO.

All in all, the Commission has enormous responsibilities and is viewed by the public as the key supranational institution in the EU.

The European Parliament

The legislative responsibilities of the EU are shared between the Council of Ministers and the European Parliament, to which we now turn. The 732-seat European Parliament (EP) is the most visible part of the EU to average citizens. Members of the EP (or MEPs) are the only EU officials for whom citizens actually get a chance to vote, which makes the EP a unique international body. The EP also differs from the other main EU institutions in that it is organized in ideological or party groups. There is a Socialist party group, a mostly Christian Democratic group, a group called the Alliance of Liberals and Democrats for Europe, and others. In each of these party groupings are citizens of different EU countries who look out not just for their country's national interests but for the agenda of their party group as well. By contrast, the Council of Ministers is based on national representation first and functional area of expertise second. So, the EP is supranational in the sense that its members are supposed to be loyal to their party ideology and Europe first.

Some powers of the EP are similar to those of national legislatures.

▮ The EP provides an arena for airing the concerns of EU citizens.

▮ It issues oral and written questions to the Council and Commission.

▮ It clarifies, criticizes, and reviews proposed legislation.

▮ It can dissolve and censure the Commission with a two-thirds vote. The EP almost dissolved the Commission in early 1999 (because of mismanagement and corruption), but the Commission, under pressure, chose to resign instead.

▮ The EP plays an important role in EU budgetary matters.

The international composition of the EU makes the EP different from national parliaments in many important respects. The most important difference is that the EP is the weakest of the EU institutions. The advice of the EP is often ignored by Council and Commission members, in large part because the EP's opinions are not legally binding. Another important difference is that the EP's political parties have members from different countries. The two largest political groups are the Christian Democrats (the European People's Party, or EPP) and the Socialists, whose members come from every EU member-state.

As noted, compared to the other EU institutions, the EP remains relatively weak. But its influence has grown steadily as EU officials and the public recognize the need for more democratic input into how the EU functions. The EP has gained influence using preexisting powers. The landmark decision by the Commission to resign in early 1999 reflected the EP's determination to force it to acknowledge and fix problems of mismanagement, corruption, and nepotism. When the Commission did not address these problems, the EP began proceedings to throw out the entire Commission (because it couldn't impeach individual commissioners).

Additional EP power has more frequently come from new treaties. The Amsterdam Treaty, which took effect in 1999, and the proposed constitution are expected to make the EP the legislative equal of the Council of Ministers in many policy areas, including judicial cooperation in civil matters (except family law), antidiscrimination measures, and specific industrial policy support measures.[41]

The European Court of Justice

The EU's judicial branch helps make the EU unique among all international organizations. In short, no other IGO in the world has such a court of justice. World War II taught many Europeans that international relations should be driven by law, not by power. The Europeans also came to understand that common policies (in agriculture, coal, and steel, for example) require a common legal framework. As a result, by the start of the twenty-first century, the EU had built up an impressive body of legal documents, although not a constitution in the American sense. In 2004, however, the EU completed work on its first constitution,[42] designed to amalgamate the various treaties and acts that had accumulated since the founding of the EU in 1957.

At the apex of the EU's legal system is the European Court of Justice (ECJ), made up of twenty-seven judges and eighteen advocates general. The ECJ is assisted by nine advocates general. They are all appointed by the member-states and serve renewable six-year terms. The extended EU's legal system consists of the Court of First Instance, the Court of Auditors (which performs functions similar to the American Government Accountability Office), and a parliamentary ombudsman (who hears complaints made against EU institutions).

The ECJ is the ultimate arbiter of laws made by the EU. As with rulings of the U.S. Supreme Court, ECJ rulings cannot be appealed. The rulings are binding on citizens of the EU as well as on the governments of the EU. What gives the ECJ considerable clout (and demonstrates its supranational character) is that when EU law conflicts with the laws of a national government, EU law takes precedence.

When countries create such an international legal structure, it of course implies that member-states have given up a lot of sovereignty. To put this in perspective, consider the following question: Would United States citizens be willing to accept an arrangement whereby the United States as a whole, its states, and its companies agreed to abide by an international legal body when the international legal body overruled the U.S. Supreme Court?

How Voting Matters in the EU and in IGOs in General

Voting in the European Union is just as important as it is in a democratic nation-state—and, as we noted earlier, how decisions are made can be just as important as the decisions themselves. We provide an overview of the EU's voting methods and note interesting parallels with what you've learned about voting in the United Nations.

The method of voting in the EU depends on many things. The most important thing is to know that each EU institution uses a different method. The European Council, for example, generally makes its decisions by consensus.[43] The Commission, ECJ, and EP tend to vote along majority lines.[44] It is the Council of Ministers, however, where we need to focus our attention. Why? Because the Council is where nation-state influence in the EU is most direct on a day-to-day basis, and because the Council often has final say on EU legislation.

As you learned in the context of UN Security Council voting, *unanimity* voting means that if just one country vetoes a proposal to use military force, the UN cannot use military force. Unanimity voting is also used in the Council of Ministers in limited circumstances, such as when a member-state fears its vital national interest is at stake. It is used, for example, on decisions to add new countries to the EU and in the areas of taxation, asylum and immigration, and foreign and security policy. Just as with the five permanent members of the UN's Security Council, each member-state of the EU has veto power when the unanimity voting rule is used.

Over time, EU member-states came to realize that the extensive use of the veto was hurting the EU's ability to get important legislation passed. The problem was summed up nicely by former Belgian Prime Minister Jean-Luc Dehaene in 1999: "If you keep unanimity, you have immobility."[45] As a result, the EU has used other voting rules for a growing number of policy issues. Sometimes, simple majority voting is used. A simple majority is achieved with support from more than 50 percent of the countries.

Another commonly used voting rule is **qualified majority voting (QMV)**. Under the QMV rule, the larger countries have more votes than the smaller countries. Since the EU expanded in 2004,[46] for example, Germany, France, Italy, and the United Kingdom each have twenty-nine votes, while smaller Austria and Sweden get ten votes each, and tiny Malta gets only three.[47] For a qualified majority to pass legislation, a total of 255 out of 354 votes must be in favor of the measure.

Qualified majority voting (QMV) Associated with the Council of the European Union (Council of Ministers), a voting rule in which the larger countries have more votes than the smaller countries and no country has a veto.

TABLE 6.2

How Different Voting Systems Matter

In IGOs, states behave differently when voting rules change. In addition, some voting systems are better than others if the IGO wants to get work accomplished. In general, for an IGO to get things done, it may need to have voting rules that limit national control. Think of voting systems as falling along a continuum, with ease of decision making at one end and safeguarding of national sovereignty at the other. Consider the following diagram.

Voting Method	Implications for Sovereignty	Implications for Efficiency	Benefits for Big vs. Small Countries	Used by (Examples)
Unanimity Voting	Best voting system for maintaining sovereignty.	Because every member has a veto, it is often hard to get things accomplished.	Because this is the best system for maintaining sovereignty, it is helpful to small as well as big states.	▮ UN Security Council ▮ EU Council of Ministers ▮ Organization for Economic Cooperation and Development
Majority Voting	Not very good for preserving national sovereignty.	Very good, because it takes many countries to block legislation.	Small countries tend to benefit most because they are much more numerous.	▮ UN General Assembly ▮ EU Council of Ministers
Qualified Majority Voting (Weighted Voting)	Not as good as unanimity voting but better than majority voting.	Not as efficient as majority voting but better than unanimity voting.	Big countries are given more votes, but small states may actually come out the winner (e.g., compare Luxembourg's population with Germany's).	▮ EU Council of Ministers ▮ The IMF and World Bank (based not on population but on level of financial contribution)

QMV matters a great deal because, unlike unanimity voting, it forces states to compromise to get what they want. Refer to Table 6.2, which compares voting methods. Note the contrast in the differing goals and outcomes of these different voting systems. Since November 2004, in response to the ten-member expansion of the EU, a qualified majority is reached if (a) a majority of member-states (in some cases, a two-thirds majority) approve, and (b) a minimum of votes is cast in favor—which is 72.3 percent of the total. In addition, a member-state may ask for confirmation that the votes in favor represent at least 62 percent of the total population of the EU. If this is found not to be the case, the decision will not be adopted. While this may sound complicated, and it is, the EU sought to meet the demands of big and small states as well as to manage better the trade-off between decision-making efficiency and the protection of individual state interests—all of which were important, by the way, during the constitutional debates among the thirteen American colonies.

The Future of the European Union

The EU faces several challenges as it looks to the future. Europeans are concerned, for example, about reducing unemployment and the corresponding challenge of improving economic competitiveness vis-à-vis the United States, Japan, and many other countries. In addition, the EU has concerns that face many nation-states, like stemming the flow of illegal drugs and reducing the threat of international terrorism. All of these issues are directly or indirectly related to globalization. The EU must also contend with two all-embracing issues: adjusting to the 2004 and 2007 membership expansions and making institutional changes to cope with it. Let's look at both of these issues in turn.

The Opportunities and Challenges of EU Expansion

The EU's 2004 expansion and the smaller expansion in 2007 are viewed with a mixture of admiration and hesitation. On the political level, the EU's embrace of many former communist countries is considered a vital step in closing a difficult chapter in European history. The countries of Central and Eastern Europe have committed themselves to a westward orientation—away from Russia—because the West offers a more secure and independent future and because of the West's greater economic opportunities compared to Russia's. They have committed themselves to a democratic, capitalistic future.

Nevertheless, it will take some time for the new members to become fully integrated, let alone economically competitive, with the rest of the EU member states. While the EU's most recent member-states add a large population to the EU, they do not add much economically and are well below the EU average in GDP per capita. According to the British magazine *The Economist,* if the new members managed only 3 percent growth (which is actually quite good), it will take them ninety years to catch up with the fifteen EU members before the 2004 expansion.[48]

A United States of Europe? Institutional Changes to the EU

If one plots the trend of political and economic integration in EU history, one may get the impression that we will soon see a United States of Europe, or U.S.E. Since its founding in the 1950s, the EU has integrated more and more. An increasing number of policy areas are within the EU's jurisdiction, including monetary policy, and others, such as common foreign and security policies, are being addressed more forcefully. In addition, EU decision making is occurring more often at the supranational level (for example, with more power granted to the European Parliament and greater use of QMV in the Council). These centralizing developments—of greater policy coordination and supranationalism—are known in EU jargon as *deepening*. One scenario for a United States of Europe envisions the following institutional arrangement as deepening continues:

▌ Judiciary: European Court of Justice

▌ Executive: Commission

▌ Legislative: Council of Ministers (similar to the U.S. Senate) and the European Parliament (similar to the U.S. House of Representatives)

This scenario is possible, but it is hard to say under what circumstances it might actually materialize.

▌ First, one should be cautious about assuming that the EU will inevitably progress, with one policy area spilling over into another until all policies are handled by the EU. Historically, Europeans have always been reluctant to give up national sovereignty to the EU. Many Europeans are unhappy about the powers that have already shifted from their own governments to the so-called Eurocrats in Brussels, Belgium (the quasi-capital of the EU). It is thus possible that the integration of EU countries will reach a certain level of deepening and then stop. Many EU states, for example, do not use the euro. Nationalist feelings run deep in Europe, and people still identify more with their own country than they do with the complicated and seemingly remote institutions of the European Union.

▌ Second, when the Commission was forced to resign in 1999 over corruption and incompetence charges, the member-states became increasingly concerned about granting it more powers. Their reluctance undermines the idea of the Commission as the only institution with executive powers.

▌ Third, even though the EP has gained considerable influence since the founding of the EU, there is still significant resistance to making it a truly effective legislative body.

▌ Fourth, the EU has exhibited and will continue to exhibit a serious legitimacy problem. To put it bluntly, the EU does not have very democratic institutions. It is often mentioned with irony that if the EU were a state and applied to join the European Union, it would be turned down on the grounds that it was not a democracy.[49] As you now know, the only democratically elected institution in the EU is the EP, but the EP does not appear to have much relative clout. Further, in the 2004 EP elections, for the first time the turnout rate was below 50 percent. As Romano Prodi, former president of the European Commission, described the link between weak democracy and the low voter turnout rate, "The message is plain and simple. Many Europeans feel the [EU] does not come up to their expectations and so they saw no point in voting."[50] Thus, a major challenge for the EP is to change this perception.

▌ Finally, the EU often does not act as a coherent organization. Remember that the EU now consists of twenty-seven countries, and that those twenty-seven voices do not always say the same thing. Historically, for example, the EU

Energy Resources under the Sea
The off-shore oil rig has become one of the symbols of the world's dependence on oil.

membership has often been at odds over foreign-policy issues. The divergent attitudes among EU member-states toward the Iraq War is an important recent example. Several eastern European countries and Britain backed the United States, while others—especially France and Germany—were vehemently opposed to the war. Perhaps most important of all, the EU has had trouble establishing policies in critical areas such as defense. Three recent examples of this problem include the EU's incoherent response in the early 1990s to the disintegration of the former Yugoslavia, its political divisions when the crisis in Kosovo erupted in 1999, and the lack of unity over the war in Iraq that began in 2003.

Thus, it is probably safe to conclude that the EU will *not* look like a United States of Europe, any time soon. But it is also unlikely that the EU will backslide much, or at all. At least for now, we are more likely to see is a United Europe of States than a United States of Europe.

We use the conclusion of this chapter as an introduction to the next. We have seen here in chapter 6 what intergovernmental organizations are, why states form them, and how some of the important ones work. An important theme of this chapter and of chapter 7 is that states drive international relations—but they do not do so alone. For a better understanding of the centralizing and decentralizing forces at work in world politics, we must not ignore the role played by IGOs and NGOs. That said, we must also be aware of the limits of what international organizations can achieve. As we saw in this chapter, for example, IGOs can be ineffective when their member-states refuse to cooperate. This reflects the natural tension between the urge to preserve national security and the urge to seek international cooperation. These themes are also at work in the following case study on the International Criminal Court.

Test Prepper 6.4

Answers appear on page A12

True or False?

_____ 1. The EU's responsibilities rest on four pillars: economic, cultural, environmental, and security.

_____ 2. The EU's Council of Ministers has significant influence as it has final say on most important pieces of EU legislation.

_____ 3. The European Commission houses most of the executive power of the EU.

_____ 4. Qualified majority voting provides smaller countries in the EU more power to ensure that minority interests are not overwhelmed by major powers.

_____ 5. Recent developments strongly point toward the establishment of a United States of Europe by the year 2012.

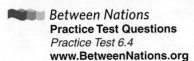 **Between Nations**
Practice Test Questions
Practice Test 6.4
www.BetweenNations.org

Multiple Choice

_____ 6. Which of the following is NOT a rationale for European cooperation:
   a. The need to rebuild war-torn economies after World War II
   b. The need to impose barriers to trade in order to protect fledgling economies
   c. Economies of scale between EU member states made them more competitive internationally
   d. A cohesive Europe was better equipped to halt the spread of communism
   e. None of the above

_____ 7. Which of the following is NOT a characteristic of unanimity voting:
   a. It is the best system for maintaining sovereignty.
   b. It makes getting things accomplished very difficult.
   c. It provides states with the most viable means of security.
   d. It is helpful to both large and small states.
   e. None of the above

Case Study

State Power, Individuals, and the International Criminal Court

See **www.BetweenNations.org**   _Between Nations_

JOIN THE DEBATE

The United States Should Leave the United Nations

Since the end of the Cold War, many Americans have become uncomfortable with U.S. membership in the United Nations. Emphasizing the altered geopolitical landscape in which the United States has become the sole superpower, opponents view the UN as anachronistic or worse. The most recent doubts about the UN's relevance came with the U.S.–led war in Iraq. While the Bush administration viewed the war as vitally necessary for U.S. national security, major UN members either opposed the United States or simply looked on. Supporters of continuing U.S. involvement in the UN, however, contend that the UN continues to play a vital role in world politics and that the United States, as its most important member, should recognize the valuable services the UN can provide. This debate explores the reasons the United States should and should not leave the UN.

THE PRO SIDE

The United States should leave the United Nations for many reasons. First, the United States should not rely on the UN for its most important national security issues. The American Sovereignty Restoration Act, yet to be passed by Congress, calls for the "American people to remain as a free and independent people of a sovereign United States of America."[1] As Ron Paul, a nine-term congressional representative from Texas, put it, UN globalists are not satisfied by meddling only in international disputes. They increasingly want to influence our domestic environmental, trade, labor, tax, and gun laws. UN global planners fully intend to expand the organization into a true world government, complete with taxes, courts, and possibly a standing army. This is not an alarmist statement, says Paul; these goals are readily promoted on the UN's own website. UN planners do not care about national sovereignty; in fact they are openly opposed to it.[2]

Another reason to oppose U.S. participation in the UN is the UN's organizational weaknesses. The UN often suffers from massive, bloated bureaucracies that can't seem to control spending or prevent the inefficient use of scarce resources. In terms of voting power, it is unfair that the United States, as the world's super-power, should have the same voting weight in the General Assembly as small, even tiny, states. This does not serve U.S. interests.

Yet another reason to oppose the UN is that repellent members sometimes have influential roles in the organization. For example, states with terrible human rights records routinely became members of the UN Human Rights Commission, and their representatives even become the chair (or head) of the commission. Members of the commission that were routinely criticized for human-rights violations included Cuba, China, and Sudan. In 2003, despite U.S. opposition, Libya was actually elected chair of the commission, backed by thirty-three states and opposed by only three. Thus, the UN's main human rights organization was headed by a country with "an appalling record on human rights."[3] Adding insult to injury, the United States was voted off the commission in 2001.[4]

THE CON SIDE

Despite the many challenges facing the UN as described in the chapter and in the pro side of this debate, one should not overlook the many contributions the UN has made, especially given its scarce political and financial resources. The interdependent character of world politics today has made the UN a valuable organization for the United States. Many of the serious challenges facing the United States are challenges that do not respect national borders. For example, international terrorism, economic instability, and environmental degradation cannot be contained in one or two countries; these are global problems and U.S. problems at the same time. If the United States leaves the UN, it is likely to lose the international cooperation required to tackle these problems.

The United States could also lose its moral authority to lead the world. It is already struggling with a poor reputation in many regions, and it could lose even more of its international prestige by leaving the UN. Ultimately, its ability to persuade states to do what it wants—in other words, to use its soft power (see chapter 4)—would also decline. The UN, fortunately, offers a forum to discuss and negotiate how challenges to the

United States and the world can be addressed in a cooperative and legitimate setting.

One should also recall many of the positive UN contributions to a better world. In 2001, the UN and Secretary-General Kofi Annan were given the Nobel Peace Prize in recognition of their work for a more peaceful world. Annan was singled out for his commitment to human rights, his campaigns to take on new challenges such as the AIDS crisis and international terrorism, and his efforts to bring new life to the UN.[5] This was the first Nobel Prize for the UN as a whole, but the organization has received seven previous awards for individual programs. For example, in 2005, the UN–affiliated International Atomic Energy Agency (IAEA) and its director General Mohamed ElBaradei were also awarded the Nobel Prize for their efforts to prevent nuclear energy from being used for military purposes and to ensure that nuclear energy is used in the safest possible way.

The United States, like most countries, has a stake in global stability, and the UN has been active in helping increase stability around the world. By 2004, the UN was deploying a monthly average of 56,000 military peacekeepers, four times the level of 1999. In 2006, the UN had about 84,000 peacekeepers involved in operations around the world. One must also remember the UN's extensive measures to address vital social and economic problems facing the people of the world. For example, the UN Development Programme has supported more than 5,000 projects in the areas of agriculture, industry, education, and the environment. UNICEF offers another example. The UN's children organization spends about $800 million a year on immunization, health care, nutrition, and basic education in more than 135 countries. The World Health Organization has been instrumental in helping eliminate contagious diseases in many parts of the world. Polio, for example, is on the verge of being wiped out worldwide.[6]

While the United States decided to go to war against Iraq in 2003 *without* UN authorization, the UN is still viewed as having a relevant role to play. By fall 2003 and early 2004, for example, even the Bush administration was making overtures to the UN for help in the reconstruction of Iraq. Many UN supporters believe the UN could help add legitimacy to U.S. efforts, thus speeding the reconstruction and saving American and Iraqi lives and financial resources.

While the jury is still out in the case of Iraq, the UN has shown its value not only to the world but to the United States as well. As a member of the UN, the United States can have considerable influence not only on security matters (because the United States has veto power in the Security Council) but also on the many economic and social issues under UN jurisdiction. For these reasons, the United States should be an active member of the United Nations.

NOTES

1. A petition in support of the bill, which is available on the Internet, says that by signing the petition, "you, as an American, demand to remain as a free American and not to become a state under the control of the United Nations nor to be assimilated in the UN's call for globalization." See http://www.petitiononline.com/HR1146/petition.html.

2. Speeches and Statements of Ron Paul, http://www.house.gov/paul/congrec/congrec2003/cr042903.htm. Ron Paul's official website is http://www.house.gov/paul/). In Utah, inspired by similar sentiments, the La Verkin and Virgin city councils in 2001 considered ordinances declaring themselves "United Nations–free zones." La Verkin's ordinance passed, making it the first city in the United States to make such a declaration. See Marla Sowards, "Resolution Calls for U.S. to leave U.N.," Brigham Young University NewsNet, http://newsnet.byu.edu/story.cfm/42399, February 19, 2003.

3. "Libya Takes Human Rights Role," BBC News, http://news.bbc.co.uk/2/hi/africa/2672029.stm, January 20, 2003.

4. The United States regained its seat in 2003.

5. Colum Lynch, "U.N. Secretary General Awarded Nobel Peace Prize," *Washington Post*, October 13, 2001.

6. According to the Global Polio Eradication Initiative, a branch of the World Health Organization. Before 1988, when the WHO started a global anti-polio campaign, there were more than 350,000 cases worldwide. In 2006, only 2,000 cases were reported, mostly in Nigeria and India. See the Global Polio Eradication Initiative website, http://www.polioeradication.org/casecount.asp. See also David Pilling, "WHO in Sight of Wiping Out Polio Worldwide," *Financial Times*, January 7, 2000.

LEARNING OBJECTIVES REVIEW

1 ▶ *Define intergovernmental organization, understanding how scope and purpose differentiate organizations from one another.*

- Intergovernmental organizations (IGOs) are organizations whose members are states. They are different from nongovernmental organizations (NGOs), whose members are individuals. International relations are usually dominated by nation-states, but non-state actors are playing an increasingly important role.

- IGOs vary depending on their scope and their purpose. IGOs can therefore fall into one of four main categories:
   - Single-purpose, regional: NAFTA (economic; North America)
   - Multipurpose, regional: the European Union (economic, political, security; Europe)
   - Single-purpose, global: World Health Organization (health; no geographic restriction)
   - Multipurpose, global: the United Nations (economic, political, social, cultural, security; with no geographic restriction)

2 ▶ *Identify the factors that lead states to join intergovernmental organizations as well as the reasons why a state might not join an IGO.*

- Governments sometimes yield some of their national sovereignty to IGOs because they perceive that international cooperation is in their national interest for economic, political, or security reasons.

- The political, economic, and military benefits of membership in an IGO, even if its institutions are powerful (that is, supranational), are often perceived as outweighing the costs. But states always face the tension between their desire to cooperate internationally and their desire to retain as much independence as possible.

3 ▶ *Understand how the UN attempts to manage security, economic, and social issues in world politics as well as issues with the management of the UN itself.*

- The United Nations is primarily an intergovernmental organization. It was developed, in part, as a collective security organization to replace the failed League of Nations. It has many functions, including the preservation of peaceful relations among states, running programs to help poor children around the world, and supporting agencies devoted to world health.

- The two most important UN bodies are the Security Council and the General Assembly.
   - The Security Council, as its name indicates, deals with the UN's military matters. It consists of fifteen members, five of whom are permanent (Britain, China, France, Russia, and the United States). A veto from any one of these five members will prevent the use of UN military force.
   - The General Assembly deals with security issues as well, but it deals extensively with all of the nonmilitary UN activities. Every country, regardless of size, has one vote. This voting method gives tiny countries the same weight as large ones like the United States or India.

- Although the UN gets a lot of press for many of its positive contributions, one should not overestimate its influence on world politics. For example, the UN cannot act militarily unless it has sufficient support from the permanent members of the Security Council. The UN is also hurt by a lack of funding and by bureaucratic problems.

4 ▸ *Be able to identify and explain the functions of the key institutions that make up the European Union and discuss its prospects for the future.*

- The European Union is a unique IGO in terms of its membership (democratic, mostly rich countries), the depth and influence of its institutions, and the number of policy areas for which it is responsible (such as a single currency, common trade policies, common regional policies, and an emerging common foreign and defense policy).

- The EU has both intergovernmental and supranational features. Countries have decided, first of all, that they want supranational institutions, and, second, that the benefits of following supranational institutions and rules outweigh the costs in lost national sovereignty. Many countries in Central and Eastern Europe agree, and that is why so many of them recently joined the EU.

- The main EU institutions are the European Council (meetings among the national leaders), the Council of Ministers (meetings of specific government ministers), the Commission (the semi-executive branch of the EU), the European Parliament, and the European Court of Justice. These institutions could potentially evolve and create a United States of Europe, but this is unlikely. EU citizens still place their loyalty in their home government first, and many are worried about too much power being shifted to the EU.

RESOURCES ON THE WEB

To use these interactive learning and study tools, including video and audio multimedia resources, go to **www.BetweenNations.org**.

Practice Tests	Case Studies	Current Events
Audio Concepts	Primary Sources	Daily Newsfeeds from *The Washington Post*
Flashcards	Historical Background	Weblinks for Further Exploration

Between Nations

Non-state Actors

The non-governmental organization Greenpeace comes under attack as it puts its ideas into practice. © Gleizes/Greenpeace.

LEARNING OBJECTIVES

1 Identify and understand the political, economic, and technological factors that have led to the rise of nongovernmental organizations (NGOs).

2 Using Greenpeace and Amnesty International as examples, identify the goals, strategies, and tactics of NGOs.

3 Identify the economic scope of international corporate actors and determine how powerful multinational corporations relate to state actors.

Chapter Outline

4 ▶ *Identify the criticisms associated with NGO interactions with states; be able to recount specific examples associated with Greenpeace and Amnesty International.*

Can One Person Make a Difference in the World?

Chapters 1, 3, and 6 introduced you to the growing visibility of non-state actors without going into much detail about them. That is the task of this chapter. A variety of non-state actors exist, including nongovernmental organizations (NGOs), international businesses, international media organizations, and even international terrorist organizations. The focus of this chapter is on two of these non-state actors: NGOs and international businesses. NGOs are organizations of individuals that seek to transform a political, economic, or social condition in one or more countries. International businesses—usually referred to as *multinational corporations*—are introduced in this chapter but are explained in more detail in chapters 12 and 13. International terrorist groups like Hezbollah and al Qaeda are addressed in chapter 10. For now, it is useful to remember that all of these organizations are non-state actors made up of individuals who seek change that may be economic, political, social, religious, scientific, or cultural in nature.

Besides the well-known NGOs like the Red Cross and Greenpeace, some rarely publicized NGOs are increasingly altering the landscape of world politics. For example, the Women in Development Movement and Women for a New Era have gotten the UN to focus on the role of women as an integrated part of a country's overall development process. Around the world, there are thousands of NGOs,[1] including:

▌ Humanitarian

▌ Scientific

▌ Educational

▌ Environmental

▌ Women's rights

▌ Religious organizations

According to the *Yearbook of International Organizations,* there are over 6,500 international NGOs and millions of exclusively national NGOs, many of which are organized into international federations.[2] The large number of NGOs is matched by their diversity. Some NGOs are single-issue oriented, while others deal with a wide variety of political, economic, and social problems. NGOs may be funded by individuals, unions, nation-states, local governments, and IGOs such as the UN.

An important issue to track in this chapter is the relationship between non-state actors and sovereign states. As we discussed in chapter 3, one of the significant characteristics of our era is the weakening of the state-dominated Westphalian system (established roughly after 1648) through the emergence of non-state actors. As many parts of this chapter show, non-state actors can be unpopular with the world's nation-states because non-state actors directly challenge government policies, and they are often perceived as threats to a country's national interests. In addition, foreign non-state actors may be viewed with suspicion because of their ideas, values, or, in the case of international businesses, their products, particularly cultural products such as films and TV programs. The result may be local resistance to non-state actors. Exposure to the globalization process associated with or nurtured by non-state actors can challenge old beliefs and social identities. People often react defensively to the forces of globalization by trying to hold on even tighter to local customs and beliefs. On the other hand, contact with non-state actors can increase people's awareness of social, political, and economic discrepancies around the world.[3]

This chapter also brings out the theme of centralizing and decentralizing tendencies in world politics. As you read in chapter 1, for example, citizen activism can reinforce centralizing tendencies through the formation of like-minded NGOs that influence policy at the local, national, and international levels. This centralizing phenomenon may come in the form of transnational religious, environmental protection, or human rights movements that go on to spawn NGOs. Sociologist Amitai Etzioni takes this idea even further. He believes we are entering a new era of global cooperation in which information is shared among NGOs and governments in order to tackle common concerns about managing global trade and banking, about dealing with international drug trafficking and terrorism, and about challenges related to human health and the destruction of the environment. In the international effort to address these problems, NGOs can bridge cultural and national divides among peoples and contribute to a *global civil society*—that is, individuals and groups united across borders in cooperation to achieve common goals.[4]

The rise in the number of non-state actors, each with its own agenda, however, also attests to the power of the decentralizing forces, or fragmentation, in world politics. International terrorist organizations, a specific type of non-state actor that seeks political change through violent means, provide a vivid example of decentralizing forces.

It is hoped that by the end of the chapter you will appreciate the variety and influences of non-state actors on the world stage. This chapter will cover the following during our discussion of non-state actors:

▌ The factors leading to so many NGOs.

▌ An examination of two highly visible NGOs: Greenpeace and Amnesty International.

▌ The variety and economic clout of corporate actors.

▌ The relationship between states and non-state actors.

▌ The chapter's case study about Doctors Without Borders draws out many of the themes you will learn about in this chapter. ▪

WHAT FACTORS EXPLAIN THE RISE OF NONGOVERNMENTAL ORGANIZATIONS?

1 *Identify and understand the political, economic, and technological factors that have led to the rise of nongovernmental organizations (NGOs).*

The international system established by the Treaty of Westphalia in 1648 enshrined nation-states as the most important unit in world politics. As we saw in chapter 6, intergovernmental organizations play an important role as well. The power of most NGOs cannot rival that of nation-states, but they are now a permanent part of the global landscape.

Some observers have even suggested that NGOs are a crucial force in world politics. Michael Edwards of the Ford Foundation, for instance, sees NGOs as

Between Nations
For more information see
Why It Matters to You:
NGOs and Citizen Activism
www.BetweenNations.org

becoming "a force for transformation in global politics and economics."[5] In this respect, NGOs contribute to the centralizing forces at work in world politics by, for example, creating a transnational sense of identity. In an era of increasing globalization, or at least regionalization, NGOs have helped establish or nurture links not just across national borders but across cultures as well.

In the following pages, we address this issue of NGOs as a centralizing force and explore why there are now so many NGOs on the international stage. Several reasons explain why NGOs are so visible in world politics today. These reasons are rooted in politics, economics, and technology.

Political Factors

A host of political factors exist that have led to the increased presence of NGOs in the international system today. These include a favorable political climate; the increase in the number of weak states around the world; the further development of international law; and for some states the politics of foreign aid.

▌ *Favorable Political Climate:* NGOs tend to thrive in democratic environments because democracies allow freedom of expression and association. By contrast, when government dominates society, as in communist and other authoritarian countries, it may be impossible for members of an NGO to meet and organize.[6] In China, for example, one of the main problems for NGOs is that they fall into a legal gray area and are often unable to register as legal organizations. This unclear legal status leaves many organizations open to government criticism or worse.[7] Elsewhere, since the collapse of communism around 1990, more and more countries have opened up politically and opted for democratic reforms, thus creating a more favorable climate for NGOs.

▌ *Weak States:* Another political reason we have so many NGOs is that more states are either falling apart or struggling to provide services that people have come to expect from the state. As you saw in chapter 1, among the new forces shaping the planet is the growing inability of states to resolve their problems. Whether the state must contend with terrorism, migration, drug trafficking, or environmental degradation, it is increasingly required to seek the cooperation of other governments and international organizations. When a country cannot even provide basic services for its people—because of poverty, its own incompetence, or deliberately harmful policies—NGOs are often there to help out.

NGOs, for example, can help by providing expert analysis and identifying and managing problems. They can deliver immediate humanitarian assistance, and they can be important links to international relief efforts.[8] We should expect, then, that as states—especially in the developing world and the former Soviet bloc—continue to face political, social, and economic upheaval, NGOs are more likely to step in as long as they are allowed to.

▌ *International Law:* Another political reason for the growing importance of NGOs relates to the development of international law over the last fifty years. For most of modern history, international law was created and managed by states. With the weakening of the state-dominated Westphalian system, however, the relationship between NGOs and international law has grown stronger. A specialized journal even addresses this topic: *Non-State Actors and International Law.* According to this journal, non-state actors are now a permanent feature of modern international relations, and they play a vital role in almost every field of international law and regulation. According to legal scholar Shirley Scott, NGOs can influence international law through scientific, technical, or statistical information. Many NGOs are also important as accredited observers at IGO meetings that influence international law. Some NGO also help implement and monitor compliance of international law. The international Commission of Jurists, for example, plays a major role in the development and implementation of international humanitarian law.[9]

▌ *Saving Face:* Yet another political explanation for the rise of NGOs is that some governments prefer to receive aid directly or indirectly from NGOs rather than other governments. Sometimes, for example, a struggling country does not have the administrative capacity to carry out humanitarian assistance, so it allows NGOs to do so. NGOs are often perceived by states to be more trustworthy and efficient at allocating funds from a donor state.

Economic Factors

More open economic environments also help explain the rise in the number of NGOs. The work of NGOs always entails money—sometimes a lot of it. Getting money from the donors to the international NGO and then to the recipient almost always takes place across borders. Open economic systems facilitate the transfer of money across international borders. Open economies also allow national governments to funnel money through NGOs to people or groups in other countries. In societies dominated by authoritarian or Marxist governments, NGOs do not tend to crop up. First, NGOs may face direct competition from governmental agencies. Second, the government may actually ban the activities or even the mere presence of NGOs.

◣◣ *Between Nations*
For more information see
Interview with Maria Stephan
www.BetweenNations.org

The International Red Cross
The Chad Red Cross deliver much needed food supplies from the World Food Programme (WFP) to the Touloum camp near Iriba town on the Chad-Sudan border. Aid workers prepare to distribute the food to the refugees using a system of ration cards under the scorching midday sun and stifling heat in the dry border area between Chad and Sudan. The United Nations says fighting between Arab Janjaweed militias and African rebels in Darfur, western Sudan, has killed some 30,000 people and created the world's worst humanitarian crisis with 1 million people forced to flee their homes.

Political Geography

The Political Power of Geography and Maps

LEARNING OBJECTIVES

1 ▶ Identify the key premises of political geography and be able to define the major terms and concepts within the field.

2 ▶ Identify and understand how certain geographic factors impact a state's power and security.

Chapter Outline

3 ▶ *Understand how human perception interacts with geographic characteristics to affect world politics.*

Political Geography:
Exploring the Power of Place

To begin this study of political geography, think about all the connections between land and politics in play around you—in your hometown and in the country at large. Local issues that may come to mind include heated debates over property taxes, land-fills, zoning restrictions, strip malls, water rights, or off-campus student housing. Within your state, you might find political hot potatoes in the form of conflicts between green-space proponents (those who believe in open space) and real estate developers, between political parties arguing over the territorial boundaries of congressional districts, and between corporations and individuals with competing views of where to dump nuclear waste. These issues fall within the domain of political geography. So does the

United States relative to its abundant natural resources, arable land, climate, and ocean frontiers. Compare U.S. access to ocean harbors relative to Russia with its problem of access to warm water ports and difficulty of extracting oil and gas from under the permafrost and transporting it.

The study of political geography's spatial relationships and political processes illustrates the many ways in which the world's geographic realms are growing both more interdependent (globalization) and more divided at the same time. A geographic *realm* refers to the large arenas of the world you very likely already know—like Europe, Russia, the Middle East, and North America.[1] A realm consists of different regions, such as Russia's Siberia.

The study of political geography at work among the states and nations that occupy realms and regions helps us explain the scope and shape of a geopolitical world undergoing rapid transformation that impacts world politics. Given the great changes since the end of the Cold War, scholars working on world politics have shown a renewed interest in political geography.[2]

Political geography's focus on the links between political power and territorial space help us understand our constantly evolving political landscape at the local, regional, and global levels. From desperate Mexican migrants traveling north over the sizzling Sonora Desert trying to cross the border into the United States to find work, to sectarian violence in Iraq, to Taliban fighters crossing from northern Pakistan into Afghanistan to launch a comeback, distinct groups of people are struggling over territorial space. States torn apart:

▌ by one group fighting another (Congo, Rwanda, Nigeria, Sudan)

▌ by gangs who control swaths of territory (Colombia and Brazil)

▌ by warlords who usurp the power of legitimate government (Afghanistan, Somalia)

▌ by conflict over holy land (Palestinians versus Israelis in Israel)

illustrate political geography's decentralizing forces. Terrorism generated by al Qaeda's radical Islamic fundamentalists—in part a reaction to modernization within their territory—reflects regional and global decentralization. The North American Free Trade Agreement (NAFTA) and the European Union (EU), on the other hand, highlight regional centralizing forces at work in political geography—given the ways in which they tie together people and states.

In this chapter, we begin by looking at what political geography is all about—its focus, assumptions, and actors. Figure 8.1 sets the scene by depicting the world's current states. Then we look at key spatial relationships that impact world politics, such as a state's or region's absolute and relative location and boundaries. Absolute location refers to place's latitude and longitude (a global location). Relative location tells us about one place relative to another in terms of landmarks, time, direction, distance, or related physical ties. As a leading video instructional series makes clear in its detailed survey of world

FIGURE 8.1

Current World Political Boundaries

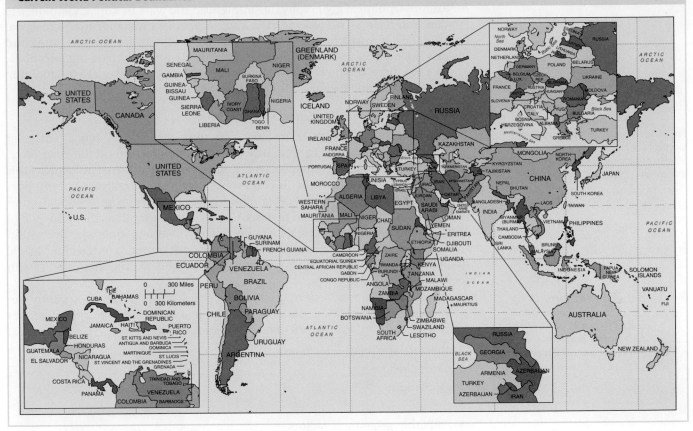

geography, different cities, regions and states around the world generate power depending on their relative location and what is happening there politically,[3] We next examine how place and territory shape human perceptions and influences foreign policy. ■

WHAT IS POLITICAL GEOGRAPHY?

1 *Identify the key premises of political geography and be able to define the major terms and concepts within the field.*

To understand the news that pours through televisions, newspapers, magazines, and increasingly, the Internet, we need at least an elementary understanding of world geography and how it intersects with politics and power. Just as geography and power have played a vital historic role in determining the growth of civilizations and empires, so they do today in the dynamics of continuity and change in the world's political landscape.[4]

 Between Nations
For more information see
*Why It Matters to You:
Iraq's Political Geography*
www.BetweenNations.org

Issues and Perspectives of Political Geography

Political geography has always influenced the news headlines. Since World War II, for example, political geography has influenced the wars in Korea, Vietnam, the Persian Gulf region (two wars against Iraq), Afghanistan, the former Yugoslavia, and the 9/11 terrorist attacks. In today's post–Cold War era, we see states and regions interconnected and interdependent in military and trade organizations. At the same time, as shown above, internal battles inside states are fragmenting them and generating regional and global conflicts.

Political Geography: A Particular Focus

Political geography—and its related field of study, *geopolitics*—has a particular focus. It looks at how, and in what ways, geographical features at the local, state, regional, and global level interact with politics and power. We can express this territory-space relationship in different ways to capture its essence. For our purposes, think of it as the study of geographic impacts on politics and political issues within and between states and regions. Conversely, it examines the influence of politics and political issues on geography and the lives of people who live within states and regions. Political geography, then, looks at power in terms of territorial spatiality, or to put it another way: how power and political processes interact with geographic features.

One thing becomes clear in the study of political geography. Geography frequently influences political decision making, just as political power influences geographical space. This means that a city's, state's or region's:

▌ absolute and relative location

▌ natural resources

▌ topography

▌ climate

▌ and other geographic factors

are subjects of study through the lenses of political geography. Iraq's oil reserves—for example, coupled to its pivotal location in the oil-rich Middle East, bounded by six neighbors (Turkey, Saudi Arabia, Jordan, Syria, Iran, and Kuwait), and locked in sectarian civil war, make it a likely candidate for a political geography assessment. Here people struggle for control of territorial space with a vengeance—and that struggle affects foreign-policy decision making and the lives of many other people outside Iraq.

Those who look at geographical factors as a way to understand world politics are concerned, as one observer puts it, with "the geographical consequences of political decisions and actions, the geographical factors that were considered during the making of any decisions, and the role of any geographical factors that influenced the outcome of political actions."[5] In other words, the spatial features of international politics are the heart of political geography. Think of political geography as a field of inquiry that studies the numerous geographic forces that drive world politics, including the following:

▌ The absolute and relative location, size, and terrain and borders of a state that influence its development, national power base, foreign policy, security concerns, and territorial disputes.

▌ Political control of key resources, such as arable land, oil, coal, water, and natural resources, drives national priorities in foreign policy.

Political geography Political geography looks at how, and in what ways, geographical features at the local, state, and regional level interact with politics and power.

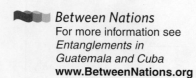

Between Nations
For more information see
Entanglements in Guatemala and Cuba
www.BetweenNations.org

▌ How spatial relationships—for example, borders and topography—affect the perceptions and decision making of key actors, such as state governments, ethnic national groups, IGOs, and NGOs.

▌ How the diversity of states and regions across the globe—for example, their differing ethnic national identities, language groups, belief systems, and territorial conflicts—interact to affect power in international economic, political, social, and military relations.

Political geography plays a huge role in who gets what, when, and how in the game of world politics. Take, for example, the costs and benefits of the U.S. occupation of Iraq. That invasion has led to the loss of an average of 2 million barrels a day of Iraqi oil from world markets. This affects economies around the globe, most notable in higher oil prices. Whereas Iraq used to produce nearly 3.5 million barrels of oil per day and exported nearly 2.5 million barrels of them when Saddam Hussein was in power, most of that oil is no longer available. For Iraqis and the world, the consequences of this loss of oil have been huge.[6]

Political Geography's Premises

Three basic premises of political geography stand out.

1. *Location's Effect on Power:* Where humans live and what territorial states they occupy in great measure conditions their level of development and power base vis-à-vis other humans in states in other parts of the world. In other words, the impact of geography and geographic location on human development is profound. Jared Diamond, a professor of physiology at the University of California, Los Angeles, School of Medicine and a Pulitzer Prize–winning author, stresses that since the beginning of human history, geography—especially in terms of the plant and animal species available for domestication in a given location—has shaped each human society's culture and competitive position.[7] This means that continental differences in levels of civilization—for example, Western Europe as compared to Africa—arise from geographical differences.[8]

2. *Competition for Territory:* Geography, however, does more than set the ground rules for human development. A second premise, also spelled out in Diamond's research, is that humans—like most animal species—compete with each other for territorial space and have been doing so since their very beginnings. Indeed, Diamond makes a compelling case for the theory that human behavior is close to animal behavior in terms of territoriality, especially given that humans share 98 percent of our genetic program with the pigmy chimp of the Congo basin and the common chimp of the rest of tropical Africa.[9] Diamond argues that territorial conflicts generally take the form of wars between adjacent groups.

3. *Perceptions Shape Reality:* A third premise of political geography is that our perceptions of the world constitute a kind of prism through which we interpret realities around us.[10] Recall chapter 2, where the constructivist position posits that policymakers and their followers act on their perceptions, on their understanding of what is going on around them. Each set of policymakers sees the world through the prism of its dominant culture's view of the world. This third premise, that perceptions shape reality, holds that the unique characteristics of each territory on which humans live—defined by its topography, resources, climate, location relative to neighboring states, and ethnic/cultural diversity—shape the perceptions of its inhabitants. When we look at territorially based perceptions, we find clues to how population groups define their national

identity and national interests (territorial security, economic vitality, political goals) and why they utilize different kinds of power and diplomacy to pursue those interests. Their perceptions generate conflict and cooperation between states, acting as either centralizing or decentralizing forces that, in turn, define the role of political geography in foreign policymaking.

Major Terms and Concepts in Political Geography

Political geography has a host of terms and concepts that illuminate the significance of geography's influence in world politics, whether of a decentralizing (conflictual) or centralizing (cooperative) nature. The following are among the most important ones. Try not to be overwhelmed by the number of "geos" in this list. They go with the territory. Most of these terms center on the conflictual side of political geography; cooperative aspects are discussed in the section on IGOs, NGOs, and international law.

- **Geopolitics**, mentioned earlier, is the study of the geographic distributions of power among states, with attention to rivalry between the major states. The global contest between the United States and Soviet Union during the Cold War is a good example. Geopolitics comes into play especially when leaders make foreign-policy decisions about military operations and assess a country's overall power, when they look at a region's balance of power or at a country that may dominate a region and/or threaten regional stability.

- **Geostrategy** is a territorial-based foreign-policy concept associated with geographic factors such as potential alliance partners, location, and terrain. The U.S. war on terrorism has distinct geostrategic overtones. The Bush Doctrine of preventive war illustrates geostrategic thinking in that it focuses on states whose foreign policies are perceived as threats to U.S. security. Geostrategy may view particular states as targets of interest—or on the strategic importance of waterways like the Suez and Panama Canals and the Straits of Hormuz (an oil route). Geostrategy was at work, too, during the days of European colonialism, as in Spain and Portugal's colonization of the Americas for God, glory, and gold.

  During the Cold War, Eurasia was extremely important in U.S. geostrategy aimed at containing the former Soviet Union. Al Qaeda is a loose collection of adherents of radical and militant Islam that has used a geostrategy of suicide attacks on U.S. and Western countries' territorial assets by penetrating weaknesses in their defense systems. Al Qaeda reasons that weakening the power of the United States and the West—as well as Western-backed elites that dominate the Middle East masses—will create opportunities to strengthen fundamentalist Islam, especially in the Middle East in lands of what had been an Arab Empire of the seventh to thirteenth centuries. We return to this point later.

- *Offensive realism* (see chapter 2) is a concept introduced by John J. Mearsheimer.[11] While traditional realists assume that a state will seek to preserve its security with military power, by joining in an alliance when necessary, Mearsheimer sees it differently. He argues that great powers constantly search for opportunities to gain power over perceived rivals—and hegemony is their final goal. This neorealist perspective is different from traditional realism that assumes states seek security rather than power per se, and thus the global political system may be less predatory and conflict-prone than Mearsheimer argues.

Geopolitics Geopolitics is a method of political analysis, made popular in Central Europe during the first half of the twentieth century that stresses the role played by geography in foreign policy and world politics. Geopolitical theorists, for example, justified German expansion during the Nazi era, emphasizing *Lebensraum*. *Lebensraum* is a German word that means "living space," a term used by Adolf Hitler to justify German territorial expansion into neighboring states. The global contest between the United States and Soviet Union during the Cold War is a good example of geopolitical thinking in foreign policy.

Geostrategy Foreign policies pursued by states or intergovernmental organizations (such as NATO) that focus on territory and the geographic distribution of power. The U.S. post–World War II policy of containment of the Soviet Union illustrates geostrategy.

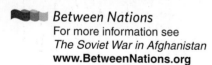

Between Nations
For more information see
The Soviet War in Afghanistan
www.BetweenNations.org

■ *America's unipolar primacy* is the concept used to describe the distribution of global power since the Soviet Union collapsed in 1989, leaving the United States as the sole superpower in the world. Much discussion in world politics today centers on the unipolar nature of the international system—albeit a unipolar world that may be fading. As G. John Ikenberry notes, while American power is not uniformly welcome around the world, no serious geopolitical balancers have emerged to challenge the United States. After the Soviet Union's collapse, scholars debated the prospect of cooperation and conflict in a post–Cold War and post-hegemonic world. Now much debate is over the character and future of world politics within an American unipolar order.[12]

■ *Geography's role in U.S. primacy* is cited by scholars who study issues of international security. Their point is that geography plays a major role in creating and extending U.S. power. The classic axiom in world politics is that a dominant hegemon—or great power—typically invites its own demise. Other countries will gang up on the big guy and form alliances to check his power, as happened to Adolf Hitler and Joseph Stalin. The rule has been: power begets countervailing superpower.

U.S. unipolar dominance after the Cold War, however, is a different kind of hegemon as some scholars see it. Stephen G. Brooks and William C. Wohlforth point to geographic location as key element of U.S. dominance in the international system.[13] It has weak and friendly neighbors to its north and south, and oceans to the east and west—unlike, say, Russia. So the United States has no great power as a threatening neighbor—in contrast to previous hegemons—and is separated from the rest of the world by two great oceans.

This geographic setting tends to make (but does not guarantee it in every state around the world) the United States perceptually less threatening—at least before the U.S.–led invasion of Iraq. The argument is that if a potential challenger were to have a go at the United States, its neighbors would fear for their local security. They most likely would form an alliance to create a regional balance in that neck of the woods, and thereby check the country challenging the United States. Finally, it has been argued that ocean space represented by the Atlantic and Pacific Oceans makes most American leaders less inclined to try to *dominate* directly other great powers.

■ *Regional hegemony* points to the power that a state exercises over more than one neighboring country. China may be seen as the hegemon actor in East Asia. Russia exerts a powerful influence over many states of the former Soviet Union. The United States dominates the rest of North America.

■ *The stopping power of water* is a phrase that comes up in discussion of offensive realism and of the United States as the dominant power in the world as we see in the discussion above. Mearsheimer makes the point that a key reason why states do not actively seek hegemony in regions lying on the other side of bodies of water is because the water space makes it difficult for them to project power. Great Britain, for this reason, has not sought to build regional hegemony on continental Europe. Wolfforth pointed out back in 1999 that the United States enjoys immense strategic territorial space advantages, because it is in North America (no threatening neighbors; protection by oceans) while other potential poles of power lie in Eurasia.[14] Enemies would find it hard to project power to North America, just as projecting North American power abroad is no easy task. The weakening of U.S. military strength due to Iraq— exhausted troops, worn-out equipment, repeated tours—underscores this

Between Nations
Audio Concept
Hegemony
www.BetweenNations.org

point.[15] The 9/11 attacks on the United States, however, raise questions about the assumption that oceans make the United States more secure.

▍ *Choke points* are strategic straits or canals that can be closed or blocked to stop sea traffic critical to the transshipment of goods and oil. Some of the more important choke points in the world are the Strait of Hormuz (oil shipments) at the entrance to the Persian Gulf (Oman), the Panama Canal (ships carrying goods) connecting the Atlantic and Pacific Oceans, and the Suez Canal connecting the Red Sea and Mediterranean Sea. See Figure 8.7 for choke points.

▍ *Shatter belt* refers to a region of chronic political splintering and fracturing—a highly unstable area in which states appear, disappear, and reappear with numerous changing names and boundaries. Central, Eastern, and Southeast Europe, with their age-old rivalries and animosities, have given this part of the world a shatter-belt identity. The breakup of former Yugoslavia, beginning in 1991, into sovereign states illustrates the shatter-belt effects of colliding ethnic identities (Slovene, Croat, Bosnian, Serb, Albanian, and Macedonian) and the Christian, Eastern Orthodox, and Muslim religions.[16] The geographic region in and immediately surrounding Israel is a shatter belt where Islam, Judaism, and Christianity collide. See Figure 8.2.

▍ *Balkanization* is a related term referring to the typical consequence of shatter-belt activity—the breakup of a region or state into smaller and frequently hostile political units. This concept is associated with the Balkan region, where the states of former Yugoslavia are located. Some scholars, such as Samuel Huntington, believe the United States runs the risk of becoming balkanized due to the inflow of non-assimilating Spanish-speaking Hispanic immigrants.

▍ *Buffer state* or *states* refers to a country or a group of countries that separate other ideological or political rivals—and that consequently come in for a good deal of buffeting from power-competing neighbors. Jordan is a buffer state between rival Middle Eastern states, just as Eastern Europe was a buffer region between Western Europe and the Soviet Union during the Cold War. As buffer states, Hungary and Czechoslovakia launched movements to become independent in 1956 and 1968 respectively, only to have them squashed by Soviet military forces. Poland has suffered dramatic consequences from its territorial buffer-state position in Eastern Europe and, in fact, has been carved up territorially more than once by rival power contenders.

▍ *Geo-Green strategy*—is a term introduced by *New York Times* correspondent, Thomas Friedman.[17] Friedman proposes that America's leaders should seek to aggressively curb America's energy consumption and make an all-out effort to develop renewable and alternative energies—including expanding nuclear power. The Geo-Green strategy aims to reduce U.S. dependence on Middle East oil, reduce the price of oil (less oil consumption and demand for it), address the global-warming crisis, and force Middle East regimes to reform. The United States, with its second-to-none production of corn (ethanol), has a natural bases on which to build a culture of biofuels.

▍ *Geography of oil power* also comes up frequently in discussions of political geography and world politics. The basic concept is that those countries with vast quantities of oil are able to wield political power within their regions and in the world. Saudi Arabia, Russia, Iran, and Venezuela come immediately to mind.

Between Nations
For more information see
Ethnic Conflict
www.BetweenNations.org

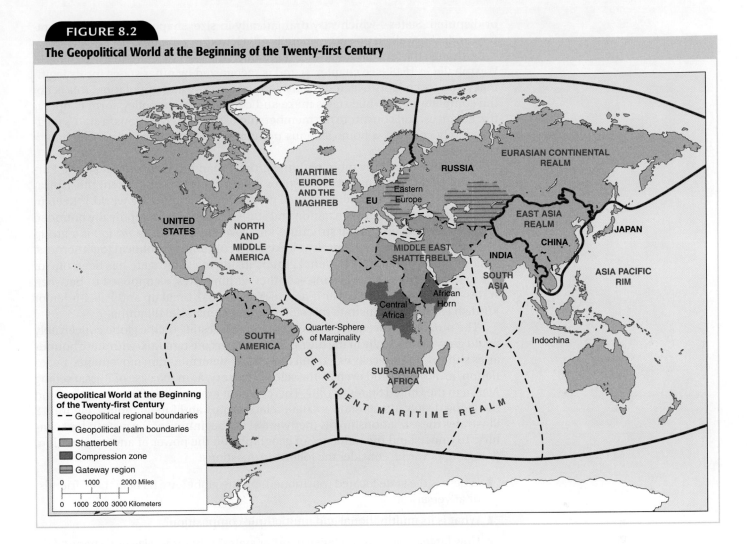

FIGURE 8.2

The Geopolitical World at the Beginning of the Twenty-first Century

Geopolitical World at the Beginning of the Twenty-first Century
- – – Geopolitical regional boundaries
- —— Geopolitical realm boundaries
- ▭ Shatterbelt
- ▭ Compression zone
- ▭ Gateway region

0   1000   2000 Miles
0   1000 2000 3000 Kilometers

The Players in Political Geography: Uniting and Dividing Forces

The key players in the world of political geography are the same as those found in the domain of world politics. They include states, nations, IGOs, and NGOs. In this section, the focus is on how and in what ways geography influences the life of the state and nation. The section also deals with IGOs and NGOs as they operate in the global geographic setting—sometimes in the context of international law and sometimes not. The players can have both uniting and dividing impacts in world politics.

State and Nation

Let's take a closer look at the geographic aspects of the state—that primary, but not exclusive, actor on the world stage for over four centuries, as discussed in chapter 3. Remember that a state occupies a portion of the Earth's territory with generally recognized limits, even though some of its boundaries may be undefined or disputed. States—which vary dramatically in size, shape, resources, topography, and, above all, in power—generally are viewed as *sovereign.*

Although the territorial state has dominated the world scene since the Treaty of Westphalia in 1648 (see chapter 3) and is recognized by other states for its legitimacy and sovereignty over a spatially defined territory and population, this is not the complete story. While states make and conduct foreign policy, form cooperative alliances, and constitute the membership of the United Nations, a state's territory rarely contains a homogeneous population, all members of which share a single national identity.

Our globe has many more national groups than it has territorial states. Further, the world's present territorial states do not necessarily represent the aspirations of the several thousand national groups found around the world.[18] Keep in mind the difference between nation and state. A *state* is a geographically bounded territory with governmental structures and sovereignty, while a *nation* is a group of people who consider themselves linked in a cultural and political togetherness. This situation of multiple national groups inside the same state has been one of the leading sources of civil wars—conflict within states, as opposed to between states—in the post–World War II period. Yugoslavia's breakup and Palestinian or Kurdish aspirations illustrate this state-national territorial dilemma.

The number of sovereign states occupying real estate on the globe conceivably could grow dramatically in the future. States are in constant flux, with state boundaries shifting dramatically as a result of war, self-determination movements, negotiation, arbitration, and even by the sale of territory, as in the case of Russia selling Alaska to the United States in 1867. This constant emergence of new states around the globe deeply affects state-to-state relationships and foreign policy. Figure 8.2 illustrates these relationships as they were at the beginning of the twenty-first century. To understand the influence of geography on the power of any state, nation, or region, however, consider the following questions:

- Where is the state located (positioned) on the globe? Are its neighbors friends or adversaries?

- What is its multinational and multiethnic composition?

- How large or small is it relative to other states? What is its size and shape?

- What natural resources are contained within its boundaries and affect its power?

- How do its topography and climate facilitate or deter security, economic development, and the acquisition of power?

- What strategic role, if any, do waterways—such as the Panama Canal or the Middle East's Straits of Hormuz—play?

Today's Iraq illustrates ethnic and national complexities inside a single state that make its future governance tenuous at best. The Kurds in the north dream of independence rather than being part of Iraq. They have a strong secular national identity. Iraq's long-suppressed Shiites in the south—the largest population group—have a strong religious identity and do not typically support secular political parties. Many Shiites believe their majority position entitles them to rule all of Iraq and to impose their version of an Islamic state. The Sunni Arabs in the center of Iraq—who dominated the Kurds and Shiites under Saddam Hussein's rule through the Ba'ath Party—are essentially nationalist in identity. They see themselves as part of a larger Arab nation. Iraq's oil, however, is concentrated in the Kurdish north and Shiite south, and the Sunnis in the center do not occupy oil-rich territory. Where Sunni concentrate is referred to as the *Sunni Triangle*.[19] The situation in Iraq is illustrated in Figure 8.3.

FIGURE 8.3

Distribution of Religious and Ethic Groups in Iraq

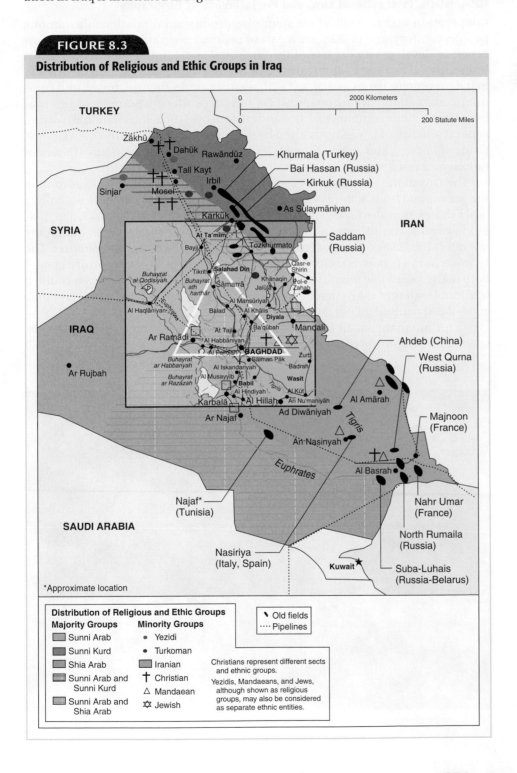

*Approximate location

Distribution of Religious and Ethic Groups

Majority Groups	Minority Groups
Sunni Arab	• Yezidi
Sunni Kurd	• Turkoman
Shia Arab	▪ Iranian
Sunni Arab and Sunni Kurd	† Christian
Sunni Arab and Shia Arab	△ Mandaean
	✡ Jewish

↘ Old fields
···· Pipelines

Christians represent different sects and ethnic groups.

Yezidis, Mandaeans, and Jews, although shown as religious groups, may also be considered as separate ethnic entities.

Keeping in mind these thoughts and questions about states and nations—many of which center on conflict and decentralization—let's look at how political geography can provide information about cooperation and centralization.

IGOs, NGOs, International Law, and the Influence of Geography

Cooperation and centralization stemming from spatial relationships among people, territory, and politics are a part of political geography. International law began to develop with the rise of the territorial state. In the twentieth century, international law grew rapidly owing to the need for rules and regulations to manage complex issues associated with security, trade, finance, travel, and communication stemming from spreading interdependence. Sources of international law include common practice and custom over time, international treaties, general practice of law as recognized by states (represented by the International Court of Justice), and international law that emanates from the many UN declarations and resolutions.

The Law of the Sea illustrates this point. It stems from a UN treaty governing the oceans and from Admiralty law. The UN Treaty on the Law of the Seas, among other things, provides for legal controls to manage marine natural resources, pollution control, navigational rights, and jurisdiction over coastal water. Admiralty law refers to a distinct body of law that governs maritime issues and offenses. The term *territorial waters* refers to waters under the sovereign jurisdiction of a state—both marginal sea and inland waters. The UN Law of the Sea Treaty (1994) codified territorial waters of twelve nautical miles (13.8 miles) and an exclusive economic zone of 200 nautical miles (230 miles).

As for international air law, each state has exclusive sovereignty over the airspace above its territory, including its territorial sea. An Outer Space Treaty (1967)

Relief Programs Needed
Regions in Africa are well known for poor production and ineffective government policies that spawn the need for international relief programs.

represents international space law that bars parties to the treaty from placing nuclear weapons or any weapons of mass destruction in orbit of the Earth.

While international law by no means always works smoothly, nor is it always obeyed, it still contributes greatly to cooperation and commonality of interests. In the wake of 9/11, a host of antiterrorist UN declarations—and hence international laws—were passed. In political geography today, international law also focuses on

- ▌ Drug trafficking
- ▌ Environment
- ▌ Women's rights
- ▌ Human rights
- ▌ Social justice
- ▌ Refugees
- ▌ Trade
- ▌ Child labor

TEST PREPPER 8.1

ANSWERS APPEAR ON PAGE A12

True or False?

_____ 1. Political geography focuses on how geography features intersect with politics at the international system level of analysis.

_____ 2. The Bush Doctrine is an example of geostrategic thinking.

_____ 3. While geography is an important element when defining a state's power, the strength of the United States rests on its people and their technological and economic capacity, rather than on geographic strengths.

_____ 4. A shatter belt refers to the area of a country that is most likely susceptible to an air or sea attack (although not a ground attack).

_____ 5. The Law of the Sea is an example of the intersection between geographic interests and international law.

Multiple Choice

_____ 6. Which of the following is not a basic premise of political geography.
   a. Where people live and what states they occupy are significant factors in explaining their level of development.
   b. Human beings, like most animal species, compete with each other for territory.

   c. Territorial features, such as topography and climate, are only important in a relative sense and there are no objective qualities to such features independent of the broader environment.
   d. The unique characteristics of a territory in which a population lives shape that population's perceptions, including how they define their national identity and national interests.
   e. None of the above

_____ 7. Which of the following is relevant when considering the influence of geography on a state or nation?
   a. Whether a state has friends or adversaries on its borders
   b. Its relative size and shape
   c. The natural resources contained in its land
   d. The climate and topography of the territory in which it resides
   e. All of the above

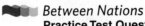 *Between Nations*
Practice Test Questions
Practice Test 8.1
www.BetweenNations.org

HOW DOES GEOGRAPHY IMPACT A STATE'S POWER AND SECURITY?

 Identify and understand how certain geographic factors impact a state's power and security.

With an understanding of major terms and concepts used in political geography—and the pivotal role played by territorial space in the life of a state and nation, we turn now to a closer look at geography's impact on a state's power and security. Every country is located somewhere on Planet Earth, and that location translates into the relative power of place. States with access to the sea are better off in terms of trade possibilities than landlocked states. A country with vast oil deposits is more likely to exert influence in regional and world affairs than a poverty-stricken country poor in natural resources, like Bangladesh or Haiti. This section focuses on location and development and then turns to location and territorial security.

Location and Power

The discussion earlier centered on the imprint of geography on a state's power and foreign policy. Among the issues are:

▮ Location

▮ Access or lack of access to water

▮ Size and shape of states

▮ Transportation routes and communication channels

▮ Boundaries

▮ Airspace

Geographic factors dramatically affects a society's economic and political development. Tied to location are such factors as climate, topography, natural resources, and other elements. Jared Diamond points out that a society's location determines how readily it can facilitate the spread of agriculture, disseminate and receive technology, and share knowledge.[20] In Figure 8.4 note the North-South axes that run from North America to South America and within Africa—compared to the East-West axis that runs through Eurasia.

The geographic effects of this axis orientation are enormous because, according to Diamond, the East-West axis generally facilitated transmission of goods and knowledge more readily than a North-South axis. In terms of food, for example, Diamond notes that "Eurasia's East-West axis allowed "Fertile Crescent" crops quickly to launch agriculture over the band of temperate latitudes from Ireland to the Indus Valley, and to enrich the agriculture that arose independently in eastern Asia."[21] This spread effect was blocked in the Americas and Africa by huge differences in latitude, climate, topographical barriers (deserts and jungles, for example), and other geographic features. As you might expect, the world's great empires—Arab, Chinese, Greek, and Roman—developed along the East-West axis. The area was the scene of the Renaissance, the center of the modern agrarian and industrial revolutions, the place where the democratic political state originated,

FIGURE 8.4

Major Axes of the Continents

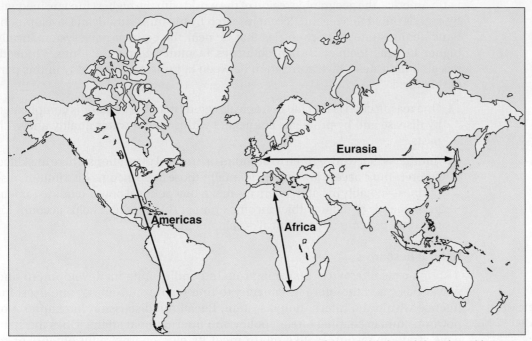

Source: Figure 10.1 *Major Axes of the Continents,* from *Guns, Germs, and Steel: The Fates of Human Societies* by Jared Diamond. Copyright © 1997 by Jared Diamond. Used by permission of W. W. Norton & Company, Inc.

and the setting for the birth of the modern powerful territorial state. Relative location along the East-West axis was a determining factor in these developments.

The Americas, to be certain, developed empires—Aztec, Mayan, and Incan—of no small significance in that part of the world. Yet these empires succumbed to Spanish and Portuguese conquest and colonization. South America, with its mountains, deserts, and jungles, became known as the "hollow continent," and urban life developed along the coastlines rather than within. Thus, the interior area remained isolated from much of the world, and many of its countries faced problems involving agriculture and the availability of arable land.

Climate

The East-West Axis lies in the temperate zone, which illustrates the important role played by climate in a society's development and power. Where a state is located affects its climate and, arguably, its potential for development. The temperate zones, as noted in chapter 4 are between 23.5 degrees and 60.5 degrees north latitude and 60.5 degrees and 23.5 degrees south latitude. The *temperate zone theory* holds that in these temperate zones a number of forces favor economic development, including an average mean temperature of around 70°F, a four-stage seasonal pattern, and adequate rainfall. The temperate zones contain the United States, Canada, Europe, the Middle East, part of South Asia, Southeast Asia, and much of the Far East (China, Japan, and South Korea).

In contrast, as we have seen, countries located near the hot and humid equator have a less favorable record in terms of economic development—as measured by rates of increased gross domestic product and equality of income distribution. Latin America, the geographic region of the world with the highest income inequality, stands out in this regard. Recent research by the Inter-American Development Bank demonstrates that countries that lie near the equator have systematically higher income inequality than countries in more temperate zones.[22] Indeed, research indicates a high correlation between latitude and inequality in this part of the world.

▌ One reason cited is that life in tropical regions near the equator is complicated by disease and by problems connected with soil and water quality and with pests.[23]

▌ Another is that work is often to be found on tropical plantations where unskilled laborers must accept low pay. Incidentally, those large income distribution disparities—notably in Latin America—mean that political power tends to remain in the hands of the wealthier income groups. This situation helps account for low rates of democratic political development.

Natural Resources

A state's **natural resources** play a big role in conditioning its development and power base, and therefore its capacity to find territorial security and exert influence within the international system. Recall the discussion in chapter 4 of power factors in shaping foreign policy and international affairs. Does the state have strategic resources, like oil, to meet its own energy requirements or to export? Does it have arable land to feed its population? If not, it will have to import energy and food. In addition to the oil producers we have discussed previously, keep in mind the world's food-producing states: the United States, Canada, and Argentina.

Natural Resource Conflict

The location of strategic natural resources—water, fish, timber, spices, gold, diamonds, and oil—can lead to both conflict and cooperation in world affairs. When Iraq invaded Kuwait in 1990, for example, world oil prices rose sharply because Iraqi and Kuwaiti oil disappeared from the market. This caused serious alarm among the oil-importing countries, such as the United States, the West European states, and Japan. Even more fearful was the specter of a possible Iraqi invasion of Saudi Arabia, with Iraq's leader, Saddam Hussein, in a position to control world oil prices. As a consequence, the United States led the Persian Gulf War to expel Iraq from Kuwait. So great was the perceived threat to oil supplies that many countries cooperated with the United States in the 1991 military action against Iraq. The Iraq War of 2003, it could be argued, was a continuation of the first Persian Gulf War—both stemming from the Carter Doctrine. In January 1980 President Jimmy Carter declared that the United States would use force if required to stop any effort by a hostile power to block the free flow of oil from the Persian Gulf.

These Gulf Wars illustrate a fundamental point: states have been fighting for control over valuable resources since the earliest wars were recorded. Michael T. Klare views natural resources as the driving force in wars between and within states.[24] Klare argues that given the past role played by natural resources in spawn-

Natural resources   A state's basic resources that spring from its physical setting, such as oil, gas, uranium, coal, and arable land, so vital to agricultural productivity.

Between Nations

For more information see
The View From:
The Caspian Sea
www.BetweenNations.org

ing conflict, we can anticipate an increase in the level of resource-driven conflict in the future. This will be caused by increased population pressure on limited resources. Such resources will include energy sources, but also transboundary water (rivers), diamonds, other minerals, and timber. In the Middle East and North Africa, for example, water is important to the different economies in the region; over 90 percent of the water resources cross international boundaries. In Sierra Leone, Congo, Liberia, and Angola, oil, diamonds, and other key minerals have fueled ongoing civil wars inside those states. In the world of political geography, as Klare sees it, natural resources likely will become more important security issues than terrorism. See chapter 14 for more on possible water wars.

Topography

Topography, or the physical and natural features of a region or state, affects its opportunity to integrate itself politically and protect its political sovereignty. Peru is less well endowed than Argentina from this perspective. Two-thirds of Peru lies on the eastern side of the Andes Mountains, much of which is unexplored even today. This makes two-thirds of Peru's territory difficult to integrate politically because so much of it is so hard to reach owing to huge mountain barriers. Although it also lies to the east of the Andes, Argentina, in contrast, has a more forgiving territorial configuration that lends itself to a nationally unified state by way of telephone, telegraph, and transportation links.

Economic integration of states in trade groupings is likewise affected by topographical relationships. Argentina, Brazil, Paraguay, and Uruguay are territorially more accessible to each other, allowing greater economic ties within their trade organization (MERCOSUR) than with Chile. That state lies on the other side of the Andes from them. Members of the European Union enjoy geographic proximity links similar to those of MERCOSUR members.

Size and Shape

The world's many small states, many with less than 200 square miles, do not carry much weight in world politics. Think of Andorra (180 square miles), Barbados (166), and Grenada (133 square miles). Bigger countries tend to be far more powerful. Yet large countries have their own problems:

▌ multinational populations living inside their borders

▌ numerous languages spoken

▌ extensive borders to be defended

▌ large numbers of people to be fed

▌ communication and transportation links to be maintained.

The largest countries in land area, in descending order are Russia, Canada, United States, China, Brazil, Australia, and India.

Size and shape help or hinder a state's unity, development, and overall power. States come in five basic shapes: compact, elongated, perforated, fragmented, and protruded.

▌ *Compact states* are those where distances from the center to boundary do not vary greatly, as in Belgium (Figure 8.5a: Belgium).

▌ *Elongated states,* like Chile and Vietnam, tend to be more difficult to manage than compact states (Figure 8.5b: Vietnam)

FIGURE 8.5

Shapes of States

a. Belgium: A Compact State

b. Vietnam: An Elongated State

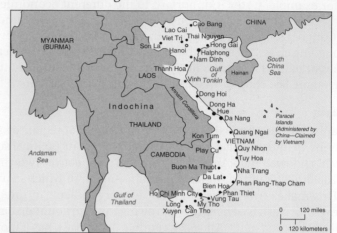

c. South Africa: A Perforated State

d. Indonesia: A Fragmented State

e. Afghanistan: A Protruded State

Sources:

a. http://www.cnr.vt.edu/boyer/geog1014/topics/108States/shape.html.

b. http://www.mapquest.com/atlas/main.adp?print=vietnam.

c. http://www.cnr.vt.edu/boyer/geog1014/topics/108States/shape.html.

d. http://www.cnr.vt.edu/boyer/geog1014/topics/108States/shape.html.

e. http://www.mapquest.com/atlas/main.adp?print=afghanis.

All used by permission.

▌ *Perforated states* (when one state completely surrounds another), like South Africa (Figure 8.5c: South Africa), which has Lesotho in its midst, and Italy, which surrounds both Vatican City and San Marino.

▌ States that are *fragmented*—also called *archipelagos*—such as Indonesia, with over 18,000 islands (Figure 8.5d: Indonesia), and the Philippines, are extremely difficult to manage, as demonstrated by self-determination movements and terrorist activities in both these states.

▌ Finally, some countries are *protruded* in that they have a panhandle or extended arm, such as Myanmar and Thailand. Benefits include possible access to water—demonstrated by the Belgians when they assumed control of the Congo and created a westward "proruption" (corridor) of about 300 miles that followed the Zaire (Congo) River and provided the colony with access to the Atlantic Ocean. A proruption can be formed for other strategic reasons—for example, to separate two states that might otherwise share a common boundary. The British did this during the nineteenth century when they controlled Afghanistan by creating a 200-mile-long, twelve-mile-wide corridor to the east to prevent their geopolitical competitor, Russia, from sharing a border with the area that later became Pakistan (Figure 8.5e: Afghanistan).

Natural Disasters

Location can create obstacles to a country's development and overall economic and political power in the global arena when it exposes a state to natural disasters such as earthquakes, typhoons, and hurricanes, which can sap financial resources needed for economic development. Think of hurricanes in the Caribbean Basin and Central America or earthquakes in India, Indonesia, Mexico, and Turkey.

Geography's Impact on Territorial Security

Geographic-power connections play major roles in a country's territorial security. The classic example is Switzerland, surrounded and protected by the majestic Alps. Thanks to the protection provided by its mountainous terrain, Switzerland remained neutral and not involved in either World War I or World War II. Its commitment to neutrality in world politics remains high, although it finally joined the UN in 2002. Poland, in contrast, has been exposed to attacks from the east and west because it has no natural territorial barriers. Let us take a closer look at geography and territorial security.

Location and Territorial Security

In addition to its effects on development, a state's absolute and relative *location* on the face of the globe is a powerful factor affecting its basic national interests (see chapter 5): territorial (physical) security, economic vitality, and political control over its territory in defense of its sovereignty. Let's first look at the issue of territorial security. In the Western hemisphere, Mexico, Cuba, and Caribbean states like the Dominican Republic, Haiti, and Nicaragua have long been concerned about the power of the United States. Cuba's location at a strategic point in the Caribbean and Mexico's border ties with the United States historically have placed both countries on the defensive in a lopsided power relationship with the United States. Cuba's proximity to the United States, moreover, led Soviet premier Nikita S. Khrushchev to use the island as a base for missiles aimed at the

United States during the Cold War in 1962, an action that brought the USSR and the United States to the brink of nuclear war.

Territorial security and defensive measures have always been a natural geographic strategy on the global chessboard. Ancient China built its Great Wall, European medieval castles had their moats, and before World War II, France built an elaborate system of heavy fortifications on its eastern frontier—a system that failed to prevent invasion by Nazi armies. Since 9/11, the United States has worried about renewed terrorist attacks across its porous borders and has built a long fence on its southwestern frontier with Mexico (which does not actually deter Mexicans who cross over illegally into the United States). Israel has built a fence or wall through the West Bank to protect against Palestinians bent on suicide bombings. The former Berlin Wall dividing East and West Germany was ninety-six miles long; Israel's wall is expected to be over 400 miles in length. The Berlin Wall was, on average, around twelve feet high; Israel's wall is about twenty-five feet tall.

Access to Water

A state's access or lack of access to water has a powerful impact on its ability to develop and acquire power for territorial security within the international system. In this respect, landlocked states, or those with no natural access to the seacoast, are not in an enviable position. The forty-two countries in this situation face huge economic and logistical difficulties in trade and transportation that entail taxes and impediments by neighboring states that, in effect, nearly cut them off from the world. Landlocked states are found in Africa, South America, Europe, Central Asia (Uzbekistan, Kazakhstan, Turkmenistan), and Northeast Asia (Mongolia). The gross domestic product (GDP) of landlocked sea countries typically is low.

While one might think a landlocked state simply could resort to flying its goods in and out of the country, think again. Most goods in daily life—food, clothing, and other commodities—arrive overseas by ship because this is the least expensive means of transportation. With no coastline or ports, as shown in Figure 8.6, you can see the problem. To complicate matters, some countries are doubly landlocked—that is, other landlocked countries surround them. Uzbekistan and Liechtenstein are cases in point.

Other countries are known as *transit states*—that is, states with or without a seacoast that are situated between a landlocked state and the sea and through whose territory traffic in transit passes. Uganda in Africa is such a transit state; it provides transit routes for both landlocked and other transit states. So is Afghanistan, discussed in the case study in chapter 2.

Boundaries and Boundary Disputes

Political boundaries have long characterized how humans organize the turf on which they live. This is so in relations between states and nations, and we also see it at the substate level, as discussed in chapter 3. Prominent physical features such as rivers and mountain ranges, as might be expected, frequently serve as boundaries. The Rio Grande, which divides the United States and Mexico, is a classic example. The Andes Mountains, which run the length of western South America, dividing Chile from Argentina, also illustrate the point. In 2007 Iran seized fifteen British Royal Marines in the Shatt-al-Arab waterway for violating Iran's territorial waters. Great Britain claimed their marines were in international waters. In any case the navy of the Iran's Islamic Revolutionary Guard Corps (IRGC) took the marines into custody.

FIGURE 8.6

Landlocked Countries

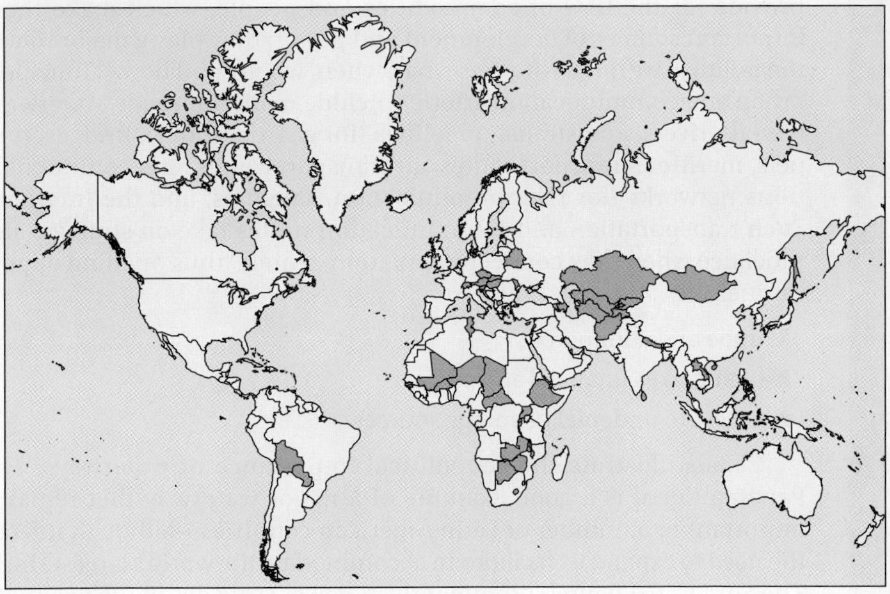

Source: http://www.cnr.vt.edu/boyer/geog1014/topics/108States/neighbor.html. Used by permission.

Boundaries are sources of conflict between states as well as between ethnic national groups inside states, which are sometimes in quest of land to create their own state, as are the Kurds and Palestinians. In another scenario, national groups divided by a state political boundary may wish that boundary removed so they can form one state. Witness the unbridled enthusiasm of East and West Germans in 1989 as they dismantled the Berlin Wall, which had divided them. Porous borders, on the other hand, can also cause tension, as with illegal immigrants and drugs pouring into the United States from Mexico.

Ocean and Airspace

Keep in mind that boundaries are *three-dimensional*.[25] They have land, water, and air dimensions—and airspace over countries also has boundaries. Planes that wander into the airspace of another country, despite the international rules of innocent passage, run the risk of being shot down. Such an event occurred on September 1, 1983, when a South Korean civilian airliner, on a flight from Alaska to South Korea carrying 269 passengers, entered Soviet airspace. A Russian Air Force fighter shot down the plane, which crashed into the international waters of the Sea of Japan, killing all aboard. Another incident of this type occurred on February 24, 1996, when two small planes from South Florida wandered into Cuban airspace and were shot down by Cuban MiG fighter jets. Because states claim and exercise sovereignty on, above, and below their territory, as well as over adjacent coastal waters, international rules governing civilian use of national airspace and coastal waters have been set forth. They articulate the principle of free international airspace. A 1944 convention created an airspace monitoring body, the International Civil Aviation Organization (ICAO) that came into being in 1947.

The Panama Canal

The Canal handles around 13,000 ships each year. It is an immense timesaver when compared to a trip passing around the tip of South America. The trip between the Atlantic Ocean entrance north of Colón and the Pacific Ocean south of Balboa is around 51 miles. The Canal opened in 1914.

Transportation and Communication

Consider global transportation and communication links within and between the world's states as key aspects of geopolitics. These systems provide for the flow of commodities and people, which make them important sources of development and power; they play a major role in the political world of who gets what, when, where, and how.[26] Transportation and communication arteries include roads, railroads, waterways (canals, rivers, and straits), pipelines (for gas, oil, water), bridges, tunnels, maritime transport routes, air transport routes, and communications networks (for telecommunication, satellites, and the Internet). Such transportation and communication routes take on strategic significance when they connect population centers, thus opening opportunities for:

- trade and commerce
- high-stakes financial advantages
- access to or denial of energy sources.

Canals illustrate the geopolitical importance of waterways. The Panama Canal is a good example of a major waterway that remains important to a number of Latin American countries—although it faces the need to expand its facilities to accommodate the world's largest ships. The Suez Canal figured prominently in power struggles in the twentieth century and today plays a significant role in international commerce as a major point of entry and exit to and from the Mediterranean Sea.

Turning now to other kinds of waterways, the Strait of Hormuz (located between Iran and Oman; see Figure 8.7) carries a huge volume of oil trade vital to the economies of the United States, Western Europe, and Japan. Thanks to the Great Lakes and the Mississippi, Missouri, and St. Lawrence rivers, the United States has achieved great economic development. Transportation and communication routes deeply affect the power of states and the power relationships between states, thus contributing to cooperation and conflict in world politics.

TEST PREPPER 8.2

ANSWERS APPEAR ON PAGE A12

True or False?

_____ 1. Being located on an East-West axis facilitated growth of an empire because it facilitated the transmission of goods and knowledge.

_____ 2. The favorable climate of countries located near the equator has facilitated their economic and political development.

_____ 3. The distribution of natural resources among different countries has been a contributing factor to conflict for well over a thousand years and is likely to increase in the future.

_____ 4. Both absolute *and* relative location of a state play an important role in its level of territorial security.

Multiple Choice

_____ 5. Which of the following is not considered when examining the role geography plays in a state's territorial security?
   a. Location
   b. Access to water
   c. Proximity to transportation or communication corridors
   d. All of the above

 Between Nations
Practice Test Questions
Practice Test 8.2
www.BetweenNations.org

How Does Geography Shape Human Perceptions?

3 ▶ *Understand how human perception interacts with geographic characteristics to affect world politics.*

At the beginning of this chapter, we noted that human perceptions form a kind of prism through which we interpret the world. Let's look at this assumption more closely and see how it applies to geography. *Perceptions* are the mental processes of leaders and followers from past to present—decision makers at the highest levels in government and leaders of IGOs, NGOs, national groups, and guerrilla and terrorist organizations. Perceptions are what people think is true about the territorial world around them and their underlying assumptions about that world.

The Power and Problem of Perceptions

Perceptions about territory—whether or not they reflect objective reality—have a potent impact on the actions of leaders and their followers. How al Qaeda members perceive the United States persuades them to undertake suicidal missions, just as how President Bush perceived Saddam Hussein's Iraq resulted in the U.S. attack on that state. Similarly, India's and Pakistan's differing perceptions of Kashmir have led them into a conflictual relationship. Perhaps the basic question is: Who is to say what reality is? Unfortunately, humans are not as rational in interpreting the outside world as they may think they are, because they have a limited capacity for remembering and processing information accurately—including geographic information. Humans are nowhere near equal to computers when it comes to high-speed information processing. Because humans are limited by what they know or can know, their perception and cognitive processes lead them to simplify the outside world. The limits to human perception and cognition mean that much of the thought and action taken in world politics is distorted in one of the following ways that are conditioned by territorial space and power. Humans:

▮ See the geographic world through the lenses of their own national identity and past.

▮ Behave on the basis of biases, stereotypes, and prejudices relative to those who live elsewhere on the planet.

▮ Ignore information inconsistent with their own core values about people living in another territory (cognitive dissonance).

▮ Oversimplify the outside territorial world of states, nations, and people.

These misperceptions and errors in cognition have a great deal to do with human decisions that lead to centralization and cooperation as well as to decentralization and conflict in world politics. The following section examines how these behavioral characteristics stem from the power of territory in shaping national, regional and religious identity that influence world politics.

 Between Nations
For more information see
Global Statistics
www.BetweenNations.org

2. Building on his 1999 *The Lexus and the Olive Tree*, Friedman's *The World Is Flat* argues that the globalized era is one where states matter less, and the principal driving force is a level playing field for international trade. The level playing field has been made possible by software and the global fiber-optic network. Onto this playing field have rushed servicing and manufacturing companies in China, India, the Philippines, and the former Soviet Union that attract the outsourcing market.[4]

3. While the state has remained the most significant political organization of human beings for over three centuries, its decline was predicted well before the intense discussion of globalization in the 1990s—preceded by discussion of interdependence in the 1970s.

4. In this era of electronic media, satellite television and the Internet increasingly are connecting people with distant images, ideas, and sources of information. This is the age of the electronic state.[5] This use of electronic media is creating a major gap between physical place and information. The emerging cyberworld opens the door to social and political actions and movements by nongovernmental actors that transcend the power and authority of the state.[6]

5. Globalization underscores economic integration and interdependence—the spread of free markets, capital moving across national boundaries without restriction, the intertwining of the economies of the world's states. The world is becoming a single, globalized marketplace.

Which side of this debate do you find more compelling? Why?

What questions do you think this debate raises that would help inform you more about political issues?

NOTES

1. "The Globalization Index," *Foreign Policy* (November/December 2006): 74–81.
2. Samuel P. Huntington, "The Clash of Civilizations," *Foreign Affairs*, 72, no. 3 (1993): 22–49.
3. Thomas L. Friedman, *The Lexus and the Olive Tree*, rev. ed. (New York: Anchor, 2000), 250.
4. Thomas L. Friedman, *The World Is Flat: A Brief History of the 21st Century* (New York: Farrar, Straus and Giroux, 2005).
5. Stanley D. Brunn, Jeffrey A. Jones, and Shannon O'Lear, "Geopolitical Information and Communications in the Twenty-first Century," in *Reordering the World: Geopolitical Perspectives on the 21st Century*, 2nd ed., George J. Demko and William B. Wood, eds., 304–305.
6. Simon Dalby, "Geopolitics, Knowledge, and Power at the End of the Century," in *The Geopolitics Reader*, Gearóid Ó Tuathail, Simon Dalby, and Paul Routledge, eds. (London and New York: Routledge, 1998), 308.

LEARNING OBJECTIVES REVIEW

▶ **1** *Identify the key premises of political geography and be able to define the major terms and concepts within the field.*

- Studies how geographic factors and power interact at the international system, regional, state, substate, and individual levels. It illuminates geography's role in world politics, from national identity to a state's power and development, to foreign-policy decision making.

- Assumes that a state's location in a realm and region influences its power, politics, and security. Location and territory go a long way in shaping the perceptions and actions of the people who live in states and identify with a nation.

- Focuses on the strategic and military power aspects of territorial spatial relations.

- Involves major actors in political geography, e.g. states and nations and their location, size, and shape relative to its neighbors, friends and adversaries, natural resources, topography, climate, and proximate waterways.

▶ **2** *Identify and understand how certain geographic factors impact a state's power and security.*

- Geography impacts a state's power and security in world politics. This influence occurs through location's influence on a state's power and on its territorial security.

- Location's power lies in: natural resources, topography, size and shape, and disasters
- Territorial security (and power) stems from: access to water, boundaries and boundary disputes, ocean and airspace, and transportation and communication.

▶ **3** *Understand how human perception interacts with geographic characteristics to affect world politics.*

- Think of perceptions as the mental processes of leaders and followers from past to present. Perceptions are what humans think is true about the territorial world around them and their underlying assumptions about that world. Leaders act on these perceptions whether or not they actually reflect the "real" world.

- Unfortunately for world peace, cooperation, and stability, human beings are not as rational in interpreting the outside world as they might think. Humans have a limited capacity to remember and process information accurately. Perceptions and cognitive processes lead to foreign policy based on biases, stereotyping, and prejudices.

- Territory shapes self-identity: national, regional, and religious.

- Maps are used extensively to shape perceptions.

RESOURCES ON THE WEB

To use these interactive learning and study tools, including video and audio multimedia resources, go to **www.BetweenNations.org**.

Practice Tests	Case Studies	Current Events
Audio Concepts	Primary Sources	Daily Newsfeeds from *The Washington Post*
Flashcards	Historical Background	Weblinks for Further Exploration

 Between Nations

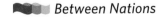

9 Nationalism's Power in World Politics

Mexican Flag-waving Football Fan at the World Cup, Germany, 2006

LEARNING OBJECTIVES

2 *Understand how history and location impact nationalism, using Russia and America as examples.*

1 *Be able to identify and explain the factors that make nationalism such a potent force in world politics.*

Chapter Outline

3 ▶ *Understand how nationalism is used by world leaders for both personal and national gain.*

Nationalism's Power in World Politics

Previous chapters introduced the concepts of *state* and *nation*. You learned that each is different in important ways. These differences have powerful implications for the study and understanding of world politics. A state, of course, must not be confused with a nation. States are geographically bounded territories, with governmental structures and sovereignty, such as China, France, Germany, Japan, Mexico, and Russia. The size and power of individual states vary greatly, but all are recognized as legally equal members of the international system of states. Chapter 8 discusses states in more detail.

A *nation*, on the other hand, need not be geographically bounded or legally defined. A *nation* is best understood as a group of people who consider themselves linked in a cultural and political togetherness, typically consolidated by past or current struggles and suffering. Think about a nation, as Benedict Anderson describes it, as a *psychological* association, or as an *imagined community*.[1] Anderson stresses that a nation is an *imagined* group of people, because fellow members of the nation likely will not meet, know, or hear about most of the nation-identifying group—even though they share in their minds their cultural and political togetherness. Look at the fan waving the Mexican flag at the World Cup matches in Germany in 2006. He is expressing the emotive side of national identity, in this case rooting for Mexico against other nations in sports competition—even though we can hardly expect that he knows every Mexican personally. A flag is a key symbol of the nation.

Keeping in mind that definitions are incomplete and partial, we can make a number of observations that at least help us understand what a nation is. A nation in essence is a group of people who consider themselves culturally, historically, linguistically—or ethnically—related.[2] Identity with a nation actually takes two distinct forms: (1) civic national identity and (2) ethnic national identity. Let's look at these distinctions more closely.

"Civic" national identity refers to groups of people bonded together through:

▮ Citizenship

▮ Political participation within a circumscribed community

▮ Shared common language and core political values regardless of the ethnic origins of the people within that group

The civic nation togetherness is basically voluntary and associated with representative democracy in countries such as the United States (U.S. Declaration of Independence) and France (Declaration of the Rights of Man and of the Citizen). This form of national identity dates back to the eighteenth century. As in the case of ethnic national identity, ties to territory play a big role in bonding people together.

"Ethnic" national identity stems from an ethnically defined group of people who share:

▮ physical characteristics

▮ a common culture, religion, language and ancestry

Ethnic group   A population of human beings who identify with each other on the basis of presumed common ancestry, culture, linguistic, ritualistic, and religious traits.

Whereas the civic nation includes people of different ethnic origins who have assimilated into a common overarching core political value system, the ethnic nation tends to be defined by lineage and closed to outsiders. To be more precise, here the nation is defined by **ethnic group** identity—that is, a population of human beings who identify with each other on the basis of presumed common ancestry, culture, linguistic, ritualistic, and religious traits. Keep in mind

Many Thousands Protest against Power of Turkey's Islamists
Tens of thousands of pro-secular demonstrators wave a huge Turkish flag during a rally in Istanbul, Turkey, Sunday, April 29, 2007. Tens of thousands of secular Turks gathered in Istanbul and chanted slogans against the pro-Islamic government, which faced severe criticism from the powerful military for allegedly tolerating the activities of radical Islamic circles. The demonstration against the government shows a deepening division between secular and Islamist nationalist camps in Turkish society. Protesters demanded a president with no Islamist ties.

Photo by Murad Sezer, Associated Press. Used by permission.

that an ethnic group typically becomes a nation when it begins to seek political control over its destiny—often by seeking its own state or more political control within the state in which it finds itself. Examples of nations that stem from ethnic identity are Tamils, Turks, Croats, Czechs, Kurds, Russians, and Serbs.

When "apprehended as an idea," to use Sir Ernest Barker's phrase, national identity becomes an exceptionally powerful force. Think of Adolf Hitler's brand of nationalism leading up to World War II, or Japanese nationalism during this same period. Here you can see national identity's power in mobilizing people into movements. For that matter, think of the assertive American national identity and nationalism expressed in the Bush Doctrine since 9/11 (see chapter 5). The Bush administration with its evangelical base, as historian Anatol Lieven points out, has invoked radical American nationalism to wage a unilateral, morally based, war against "evil-doers."[3] In Lieven's view, this struggle between "good," that is, America and those who agree with it, and "evil," those opposing freedom and liberty, has fueled a self-righteous nationalist extremism that has strained America's relations with the outside world. We look at radical American nationalism later in this chapter.

This chapter examines how national identity becomes nationalism and how nationalism dramatically decentralizes world politics. While nationalism integrates people who identify with the same nation, it divides the people of one nation from those of another and all too frequently leads to conflict. This consequence is vividly seen in Serb nationalism versus Croat nationalism in the fierce fighting involved in the breakup of former Yugoslavia in the first half of the 1990s. How the population of a nation sees itself, however, can divide perceptions within the same nation. Turkish nationalists are divided over how much Islam to bring into government policies. In April 2007, 700,000 people, waving the red national flag, gathered in Istanbul to protest the Islamic tilt of Turkey's ruling party and the ruling party's then presidential candidate, Foreign Minister Abdullah Gul.

The first section of this chapter examines the nature of nationalism in more depth and its world political consequences. Next the discussion turns to how nationalism is manifested across the world and acts as a decentralizing force. This understanding of nationalism leads on to how leaders have used nationalism as a powerful emotive force in domestic and foreign policy. ■

WHAT IS NATIONALISM?

> **1** ▷ *Be able to identify and explain the factors that make nationalism such a potent force in world politics.*

A sensible place to begin to explore the force of nationalism in world politics is to take a closer look at national identity and its many forces across the globe. In essence, nationalism is basically how national identity is expressed by an individual member, group, or mass constituents of a nation—from flag waving to singing the national anthem to waging war in defense of the homeland as America did in World Wars I and II.

National Identity: Taproot of Nationalism

National identity, as discussed above, is in part an identity with a piece of territory. As a well-known observer of nationalism, Anthony D. Smith, puts it, national identity has a strong spatial or territorial conception, where a nation of people identify with a well-defined territory.[4] **Civic national identity** as it evolved from the late eighteenth century onward came to encompass the idea of a political community of laws and institutions that reflect the national people's political will and express their political sentiments and purposes within a given territory.[5] National identity then, is a "we" feeling, a collective identity of "a people," bound by culture and a sense of shared territory.

Anthony D. Smith's book *National Identity* provides a good summary of the underlying assumptions in a people's sense of national identity in either its civic or ethnic types.[6] It is an identity with shared:

- Historic territory or homeland
- Myths and historical memories
- Mass public culture
- Legal rights and duties for all members
- Economy

It would be difficult to overstate the powerful impact of nationalism on world politics. As a remarkably potent magnet that crystallizes people's loyalty to a home country and cultural hearth, its uniquely diverse faces have produced both

---

Between Nations
Audio Concept
Civic National Identity
www.BetweenNations.org

Civic national identity   A group of people bonded together through citizenship, political participation within a circumscribed community, and a shared common language and core political values regardless of the ethnic origins of the people within that group.

centralizing (within a nation) and decentralizing (nation versus nation) consequences for the world political system.

As a centralizing force, nationalism has brought people with shared roots together inside new states, promoted unified democratic governments, challenged imperialism, and spurred economic development. These effects might well be classified as positive. Yet on the negative, decentralizing side, nationalism has led to horrific world wars (German and Japanese aggressive nationalism in World War II), unspeakable genocide of a people (German nationalism against the Jews in the 1940s, and mass killings of Bosnians by Serb nationalists in the 1990s).

Nationalism has less horrific, yet still decentralizing, influences too. Both French and Dutch voters rejected the European Union (EU) constitution in May and June 2005. French and Dutch opponents to the EU constitution worried, among other things, about loss of national control and identity to a large impersonal bureaucracy. This nationalist rejection sent the EU reeling, because the charter requires approval from all EU states to take effect.

Now let us look at the nature of nationalism. A close examination of this key driving force in world politics reveals that at heart, in both its civic and ethnic types, it is:

1. A psychological group identity among people
2. An emotional force that ignites people's passions
3. A power factor with strong historical roots
4. A driving force that leads to positive and negative impacts in international relations

A Psychological Group Identity among People

From the psychological point of view—that "imagined community" in Benedict Anderson's terms—nationalism works as a bonding agent. It ties people together with a common set of reference points and perceptions of reality. This group identity separates one national group from another across the world. It creates unity among group members and separates them from other groups. This bonding occurs through shared language as well as art, culture, heroes, religion, and customs. Flowering in Europe in the revolutionary fervor of the late eighteenth and early nineteenth centuries, nationalism united people around a multitude of flags and pieces of territory all over the world. The United Nations, with its original fifty-one member-states, now includes 191 countries, many of which have more than one national self-identifying group inside them.

Nationalist sentiments, as noted above, proved a strong psychological force in the Soviet Union after 1917. Throughout the Soviet years, Moscow wrestled with how to keep its restless nationalities under control and devised an elaborate federal political system to do so. In the end, these efforts proved useless. The Soviet Union broke up in 1991, which set the scene for Yugoslavia to follow a similar and far more violent path. At the beginning of the twenty-first century, Russia is still struggling with determined nationalist groups seeking autonomy, as vividly demonstrated not only by the tenacious Chechnya nationalist breakaway movement in the Transcaucasian region—an area of many contentious nationalities—but also by restive militants in Dagestan.

Nationalism as a psychological force is fostered in a variety of ways. The mass media are perhaps the most effective means of triggering its appeal. In many countries, the government controls the instruments of mass communication, such as mail, newspapers, telephone, telegraph, and television, Internet, radio, and satellite transmissions. By promoting the symbols of the nation, governments can motivate their people to all kinds of endeavors. Following 9/11, for example, Americans came together in a psychology of defense of the nation—when the administration used many symbols of the nation (national anthem, flag, references to previous wars and others, defense of liberty and freedom) against al Qaeda forces. In contrast, a nationalist mural in Baghdad before the U.S.–led invasion depicted Saddam Hussein fighting a three-headed serpent representing British Prime Minister Tony Blair, President George W. Bush, and then Israeli Prime Minister Ariel Sharon.[7]

An Emotional Force that Ignites People's Passions

Nationalism is a deeply felt emotional force. Nationalist emotions are deeply present in sporting events, such as the Olympic Games and World Cup soccer (football) matches. The Olympics are of course the premier state for nationalist competition, and these games have a history of political conflict. In the 1936 games held in Berlin, Germany, for example, Adolf Hitler tried to use them to propagandize Aryan race superiority. This goal was undercut by the black American track star, Jesse Owens, who won four gold medals. The German public followed him wherever he went in Germany. The dark side of nationalism and sport appeared in 1972 at the Munich Olympics, when Palestinian nationalists murdered Israeli athletes.

Yet nationalism can work in positive ways to spur defense and industrial power. After the Japanese attack on Pearl Harbor in December 7, 1941, the United States mobilized rapidly to go into high-gear wartime production. America's women and national patriotism played a major role in this wartime effort. See the photo of "Rosie the Riveter." Meanwhile, nationalism is constantly at work in political parties during elections around the world—from the Scottish National Party to the Chinese Nationalist Party in Taiwan. It remains a strong force within the countries that make up the European Union (EU).

Nationalist Passion and World Politics

When the psychological power of nationalism is sparked by leaders, it makes an enormous imprint on the world stage. Nationalist passions have been used to:

▌ Rally a people in time of war, as in Adolf Hitler appealing to German nationalism, Japan's leaders to Japanese nationalism, and Franklin D. Roosevelt to American nationalism after Pearl Harbor.

▌ Seek territorial control over disputed land in order to create a new state for a stateless people (Palestinians in Israel).

▌ Fight for independence against foreign oppressors (Vietnamese against their many invaders from China, France, Japan, and the United States).

▌ Eliminate alien national groups inside or in nearby states (Hitler's Germans against the Jews; Serb ethnic cleansing of Croats and Bosnians in Yugoslavia).

▌ Spark breakaway nationalist movements from inside an existing state to form a new state with its own sovereign institutions (Biafra in Nigeria; Chechnya in Russia; Basques and Catalans in Spain; Quebec in Canada; East Timor in

Rosie the Riveter

Six million U.S. women began to work in manufacturing plants that produced munitions and materiel during World War II, when the men normally doing factory work went to fight in the European and Pacific fronts. The U.S. women's role in the war effort is depicted by the character whose name was "Rosie the Riveter." Rosie is a feminist icon and symbol of women's economic power.

Image courtesy of US National Archives. Produced by Westinghouse for the War Production. Created by J. Howard Miller. Modifications © Jone Lewis 2001. Used by permission.

Indonesia; Eritrea in Ethiopia). These **national self-determination** movements frequently lead to bloodshed. For example, Indonesian militia groups went on a killing rampage against pro-independence people in East Timor after they voted for independence in 1999.

National self-determination The right of all people to determine their own government.

The following brief list captures nationalism's wide-ranging possibilities and shows how over time it has united and divided peoples occupying the same territory in the international political system. It is a force at work at all levels of analysis. Studying nationalism helps explain how and why:

▮ Violence and war occur in the international political system.

▮ People act as they do toward each other across state boundaries and within multinational states.

▮ Misunderstanding occurs so frequently in world politics.

▮ Diplomatic negotiations can be exceedingly difficult over many issues.

▮ Perceptions form an important element in assessing conflict and cooperation.

▮ Leaders manipulate the masses.

Ethnic national identity, discussed above, has become more pronounced in spawning ethnic nationalism in world politics in the twentieth and twenty-first centuries. It has led to frequently expressed emotionally bitter grievances against foreigners, passionate struggles for national self-determination and independence, and longing desires for a separate territorial state. As one scholar of ethnic nationalism, Eric Hobsbawm, notes:

Between Nations
For more information see
Terrorism
www.BetweenNations.org

> Every separatist movement in Europe that I can think of bases itself on "ethnicity," . . . that is to say, on the assumption that "we"—the Basques, Catalans, Scots, Croats, or Georgians—are a different people from the Spaniards, the English, the Serbs or the Russians, and therefore we should not live in the same state with them.[8]

This obsessive ethnic nationalism, for example, lies at the heart of the post–Cold War breakup of Yugoslavia, in the wrenching upheavals in the Transcaucasian region, and in many other geographic regions of the world.

American civic nationalism is different; characterized not by a particular ethnic group but by a melting pot of ethnic groups who adhere to a political creed embedded in American democratic institutions and ideals deemed superior to all others.[9] Like its more ethnic-based counterparts, American nationalism—a kind of patriotism rather than ethnic superiority—has strong emotional patterns too. President Woodrow Wilson tapped into American nationalism as a reason for entering World War I, President Roosevelt for entry into World War II, and President George W. Bush for the wars in Afghanistan and Iraq and the more amorphous war against "terrorism."

While new driving forces of globalization, interdependence, and the information revolution are transforming world politics, as discussed in chapter 1, nationalism simply refuses to go away. Its power to mobilize people through high drama and intense emotions, and its universal presence from around the world, left an unmistakable imprint on the twentieth century. Nationalist sentiments became powerful forces in world politics right after World War I, when the Ottoman Empire fell apart, when colonial powers like Great Britain and France assumed League of Nations mandates to control places like Egypt and

NEGATIVE SIDE

No, absolutely not. America should not try to transplant its core values abroad.

1. Look at what has happened to the U.S. image abroad since the Bush Doctrine began to push American ideals in Iraq. The United States has become the most disliked country in the world. Thanks to the U.S. occupation of Iraq, al Qaeda is now a brand of militant Islam franchise. Its anti-American, anti-West religious ideology has spread across the world.

2. American citizens do not have a corner on the market of core values by which to live. They have no business pushing their culture on others. When they do, they all too easily can embrace a doctrine of force and become cultural imperialists—forcing their nationalism on others.

3. U.S. citizens do not follow world events in depth. In fact, no more than 22 percent of the U.S. public follows, or even knows much about, world affairs. How can Americans possibly have the remotest idea, therefore, of what is best for the rest of the world?

4. If American values are pushed on the rest of the world, the United States—in the context of "good" versus "evil"—will stand out like a sore thumb and become the target of suicide bombers here and around the world.

5. U.S. nationalism lately has taken a Christian evangelical religious tilt that followers of other religions, or no religions, around the world find particularly offensive. Anatol Lieven's *America Right or Wrong: An Anatomy of American Nationalism* stresses that in waging a crusade abroad American nationalism has taken a radical, evangelical, and counterproductive form.

6. Because such a low percentage of U.S. citizens actually vote, the U.S. form of government is far less representative than it appears in theory. This point alone invalidates the U.S. government's export of national core values

7. The downside of American nationalism is its false sense of moral superiority and racism.

QUESTIONS

1. Which side of the debate makes the most sense to you?

2. What factors to you think have most contributed to America's type of nationalism?

3. How strongly do you think Americans disagree on the core values of their national identity and how they should be expressed in terms of domestic and foreign policies?

LEARNING OBJECTIVES REVIEW

▶ *Be able to identify and explain the factors that make nationalism such a potent force in world politics.*

- States, nations, and nationalism are key features and driving forces in today's international system. Whereas a state is a piece of territory with a government possessing sovereignty and inhabited by people, a nation is a psychological identity of people who see themselves as part of a common group.

- Nationalism springs from national identity that comes in two distinct forms: civic national identity and ethnic-national identity.

- Nationalism of the twentieth century increasingly had ethnic identity as its base, and therefore was frequently expressed in terms of grievances against foreigners, struggles for independence, and the right to a separate territorial state.

- Hyper-nationalism or ultranationalism—also known as *xenophobia*—as it appeared in Germany, led to the European Jewish Holocaust.

- Nationalism can best be thought of as
  - a psychological group identity
  - an emotional force that ignites people's passions
  - a power factor that dates back in time
  - a driving force with positive and negative impacts on world politics
  - an identity that competes with transnationalism for a people's loyalty.

- Nationalism has both positive and negative effects on world politics. On its dark side, American nationalism under the influence of the Bush Doctrine (see chapter 5), has become jingoistic and militaristic—undermining American influence abroad, according to Anatol Lieven, one observer among many.

2 ▸ *Understand how history and location impact nationalism, using Russia and America as examples.*

- Both history and location shape nationalism. Numerous distinctions are expressed in ethnic identity; some lead to cooperation, while others, more frequently, lead to tensions and conflict.

- American and Russian versions of nationalism illustrate vivid contrasts.

- American nationalism is less focused on ethnicity than "Russian" nationalism.

- Religious nationalism has demonstrated a particular tendency to violence and conflict. Sudan illustrates violent religious nationalism at work today, as did radical Islam under Afghanistan's Taliban before 9/11.

3 ▸ *Understand how nationalism is used by world leaders for both personal and national gain.*

- Some states try to control disparate nationalist forces inside their borders by creating a power-sharing federal form of government, as in the Soviet Union and Yugoslavia. The principal ways leaders use nationalism to try to:
  - Legitimize their power
  - Conquer perceived enemy ethnic groups
  - Promote state political unity and economic development by overcoming separatist sentiments within the state
  - Lead self-determination movements
  - Legitimize their preferred policy direction

- Nationalism helps political scientists understand why:
  - Violence and war occur in the international political system.
  - People act as they do toward each other across state boundaries and within multinational states.
  - Misunderstanding occurs so frequently in world politics (a result of differing perceptions of nationalist realities).
  - Diplomatic negotiations can be so difficult (diplomats approach negotiations from different nationalist perspectives).
  - Perceptions play such important roles in assessing conflict and cooperation.
  - Leaders manipulate the masses.

RESOURCES ON THE WEB

To use these interactive learning and study tools, including video and audio multimedia resources, go to **www.BetweenNations.org**.

Practice Tests	Case Studies	Current Events
Audio Concepts	Primary Sources	Daily Newsfeeds from *The Washington Post*
Flashcards	Historical Background	Weblinks for Further Exploration

 *Between Nations*

10 Global Violence:
Wars, Weapons, Terrorism

The Pentagon Rebuilds after the 9/11 Attack

LEARNING OBJECTIVES

1 *Be able to identify the various reasons why war occurs.*

2 *Be able to identify the different types of weapons used in war and understand the methods used to control these weapons.*

3 *Define terrorism and understand the objectives and tactics of terror groups; also identify methods for dealing with the problem of terrorism.*

> *"It is well that war is so terrible, or we should grow too fond of it."*
>
> —Robert E. Lee

Chapter Outline

4 ▶ *Identify and be able to explain what methods are available for deterring global violence.*

Explaining the Nature and Causes of War

When the Cold War confrontation between Soviet communism and Western democratic capitalism ended in 1991, there was a sense of optimism that a new and more peaceful world order would emerge. Despite the end of the Cold War, however, violence in many parts of the world occurred throughout the 1990s and in some places actually increased. The first few years of the twenty-first century gave the impression that for most of the world, war and the prospects for war would be as prevalent as ever. As we look to the future, the threat of nuclear war persists because of tensions between India and Pakistan, because of Russia's inability to control its vast supplies of nuclear materials, because of tensions between North Korea, its neighbors, and the United States, also possible that Iraq's WMD could have been used by terrorists in attacks against the United States and other targets.

After Iraq failed to provide the UN with adequate explanations for its weapons programs and after the UN chose not to authorize force against Iraq, the United States and a coalition of countries used military force to achieve "regime change" in Iraq. Nevertheless, controversy persists over the Bush administration's decision to go to war.

■ First, after extensive searches, no significant numbers of WMD were found.

■ Second, some doubt that the government of Saddam Hussein would have ever used WMDs against the United States. Moreover, many analysts believed that the Iraqi leader had been contained after the Persian Gulf War because of U.S. and British patrols of the no-fly zones and because of the UN sanctions.

■ A third point of contention has to do with the very definition of preemptive war. As explained above, a preemptive war occurs when a country feels there is a clear and present danger of attack. A *preventive* attack, by contrast, occurs out of fear that another country might pose a danger in the medium or long term. Most analysts now conclude that Iraq did not pose a clear and present danger to U.S. interests. Since Iraq might have posed a serious threat at some distant time, the Iraq War is more appropriately viewed as a preventive war.

Ethnic and Religious Differences

As you saw in chapter 9, ethnic national and religious differences can lead to international violence. Religious differences are at work in the wars between Israel (primarily a Jewish state) and many of its neighbors (which are primarily Islamic). Religious differences are also at the core of many internal conflicts, like the one between Catholics and Protestants in Northern Ireland (a part of the United Kingdom), and those between Hindus and Muslims in India, Pakistan, and elsewhere. Ethnic differences often lead to violence among groups, as shown in the Transcaucasus region of Asia, Rwanda in Africa, and in the Middle East among Kurds, Arabs, and Turks.

Gender-based Causes

Another more recent trend of analysis by feminist political researchers points to gender as a reason states go to war. As we saw in chapter 2, there are many strains of feminist thought in international relations. Some feminists believe natural differences (nature) exist between the sexes. Others believe the social environment (nurture) in which people are raised—an environment that encourages males to be aggressive and violent, and females to be quiet and cooperative—is more important. Both the "nature" and the "nurture" feminists might agree that war is essentially a male enterprise, but they might disagree as to why. Feminists also disagree on why, when women reach the apex of political power, like England's Queen Victoria in the nineteenth century and Margaret Thatcher in the twentieth, they seem as ready to go to war as their male counterparts.

Structural Causes of War

Yet another important cause of war can be the structure of the international system. In fact, most international relations scholars view this factor as a primary cause of war, but they disagree over how it operates.

The Structure of the International System

What do we mean by *structure?* Most observers agree the international system can have three basic structural patterns; you are familiar with these concepts from chapters 3 and 4.

▌ A *multipolar structure,* which has many great powers in the international system

▌ A *bipolar structure,* which has two dominant countries

▌ A *unipolar structure,* which has one country with predominant power

In addition, most observers agree with the following three points, all of which should sound familiar.

▌ First, anarchy in the international system makes wars more likely because of the tension created by uncertainty over what other countries will do.

▌ Second, we live in a world where each country must rely on itself for survival (it is a self-help system).

▌ Third, as we have stressed in many parts of this book, the world has no world government or global police force to enforce international rules for keeping troublesome countries in line.

Moreover, as the old saying goes, there are no permanent allies or enemies in this uncertain world. Differences of opinion appear, however, when analysts ponder which international structure is the most dangerous or the most likely to produce peace.

Some people believe multipolar systems are more peaceful because countries have more choices in forming alliances, and they can better balance each other's power to prevent war. Others argue that bipolar systems (as during the Cold War) are safer because the two main countries (the United States and the USSR, in that case) know that the risks of going to war are high and therefore will avoid doing so. A major dispute revolves around the unipolar international system structure. Some analysts believe that because "power corrupts, and absolute power corrupts absolutely," a single country dominating the international system creates the most dangerous situation. Proponents of the Hegemonic Stability Theory, however, argue that a single dominant country, a hegemon, is required to help maintain a peaceful global political economy.

Many believe that power shifts or changes in the international distribution of power can be a primary source of instability, international friction, and, ultimately, major conflagration among states. In short, the transition from one international power structure to the next can be an extremely dangerous situation.

War: A Complex Issue

Now that you have read about the many reasons for wars, you should have a better appreciation for the complexity of the question. From the above discussion, we may draw several conclusions. First, there does not appear to be one overarching cause for all wars. Second, keep in mind that several causes may explain why states go to war. Finally, people commonly assume that all wars are offensive wars. However, as we mentioned, states may go to war for defensive reasons (as Britain did in World War II because it was attacked by Germany) or for national liberation (as Algeria did against France in the late 1950s and early 1960s).

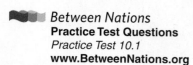

Test Prepper 10.1

Answers appear on page A12

True or False?

_____ 1. We can divide the reasons for going to war into two categories: long-term and historic.

_____ 2. The security dilemma illustrates how preparing to defend against a potential attack may actually increase the likelihood that you will be attacked.

_____ 3. While there are a variety of reasons that explain why a country may go to war, all of these explanations center around international (not domestic) factors.

_____ 4. Misperceptions in world politics can result in wars that none of the warring parties had desired.

_____ 5. Virtually all scholars of world politics argue that multipolar balances of power lead to the most stable international systems.

 Between Nations
Practice Test Questions
Practice Test 10.1
www.BetweenNations.org

Multiple Choice

_____ 6. Which of the following is a material or political motivation for going to war?
   a. Desire for territorial gain
   b. Bids for national independence
   c. Economic causes
   d. Domestic political pressures
   e. All of the above

_____ 7. Which of the following statements is false?
   a. Anarchy in the international system makes wars more likely.
   b. In terms of security, the world is a self-help system.
   c. Except for the United Nations, the world has no world government.
   d. There is no such thing as a permanent ally or enemy in world politics.
   e. None of the above

What Are the Weapons of War, and Can They Be Controlled?

2 *Be able to identify the different types of weapons used in war and understand the methods used to control these weapons.*

Global violence is affected not simply by the outbreak of war but also by the type and number of weapons involved. This section deals with the tools of global violence. Most people are aware, at least vaguely, of the destructive power of nuclear weapons. (The bomb dropped on Hiroshima in 1945 killed about 100,000 people.) Increasingly, however, people are becoming aware of the threats posed by biological and chemical weapons. Compared to nuclear weapons, these weapons are cheaper to make, easier to make, and easier to make in secret. They are often called the poor man's weapon of mass destruction. Atop a missile, fired from an advanced bomber, or even delivered by foot, biological and chemical weapons can have an enormous impact. The United States, its allies, and its rivals are all heavily involved in research in or acquisition of weapons technology, with the hope of gaining the edge. Advanced technology improves the force of explosives, makes targeting more accurate, makes information processing more efficient, and, ultimately, determines how well aggression is deterred and who wins a war. Let's take a closer look at the weapons of violence in world politics.

Weapons of Mass Destruction

The term *weapons of mass destruction* (WMD) encompasses nuclear, biological, and chemical weapons. The paragraphs below describe each of these types of weapons, but you should first be aware of two controversies surrounding the expression *WMD*.

▌ First, some weapons experts believe that attacks with chemical and biological weapons will not result in mass casualties. The attacks could be lethal but not necessarily result in mass destruction. (Of course, much depends on one's definition of *mass*, and there is no commonly accepted definition.) Nevertheless, these weapons are likely to lead to massive clean-up operations affecting health-care professionals, businesses, civil engineers, and so on. Thus, perhaps a better expression for these weapons is "weapons of mass disruption."

▌ Second, some believe the expression is heavily politicized. According to New York University professor Andrew Flibbert, *WMD* is more "a political term and a rhetorical device used with the clear purpose of describing the kinds of weapons that American adversaries may seek and that the United States and the international community does not want them to have."[7] Thus, one should keep in mind, for example, that U.S. nuclear weapons, numbering almost 10,000, should also be considered weapons of mass destruction. Before turning to descriptions of these weapons, take a look at Figure 10.2, which shows states possessing nuclear, biological, and chemical weapons.

Nuclear Weapons and Radiological Bombs

For most of the Cold War, only five countries admitted to having nuclear weapons:

▌ United States   ▌ China

▌ Britain   ▌ Soviet Union

▌ France

However, others, including Israel, have been suspected of having them for some time. The most recent members of the nuclear club are India and Pakistan, each of which conducted nuclear blast tests in 1998, and North Korea. In addition, Iran may join the club in the near future. Stopping the spread (or proliferation) of nuclear weapons is a daunting challenge for the international community. Aside from the existence of today's 28,000 nuclear devises, the concern is not just that new nuclear states will emerge but that terrorists might get a hold of either nuclear weapons, or more likely, nuclear material that can be used in a conventional explosion. According to Harvard's Graham Allison, the world is losing the race to secure a growing amount of nuclear material. Part of the problem is that the Nonproliferation Treaty allows states to build nuclear material facilities for peaceful purposes, but the nuclear material produced in those facilities can also be used in nuclear weapons.[8]

Few expect nuclear weapons to be used any time soon, now that the Cold War is over. A more pressing concern is the use of nuclear material in radiological, or dirty, bombs. These bombs use conventional explosions to spread radioactive contamination. They are easier and cheaper to make than nuclear bombs, but they are not as devastating as nuclear explosions. There is a growing fear that terrorists could obtain nuclear material through theft or illegal purchases from many of the world's nuclear laboratories. The biggest source of "loose nukes" that could fall into the wrong hands is Russia. Studies by the International Atomic Energy Agency reveal that thousands of radioactive sources worldwide, designed to generate high levels of radiation for industrial and medical equipment, are lying virtually unguarded in factories and hospitals, and more than 100 countries may have inadequate programs to prevent or detect thefts.[9]

Problems exist even in states that have relatively good records of keeping track of nuclear material. For example, Austrian nuclear physicist Fritz Steinhausler notes that the U.S. Nuclear Regulatory Commission lists an average of 200 radiation sources that are stolen, lost, or abandoned within the United States every year.[10]

Biological and Chemical Weapons

Like nuclear weapons, chemical and biological weapons do not discriminate between soldier and civilian. Figure 10.2 breaks down the distribution and use of these weapons across the globe.

FIGURE 10.2

Proliferation of Nuclear, Biological, and Chemical Weapons, 2007

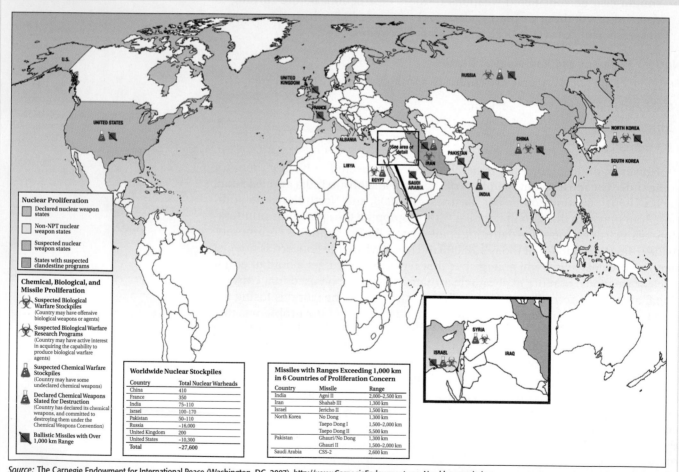

Source: The Carnegie Endowment for International Peace (Washington, DC, 2007), http://www.CarnegieEndowment.org. Used by permission.

- **Biological weapons** contain living organisms. Such weapons, developed by the United States and other countries, include lethal agents such as *Bacillus anthracis* and botulinum toxin; incapacitating agents, including *Brucella suis* and *Coxiella burnetii*; and anti-crop agents, such as rice blast and wheat stem rust.[11]

- **Chemical weapons** do not contain living organisms. They include harassing agents, irritants (for example, tear gas), and casualty agents, such as poison gas and nerve gas. Some nerve gases are so strong that a milligram is enough to kill a human being. Another category of chemical weapon includes incendiary devices, such as napalm; anti-plant agents, such as defoliants; and anti-crop agents, such as soil sterilants.

In light of the inadequate surveillance of Russia's chemical and biological weapons, U.S. Senator Richard Lugar has described the threat of "catastrophic terrorism" from bioweapons as possibly the gravest challenge to global security.[12] Since anthrax letters were sent through the U.S. postal system in the fall of 2001, much greater attention is now paid to the potential use of biological weapons. Anthrax occurs naturally, and about 2,000 people worldwide contract anthrax annually through the skin, mostly from handling contaminated wool, hides, or leather.[13] It is also developed in laboratories by several countries, including the United States. According to a congressional report, if an estimated 60 pounds or so of anthrax spores were released upwind of Washington, D.C., 13,000 to 3 million people could be killed.[14] Antibiotics can stop anthrax if taken in time. If not, the mortality rate is estimated to be 90 percent.[15]

Conventional Weapons Versus Unconventional Weapons

Any weapon that is not nuclear, biological, or chemical is typically considered a traditional or **conventional weapon**. However, a growing number of other weapons are quite unconventional. In the following paragraphs we review several of these types of weapons.

Conventional Weapons

Most conventional weapons have been around for a long time or are simply modern variants of weapons that predate the twentieth century. For example, all the armed services make use of various kinds of guns, bullets, and bombs. Other common weapons include hand grenades, cannons, artillery shells, and improvised explosive devices (IEDs) as well as various platforms for firing weapons, such as submarines, planes, helicopters, and aircraft carriers. Furthermore, radar-evading cruise missiles guided by global positioning systems (GPS) can be launched from ships or jets. Smart bombs have sophisticated tracking and targeting systems, while dumb bombs (or gravity bombs) basically get dropped from a plane and land on their target by gravity. An unusual bomb is the GBU-43/B Massive Ordnance Air Blast Bomb (MOAB) weapon, also know as the Mother of All Bombs. It weighs 21,000 pounds, is GPS-guided, and is designed to spread devastation over a broad area—much like its smaller predecessor, the Daisy Cutter, which was used in Vietnam and the Persian Gulf wars.[16] The world's biggest conventional bomb, it is designed to spread devastation over a broad area or to penetrate "hard and deeply buried targets," like the caves of Afghanistan.[17]

The term *light weapons* encompasses some of the weapons already mentioned but characterizes those that are light in weight, such as pistols, rifles, and

Biological weapon   A weapon that utilizes living organisms such as anthrax or botulinum toxin. It is a weapon of mass destruction in that it does not distinguish between soldier and civilian.

Chemical weapon   A weapon consisting of harmful chemicals including tear gas, napalm, or poison gas. It is a weapon of mass destruction in that it does not distinguish between soldier and civilian.

Conventional weapon   A loose term referring to any weapon that is not a weapon of mass destruction.

hand grenades. Light weapons may not seem as effective as weapons of mass destruction, or as powerful and precise as cruise missiles, but they are the weapon of choice in much of the developing world, and they can also lead to devastating results. In Rwanda in 1994, for example, 800,000 to one million people were killed after the Hutu-dominated government spent millions of dollars on rifles, grenades, machine guns, and machetes. These were later used to slaughter Tutsi civilians.[18]

In brief, then, *conventional weapons* is a loose term encompassing a wide range of offensive and defensive weapons.

Other Weapons

It is worth noting several other types of weapons. As a result of scientific and technological advances, scientists, engineers, and weapons manufacturers have become increasingly imaginative and innovative in finding new ways to subdue a foe. Some of the new or proposed weapons are designed to incapacitate a soldier, while others are designed to render military hardware useless. Many are also being designed to help acquire battlefield intelligence. Laser weapons, for example, are designed to inflict temporary or permanent blindness on the enemy. Weapons designers are working on non-illuminating paints to make military vehicles invisible to radar. They are also developing armor as flexible as skin, tough as an abalone shell, and enhanced with "living characteristics" such as the ability to heal itself when torn."[19]

Some of these weapons will not be developed for technical reasons; others may not be developed for political or ethical reasons. For example, even though supporters of blinding laser weapons believe the weapon is a nonlethal way of stopping an opponent, others—including the Red Cross—argue that such weapons should be outlawed because they are inhumane.

The Israeli-Hezbollah Conflict in Lebanon

Lebanese trucks remove debris from sites bombed by Israel in the July–August 2006 conflict between Israel and Hezbollah fighters based in Lebanon.

Associated Press, Andrew England ,"Lebanese Industry Counts Costs of Reconstruction," *Financial Times*, September 26, 2006. Used by permission.

Air Power without Pilots
Unmanned aerial vehicles (UAVs), such as the Predator pictured here, began to prove their worth as reconnaissance and attack vehicles at the start of the twenty-first century.

Land Mines: The World's Most Dangerous Weapons

When asked, "What is the world's most dangerous weapon?" most people quickly say, "Nuclear weapons." One should keep in mind, however, that the degree of danger a weapon poses is determined both by its destructive capacity *and* the likelihood of its use.

A good case can be made for land mines being the world's most dangerous weapon. They have killed or maimed far more people than all victims of chemical, biological, and nuclear warfare put together. The production of land mines requires no fancy technology. Land mines are generally inexpensive, and they are often hard to detect and eliminate. It is estimated that between 80 and 100 million mines are still active, some in areas never identified as mine fields. Every twenty minutes, someone, somewhere, is injured by a mine, and every year 26,000 people are maimed or killed. Eighty percent of victims of land mines are civilians. In Cambodia, for example, 1 out of every 384 people is an amputee.[20] Recently in Colombia, in a one-year period, 1,100 people were killed or maimed by mines, more than in Afghanistan, Cambodia, or Chechnya. Most of the mines were laid by Marxist rebels, and according to the Colombian Campaign Against Mines, more than 30 percent of the casualties are civilians.[21]

The 1980 Geneva Convention governing the use of conventional weapons limits the use of weapons such as land mines, which are deemed to be "excessively injurious or to have indiscriminate effects." The United States, however, is one of the few countries unwilling to sign an international convention that would ban the use of land mines. It argues that the dangerous border between North and South Korea makes land mines indispensable and that any treaty banning land mines would be impossible to monitor or implement.

International efforts to reduce the dangers of land mines have made some progress in recent years. A total of 138 countries have signed the Ottawa Treaty banning the manufacture, trade, and use of land mines, and 110 of those countries have ratified it. In addition, 22 million stockpiled land mines have been destroyed over the past few years by more than fifty nations. The number of countries producing

As we saw in chapter 1, terrorism is a problem that one state cannot solve on its own, especially when terrorist organizations are using the benefits of the technological revolution to coordinate their activities.

Future Terrorist Threats

Between Nations
For more information see
The View From:
The Most Wanted Terrorist
www.BetweenNations.org

Terrorists pose many kinds of threats to countries around the world. Car bombings, kidnapping, radiological bombs, and cyberattacks on vital economic, administrative, and military computer networks are just a few possibilities. Suicide bombings, another terrorist threat, have been used extensively, for example, in Israel by Palestinian militants, in Sri Lanka by Tamil Tigers fighting an ethnic war for a separate state, and in Iraq since the U.S.–led occupation, as Islamic insurgents have gone after foreigners as well as Iraqi citizens seen to be working with foreigners.

There is some concern that the Iraq War is increasing the threat of future terrorist attacks. The instability in Iraq since 2003 appears to offer both recruiting opportunities and on-the-job training for new terrorist elements. Thus, despite the fact that the war in Iraq was incorrectly viewed as part of the war on al Qaeda–inspired terrorism, it is becoming so as time passes. If we combine the problems of the Iraq War with disputes between the Palestinians and Israelis, the tensions within Lebanon, and the struggle of the international community to prevent Iran from acquiring nuclear weapons, the Middle East has become a major incubator of international terrorism.

Nuclear, Biological, and Chemical Materials

It is unclear how well prepared states are to face these terrorist threats, although many signs suggest that much needs to be done. A 1999 study commissioned by the U.S. government to look into the threats posed by the proliferation of weapons of mass destruction around the world found the U.S. government was poorly organized to combat the proliferation of nuclear weapons and lacked the necessary technology to protect soldiers from nuclear and chemical attacks. Of the thousands of possible chemical and biological threats, only a few can be detected by sensors, which have a very limited range.[34] An audit of both the Energy Department and Nuclear Regulatory Commission found that neither agency was keeping accurate inventory of nuclear materials loaned out for domestic research.[35] Much has been done since the 9/11 attacks, but it is unclear whether those efforts have significantly reduced the threat of terrorist attacks.

Between Nations
Audio Concept
Infrastructure
www.BetweenNations.org

Arms Smuggling

Another source of concern is the many ways weapons or terrorists might be smuggled into the target country. For example, in 2000 alone the following passed through U.S. border inspection systems:

- 489 million people
- 127 million passenger vehicles
- 11.6 million maritime containers
- 11.5 million trucks
- 2.2 million railroad cars
- 829,000 planes
- 211,000 vessels

The magnitude of the trade in goods and the mobility of people make it impossible to track everything. In October 2001, an al Qaeda suspect was found inside a Canada-bound container in an Italian port. The container had arrived from Egypt, and the man inside it was equipped with a laptop computer, a mobile phone, a bed, and food and water for the voyage to Halifax.[36] In March 2002 alone, some twenty-five Middle Eastern men were smuggled into the United States in shipping containers. According to one estimate, it takes five inspectors three hours to conduct a physical examination of a loaded forty-foot container or an eighteen-wheel truck, making it almost impossible to inspect everything.[37]

Vulnerable Infrastructure Targets

As 9/11 showed, future terrorist threats could involve a variety of unexpected methods. For example, in October 2001, a drunken man with an extensive criminal background took a high-powered rifle and fired several shots at the Trans-Alaska pipeline. One shot punctured the pipeline's protective layer of galvanized steel and four inches of insulation, spilling over 285,000 gallons of oil. The pipeline, the most important link in the U.S. domestic oil network, is 800 miles long, about half of it above ground on open public land and thus difficult to protect.[38] Other vulnerabilities exist as well. Less than 1 percent of U.S. imported foods are tested by government authorities at the Food and Drug Administration (FDA). The Bush administration proposed funding increases for both the FDA and the Department of Health and Human Services, but critics believe the resource allocations to these organizations will still be inadequate to the task. Yet another fear is that terrorists might strike some of the 15,000 chemical plants and chemical storage sites that handle hazardous chemicals in the United States. According to a study by the Environmental Protection Agency, at least 123 chemical plants keep amounts of toxic chemicals that, if released, could form deadly vapor clouds that would put more than a million people at risk.[39]

So, in terms of terrorist activities, what will we see as the century progresses? First, we can, unfortunately, be quite sure that terrorism will still be around as a powerful force. Both old and new methods are available to terrorists with the motivation, money, and organizational skill to carry out attacks. Terrorists are likely to find ways of using old technology in new ways, just as they did for 9/11. For example, terrorists might use a dirty nuclear bomb, which is believed to be easier to build and use than an actual nuclear bomb. Cyberterrorist attacks are also increasingly viewed as a threat to all countries, especially those heavily dependent on the Internet. Computer hacking can cause millions of dollars in damage, shut down vital government websites, and so on.

The tentative efforts by the United States and other countries to prepare for terrorist attacks have become significant efforts since 9/11. As we described earlier, many ideas considered radical, politically impractical, or simply unnecessary before 9/11 are now turning into reality. But as long as potential terrorists believe that political authorities will yield to their pressure, terrorism will persist. It is in this context that the U.S. 9/11 Commission Report has urged dramatic changes in the U.S. intelligence-gathering and processing structure.

Finally, because political and social unrest are likely in the future of many emerging nuclear states, the risks increase for accidental and unauthorized weapons detonations. Disgruntled operators, for example, might engage in acts of sabotage that could inadvertently or deliberately produce accidents.

These problems call for serious attention, but they neglect to mention that even the major nuclear powers have not always been in complete control of their own nuclear weapons. Consider the following examples—not from India, Pakistan, Israel, or even Iraq—but from the United States. In Damascus, Arkansas, in September 1980, "during routine maintenance in a missile silo, a technician caused an accidental leak in a Titan II missile's pressurized fuel tank. Nearly nine hours after the initial leak, fuel vapors within the silo exploded. The pair of doors covering the silo, each weighing 740 tons, were blown off by the blast, and the nine megaton warhead was hurled 600 feet away. The warhead was recovered intact. One technician was killed in the explosion."[4] More recently, the U.S. General Accountability Office reported that the Los Alamos and Lawrence Livermore laboratories were guilty of safety violations, including exposing their employees to radiation and inadequate monitoring of radiological contamination.[5]

In a major effort to limit the development of nuclear weapons, most of the countries of the world have sought to implement a Comprehensive Test Ban Treaty (CTBT). The treaty assumes that if countries give up their right to test nuclear weapons, they will not try to develop them. By the end of 1999, 152 countries had ratified the global Comprehensive Test Ban Treaty. President Clinton signed the treaty in 1996, but the Senate has yet to give its approval.

Given the information above, it seems obvious that more nuclear states make the world more dangerous. However, could more nuclear states actually make the world safer because of deterrence?

NOTES

1. The following discussion borrows generously from Kenneth Waltz and Scott D. Sagan, *The Spread of Nuclear Weapons: A Debate* (New York: W. W. Norton, 1995), 80–85.
2. "How MAD can they be?" *The Economist*, February 10, 2007.
3. See also Seymour Hersh, "On the Nuclear Edge," *The New Yorker*, March 29, 1993, p. 56–73.
4. CNN, http://cnn.com/SPECIALS/cold.war/experience/the.bomb/. CNN cites the following sources for this information: The U.S. Defense Department; *Arkansas Democrat Gazette*, September 20, 1981; Stephen Schwartz, letter to the editor, *Commentary*, January 1997.
5. "Periscope," *Newsweek*, June 28, 1999, p. 4.

LEARNING OBJECTIVES REVIEW

1 *Be able to identify the various reasons why war occurs.*

- Wars are caused by many factors, and not all wars are caused by the same things. These factors include:
  - The desire for territorial gain and independence
  - Economic causes
  - Ideology
  - Psychological causes
  - Ethnic and religious differences
  - Domestic political causes
  - Misperception
  - The structure of the international system
- Immediate causes of war are the short-term factors that spark its outbreak. Underlying causes of war are the long-term trends that create tension between states.

2 *Be able to identify the different types of weapons used in war and understand the methods used to control these weapons.*

- Weapons of mass destruction (WMD), such as nuclear, biological, and chemical weapons, do not discriminate between soldier and civilian.
- Weapons that are not WMDs are called *conventional weapons*. Some conventional weapons are extremely dangerous. Land mines, for example, pose the greatest threat to the largest number of people on a day-to-day basis.
- New weapons inspired by high-tech advances are changing the face of warfare. These include unmanned aerial vehicles (UAVs), lasers weapons that can inflict

temporary or permanent blindness, and high-powered microwaves that can melt electronic systems.

- The global demand for weapons has remained robust in the post–Cold War era. Countries want to be well armed for many reasons, including preparation for waging offensive or defensive war. Countries also acquire weapons to deter potential attackers.

- Structural arms control agreements attempt to limit the number of weapons in existence.

- Operational arms control doesn't directly limit the flow of weapons but reduces tensions, and hence the need for weapons, through measures that foster trust among adversaries, such as notifying the "other side" of war games, hotlines, and public disclosure of weapons sales.

3 *Define* terrorism *and understand the objectives and tactics of terror groups; also identify methods for dealing with the problem of terrorism.*

- The short-term aim of terrorists is to instill fear in a civilian population. Their longer-term objectives are political in nature. This helps distinguish terrorists from (common) criminals.

- International terrorist organizations have been, and will continue to be, influential actors in the politics of many countries, as in the case of religious-inspired attacks in Northern Ireland, suicide bombers in Israel, ETA in Spain, and al Qaeda in many parts of the world.

- Al Qaeda may be thought of as an ideology. It seeks, by force, to overthrow the "false" Muslim states of the Middle East and to attack Western countries that get in the way.

- Terrorists may be stopped by military confrontation (such as the war in Afghanistan) or by effective antiterrorist efforts, such as capturing and killing terrorists or cutting off their funding. But as long as terrorists believe terror is their only weapon and that political authorities will yield to their demands for political change, terrorism will persist.

4 *Identify and be able to explain what methods are available for deterring global violence.*

- Countries may be dissuaded from starting a war because of deterrence. International organizations like the UN can help make countries see the merits of cooperation and, at the same time, provide a military response to those who engage in aggressive activities.

- Terrorists, on the other hand, are much less susceptible to deterrence because their whereabouts are unknown, thus making it difficult for a state to threaten unacceptable damage on the terrorists' and their allies.

- International law, while easily ignored because of the lack of a global police force, can still help states resolve differences peacefully, especially through the concepts of reciprocity and reputation. Controlling global violence has never been easy. Deterrence can fail, and both international organizations and international law may be ignored by determined, aggressive states.

RESOURCES ON THE WEB

To use these interactive learning and study tools, including video and audio multimedia resources, go to **www.BetweenNations.org**.

Practice Tests	Case Studies	Current Events
Audio Concepts	Primary Sources	Daily Newsfeeds from *The Washington Post*
Flashcards	Historical Background	Weblinks for Further Exploration

Between Nations

Afghani women brave possible retaliation to cast their first votes in 2004. Because women had endured cruel suppression under Taliban rule, the United Nations insisted that women's rights be at the forefront of the Afghan agenda to rebuild the nation.

LEARNING OBJECTIVES

3 *Identify the different types of feminist theories and how they approach the topic of human rights.*

2 *Understand why women's rights should be given special standing in the study of world politics.*

1 *What is meant by the term* human rights? *Understand the origins of these rights and the international conventions that support their existence.*

Chapter Outline

4 ▶ *Understand how the international community addresses human rights violations, especially in the case of women's rights.*

Human rights   Universal rights held to belong to individuals by virtue of their being human, encompassing civil, political, economic, social, and cultural rights and freedoms, and based on the notion of personal human dignity and worth.

Convention   An agreement between states, sides, or military forces, especially an international agreement, dealing with a specific subject, such as the treatment of prisoners of war; an international treaty.

Human Rights in an Imperfect World

This chapter focuses on **human rights**, women, and global justice. The issue of universal human rights rose to the top of the international agenda in the years immediately following World War II with the adoption of the **Convention** Against Genocide in 1948, the Universal Declaration of Human Rights that same year, and the Convention on the Status of Refugees in 1951. Since that time, the international community has drafted and signed many other conventions designated to protect the human rights of the most vulnerable groups on our planet, including women, children, and migrant workers.

If the record of conventions is admirable, the record since 1945 of abuse of human rights on a global scale is far from laudable. For all the talk of human rights, the twentieth century was one of the

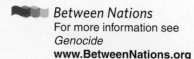

Between Nations
For more information see
Genocide
www.BetweenNations.org

most violently abusive, especially toward women. Throughout the century, predatory and unscrupulous rulers used man-made famines as a way to keep their populations in line. The most famous was the famine in the Ukraine in 1932–1933, engineered by Joseph Stalin, dictator of the Soviet Union, to eliminate all Ukrainian resistance to communist rule. Ukrainian scholars estimate that from 1920–1939, from 25 to 30 percent of the total Ukrainian population of 31 million died.[1] Another massive famine occurred in 2002 in Zimbabwe. Tragically, women and children bear the brunt of these cruelties.

The twentieth century is also famous for its renewal of the practice of genocide. In 1915, the Ottoman Empire conducted the century's first genocide against the Armenian population within its territory. In the 1930s and 1940s, Adolf Hitler sent an estimated six million Jews[2] to the gas chamber in an attempt to exterminate the Jewish people. In the 1970s, the regime of Pol Pot in Cambodia murdered over two million Cambodians who *might* have opposed his plan to reconstruct Cambodia into his ideal of a communist society.[3] During the 1990s, in the Bosnian civil war and the war in Kosovo, the Serbs tried to uproot all Muslims in Bosnia by breaking into their homes and burning them down. In 1994, up to a million Tutsis were savagely murdered by extremist Hutus in the ethnically divided state of Rwanda.[4]

States that join the Union Nations must accept the obligations of its Charter, one of which is the promotion of respect for human rights.[5] Yet, as we saw in chapter 7, even states like the United States that are in principle committed to upholding human rights have been accused of serious abuses by international NGOs, like Amnesty International and Human Rights Watch.

Children are the helpless victims of these events. War and environmental disaster have orphaned millions of them. Many children suffer acts of discrimination, abuse, and sexual violence inside the classroom and in refugee camps. In 2004, terrorists seized a school in southern Russia. The majority of the victims killed in the bomb explosion and subsequent shootout were women and children. A new and disturbing problem is the recruitment of hundreds of thousands of young boys who have been orphaned or are otherwise without resources as soldiers into impromptu armies to risk their lives for whatever cause their mentors espouse. Child soldiers are being used in more than thirty countries around the world.[6]

Three hundred million indigenous peoples, stretching from the Arctic to the South Pacific and the Amazon, find their culture and lifestyle at risk by the advance of globalization. The lives of religious and ethnic minorities are also at risk. So severe has been their persecution in the past 50 years that the UN has brought back to life the international treaties on identifying crimes against humanity and established the International Criminal Court to try persons accused of such crimes.

One human rights situation that has improved is the status of refugees. With the return of millions of people to Afghanistan, Angola, and Sierra Leone, the number of refugees dropped from a high of 17 million in 2004 to 9.2 million in 2006, the lowest number in twenty-five years. However, the number of displaced people within their own country is growing. The UN High Commission for Refugees (UNHCR) is expanding its role in this area. Tragically, women and children under seventeen represent 73 percent of this number.[7] Of this 73 percent, 70 percent will be uprooted women and girls.

Of all these abused groups, women and girls are the most vulnerable. Not only do they suffer abuse and discrimination as a result of their refugee status but they are also maltreated simply because they are women. During World War II, the Japanese military practiced the mass rape of women in China and Korea as part of its strategy to subdue the country. During the civil war in Bosnia-Herzegovina in the 1990s, the Serbian army systematically raped Muslim women so that they would be rejected by their families and communities. In many countries today, women continue to be considered and treated as second-class people.

- In India, husbands and mothers-in-law sometimes burn women if they do not give birth to a boy child or if their dowry is judged too small.[8]
- In China, women sometimes kill their girl children at birth or abandon them on the steps of orphanages because China's one-child policy permits only one child per family, and most families want boys.
- In Iran and Afghanistan outside of Kabul, women can be beaten to death because their dress—known as a *burka,* and legally required to cover them from head to toe—is too short.
- All over Asia and in Central and Eastern Europe, women are sold into slavery for the sex parlors of the prosperous industrialized countries. Our case study examines the global sex trade and the challenges the international community faces in alleviating the suffering of the victims.

The plight of the victims calls forth our concern and our compassion. Why isn't the international community doing more about human rights? This chapter moves issues of human rights and women's rights from the periphery to the center of world politics. In so doing, we follow the neoliberal paradigm and environmental paradigms, which include the well-being of *all* humankind as a key value of international relations. Liberals consistently attach great importance to human rights and support humanitarian aid to correct the worst abuses. Concerned as realism is with interstate relations and the dominant role of power in the global jungle, realists traditionally consider human rights as marginal to the central problem of power. In their scenario, women's issues are a domestic problem that national governments should solve within their own territory.

The attacks of 9/11 forcefully challenged liberal and realist assumptions. Political observers were unanimous in their opinion that endemic poverty and inequality were root causes of the tragedy. As a result, in post-Taliban

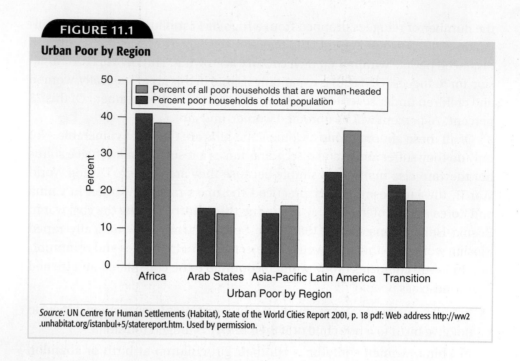

FIGURE 11.1

Urban Poor by Region

Source: UN Centre for Human Settlements (Habitat), State of the World Cities Report 2001, p. 18 pdf: Web address http://ww2
.unhabitat.org/istanbul+5/statereport.htm. Used by permission.

Afghanistan, the international community not only insisted that women be given a role in the new government but also that they have complete access to education. In January 2002, the International Monetary Fund (IMF) sponsored an international conference on poverty-reduction strategies where women were front and center in the sessions on poverty and inequality.

If terrorism is rooted in inequality, then liberals and realists must recognize that the abusive treatment of women and other minorities in poor countries contributes in ways we do not yet fully understand to the formation of the terrorist mentality. The relationship between urban poverty and women-headed households in the developing regions of the world is shown in Figure 11.1.

Our book's theme of centralization/decentralization comes into play here. The IMF 2002 Conference on Poverty-Reduction Strategies started from the realization that a country's societal attitudes, violence, and lack of education *taken together* foster poverty. The international community has a track record of helping states in the areas of economic development, education, and health, but societal attitudes and human rights are traditionally considered problems to be solved at the state level. However, economics is not and should not be, the only centralizing issue where the international community can come together and cooperate. The very concept of human rights means that rights accrue to *all* the world's people, not just some of them. The challenge of the twenty-first century is to make that happen.

This chapter is divided into four parts:

1. The first asks what human rights are and looks for answers in people's search for global justice and the Universal Declaration of Human Rights.

It concludes with a brief discussion of the major UN human rights conventions.

2. Because it is beyond the scope of this book to discuss all forms of human rights abuse in detail, we focus on discrimination against women in the second section. When our attention centers on human rights in general, women become marginal to discussions of discrimination against religious, ethnic, and refugee groups, or crimes against humanity, such as genocide. But women represent half or more of the victims in all these groups, and thus deserve to be placed at the center of the issue. In the second section, we turn the human rights question on its head to ask, How does the socially and culturally determined low status of women affect the promotion of human rights? In this section, we take a brief look at the status of women in the past and present and at the strategic role women play especially in the developing economies.

3. The third section presents the unique aspects of a feminist perspective in international relations and explores how feminist international relations theory contributes to our understanding of human rights issues.

4. In the fourth and last part, we look at the international response to violations of human rights. In this section, we examine the UN response to two kinds of violations: violations by states based on economic, social, and cultural conditions, and gross violations of human rights, such as genocide. In the discussion of the first kind of violation, we use the problem of women's rights and unequal treatment of the sexes as an example of UN response to similar violations of other human rights. The case study highlights one of the consequences of unequal treatment of men and women around the globe: the increase in the global slave trade in women and children. ■

WHAT ARE HUMAN RIGHTS?

 What is meant by the term human rights? *Understand the origins of these rights and the international conventions that support their existence.*

The typical dictionary definition of a *right* is "a just and fair claim to anything whatever that belongs to a person by law, nature, or tradition."

The Origin of Human Rights

The concept of inalienable rights, rights that cannot be taken away from any human being, is relatively new, essentially the product of seventeenth- and eighteenth-century European thought. Traditionally, religions as well as the great legal systems, such as that of ancient Rome, have dealt with the duties and obligations of the individual. In 1215, the British feudal lords joined at Runnymede to force upon King John the Magna Carta, or Great Charter. The landmark document established the legal rights of Englishmen, such as no taxation without the consent of Parliament, the right to petition the king, and the right to a fair and speedy trial. To address the deeper issue of what kind of government the English would accept, however, political philosophers such as Hobbes (see chapter 2) and John Locke asked fundamental questions such as these: How did governments originate in the first place? Why would anyone want to be subjected to one?

The answer came from an unexpected source. At that time, Europeans were rapidly colonizing the New World. Their first impressions of the Native Americans was that they were uncivilized, or, to put it more kindly, living in a state of nature. A *state of nature* meant to the Europeans that there was no established government. So the question, became: What would urge a person living in a state of nature to agree to submit to a government? Hobbes and Locke answered the question by arguing that a person in a state of nature enjoyed life and liberty but lived in constant fear losing of both. If a person had property, it could be taken away at any time by anyone stronger. So the answer to why would one enter into a contract to form a government was that he would do so to secure his prior right to life, liberty, and property. So basic were these rights that Hobbes and Locke asserted they were given by God as a natural right, and thus could not be taken away by any government.

This concept of rights was cogently set forth by Thomas Jefferson and others in the U.S. Declaration of Independence. "We hold these truths to be self-evident: that man is endowed by his Creator with certain unalienable rights; that among these rights are the right to life, liberty and the pursuit of happiness." Essentially, Jefferson's inalienable rights are human rights that we claim at birth by the sheer fact of being human. Jefferson and others insisted that a list of rights be appended to the Constitution, and so in 1791 Congress passed the first ten amendments, known as the Bill of Rights. The United States was the second state to endorse such a comprehensive list. In 1789 the revolutionary French government passed the Declaration of the Rights of Man and the Citizen universalizing the concept of human rights. The UN Universal Declaration of Human Rights derives essentially from the *Declaration des droits de l'homme et du citoyen* rather than from the U.S. Bill of Rights.[9]

Between Nations
Audio Concept
Declaration of the Rights of Man and the Citizen
www.BetweenNations.org

The UN Universal Declaration of Human Rights

It is important to note that the concept of human rights as God-given and rooted in some vague assumption of how governments come into being is not universally accepted. The UN Universal Declaration of Human Rights is the first multinational document mentioning human rights by name. It is ironic that while the declaration satisfies no one state, it is the best consensus the international community was able to achieve on the subject at the time. We have a woman, Eleanor Roosevelt, the wife of U.S. President Franklin Roosevelt (1932–1945) to thank for her persistence and diplomacy in getting any declaration of rights appended to the UN Charter. As chair of the newly formed UN Commission on Human Rights in 1945, she became a passionate advocate for the world's weak and forgotten. She was convinced the world needed a statement that set forth the goals of global justice. In her own words to the Third General Assembly of the United Nations in 1948, the declaration was not an agreement or a treaty. "It is a declaration of basic principles of human rights and freedoms, to be stamped with the approval of the General Assembly by formal vote of its members, and to serve as a common standard of achievement for all peoples of all nations."[10]

We must emphasize that the Universal Declaration of Human Rights is not a legal document; it does not state unequivocally that humans have the right to life or liberty and that it is the duty of the state to provide these. It is a document intended as "a common standard" of achievement of global justice. What does this mean? To understand human rights as a standard, we must understand what global justice is.

Global Justice

One way to define global justice is to look at it is as a sort of balance or equilibrium between one state's assets and those of other states (wealth, power, status, health, welfare, education) and the distribution of these assets among the state's constituent groups. This definition highlights the fairness aspect of justice. Let's look a little bit more at this concept of justice.

Justice as Equal Shares

First of all, let us look at justice as equal shares—for example, in the world's resources, as discussed in chapter 8. As the ecojustice movement rightly says, there is no such thing as equal shares. About a fourth of Russia is above the Arctic Circle, where farming is very difficult and where most people do not want to live. Large portions of Canada's territory are also unsuitable for agriculture or for habitation by large numbers of people, while the African state of Chad is almost all desert. Some states, like Saudi Arabia and Venezuela, are rich in natural resources; others, like Japan, have few natural resources.

Nor are states equal in size, in the educational achievement of their population, in technological development, or in economic prosperity. To realize justice as an equilibrium where every state is equal to every other state in even one dimension, such as per capita income, would mean a gigantic transfer of wealth from the rich industrialized states to the three-fourths of the world living in poverty. While much needs to be done and can be done to lift the world's poor out of poverty, few would argue that everyone or every state sharing all the world's resources equally is either realizable or practical.

Justice as Due Process

If justice is not about equal shares for all, what is it about? When we think about justice as a balance, two meanings of the word come to mind.

▌ The first is contained in the idea that *justice involves* a process that operates the same way for everyone according to a standard set of accepted rules and regulations.

▌ The second involves the idea of *fairness,* which we discuss later.

In the United States, the standard set of rules that defines the judicial process is contained in the first ten amendments to the Constitution. When we talk about *global justice* as "due process"—a process that considers everyone in the global community impartially on the same

 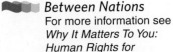
Between Nations
For more information see
Why It Matters To You:
Human Rights for
Nonstate Actor-Detainee
www.BetweenNations.org

Between Nations
For more information see
International Law
www.BetweenNations.org

Detainees at Guantanamo
Their treatment has become the subject of worldwide interest because the way the United States treats its prisoners is seen by many as an indication of its commitment to equal justice for all.

terms—we see immediately that an accepted global standard or set of principles must exist to enable due process to take place. We find this global standard in the UN Universal Declaration of Human Rights.

The UN Declaration sets forth general principles for a common judicial, political, and social process that the member-states assert to be universal. Selected principles are covered in Figure 11.2.

▌ The first set of principles assures equality before the law and redress of grievances. These concepts of justice are those that U.S. citizens generally associate with the notion of a fair trial.

▌ The second set comprises principles associated with the building of a democratic society, such as freedom of speech and association. But because these rights are universal, the UN Declaration goes further to assure the right of asylum, the right to information wherever obtained, and the right to a nationality.

▌ The third set of principles delineates an individual's economic, social, and cultural rights, including not only the right to work and to receive an education but also the right to marry whomever one chooses.

▌ The final set binds both individuals and member-states to furthering the principles described in the UN Declaration. These articles set the ground rules for all states that, if adopted, lead to the development of legal processes that support the rule of law, democracy, and equal opportunity, as institutionalized in the Western parliamentary states.

Not all states adhere to the principles of the Declaration. Many countries today still do not assure the accused a fair trial, permit freedom of speech and assembly, or have a free and fair electoral system. In many states, education remains the province of wealthy and privileged men. There are millions of refugees in the world with no rights at all. Indigenous peoples are being denied their right to lead their traditional lifestyle. Women in most of Asia and Africa do not have the same rights as men either before the law or in guarantees of equal access to education, health care, and work. In particular, women do not have the same rights as men to marry and have a family. We talk more about human rights and women later.

Justice as Fairness

The second way to view justice is as *an equalizing factor for the human condition.* This aspect makes us think a little harder about the idea of fairness. What do we mean when we say it isn't fair that some people are born into poverty and some into wealth? It isn't fair that there is no gender equality or that people are judged by their race. In these instances, our talk of fairness refers to a condition that seems to exist in society or is inherent in the biological condition of a human being. In our best moments, we would like to even the odds a little. The U.S. Declaration of Independence rather grandiosely asserts that all men (and women) are born with the right to life, liberty, and the pursuit of happiness. That's a tall order for any country to deliver, let alone the international system. But the liberal and idealist side of us would like to believe that human-made institutions can and will rectify the most egregious inequities of the human condition.

Rise of Concern for Fairness

During the nineteenth century, the Industrial Revolution created more wealth in a few generations than had been created in the previous history of humankind. This

FIGURE 11.2

Selected Universal Human Rights as Set Forth in the UN Universal Declaration of Human Rights, 1948

Equality before the Law, Articles 1–16

All human beings born free and equal in dignity and rights.

Everyone has the right to life, liberty and security of person.

No one shall be held in slavery and slavery shall be prohibited.

No one shall be subject to torture.

Everyone has the right to recognition before the law.

All are equal before the law and entitled to equal protection without discrimination.

Everyone has the right to an effective remedy by national tribunals for violations of rights.

No one shall be subject to arbitrary arrest, detention or exile.

Everyone is entitled in full equality to a fair public hearing by an impartial tribunal in the determination of his rights.

Everyone has the right to be presumed innocent until proved guilty.

No one shall be subject to arbitrary interference with his privacy.

Everyone has the right to freedom of movement within the borders of each state and to leave any country and to return to his country.

Everyone has the right to seek asylum in other countries and that right may not be revoked.

Everyone has the right to a nationality and no one shall be arbitrarily deprived of his nationality nor denied the right to change his nationality.

Building of Democratic Societies, Articles 18–21

Everyone has the right to freedom of thought, conscience and religion.

Everyone has the right to freedom of opinion and expression.

Everyone has the right to freedom of peaceful assembly and association.

Everyone has the right to take part in the government of his country, directly or through freely chosen representatives, through public service. The will of the people shall be the basis of the authority of government expressed through periodic and genuine elections held by universal suffrage and secret ballot or their equivalent.

Social, Economic, and Cultural Rights, Articles 16–17, 22–27

Men and women of full age have the right to marry and found a family. They are entitled to equal rights as to marriage.

Marriage shall be entered into only with the free and full consent of the spouses.

The family is the natural and fundamental group unit of society and entitled to protection by society and the State.

Everyone has the right to own property and no one shall be arbitrarily deprived of his property.

Everyone has the right to social security and is entitled to realization of the economic, social and cultural rights.

Everyone has the right to work.

Everyone has the right to equal pay for equal work.

Everyone has the right to form and join trade unions.

Everyone has the right to rest and leisure.

Everyone has the right to a standard of living adequate for the health and well-being of himself and his family, including food, clothing, housing and medical care, the right to security in the event of unemployment, sickness, disability, widowhood, old age, etc. Motherhood and childhood are entitled to special care and assistance. All children shall enjoy the same social protection

Everyone has the right to education. Education shall be free, at least in the elementary stages. Elementary education shall be compulsory.

Universal Obligations, Articles 28–30

Everyone is entitled to a social and international order in which the rights and freedoms set forth in the Declaration can be fully realized.

Everyone has duties to the community. In the exercise of his rights and freedoms, everyone shall be subject only to such limitations as are determined by law solely for the purpose of securing recognition and respect for the rights and freedoms of others.

No state has the right to engage in any activity aimed at the destruction of any of these rights and freedoms.

Source: UN Universal Declaration of Human Rights, http://www.un.org/Overview/rights.html. Used by permission.

FIGURE 11.3

Principal Human Rights Conventions

Convention	Date of Adoption	Name of Monitoring Agency
Protection of Individual Rights		
International Covenant on Civil and Political Rights	1966	Commission on Human Rights
*International Covenant on Economic, Social and Cultural Rights	1966	Economic and Social Council
Protection of Minority Group Rights		
Convention on the Prevention and Punishment of Crime of Genocide	1948	Judiciary of member-states
*Convention for the Suppression of the Traffic in Persons and of the Exploitation of the Prostitution of Others	1949, updated 2001	Member-states
Convention for the Amelioration of the Condition of the Wounded and Sick in Armed Forces in the Field (Geneva Convention)	1949	International Red Cross
Convention on the Political Rights of Women	1953	Commission on Human Rights
*Convention on the Nationality of Married Women	1957	
*Convention on Consent to Marriage, Minimum Age for Marriage, and Registration of Marriages	1962	Member-states
International Convention on the Elimination of All Forms of Racial Discrimination	1966	Sub-Commission on Prevention of Discrimination and Protection of Minorities
*International Convention on the Suppression and Punishment of the Crime of Apartheid	1973	Commission on Human Rights
*Convention on the Elimination of All Forms of Discrimination against Women	1979	Committee on the Elimination of Discrimination against Women
Convention against Torture and Other Cruel, Inhuman, or Degrading Treatment or Punishment	1985	Committee Against Torture
*Convention on the Rights of the Child	1989	Committee on the Rights of the Child
*Convention on the Rights of Migrant Workers and the Members of Their Families	1990	Committee on the Protection of the Rights of Migrant Workers and Their Families
Convention on the Rights of Indigenous Peoples, Draft only, 1994		Working Group on Indigenous Populations
*The US has not ratified these conventions.		

Source: Nancy Flowers, ed., "Human Rights Here and Now: Celebrating the Universal Declaration of Human Rights." From http://www1.umn.edu/humanrts/edumat/hreduseries/hereandnow/Part-1/from-concept.htm. Used by permission of University of Minnesota Human Rights Center.

Sovereignty Versus Global Rules

You have spent enough time studying world politics to grasp the real reason the United States and other states are not quick to ratify UN conventions regarding human rights. The basic issue is sovereignty. The U.S. government, from the beginning of the UN, has been reluctant to give up decisions about human rights, among other issues, to an international organization. By contrast, the member-states of the European Union were required to give up part of their sovereignty to the European Union, and many of them now have considerable experience accommodating their culture and values to supranational legislation.

Other countries that either have not signed or not ratified the various conventions have reservations similar to those of the United States. If anything, their objections touch the deeper cultural chord that echoes in the debate on whether women's rights are human rights. To a large number of member-states, the conventions on human rights reflect Western values and Western culture. In addition, these states are reluctant to endorse economic, social, and cultural covenants that would put their economies at a disadvantage with the states they perceive to be pushing the human rights agenda. The world remains decentralized clusters of conflicting views and values.

TEST PREPPER 11.1

ANSWERS APPEAR ON PAGE A12

True or False?

_____ 1. The UN Universal Declaration of Human Rights is accepted in whole by all member-states of the organization.

_____ 2. The UN Declaration covers the following areas of rights: equality before the law; rules to foster a democratic society; economic, social, and cultural rights; and other principles designed to support the Declaration.

_____ 3. The key issue that makes the enforcement of human rights at the international level difficult is state sovereignty.

_____ 4. Humanitarian law seeks to limit the effects of armed conflict.

Between Nations
Practice Test Questions
Practice Test 11.1
www.BetweenNations.org

Multiple Choice

_____ 5. Which of the following best describes the nature of the UN Universal Declaration of Human Rights?
    a. A legally binding document
    b. A resolution of the UN General Assembly
    c. A common standard of achievement regarding social justice
    d. All of the above

_____ 6. Which of the following is not a provision of the UN Declaration?
    a. No one shall be subject to torture.
    b. Everyone has the right to freedom of opinion and expression.
    c. Everyone has the right to own property.
    d. Marriage shall be entered into only with the free and full consent of both spouses.
    e. No one shall be required to live under a totalitarian government.

forced to serve in the military where there is a draft. In countries where they participate in some form of combat, such as flying planes, women are questioning the appropriateness of their role. Women have always defended their home and family. In a world fraught with terror, women should not be the ones to sacrifice their lives for the next generation.

4. *To ensure the human family continues,* throughout history, women have needed specific rights accorded to them alone to protect the institution of motherhood and the education of children. Where women are largely viewed negatively, as other than males, as in the Western world, we see these institutions downgraded. In all countries where women are achieving so-called unisex quality with men, the birthrate has plummeted. Women's rights are *not* human rights.

We need a Universal Declaration of Women's Rights!

Using any of the five feminist theories of international relations, defend or refute the arguments of this thesis.

NOTES

1. Dr. Louis Lanya' al Farugi, "Islamic Tradition and the Feminist Movement: Confrontation or Cooperation," Islam for Peace, http://www.jannah.org/sisters/feminism.html.

2. Hinduism and the status of women, http://hinduwebsite.com/hinduwomen.htm.

3. Information cited from a study by Hindus Against the Abuse of Women, presented at the Second International Conference on Bride Burning and Dowry Deaths in India, "Women in Hinduism," http://www.atributetohinduism.com/Women in Hinduism.htm. This information is also found in *Violence Against Women: A Violation of Human Rights, A Resource Guide to the Video*. Institute for Development Training, RFD 1, Box 267 B Route 230, Trention, Maine 04605, http://www.curowrc.org/06.contributions/1.contrib_en/27.contrib.en.htm.

4. Statistics from V-Day Loyola, Women's Studies and Women's Resource Center, Loyola University, New Orleans, http://www.loyno.edu/womens.center/vday.html.

LEARNING OBJECTIVES REVIEW

1 ▶ *What is meant by the term* human rights? *Understand the origins of these rights and the international conventions that support their existence.*

- Human rights are rights that human beings claim at birth and that governments ought not to take away. A sense of justice, or equality, informs how states address these rights.

- Justice may be seen as due process, with its emphasis on a legal system in which everyone is treated equally under the law regardless of wealth, race, sex, or religion.

- Human rights, the principles or standards on which due process is built, are set forth in the UN Universal Declaration of Human Rights, and in international humanitarian law.

- Justice, as fairness, seeks to redress the inequality of condition among human beings by redistributing resources.

2 ▶ *Understand why women's rights should be given special standing in the study of world politics.*

- Women's history is one of almost universally low political, economic, and social status. No culture has considered women human in the same way it considers men to be human.

- Few women have been influential individuals, and most of these were upper-class women, women rulers, or, in rare instances, philosophers and writers. The situation did not change with the Industrial Revolution.

- In the 1800s, women in Europe and America organized to protest their lack of equal rights. The women's movement dates from 1848. It had essentially two branches:
  - The American and British movement focused on due process
  - The continental European movements focused on equality of condition, utilizing Marxist arguments to advance their cause.

- While the modern-day women's movement has helped achieve economic progress and human rights for women in many countries, the United Nations has yet to endorse the statement that women's rights are human rights.

---

3 ▶ *Identify the different types of feminist theories and how they approach the topic of human rights.*

- Feminist theories of international relations help us uncover gender bias in world politics.

- There are five kinds of feminist international relations theory: radical feminism, socialist feminism, liberal feminism, postcolonial feminism, and postmodern feminism.

- We used these approaches to uncover gender bias in three areas of international relations: international security, the international economy, and the global environment.

- We noted that feminist theories emphasize cooperative centralizing tendencies in world politics over what feminists see as divisive decentralizing tendencies in male theories of international relations.

---

4 ▶ *Understand how the international community addresses human rights violations, especially in the case of women's rights.*

- The international community has responded in different ways to different kinds of violations. In the case of women's rights, the UN has responded as follows:

- The profiling of women's issues in four world conferences on women
- The adoption (in 1979) by the UN General Assembly of the UN Convention on the Elimination of All Forms of Discrimination Against Women
- Development of a comprehensive data-collection system that measures and compares states' economic development, the status of women, and the empowerment of women in public life (HDI, GDI, and GEM indices)
- The elaboration of investments and aid programs specifically targeted toward women, microinvestment strategies in the economic area, and combined macrofunding strategies to combat HIV/AIDS

- The United Nations has responded to state violations of human rights in the following ways:
- Passage of international laws, after World War II, identifying crimes that can be prosecuted at the international level: crimes of war, crimes of peace, and crimes against humanity
- Sanctions, peacekeeping, ad hoc international tribunals, Conference on Human Rights
- Direct intervention (There have been three cases of UN intervention on charges of a state's violation of human rights and commission of crimes against humanity, and two instances of non-UN sanctioned intervention.)

- Current arguments for and against intervention pit issues of human rights against state sovereignty.

RESOURCES ON THE WEB

To use these interactive learning and study tools, including video and audio multimedia resources, go to **www.BetweenNations.org**.

Practice Tests	Case Studies	Current Events
Audio Concepts	Primary Sources	Daily Newsfeeds from *The Washington Post*
Flashcards	Historical Background	Weblinks for Further Exploration

 Between Nations

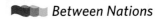

Global Trade Occurs on a Massive Scale, 24-7

LEARNING OBJECTIVES

1 *Be able to define* international political economy *and understand its key theories.*

2 *Identify the different views held by advocates of free trade and protectionism; explain how global trade is managed.*

"The world is flat."

—Thomas Friedman

Chapter Outline

3 ▶ *Understand how the international
monetary system is managed,
identifying the primary international
institutions that handle monetary
issues.*

Where Politics and
Economics Meet

No major event around the world can be explained without considering the links between politics and economics. Economics influences every political issue, and every economic issue takes place within a political context, whether the event involves war, trade disputes, international loans, the expansion of a security organization, or the decision to create a single currency for many countries. Surprisingly, though, undergraduate students majoring in economics do not receive much training in politics. Likewise, political science or government majors are not required to take many economics courses. What's more, few undergraduate political science and economic majors learn very much about political-economic links at the international level. Unfortunately, the real world is not divided as neatly as it is for many college majors. ■

13 The Politics of Development

Worlds collide: The poor and the well-off live side-by-side in most countries

LEARNING OBJECTIVES

1 Identify what is meant by development *while understanding the difficulties associated with arriving at a commonly accepted definition of the term.*

2 *Understand how different theories approach the issue of development and how each explains why some countries are rich while others are poor.*

3 *Identify and understand the political factors that affect the development process.*

"The forgotten world is made up primarily of the developing nations, where most of the people, comprising more than fifty percent of the total world population, live in poverty, with hunger as a constant companion and fear of famine a continual menace."

—Norman Borlaug

Chapter Outline

4 ▶ *Be able to discuss the relationship between development and democracy.*

Searching for the Keys to Development

Despite the technological and scientific advances of the twentieth century, poverty remains an unrelenting challenge in many of the world's countries. Although global poverty rates have been falling, half the world—nearly three billion people—live on less than $2 a day.[1] In some countries the literacy rate is 40 percent or lower (Sierra Leone, Burkina Faso, Niger), and in the least developed countries, where the prevalence of HIV/AIDS is high, life expectancy is in the thirties, compared to the upper seventies in the advanced industrial democracies.

The largest concentration of poor people is in Asia, but most of Africa is also a serious concern, as are many parts of Latin America. Conditions have improved in many countries in the past fifty years—in parts of India and China, South Korea, Taiwan, and

Between Nations www.BetweenNations.org

Chile, for example—but the solution to poverty and political instability remains elusive. It is likely that in the twenty-first century, large numbers of people will remain mired in distressed economic, political, health, and environmental conditions. A helpful indicator of the gap between the world's haves and have-nots is purchasing power parity (PPP). See Figure 13.1 for a better understanding of the relative wealth of people living in different countries.

This chapter looks not only at the problems facing the developing countries but also the reasons for the existence of poor (and rich) countries. In addition, it explores a variety of policy recommendations for improving the political and economic conditions of the world's less developed countries (LDCs). Because there is much disagreement as to which paths successfully lead to development, it is expedient to rely on several theoretical approaches as guides. Fortunately, the theories discussed in previous chapters provide a solid foundation. With this chapter overview in mind, the sequence of topics is as follows:

❚ First, the chapter looks at what is meant by *development,* with a focus on the politics of development.

❚ It then examines key theories that explain why there are rich and poor countries.

❚ The next section studies the factors that affect the politics of development, by which is generally meant whether countries are governed in ways that initiate and sustain the process of development or hold it back interminably.

FIGURE 13.1

Relative Wealth of Nations: Purchasing Power Parity, IMF 2006

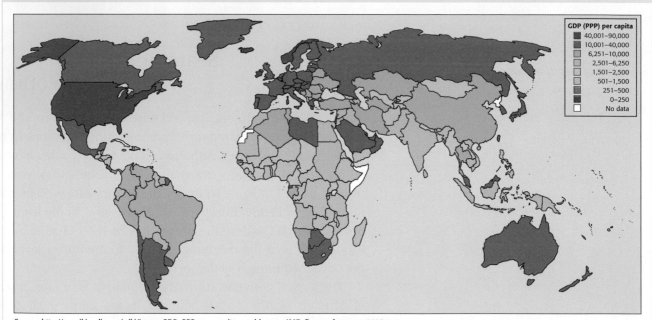

Source: http://en.wikipedia.org/wiki/Image:GDP_PPP_per_capita_world_map_IMF_figures_for_year_2006.png.

▌ The final section discusses how states have approached development, with a look at some of the links between democracy and development. This chapter's online case study (**www.BetweenNations.com**) on the pros and cons of job outsourcing and its effect on development carries this discussion more deeply into the sphere of development, with its overall impact on centralization and decentralization. ▪

WHAT IS MEANT BY *DEVELOPMENT?*

1 ┃ *Identify what is meant by* development *while understanding the difficulties associated with arriving at a commonly accepted definition of the term.*

A useful way to begin a discussion of development is to look at poverty—the very thing development tries to erase. Poverty in some developing countries today is truly monumental, and in certain countries it has gotten worse as the gap between rich and poor countries widens and as the world's poorest states become more vulnerable than before. Many policymakers and scholars worry that poverty—in itself a terrible condition for people to endure—and violence interact to drive each other.[2] This connection between poverty and worldwide violence is a dangerous example of decentralization in the international system. Examples of growing lawlessness associated with poverty can be seen, among other places, in Haiti and in Sudan's Darfur region. Eighty percent of the world's twenty poorest countries have suffered a major civil war since 1990, as in Afghanistan, Angola, Cambodia, the Democratic Republic of Congo, Eritrea, Ethiopia, and Haiti. Behind rising global anarchy lies the growing gap between the world's rich and poor countries and the failure of globalization to improve the lives of the vast majority of the world's poor.

In addition to purchasing power parity, a useful way to understand levels of development in countries is to designate them in terms of Gross National Income (GNI), the method used by the World Bank. Previously known as Gross National Product, Gross National Income comprises the total value of goods and services produced within a country in the form of wages, profits, rents, interest on the activities produced in a particular country plus all transfers of income from other countries—such as profits on foreign investment, remittances of migrants, foreign investment inflows—minus all such transfers of income to other countries. Gross National Income Per Capita is the GNI divided by population. This designation leads to the following country comparisons of annual per capita income:

1. In low-income countries the GNI per capita is $745 or less;
2. In lower middle–income the GNI per capita is $746–$2,975;
3. In upper middle–income countries the GNI per capita is $2,976–$9,205;
4. In high-income countries the GNI per capita is $9,206 or more.

The less or least developed countries are those in the low- and lower middle–income groups, while the developed countries fall into the high-income group. When you read about the *developing countries,* the reference typically is to those not in the high-income group. The World Bank calculates the GNI of countries by means of a conversion method that reduces the impact of exchange rate fluctuations in the comparison of national incomes.

Between Nations
For more information see
Globalization
www.BetweenNations.org

TABLE 13.1

The Eight UN Millennium Development Goals

1. Eradicate extreme poverty and hunger.

   Halve the proportion of people living on less than $1 per day.

   Halve the proportion of people who suffer from hunger.

2. Achieve universal primary education.

   Ensure that boys and girls alike complete primary schooling.

3. Promote gender equality and empower women.

   Eliminate gender disparity at all levels of education.

4. Reduce child mortality.

   Reduce by two-thirds the under-five mortality rate.

5. Improve maternal health.

   Reduce by three-quarters the maternal mortality rate.

6. Combat HIV/AIDS, malaria, and other diseases.

   Reverse the spread of HIV/AIDS.

7. Ensure environmental sustainability.

   Integrate sustainable development into country policies and reverse loss of environmental resources.

   Halve the proportion of people without access to potable water.

   Significantly improve the lives of at least 100 million slum dwellers.

8. Develop a global partnership for development.

   Raise official development assistance.

   Expand market access.

Source: World Bank, "World Development Report 2004: Making Services Work for Poor People," 2004.

Poverty, of course, has many dimensions. Its multiple aspects include:

▌ Illiteracy

▌ Poor health

▌ Gender inequality

▌ Environmental degradation

▌ Gross inequality in political power and access to social services

These aspects of poverty are reflected in the UN's Millennium Development Goals, a pledge made at the UN Millennium Summit in September 2000. At the summit, these eight goals, to be achieved by 2015, were made. They are shown in Table 13.1. Behind these goals—tracked annually by the UN—lies a pledge by developed states to provide 0.7 percent of their gross national product (GNP) as development aid for the poor.[3]

Six years after the Millennium Development Goals were set (2006), only Denmark, Norway, Sweden, the Netherlands, and Luxembourg had achieved or surpassed the 0.7 percent target for development aid. Overall, the world was spending far less on development aid annually compared to the over $1 trillion in military spending. Meanwhile, the faces of global poverty persist, as reflected in Table 13.2 Some of the more prominent features of poverty are shown in Table 13.3.

TABLE 13.2

Poverty in Developing Countries

Region or Country Group	Life Expectancy at Birth 2002	Adult Literacy Rate (% ages 15 and above) 2002	GDP per Capita (PPP US $) 2002	Population Lacking Access to Safe Water (% of pop) 2000	Undernourished People (% of total population) 1999/2001
Developing Countries	64.6	76.7	4,054	22	17
Least developed Countries	50.6	52.5	1,307	38	37
Arab States	66.3	63.3	5,069	14	13
East Asia	69.8	90.3	4,768	24	
Latin America and Caribbean	70.5	88.6	7,223	14	11
South Asia	63.2	57.6	2,658	15	22
Sub-Saharan Africa	46.3	63.2	1,790	43	32

Source: World Bank, "World Development Report 2004: Making Services Work for Poor People," 2004. Used by permission.

Conditions in developing countries vary considerably. A study by the Brookings Institution explored the gap between rich and poor states between 1980 and 2000. The study found that the gap is widening. However, the study also found that, in general, people in developing countries are living longer, the number of countries that have negative growth is lower than in 1980, and Asia expanded faster than all

TABLE 13.3

Poverty's Facts and Statistics

1. Half the world, nearly 3 billion people, live on less than two dollars a day; 1.3 billion people have no access to clean water; 3 billion have no access to sanitation; 2 billion have no access to electricity.

2. The GDP (gross domestic product) of the poorest countries (a quarter of the world's countries) is less than the wealth of the world's three richest *people* combined.

3. Nearly one billion adults entered the twenty-first century unable to read a book or sign their names.

4. Less than 1 percent of what the world spent every year on weapons was needed to put every child into school by the year 2000, and yet this did not happen.

5. Fifty-one percent of the world's 100 wealthiest bodies are corporations.

6. Twenty percent of the population in the developed states consume 86 percent of the world's goods.

7. The lives of 1.7 million children were needlessly lost in 2000 because world governments failed to reduce poverty levels.

8. A mere 12 percent of the world's population uses 85 percent of its water, and these 12 percent do not live in the developing countries. Remember that water is not distributed equally over the globe. That cannot be changed.

Source: http://www.globalissues.org/TradeRelated/Faces.asp. Used by permission.

Contrast of Rich and Poor in Developing Countries

A long line of South Africans wait for their minibusses home to their townships as a luxury car drives past in Johannesburg, South Africa, April 2004. More than ten years after South Africa's first free and fair elections, the country still has huge differences in income and wealth. Millions of black people are still poor with no basic human needs such as running water.

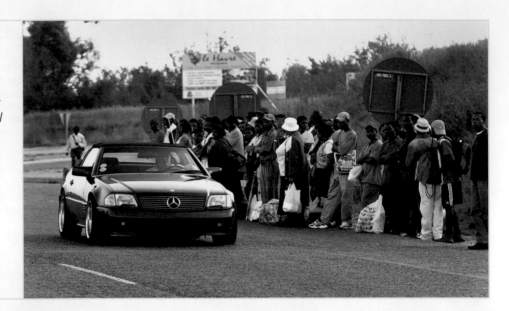

other areas of the world. In fact, incomes there rose much faster than among developed countries.

Poverty and economic inequality continue, as in the past, to be linked to political inequality. One consequence of poverty and political inequality is that the majority of victims of human rights violations are peasants and rural and urban laborers.[4] They, along with indigenous groups and women, fall into the category of the suppressed—with far less political power than landed elites, military officers, business and commercial groups, industrialists, and other power elite groups. The depth and spread of poverty, and its vast system of social and political inequalities, call into question the value or credibility of the legally guaranteed constitutional rights of citizens to a fair trial, a job, medical care, and access to education. This is true despite the appearance of new democratic governments that are supposed to promote citizenship rights. Behind these deplorable conditions lies the legacy of a state's colonial heritage, geographic location, depth and scope of corruption, inadequate formal government institutions, and poor leadership. Each of these factors is discussed later in the section about the politics of development.

Given the scope of poverty in the world and the large number of developing countries, scholars of world politics have devoted much attention to the developing world and the political dynamics that drive it. To borrow a phrase from Thomas Hobbes (1588–1679), life in the Third World can be "nasty, brutish, and short."[5] Given this dour perspective, the obvious questions to ask are, why are conditions in developing countries so bad, and how can these countries develop? The answers are explored in the following sections.

A Transformation of a Country's Underdevelopment

Between Nations
For more information see
*The View From:
China: Market Socialism*
www.BetweenNations.org

Fortunately, Hobbes's pessimistic predictions and observations do not apply to everyone in every country.

▌ First, not all poor countries today were always poor, and some countries are growing out of poverty. For example, China at one time was the richest country in the world, and India was thriving up to the end of the eighteenth century. Both were ranked as very poor countries in 1980, but neither country is among the ranks of the very poor today.

❚ Second, and more important, some countries have made great strides in the past fifty years—a relatively short time.

With luck, more countries will solve such seemingly intractable problems as poverty, political instability, illiteracy, discrimination against women and other minorities, child labor practices, and even slavery. Along the way, however, developing countries face many internal and external obstacles to improvement. Internal obstacles include lack of social cohesion, political inequality, and problems determining effective governmental policies. External obstacles include global economic competition, trade imbalances, dependency on single-export economies, and political pressure from other countries.

Despite interest in development over the past half-century and the post–World War II explosion in the number of newly independent underdeveloped states in Africa, Asia, and Latin America, the concept of development does not have a commonly accepted definition. Most people would agree, however, that **development** is an overall process of change over time in a country's economy, political system, and social structure that improves the quality of human life and makes possible widened civic participation and sharing in political decisions. The key point here, drawing on Monte Palmer, a leading scholar of comparative politics and development, is that development is not random change and transition but rather "purposeful change that moves toward the attainment of a specific goal."[6] It helps to think in terms of a finish line in the process of development, which allows you to measure the actual development in a country's economy, polity, or society. When you think of the finish-line idea, think about purposeful change in a specific direction—like human beings growing or developing into mature adults.[7]

Development   Overall change in a country's economy, political system, and social structure that improves the quality of human life.

An Improvement in Economic, Political, and Social Life

Development, then, may be thought of as an improvement in a country's economic, political, and social life. Economists look at **economic development**, which is the easiest to follow because it involves physical progress in standards of living that can be empirically measured. Political scientists emphasize **political development**, which is harder to measure: among other things, it refers to wider civic participation among a country's population—or less inequality in political power. Each country's level of political equality and civic participation is, of course, linked to its history and culture. Sociologists and anthropologists write about **social and cultural development**, which is equally important but even more difficult to chart and measure.

Given these three aspects of the development process, how can we make sense of the changes taking place in the world's poor countries?

❚ First, we know *under*development when we see it in Africa, Asia, and Latin America, because poverty conditions are crystal clear, as indicated in the data presented in this chapter. Yet debate still surrounds how one measures overall development, especially in the political and social realms. Some observers, for example, criticize modern concepts of political development that stress democracy and emphasize the creation of market economies by a country's political leaders. They say such concepts are Western-based in that they reflect the experiences and values of Western Europe and the United States. As such,

Economic development   The use of land, labor, and capital to produce higher standards of living, typically measured by increases in gross national product (GNP) and more equitable distribution of national income.

Political development   An intangible concept measured, to some extent, by civic participation in government and political equality among citizens.

Social and cultural development   Progress in a country's standards of living and quality of life, characterized by a growing middle class.

the argument is that they may not reflect the culture, religion, attitudes, and values practiced in a developing country.

▌ Second, rates of development, as in economic development, vary greatly from one country to the next. China is moving rapidly in economic development, while Haiti and African states south of the Sahara are not. South Korea is far ahead of North Korea in economic growth, while Mexico is ahead of Guatemala, and Taiwan is doing much better economically than Sudan. Rates of development are by no means the same across countries, nor do they affect everybody within a country in the same way. A country may look like it is making economic progress, while in fact inequality may remain high among its population. As to alternative paths to economic growth, these vary widely from state to state. China, Vietnam, and Cuba follow variations of single-party rule (the Communist Party) that exist within the context of market economics. Bhutan, a small country in the Himalayas, pursues a philosophy of gross national happiness that recognizes the individual's spiritual needs, not defined simply as fulfillment of material wishes.

▌ Third, when development occurs in one sector of a country, such as its economy, that sphere of development tends to change other sectors, like the political and social systems. Indeed, many political economists believe economic development is a precondition for political (democratic) and social development (a growing middle class). If standards of living rise and an economy becomes more modern and diversified, it can generate movement toward a more democratic system—as occurred in Mexico just over a century ago. In fact, a look at the history of Latin America indicates that economic development typically leads to major change in a country's political system, including the emergence of multiple political parties. Such a political transition might occur because a more diversified economy tends to produce more interest groups and political parties, higher literacy, and the spread of mass communication media like newspapers and television. A thriving economy, moreover, should generate more opportunities for upward mobility and higher standards of living for women as well as men.

▌ Fourth, most of the developing countries have been affected by *globalization,* especially the technology revolution (see chapter 1). If you travel through developing countries—from China and Vietnam to Mexico and Guatemala— you can see the presence of Internet cybercafes, IGOs, NGOs, MNCs, and global banking and financial institutions. Coca-Cola and Pepsi-Cola have been globalized, along with McDonald's and K.F.C. (formerly Kentucky Fried Chicken). Still, opposition to globalization is common in some parts of the developing world. The reaction is caused by the perception that the development process is not homegrown but generated from abroad—and, specifically, by the West (think of al Qaeda). It is also a response to the conflicts in identity arising from the interplay of changing economy, a changing social and cultural system, and the political regime.

Crafting a Definition of Development

Development has traditionally been defined in economic terms, first in terms of overall economic growth (as measured by GNP or by gross domestic product, GDP) and later in terms of economic growth per person (GDP per capita). Such measurements are useful but incomplete. They are useful because they indicate

North Korea's Leader Kim Jong Il
The son of, and successor to, long-time North Korean leader, Kim Il Sung, Kim Jong Il is known as "Dear Leader." An autocratic leader of enormous power and influence, he has dramatically impoverished his country.

whether or not a country is doing well economically and whether or not it is doing better or worse over time. A country, however, could have a rising national income but still exclude much of its population from the political process. Similarly, a country may be growing economically in the short run but destroying its environment in the process, thus hurting long-term economic growth. To encompass these and other definitional problems, we propose five components to the definition of development.

▌ The first component is *economic*. Because the equitable distribution of wealth (equity) matters just as much as overall economic growth, the notion of economic health is measured by GDP per capita. It is necessary to focus on not only the size of the economic pie, however, but also on how the pie is divided. For example, a country's development would be very restricted if only 1 percent of the population benefited from 99 percent of the economic growth.

▌ A second component of development is the *health of the population*. The most useful measurement is the infant mortality rate, which reflects the quality and quantity of food, the availability of housing, and the quality of and access to medical care.

▌ A third component of development is *literacy*. A country's literacy rate is a useful indicator of development because it measures quality and access to education. Most people in the rich industrialized countries take for granted the ability to read and write, not to mention basic math skills. Illiteracy is a terrible problem in many countries, as shown in the tables above. Around the world, about one billion people are illiterate.

▌ *Environmental sustainability* is the fourth component of development. This is the ability of a country to advance in economic development without destroying the environment in the process (see chapter 14 for more details).

▌ The fifth component of development is *civil rights,* particularly *gender rights.* In most countries, women play a relatively small role politically as well as economically (by traditional measurement). Thus, improvements in this area would see greater participation of women in political and economic life. (The fourth and fifth components of development are not yet widely accepted among mainstream political scientists and economists. Historically, few people paid attention to these two issues, and there is still reluctance to include them.

In short, then, *development* has come to encompass many elements besides economic progress. Development, then, is movement toward higher standards of living, widening opportunities to live a better life, upward social and economic mobility, and expanding participation in government. Explicit definitions of economic, social, and political development are the next topics to consider.

Classifying the World's Countries

By using one or more indicators, it is possible to rank countries in terms of development. A relatively complex system of ranking countries, the Human Development Index (HDI), was presented in chapter 11. As you learned, a variety of political, economic, and social elements are factored in so countries can be compared by their HDI score.

From your reading of chapter 3 and this chapter thus far, you know that categorizing countries in terms of development can be confusing. To simplify matters, this chapter uses the World Bank method of low-, lower middle–, upper middle–, and high-income groups. Think of developing countries as those *not* in the high-income groups. (See Figure 13.2.) An older, but still widely used, method for categorizing countries evolved during the Cold War. In this system,

▌ *First World* countries are developed, rich, and democratic.

▌ *Second World* refers to the world's communist or former communist countries. These countries are also referred to as *countries in transition.*

▌ *Third World* covers the rest of the world's countries—those that are relatively poor and politically unstable. A common expression that encompasses Third World countries is the global *South,* after the hemisphere where most Third World countries are located. This term contrasts with the *North,* after the hemisphere where most of the First World and Second World countries are found. Other terms commonly used to describe the Third World are *less developed countries* (LDCs), *underdeveloped countries,* and *undeveloped countries.*

▌ *Fourth World* is sometimes used to refer not to countries but to indigenous peoples, such as the Tamils in Sri Lanka and the Mayans of Guatemala. It is important to note that there is no

FIGURE 13.2

People Living on a Dollar a Day

People in poor countries struggle in many social, political, and economic areas. However, over the past 15 years or so, progress has been many at least in terms of the number of people living on less than a dollar a day. Unfortunately, as we noted at the start of the chapter, half the world—nearly three billion people—live on less than two dollars a day.

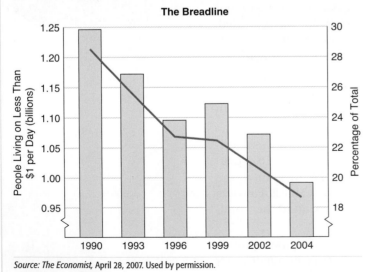

The Breadline

Source: The Economist, April 28, 2007. Used by permission.

progression from Fourth World to First World—that is, it doesn't make sense for countries to go from Fourth to Third to Second to First World status. If so, it would mean a Third World country would have to become a communist country (Second World) in order to become a First World country.

This system is a useful way to make sense of the world's many countries, but it is full of nagging problems.

1. Some countries do not fit neatly into one category. China, for example, may be classified as a Second World country from a political perspective because a single political party, the Communist Party, dominates it. However, China has added so many capitalist elements to its economic system that the term *Second World* no longer makes perfect sense.

2. It makes sense to create certain exceptions to the First, Second, and Third World categorization system. This is often done for oil-rich countries, such as Saudi Arabia and Kuwait, and for the **newly industrializing countries (NICs)**, such as South Korea, Taiwan, and Singapore.

3. Many people object to the term *Third World* because it has a negative or pejorative connotation; it is viewed as implying inferior status.

4. Another problem with this commonly used category system is that some Third World countries have regions that could well be defined as developed. India, for example, is more developed than China in some ways but not in others. For instance, India is much more democratic than China and has a much freer press. It also has a much lower literacy rate than China. Likewise, some developed countries—that is, countries in the First World—have regions that resemble the Third World. Consider, for example, which parts of the United States may have Third World features.

Thus, the terms *First, Second,* and *Third World* are useful but crude shortcuts for categorizing the world's countries; they are helpful, but only to a point.

Newly industrializing countries (NICs)
Those countries previously classified as less developed countries (LDCs) that have raised significantly their levels of production and wealth typically through export-led growth.

TEST PREPPER 13.1

ANSWERS APPEAR ON PAGE A12

True or False?

_____ 1. A key decentralizing force in world politics today is the interaction between poverty and violence.

_____ 2. As a result of the UN's Millennium Development Goals pledge, many developed countries now contribute 0.7 percent of their GNP to development aid.

_____ 3. The GDP of the poorest countries is less than the wealth of the world's three richest *people* combined.

_____ 4. An acceptable definition of *development* focuses on two types of change in a country's condition: economic and political.

_____ 5. Countries that have industrialized in recent years but have not yet obtained high levels of economic wealth are characterized as Second World countries.

Multiple Choice

_____ 6. Which of the following components would you leave out when crafting a definition of development?
   a. Economics
   b. Civil rights
   c. Literacy
   d. Culture
   e. None of the above, all are important

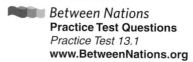
Between Nations
Practice Test Questions
Practice Test 13.1
www.BetweenNations.org

WHAT THEORIES EXPLAIN RICH AND POOR COUNTRIES?

> **2** ▶ *Understand how different theories approach the issue of development and how each explains why some countries are rich while others are poor.*

In many of the chapters, you have considered extremely difficult questions, such as, Why are there wars? In this chapter, you consider an equally daunting question: Why are some countries rich and politically stable, whereas others, are poor and politically unstable? This question leads to a host of other challenging questions: How can poor countries improve their economic situation? Must countries trying to develop economically also be democratic, or can a country be too poor to be democratic?[8] Should the state play a dominant role in the economy, or should a hands-off approach—letting the market drive the economy—be chosen? Should all states try to develop by creating a U.S.–style economy? Unfortunately, there are no easy answers to these questions, nor is there a consensus among academics or practitioners. Nevertheless, you can make significant progress in addressing these questions by building on the theoretical foundations from earlier chapters.

Three Main Theoretical Approaches

The three approaches that follow offer different explanations for why there are rich and poor countries. They also offer different prescriptions, or policy recommendations, for helping developing countries improve their lot. Chapter 12 provides a head start in understanding the following theories. Specifically, this discussion briefly reviews the economic liberal and neo-mercantilist approaches. It then explores in greater depth the neo-Marxist and dependency theories introduced in chapter 2. These approaches are shown in Table 13.4.

Economic Liberalism

As chapter 12 showed, **economic liberalism** (neoliberal economics) grows out of the classical economics tradition. It is a variation on the classical free-trade and free market–economy liberalism of the nineteenth century, made famous in Europe with the 1776 publication in England of Adam Smith's *The Wealth of Nations*. According to this approach, free-market principles should dominate a country's political economy. Domestically, the state should limit its regulation of the economy. Internationally, the state should not construct barriers to trade and investment with other countries. When individuals can buy, sell, and trade freely across borders, everyone is better off in the long run. Since the 1960s, U.S. foreign policy toward developing countries has essentially relied on this approach. A look at the third edition of Walt W. Rostow's 1991 book, *The Stages of Economic Growth*,[9] shows how little the approach has changed since then. The **modernization school**, espoused by Rostow and others, attempts to modernize "backward" countries by encouraging the kinds of policies that helped the United States become so successful. The modernization theory also stresses the internal obstacles to development, that is, those located inside the developing countries themselves.

How does this economic liberal approach answer the question, Why are there poor countries? The primary response is that in developing countries problems

Between Nations
Audio Concept
Adam Smith's
"The Wealth of Nations"
www.BetweenNations.org

Economic liberalism   An approach to IPE based on free-market principles and open international trade and monetary systems. Founded, in part, on the belief that the role of the state should be minimized because of potential inefficiency as well as the fear of states abusing their power.

Modernization school   An approach to development that seeks to modernize "backward" countries through the adoption of policies consistent with economic liberalism and free trade. The United States is usually seen as the successful model to emulate.

TABLE 13.4

Three Theoretical Approaches to Development

	Economic Liberalism	Mercantilism, Economic Nationalism	Neo-Marxism Dependency
General comments about the political economy:	Free-market principles should dominate the political economy.	The state uses the economy to increase its political power.	Economic factors dominate politics and society.
Most important unit of analysis:	The individual or the firm.	The state.	Class (capitalist and proletariat) or the international capitalist system.
Expectation about the IPE:	Harmonious and self-regulating international economic integration through the world market.	Inherent struggle among states; regulated by a balance of power.	Inherent conflict, especially class conflict; revolutionary change until Marxist utopia.
Main obstacles to development:	Mostly internal.	Internal and external	Mostly external.

are created or made worse by failed government policies. Policies that restrict trade, for example, can lead to what economists call *market imperfections* that hinder the efficient use of land, labor, and capital. Governments that meddle too much in the economy, that are excessively incompetent, or that are exceedingly corrupt also hurt development prospects. In some troubled countries, for instance, government policies favor a small minority of wealthy people. *Kleptocracies* are governments that essentially steal from the people; this was the case in the Philippines under the regime of Ferdinand Marcos (1965–1986). These political factors are discussed in greater depth later in the chapter.

Proponents of the neoliberal economic approach admit that the international political and economic environment is competitive and sometimes even hostile. In the long run, however, there is no substitute for sound domestic policies. This point was recently echoed by the United Nations, which argued that effective governance, in conjunction with sound international assistance, is essential for development. As Mark Malloch Brown, the former head of the UN's Development Program, put it, "Governance is a critical building block for poverty reduction."[10]

Neoliberalism in Practice

From the 1990s onward, in many developing countries, neoliberalism has emphasized:

▌ Free trade

▌ Market economies

▌ Selling off inefficient state-owned enterprises

▌ Exports

▌ Decreased tariffs

▌ Streamlining bureaucratic processes

▌ Attempts to diversify economies

14 The Global Environment

The habitat of the Arctic polar bear is threatened by the rapid melting of the Arctic ice attributed to a combination of natural and cyclical increases in south to north energy flows in the atmosphere and global warming.

LEARNING OBJECTIVES

1 *Define* sustainable development *and understand the factors that influence the viability of sustainable development within a state.*

2 *Be able to identify and explain the major challenges to sustainable development.*

Chapter Outline

3 ▶ *Identify the major environmental
issues the world currently faces and
understand how the international
community is addressing these issues.*

Sustainable development   We use the
Brundtland Commission definition: Sustainable
development is development that meets the
needs of the present without compromising
the ability of future generations to meet their
own needs. (See chapter 2.)

Climate change   Any change in climate over
time whether due to natural variability or as a
result of human activity.

Global Environmental
Challenges and Concerns

The principal challenge to our Earth in the twenty-first century
is ensuring the **sustainable development** of the planet. The greatest
threat to our Earth for the next century is **climate change**. According
to the International Panel on Climate Change (IPCC), climate
change is "any change in climate over time whether due to natural
variability or as a result of human activity." The Panel was established under the UN in 1988 to investigate and report on warming
trends on the globe.

Three earlier IPCC reports found a warming trend in global
temperature. The fourth report of April 2007 confirmed that trend
in the strongest terms the IPCC has ever used:

▌ There was "*very high confidence* that the global average net effect of human activities since 1750 has been one of warming."[1]

❚ "It is very likely that climate change can slow the pace of progress towards sustainable development, either directly through increased exposure to adverse impact or indirectly through erosion of the [*planet's*] capacity to adapt."[2]

Climate change is real: The polar icecaps are melting, polar bears are endangered, sea levels are rising in coastal areas around the globe. Worse case scenarios predict that the temperate climates of the globe will dry up and become desert, the Arctic will warm, and the Gulf Stream may turn around and head south. If the cost of climate change is high—namely, the collapse of the Earth's environment and global social chaos, the cost of doing something about climate change is also high and there is no certainty that the measures will be effective.

As we stated in chapter 1, the twenty-first century is the century of the ecological paradigm. Today, for the first time in human history we are face-to-face with the fact that human institutions and societies are not *above and master of* the natural world but are an integral part of the global ecosystem.

The main concern of the human race today is to keep the Earth sufficiently people-friendly so that the 9.3 billion human beings projected[3] to inhabit it by 2050 will be able to survive. Keeping the planet people-friendly means understanding the complex relationships among the:

❚ Global biochemical cycles

❚ Human society

❚ World's ecosystems

so the environmental damage that now threatens human and other forms of life may be repaired. Sustainable development means developing sustainable forms of agriculture, animal and fish husbandry, industry, and lifestyles that can accommodate increased numbers of humans without ecosystem collapse. It also means preserving wild spaces that maintain and preserve our planet's extraordinary biodiversity.

These tasks are global in scope but demand continuous local attention. Environmental problems are thus among the most centralizing of all world problems—and the most decentralizing. Most environmental problems cross state borders or are inter-state in character. Hence, the environmental pollution of one country or failure to solve jointly an inter-state environmental problem affects the environmental conditions of many states. A single state, acting alone, cannot realize the solution to such problems; they require dedicated, focused, long-term international cooperation. Realists have come to share the idealist and environmentalist view that humankind cannot continue the same exploitative behavior as in the past. They also have come to believe that planning for the future must include environmentally sustainable programs and technology.

Human beings have caused and overcome environmental problems since the dawn of the species. The first humanoids may have come down out of the trees looking for food when the harvest of fruits and nuts became scarce. Historical evidence shows that the first city-states between the Tigris and Euphrates rivers and along the Indus River between India and Pakistan ceased to exist because of the salting of the irrigation channels caused by primitive ditch construction and erosion from the cutting of forests ever farther up river.

The difference between the impact of earlier human societies on the environment and the impact of modern society today is one of scale. In early human history, humans were few, environmental damage was local and frequently could be remedied by a local solution or by migration to another location. In the twentieth century, the human race spread all over the globe, and except for the high mountains and the Arctic regions, now dominates the planet. As a result, problems such as poor water quality, air pollution, and soil degradation have become global in scale, requiring solutions at a global level that address specific ecological conditions at the local level. This chapter addresses these global problems and discusses potential solutions.

The environmental challenges facing our world come in different forms; all of them involve pollution. Traditional pollution is the main problem of the developing countries: poor water quality, soil degradation, deforestation, **desertification**.

Desertification The process of land becoming desert due to mismanagement or climate change.

▌ The major polluter is agriculture. Seventy percent of the world's poor live in rural areas. Agriculture takes up more than one-third of the planet's area and accounts for more than two-thirds of the world's water withdrawals. Competition for water and land is increasing as urban populations grow and with them the demand for food. Forests are cut down to plant crops with the inevitable result of soil erosion. Climate change is altering the patterns of rainfall and the temperatures on which agriculture depends. The depletion and exhaustion of these resources poses a serious threat to our capacity to produce enough food and other agricultural products to feed the world's people.[4] Around the world, 1.1 billion people lack access to a clean water supply and 2.6 billion lack improved sanitation.[5]

▌ A second and possibly even more damaging form of pollution comes from advances in technology and the production of chemicals and man-made materials that have only recently been developed. The atomic age began when the United States dropped the first atomic bombs on the Japanese cities of Hiroshima and Nagasaki in 1945. Nuclear energy raised the twin horrors of planetary collapse through nuclear war and the danger of worldwide radioactive fallout through nuclear accidents, such as Chernobyl, Ukraine in 1987, or the improper storage of nuclear waste.

▌ Chemicals pose an equal risk to the planet.[6] The impact of pesticides, such as DDT, and herbicides on human health and the environment are major global concerns. The most recent global outcry has been over advances in biotechnology that allow for alteration of gene systems in plants and the cloning of animals. Genetically modified foods are the subject of the chapter's online case study (**www.BetweenNations.org**). To date, every scientific advance in warfare, agriculture, and health has brought unanticipated consequences. We will talk more about that in a later section.

The question is: Can the peoples of the Earth, through international cooperation, learn to alleviate both the old and the new environmental threats? This chapter is designed to start you thinking about how you would answer that question.

▍ Our discussion focuses first on the major components of the environmental problem: natural resources and population.

▍ The next section examines the challenges to the global environment, describing the positive and negative effects on the Earth of the increased application of science and technology.

▍ The third section looks at what the international community is doing to alleviate environmental problems. Although cooperation among the world's states seems an obvious strategy, the drive to secure the short-term economic and political survival of individual states and substate units (ethnic groups) has brought the negative decentralizing tendencies to the fore.

▍ The last section asks: Why can't the international community agree on solutions to environmental problems? ■

WHAT FACTORS INFLUENCE SUSTAINABLE DEVELOPMENT?

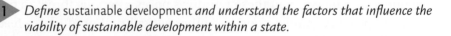

1 ▶ *Define* sustainable development *and understand the factors that influence the viability of sustainable development within a state.*

In chapter 8, you learned that geography has a profound impact on human development. The territories people inhabit condition their level of development and their ability to become powerful on the world stage. For some regions, notably Saharan Africa, Siberia, and the Canadian Arctic, the environmental conditions are so unfavorable as to make sustaining human life very difficult. This section is divided into two parts:

▍ The first deals with the role of natural resources in human development.

▍ The second looks at the impact of population on those resources.

Natural Resources

Natural resources include all the resources on Earth that sustain human life: air, water, soil, and climate, as well as energy and construction resources, forests, coal, oil, gas, and mineral deposits. The first group are termed *renewable resources,* because while some, like water and soil, may become exhausted, or like air, polluted, they can be rehabilitated and used again. The second group (with the exception of forests), falls into the category of *nonrenewable* resources. Coal, natural gas, oil, and all mineral deposits were formed millions of years ago in a long, slow process of decay. Once humankind has extracted all the coal there is from the Earth, there will be no more. That resource will be no longer available.

Renewable Resources

The first factor that most people mention as essential to life on Earth is air—not frigid Arctic air but air that blows not too hot and not too cold, providing a temperate climate where the growing season lasts a long time and it is easy to keep warm. Until recently, no humans lived on Antarctica, and only a few hardy tribes lived in the Arctic. Until *very* recently, there were no large cities in the Arctic. Even now, the populations of the largest Arctic cities do not exceed the populations of medium-sized cities in the rest of the world.

The tropics also were not densely settled until recent times. While their warm climate is favorable to human beings, it is also favorable to disease-causing microbes. Neither the Congo River basin nor the Amazon River basin was densely settled until modern times. The indigenous tribes that formerly occupied the tropics were largely hunter-gatherers who had, over the millennia, adapted to a climate rife with lethal infections and where crop growing was difficult. The soil of the rainforest provides few of the nutrients for its trees and plants and hence few nutrients for an agricultural crop like corn. Dense mangrove forests protect coastlands from killer waves and, once gone, take a long time to regrow.

Because climate plays such a substantial role in where human beings choose to settle, dense human settlements inevitably create air pollution and heat islands, and thus, to a degree not yet totally understood, affect climate change. How climate change will play out in terms of the modification of worldwide population distribution and the location of suitable land for industrial and agricultural use, no one knows.

A steady and dependable source of fresh water is the second crucial component for the emergence of settled human society. The first agricultural communities were in the river basins of the big rivers, the Nile, the Indus, the Tigris and Euphrates. Water today remains one of the Earth's most precious resources. Large numbers of people live without adequate access to water, and the situation will only get worse. In the third section we discuss the new phenomenon of **water stress**.

Today, all around the globe, the temperate lands retain their geographic and ecological advantages over areas of climate extremes. The highest population density is in this area. The most trade and sharing of information occurs between states in the temperate climate zones. The states located in the tropics continue to have major difficulties with disease (AIDS, malaria, TB), agricultural and industrial development (land reform, technology), and the establishment of stable forms of government.

Water stress   A term used by the United Nations to indicate consumption levels that exceed 20 percent of available water supply.

Nonrenewable Natural Resources

Sooner or later, human societies exhaust the resources closest to them and need to exploit resources farther afield. The resources farther away are the tin mines, the gold mines, the oil fields—in other words, the nonrenewable natural resources. As society moves to these new sources, it must develop new tools and new approaches to use them. The invention of the new methods and their practical application we call *technology*. The close connection between the exploitation of natural resources, technology, and the environment has proved both a blessing and curse for our planet.

In today's world, the two kinds of natural resources most in demand are energy resources and mineral resources. The country with the richest mineral reserves and oil and gas resources is Russia. However, most of these reserves lie in Siberia, where the harsh climate makes it difficult to build permanent settlements, attract people to live, and bring the minerals and oil out of the ground. In addition, Siberia is a long way from everywhere. To get the resources to market, the Russians must build lengthy pipelines and maintain a long transportation infrastructure, once again under the harshest climatic conditions.

By contrast, the only energy resource of Western Europe is coal, and compared to the reserves in China, the United States, and Russia, the amount is small indeed. Western Europe is also lacking in mineral resources. Hence, most of the efforts of the European industrial states have been put toward either acquiring colonies rich in natural resources or making trade deals to secure them. The developed states consume so large a share of the mineral and energy resources that one of the big tensions in the growth of the developing countries, as you saw in chapter 13, is how to secure for the poor countries the materials and energy necessary for indus-

FIGURE 14.1

Crude Oil Reserves Worldwide

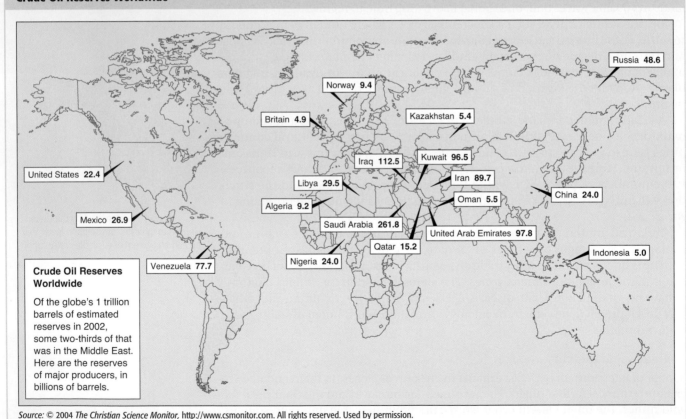

Crude Oil Reserves Worldwide

Of the globe's 1 trillion barrels of estimated reserves in 2002, some two-thirds of that was in the Middle East. Here are the reserves of major producers, in billions of barrels.

Russia **48.6**
Norway **9.4**
Britain **4.9**
Kazakhstan **5.4**
United States **22.4**
Iraq **112.5**
Kuwait **96.5**
Iran **89.7**
China **24.0**
Libya **29.5**
Oman **5.5**
Mexico **26.9**
Algeria **9.2**
Saudi Arabia **261.8**
United Arab Emirates **97.8**
Indonesia **5.0**
Venezuela **77.7**
Qatar **15.2**
Nigeria **24.0**